GLOBAL 🌐 STUDIES

INDIA AND SOUTH ASIA

TENTH EDITION

Dr. Ramesh Dhussa
Drake University
Des Moines, Iowa

Series Consultant
Christopher J. Sutton Western Illinois University

OTHER BOOKS IN THE GLOBAL STUDIES SERIES
- Africa
- Europe
- Islam and the Muslim World
- India and South Asia
- Japan and the Pacific Rim
- Latin America
- The Middle East
- Russia, the Baltics and Eurasian Republics, and the Central/Eastern Europe

GLOBAL STUDIES: INDIA AND SOUTH ASIA, TENTH EDITION

Global Studies is published by the **Contemporary Learning Series** group within the McGraw-Hill Higher Education division.

1 2 3 4 5 6 7 8 9 0 QDB/QDB 1 0 9 8 7 6 5 4 3 2 1

MHID 0-07-802617-2
ISBN 978-0-07-802617-1
ISSN 1080-4153

Managing Editor: *Larry Loeppke*
Senior Developmental Editor: *Jill Meloy*
Senior Permissions Coordinator: *Shirley Lanners*
Senior Marketing Communications Specialist: *Mary Klein*
Lead Project Manager: *Jane Mohr*
Design Coordinator: *Brenda A. Rolwes*
Cover Graphics: *Rick D. Noel*
Buyer: *Nicole Baumgartner*
Media Project Manager: *Sridevi Palani*

Compositor: Laserwords Private Limited
Cover Image: © Getty Images/RF

www.mhhe.com

INDIA AND SOUTH ASIA

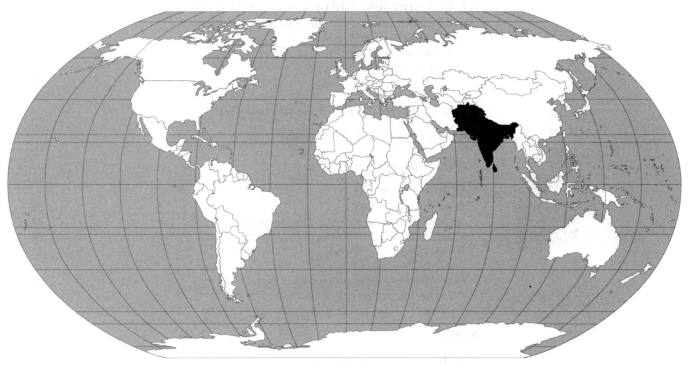

AUTHOR/EDITOR

Dr. Ramesh C. Dhussa

Dr. Ramesh Dhussa is an associate professor of geography at the Drake University, Des Moines, Iowa. He teaches classes in geography of India and South Asia, human geography, world regional geography, cultural geography of Islam, landscape in literature, and various other regional geography courses. He received his MA degree in geography at the Akron University, and PhD in geography from the Kent State University. Before coming to the United States, Dr. Dhussa completed his undergraduate work (BA, Honors in geography) at the Patna University, Patna, India. After completing his Master in geography from the Patna University, he taught in the post-graduate department of geography at the Magadh University at Bodh Gaya, Bihar, India. Professor Dhussa's main research interests are in the field of cultural, humanistic, literary geography, and ethnic geography of India. He has published numerous research papers in various national and international journals. He has been a member of the steering committee of the Geographic Alliance of Iowa (GAI) for over twenty years and regularly serves as a judge in the state Geography Bee of Iowa.

Professor Dhussa is a life member of the National Association of Geographers, India. He is also a member of the Association of American Geographers, and member of ASIANet.

Contents

Articles

India

Pakistan

Bangladesh

Nepal

Sri Lanka

Bhutan

Afghanistan

Maldives

Using *Global Studies*: India and South Asia

THE GLOBAL STUDIES SERIES

The Global Studies series was created to help readers acquire a basic knowledge and understanding of the regions and countries in the world. Each regional volume provides a foundation of information—geographic, cultural, economic, political, historical, artistic, and religious—that will allow readers to better assess the current and future problems within these countries and regions and to comprehend how events there might affect their own well-being. In short, these volumes present background information necessary to respond to the realities of our global age.

Each of the volumes in the Global Studies series is crafted under the careful direction of an author/editor—an expert in the area under study. The authors/editors teach and conduct research and have traveled extensively through the regions about which they are writing.

In this *India and South Asia* edition, the author/editor has written introductory essays on the South Asia region and country reports for each of the countries included.

MAJOR FEATURES OF THE GLOBAL STUDIES SERIES

The Global Studies volumes are organized to provide concise information on the regions and countries within those areas under study. The major sections and features of the books are described here.

Regional Essays

For *Global Studies: India and South Asia,* the author/editor has written an essay, "Five Images of South Asia," focusing on the social, cultural, political, regional and post-colonial South Asia. A detailed map accompanies the essay.

Country Reports

Concise reports are written for each of the countries within the region under study. These reports are the heart of each Global Studies volume. *Global Studies: India and South Asia, Tenth Edition,* contains eight country reports, including India.

The country reports are composed of five standard elements. Each report contains a detailed map visually positioning the country among its neighboring states; a summary of statistical information; a current essay providing important historical, geographical, political, cultural, and economic information; a historical timeline, offering a convenient visual survey of a few key historical events; and four "graphic indicators," with summary statements about the country in terms of development, freedom, health/welfare, and achievements.

A Note on the Statistical Reports

The statistical information provided for each country has been drawn from a wide range of sources. (The most frequently referenced are listed on page ix.) Every effort has been made to provide the most current and accurate information available. However, occasionally the information cited by these sources differs to some extent; and, all too often, the most current information available

for some countries is dated. Aside from these difficulties, the statistical summary of each country is generally quite complete and up to date. Care should be taken, however, in using these statistics (or, for that matter, any published statistics) in making hard comparisons among countries. We have also provided comparable statistics for the United States and Canada, which can be found on pages x and xi.

World Press Articles

Within each Global Studies volume is reprinted a number of articles carefully selected by our editorial staff and the author/editor from a broad range of international periodicals and newspapers. The articles have been chosen for currency, interest, and their differing perspectives. There are 25 articles in *Global Studies: India and South Asia, Tenth Edition.*

A brief summary of each article can be found in the table of contents.

Websites

An extensive annotated list of selected World Wide Web sites can be found on page ix in this edition of *Global Studies: India and South Asia.* In addition, the URL addresses for country-specific websites are provided on the statistics page of most countries. All of the website addresses were correct and operational at press time. Instructors and students alike are urged to refer to those sites often to enhance their understanding of the region and to keep up with current events.

Glossary, Bibliography, Index

At the back of each Global Studies volume, readers will find a glossary of terms and abbreviations, which provides a quick reference to the specialized vocabulary of the area under study and to the standard abbreviations used throughout the volume. Following the glossary is a bibliography, which lists general works, national histories, and current-events publications and periodicals that provide regular coverage on India and South Asia. The index at the end of the volume provides reference to the contents of the volume. Readers seeking specific information and citations should consult this standard index.

Currency and Usefulness

Global Studies: India and South Asia, like the other Global Studies volumes, is intended to provide the most current and useful information available necessary to understand the events that are shaping the political events, history, and cultures of the region today.

This volume is revised on a regular basis. The statistics are updated, regional essays and country reports revised, and world press articles replaced. In order to accomplish this task, we turn to our author/editor, our advisory boards, and—hopefully—to you, the users of this volume. Your comments are more than welcome. If you have an idea that you think will make the next edition more useful, an article or bit of information that will make it more current, or a general comment on its organization, content, or features that you would like to share with us, please send it in for serious consideration.

Selected World Wide Web Sites for India and South Asia

(Some websites continually change their structure and content, so the information listed here may not always be available.)

GENERAL SITES

CNN Online Page
www.cnn.com

This is a U.S. 24-hour video news channel. News, updated every few hours, includes text, pictures, and film. Good external links.

C-SPAN ONLINE
www.c-span.org

See especially C-SPAN International on the Web for International Programming Highlights and archived C-Span programs.

Penn Library: Resources by Subject
www.library.upenn.edu/eresources

Rich in links to information about Asian studies, this vast site includes population and demography data.

Political Science RESOURCES
www.psr.keele.ac.uk

On this Web site, find a dynamic gateway to sources available via European addresses. A list of country names is available.

ReliefWeb
www.reliefweb.int

UN's Department of Humanitarian Affairs clearinghouse for international humanitarian emergencies.

Social Science Information Gateway (SOSIG)
www.galaxy.com

The project of the Economic and Social Research Council (ESRC) is located here. It catalogs 22 subjects and lists developing countries' URL addresses.

Special Issues
http://specialissues.com

This unusual site is the repository of transcripts of every kind, compiled by Gary Price, from radio and television, of speeches by world government leaders, and the proceedings of groups like the United Nations, NATO, and the World Bank.

United Nations System
www.unsystem.org

The UN's system of organizations presents this official Web site. An alphabetical list is available that offers: UNICC—Food and Agriculture Organization.

UN Development Programme (UNDP)
www.undp.org

Publications and current information on world poverty, Mission Statement, UN Development Fund for Women, and more can be found here. Be sure to see Poverty Clock.

U.S. Agency for International Development (USAID)
www.usaid.gov

The U.S. policy toward assistance to Asian countries is available at this site.

U.S. Central Intelligence Agency Home Page
www.cia.gov

This site includes publications of the CIA, such as the World Factbook, Factbook on Intelligence, Handbook of International Economic Statistics, and CIA Maps.

U.S. Department of State Home Page
www.state.gov/index.html

Organized alphabetically, this Web site presents: Country Reports, Human Rights, International Organizations, etc.

World Bank Group
www.worldbank.org

News (i.e., press releases, summary of new projects, speeches), publications, topics in development, countries and regions are available here. Links to other financial organizations are possible.

World Health Organization (WHO)
www.who.ch

Maintained by WHO's headquarters in Geneva, Switzerland, this comprehensive site includes a search engine.

World Trade Organization (WTO)
www.wto.org

Topics include a foundation of world trade systems, data on textiles, intellectual property rights, legal frameworks, trade and environmental policies, recent agreements, and other data.

The Economist
www.economist.com/asia

The Economist is a weekly international news and business publication offering clear reporting, commentary and analysis on world politics, business, finance, science and technology.

Foreign Affairs
www.foreignaffairs.org/regions/asia

Founded in 1921, the Council on Foreign Relations is a non-profit and nonpartisan membership organization dedicated to improving the understanding of U.S. foreign policy and international affairs through the free exchange of ideas.

Human Rights Watch
www.hrw.org/asia

Human Rights Watch is dedicated to protecting the human rights of people around the world.

South Asia Terrorism Portal
www.satp.org

South Asia Intelligence Review (SAIR) brings regular assessments, data and news briefs on terrorism, insurgencies and sub-conventional warfare, counter-terrorism responses and policies, as well as on related economic, political, and social issues, in the South Asian region.

Wikipedia
www.wikipedia.org/(Country)

Wikipedia is a multilingual, web-based, free content encyclopedia project. Wikipedia is written collaboratively by volunteers from all around the world.

World Newspapers
www.world-newspapers.com(Country)

A collection of world newspapers, magazines, and news sites sorted by country and region.

GENERAL INDIA AND SOUTH ASIA SITES

Asia Web Watch
www.ciolek.com/Asia-Web-Watch/main-page.html

Here is a register of statistical data that can be accessed alphabetically. Data includes Asian Online Materials Statistics and Appendices about Asian cyberspace.

Asian Arts
http://asianart.com

This online journal for the study and exhibition of the arts of Asia includes exhibitions, articles, and galleries.

Asian Studies WWW Virtual Library
http://coombs.anu.edu.au/WWWVL-AsianStudies.html

Australia National University maintains these sites, which link to many other Web sources, available at each country's location.

Asia-Yahoo
www.yahoo.com/Regional/Regions/Asia/

Access a specialized Yahoo search site that permits key-word searches on Asian events, countries, and topics from here.

South Asia Resources
www.lib.berkeley.edu/SSEAL/SouthAsia/

From this University of Berkeley Library site there is quick access to online resources in Asian studies as well as to South Asian specialists and other special features.

See individual country report pages for additional websites.

The United States (United States of America)

GEOGRAPHY

Area in Square Miles (Kilometers):
3,794,085 (9,826,630) (about 1/2 the size of Russia)

Capital (Population): Washington, DC (563,400)

Environmental Concerns: air and water pollution; limited freshwater resources, desertification; loss of habitat; waste disposal; acid rain

Geographical Features: vast central plain, mountains in the west, hills and low mountains in the east; rugged mountains and broad river valleys in Alaska; volcanic topography in Hawaii

Climate: mostly temperate, but ranging from tropical to arctic

PEOPLE
Population
Total: 301,139,947

Annual Growth Rate: 0.89%

Rural/Urban Population Ratio: 19/81

Major Languages: predominantly English; a sizable Spanish-speaking minority; many others

Ethnic Makeup: 82% white; 13% black; 4% Asian; 1% Amerindian and others

Religions: 52% Protestant; 24% Roman Catholic; 1% Jewish; 13% others; 10% none or unaffiliated

Health
Life Expectancy at Birth: 75 years (male); 81 years (female)

Infant Mortality: 6.37/1,000 live births

Physicians Available: 2.3/1000 people

HIV/AIDS Rate in Adults: 0.6%

Education
Adult Literacy Rate: 97% (official)

Compulsory (Ages): 7–16

COMMUNICATION
Telephones: 177,900,000 main lines

Daily Newspaper Circulation: 196.3/1,000 people

Televisions: 844/1,000 people

Internet Users: 208,000,000 (2006)

TRANSPORTATION
Highways in Miles (Kilometers): 3,986,827 (6,430,366)

Railroads in Miles (Kilometers): 140,499 (226,612)

Usable Airfields: 14,947

Motor Vehicles in Use: 229,620,000

GOVERNMENT
Type: federal republic

Independence Date: July 4, 1776

Head of State/Government: President Barak H. Obama is both head of state and head of government

Political Parties: Democratic Party; Republican Party; others of relatively minor political significance

Suffrage: universal at 18

MILITARY
Military Expenditures (% of GDP): 4.06%

Current Disputes: various boundary and territorial disputes; Iraq and Afghanistan; "war on terrorism"

ECONOMY
Per Capita Income/GDP: $43,800/$13.06 trillion

GDP Growth Rate: 2.9% (2006)

Inflation Rate: 3.2%

Unemployment Rate: 4.8%

Population Below Poverty Line: 12%

Natural Resources: many minerals and metals; petroleum; natural gas; timber; arable land

Agriculture: food grains; feed crops; fruits and vegetables; oil-bearing crops; livestock; dairy products

Industry: diversified in both capital and consumer-goods industries

Exports: $1.023 trillion (primary partners Canada, Mexico, Japan, China, U.K.)

Imports: $1.861 trillion (primary partners Canada, Mexico, Japan, China, Germany)

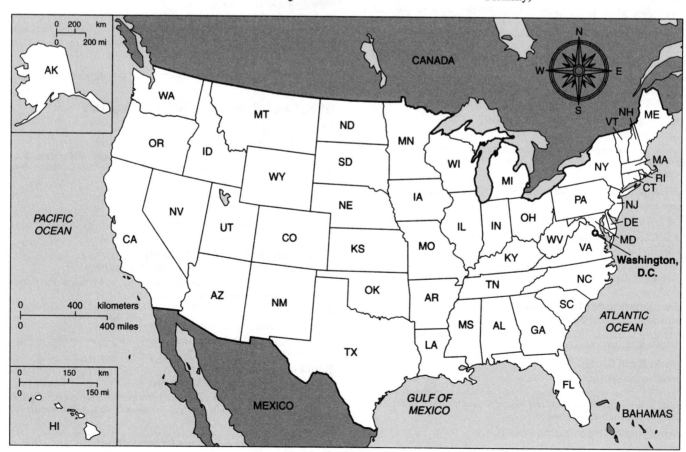

Canada

GEOGRAPHY

Area in Square Miles (Kilometers):
3,855,103 (9,984,670) (slightly larger than the United States)
Capital (Population): Ottawa (1,560,000)
Environmental Concerns: air and water pollution; acid rain; industrial damage to agriculture and forest productivity
Geographical Features: permafrost in the north; mountains in the west; central plains; lowlands in the southeast
Climate: varies from temperate to arctic

PEOPLE

Population

Total: 33,390,141(2007)
Annual Growth Rate: 0.87%
Rural/Urban Population Ratio: 20/80
Major Languages: both English and French are official
Ethnic Makeup: 28% British Isles origin; 23% French origin; 15% other European; 6% others; 2% indigenous; 26% mixed
Religions: 42.6% Roman Catholic; 27.7% Protestant; 12.7% others; 16% none.

Health

Life Expectancy at Birth: 77 years (male); 84 years (female)
Infant Mortality: 4.63/1,000 live births
Physicians Available: 2.1/1,000 people
HIV/AIDS Rate in Adults: 0

Education

Adult Literacy Rate: 97%
Compulsory (Ages): 6–16

COMMUNICATION

Telephones: 20,780,000 main lines
Daily Newspaper Circulation: 167.9/1,000 people
Televisions: 709/1,000 people
Internet Users: 22,000,000 (2006)

TRANSPORTATION

Highways in Miles (Kilometers): 646,226 (1,042,300)
Railroads in Miles (Kilometers): 29,802 (48,068)
Usable Airfields: 1,343
Motor Vehicles in Use: 18,360,000

GOVERNMENT

Type: federation with parliamentary democracy
Independence Date: July 1, 1867
Head of State/Government: Queen Elizabeth II; Prime Minister Stephen Harper
Political Parties: Conservative Party of Canada; Liberal Party; New Democratic Party; Bloc Québécois; Green Party
Suffrage: universal at 18

MILITARY

Military Expenditures (% of GDP): 1.1%
Current Disputes: maritime boundary disputes with the United States and Denmark (Greenland)

ECONOMY

Currency ($U.S. equivalent): 0.97 Canadian dollars = $1 (Oct. 2007)
Per Capita Income/GDP: $35,700/$1.181 trillion
GDP Growth Rate: 2.8%
Inflation Rate: 2%
Unemployment Rate: 6.4% (2006)
Labor Force by Occupation: 75% services; 14% manufacturing; 2% agriculture; and 8% others
Natural Resources: petroleum; natural gas; fish; minerals; cement; forestry products; wildlife; hydropower
Agriculture: grains; livestock; dairy products; potatoes; hogs; poultry and eggs; tobacco; fruits and vegetables
Industry: oil production and refining; natural-gas development; fish products; wood and paper products; chemicals; transportation equipment
Exports: $401.7 billion (primary partners United States, Japan, United Kingdom)
Imports: $356.5 billion (primary partners United States, China, Japan)

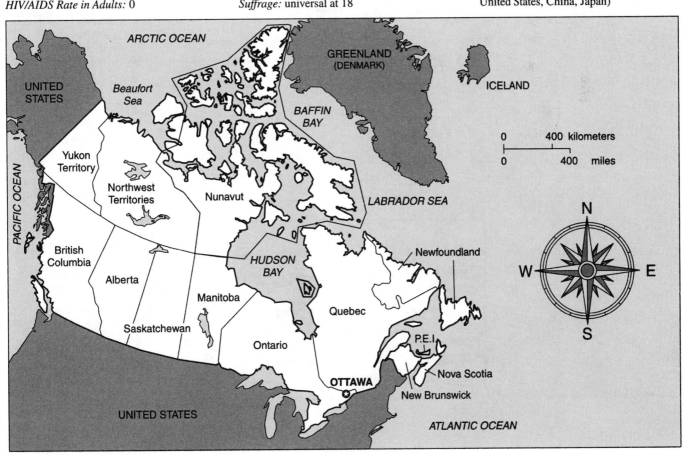

GLOBAL ⬤ STUDIES

This map is provided to give you a graphic picture of where the countries of the world are located, the relationship they have with their region and neighbors, and their positions relative to major trade and power blocs. We have focused on certain areas to illustrate these crowded regions more clearly. The India and South Asia region is shaded for emphasis.

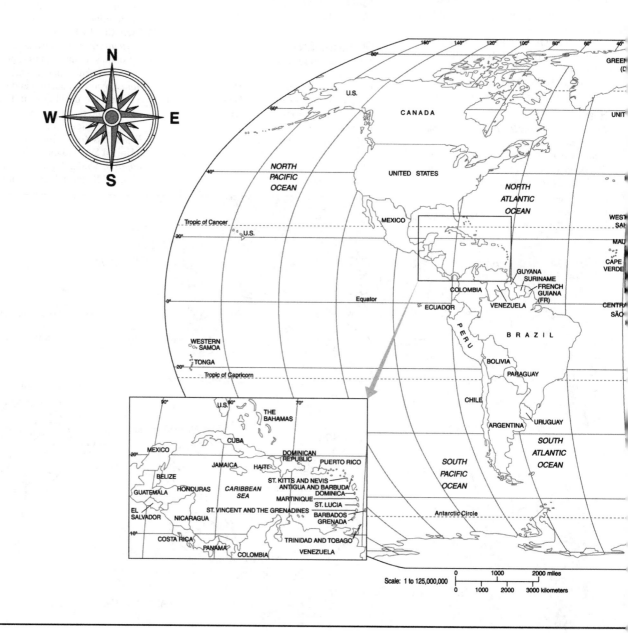

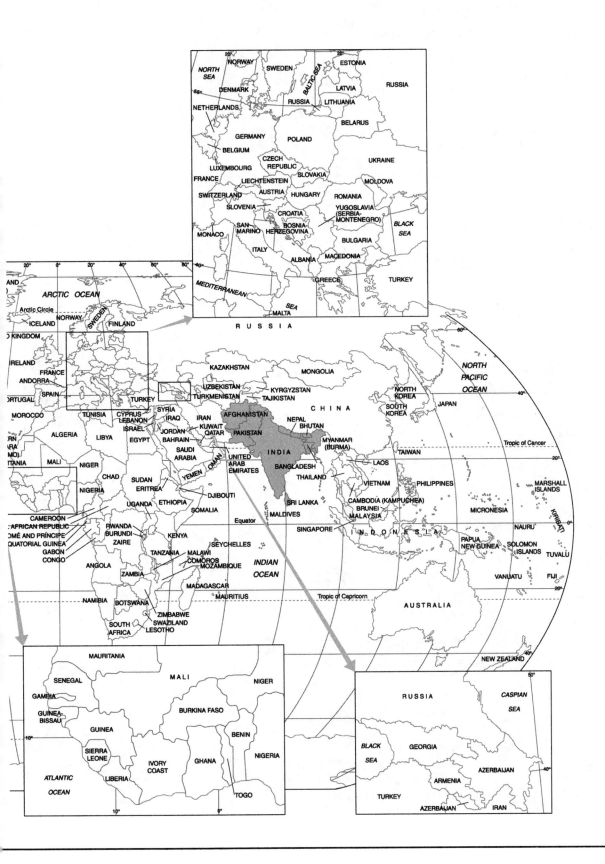

India and South Asia

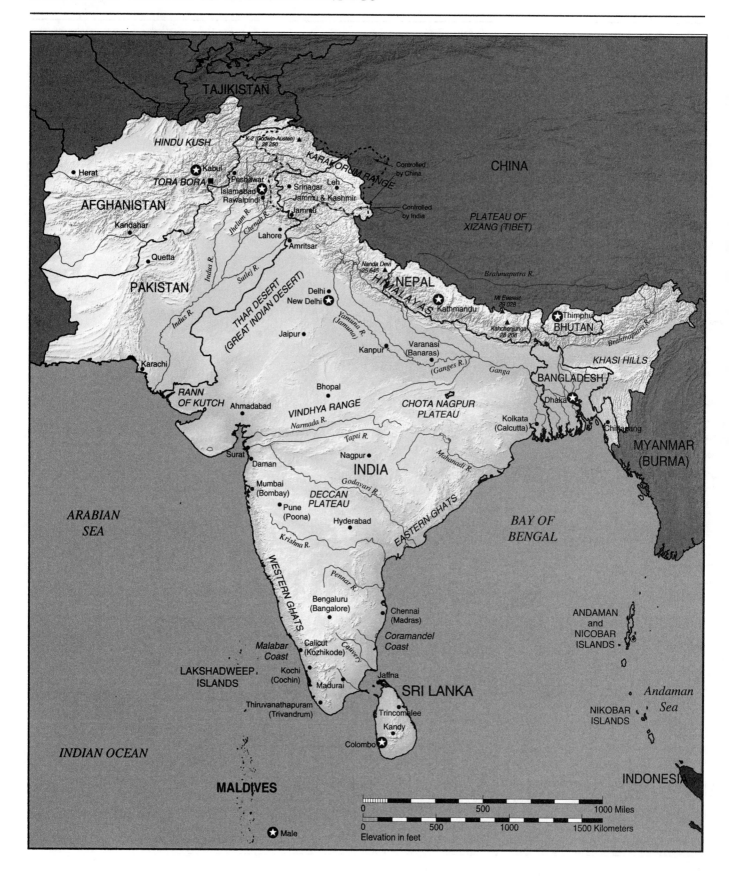

Five Images of South Asia

OUT OF MANY VIEWS, A PORTRAIT

We begin with five images to portray the uniqueness of South Asia. Of course, many more images of South Asia can also be portrayed. Every assertion about the subcontinent, it is said, is a contradiction. Rather, they intend to create illuminating foci toward a picture of this immensely varied, fascinating, and increasingly important part of our world.

IMAGE I: SOUTH ASIA, A DISTINCT LAND AND AN ANCIENT CIVILIZATION

> The diversity of India is tremendous; it is obvious; it lies on the surface and anybody can see it. It concerns itself with physical appearances as well as with certain mental habits and traits. There is little in common, to outward seeming, between the Pathan of the North-West and the Tamil in the far South. Their racial stocks are not the same; though there may be common strands running through them, they differ in face and figure, food and clothing, and of course language. . . . Yet, with all these differences, there is no mistaking the impress of India on Pathan, as this is obvious on the Tamil.
> —Jawaharlal Nehru,
> *The Discovery of India*,
> (Thirteenth Impression), New Delhi: Jawaharlal Nehru Memorial Fund, Teen Murti House, 1993. p. 61. (First published Calcutta: Signet Press, 1946.)

A DISTINCT LAND

South Asia is clearly set apart from the rest of Asia. Geologically speaking, it is a recent addition to the continent. Initially on a separate tectonic plate attached to the east coast of Africa, it broke away about 100 million years ago and drifted slowly east and north across the Indian Ocean. Seventy-two million years later it collided into the southern edge of the Asian continent.

The immense power of this impact pushed the Tibetan plateau more than 3 miles into the air and created a high ridge of snow-clad mountains. The Himalayan range, the highest in the world, is still rising at a rate of about 10 inches per century as a result of that massive collision.

The India tectonic plate is still sliding, pushing down the Burma plate to the east. A sudden springing free of the western edge of the Burma plate caused the devastating earthquake and tsunami that brought such wide-spread death and havoc to Indonesia and the South Asian coastlands on December 26, 2004.

The Himalayas set the subcontinent apart from the rest of Asia to the north. The waters of the Arabian Sea, the Bay of Bengal, and the Indian Ocean enclose its coastal shores to the south. The westerly winds crossing these vast ocean waters and rising over the mountains produce the annual monsoons, seasonal torrents of rain and snow upon which the peoples of South Asia depend for their livelihood.

The subcontinent is divided into four distinct regions by topography and climate. To the north are the frigid south slopes of the Himalayas. All of Bhutan, most of Afghanistan and Nepal, and smaller portions of India and Pakistan fall in this region.

Three wide, alluvial river valleys form the second great plains region across the north-central portion of the subcontinent. The Indus, the Jumna-Ganga (Ganges), and the Brahmaputra all begin within 100 miles of each other in the Himalayas, but flow in different directions. The Indus flows to the west through Ladakh and Pakistan to the Arabian Sea. The Jumna and Ganga (Ganges) Rivers flow to the south, where they join to flow east across the great northern plain of India. The Brahmaputra flows to the east from its Himalayan source, then south into Bangladesh. There it joins the Ganga (Ganges) and Maghna Rivers to flow through hundreds of tributaries into the Bay of Bengal.

These river systems provide the temperate north-central plains region with a steady, though uneven, flow of melting snow. This region is widely irrigated to nourish the most productive agricultural lands of the subcontinent.

To the south of the northern plains is the highlands region of peninsular India. It rises to a wide plateau, called the Deccan, bordered to the east and west by mountains smaller, but older, than the Himalayas. The central portion of Sri Lanka also rises to highlands, which, together with the Deccan, form the third geographical region of the subcontinent. Because these highlands are not high enough to be snow-covered, farmers in this region are entirely dependent upon the seasonal monsoons for sufficient water to cultivate the land.

From these highlands the land slopes down into the fourth region, the coastal plains and tropical beaches of India, Pakistan, Bangladesh, and Sri Lanka. Most of South Asia's largest cities, which developed as trading posts during the seventeenth century and are now great centers of commerce, are in this coastal region.

These four distinct regions, which also include desert and rain forest, contain as wide a range of topography and climate as exists anywhere in the world.

AN ANCIENT CIVILIZATION

The Harappan city culture, the world's earliest known urban civilization, flourished in the Indus River valley, in the northwestern portion of the subcontinent, from 3000 to 1500 B.C. Excavations of their archeological sites and seals reveal that the Harappans produced enough surplus, primarily in cotton and grains, to carry on trade well beyond their own settlements. This commercial activity extended into the developing civilizations in the Fertile Crescent, Africa and Europe to the west, and Southeast Asia and China to the east. It later brought peacocks from the subcontinent to embellish the throne of King Solomon in ancient Israel. It also transported Buddhism to become a major religious faith in East Asia and the rest of the world. And during the Renaissance, it introduced the number zero to change the calculations of mathematics in the Middle East and across Europe.

(Copyright © David Zurick (DAL 57230006))

Indus valley region located in the northwestern section of South Asia is a semi-desert to desert region. Rainfall here is very meager. But with the help of irrigation from the perennial river Indus people grow crops for their need. In this picture one can clearly see agricultural patches developed with the help of irrigation along the side of dry barren land.

South Asia remained strategically at the center of commerce through the era of silk trade, to the fiercely competitive activity of European trading companies in the seventeenth and eighteenth centuries, and into the universal scope of information technology in the present day.

Because of the extent and intensity of this trade, it is difficult to trace the origin of many of the concepts and practices which came the other way—brought from other parts of the world to become part of South Asian daily life. We do not know, for example, the origin of the Harappan city builders, whose layout of streets and water use reveal a clear understanding of urban planning. We have no earlier instances of city dwelling to learn how or where these skills were developed. The practice of spiritual discipline called yoga is also of unknown origin, as is the Dravidian culture of south India. Both are old enough to have developed within the Harappan city culture. Attempts have been made to establish links between them. But they could have come from other sources which have been lost, and of which they are the only trace.

Also difficult to unravel is the persistence of so many indigenous cultural threads that have continued to evolve into a wide variety of patterns. So much has been added and nothing ever appears to be thrown away.

Early agrarians on the subcontinent used a large slab and rolling stone, called a saddle-quern, over 6,000 years ago to grind grain into flour. This implement was made obsolete long ago by grinding mills. But it is still used in village kitchens to pulverize condiments to season food and to crush peanuts into peanut butter.

Old practices, many times intermingled with newer things, are still recognizable as significant elements in the heritage of the peoples of South Asia. In the western world of planned obsolescence, such tenacity is hard to imagine. Geeta Mehta, in *Snakes and Ladders,* describes this contrast in a slightly different way: Whereas westerners struggle to recover their past, the problem for the people of India is to discover their present.

The Aryan Migration

In contrast to the more elusive impact of maritime commerce on South Asia, migrations of peoples from other parts of the world are a clearer source of new life and perspective in South Asia. They have come, for the most part, overland, across the Central Asian trade routes between China and the Middle East, down into the northwestern approach to the north-central plains region of the subcontinent.

The Aryan people are the earliest recorded migrants of major impact. Around 1500 B.C., this tribal, martial, and pastoral people from Central Asia drove their horse-drawn chariots and herds of cows into the subcontinent, destroying what remained of the Harappan cities and irrigation channels in their path.

They brought with them an Indo-European language which later evolved into Sanskrit, the classical language of ancient India, and the many contemporary languages that are spoken throughout the northern portion of the subcontinent and on the islands of Sri Lanka and Maldives. They also brought collections of religious songs, which formed the basis of a tenth century B.C. anthology of 1,028 poems called the Rg-Veda, the oldest surviving religious literature in the world. The Veda is still considered *sruti*—that is, inspired; literally, "heard by ancient seers"—the most sacred of all Hindu religious texts. And the Aryans either brought or soon developed

(Copyright © Guarav Sharma (DAL mhhe015300))

This is the idol of Goddess Durga in Kolkata, India. Goddess Durga, who is the symbol of power, is worshipped all over northeastern India. With the diffusion of people from Bengal in various parts of India, now Goddess Durga is worshipped in other parts of the country also. 'Durga Puja', as the festival is called, is generally celebrated in the month of October. It is based on the lunar calendar, thus the date on the solar calendar varies from year to year.

a mythic understanding of the world as a sacred reality. This perspective blossomed as Vedic culture during the time of their expansion and settlement across the northern plains of the subcontinent.

During the era of the Aryan settlement, Brahmin priests developed, celebrated, and interpreted an elaborate scheme of sacrifices as expressive of the total sanctity of the world in which they lived. They instituted daily rituals to assure long life, progeny, and prosperity, ceremonies to celebrate the consecration of their leaders and assure them of victory in battle, and disciplines to enhance their sacred powers. They also asserted a dominant role in restructuring Aryan society around their religious activity. One of the later Vedic hymns celebrates the creation of the universe through a cosmic sacrificial offering of primordial man. It sets forward the earliest description of the **varna,** or classical, model of the hierarchical caste system, which divided mankind into four groups. And it placed the priesthood at the top:

> When they divided the Man [in the cosmic sacrifice],
> into how many parts did they apportion him? What do
> they call his mouth, his two arms and thighs and feet?
>
> His mouth became the Brahmin; his arms were made
> into the Warrior, his thighs the Peasant, and from his feet
> the Servants were born.
> —Rg-Veda 10.90,11-1 (O'Flaherty translation)

Next to the Brahmins in order of preference on this scale are the Kshatriya, the warriors, or rulers by might. Then came the Vaisya, citizens, with landholding or commercial status. And at the bottom were the Sudra, laborers, and craftspeople.

People were grouped on this scale according to the inherited occupation of their extended family, community, or tribe. The ranking was based on a combination of the ritually purifying-polluting status in a sacrifice of a group's traditional occupation, as determined by the priesthood, and the ability of that social group to maintain social order. Maintaining social order was everyone's responsibility, but it held a specific and elevating prerogative for the priests because they had unique recourse to sacred power, *brahman,* which emanated from their performance of sacrificial rites. This scale clearly envisioned a Brahmin-dominated society.

Subsequent periods in South Asian history and literature do not show general acceptance of this dominant role for the priesthood. In the period between 500 B.C. to A.D. 200, the Sanskrit epics, the Mahabharata and the Ramayana, and early Buddhist literature, give more prominence to the warrior, or princely community, to which the heroes of the epics and the Buddha belonged. Social and world order was not based on the rite of sacrifice, nor was it maintained by the Brahmin priests. It was based, rather, upon princes' strict adherence to their chivalrous obligations, called Dharma.

Rama, the hero of the Ramayana, is portrayed as a prince who is severely righteous in order to assure the peace and well-being of the people over whom he is called to govern. In that same tradition, Siddhartha Gautama, the prince who became the Buddha, the "Enlightened One," taught to his religious community an eight-fold path of righteousness, which he called *dhamma,* the "Way." Heinrich Zimmer, in *Philosophies of India,* describes this path as a "spiritual physician's program of psycho-dietetics" to lead them to realize their Buddha nature and, ultimately, attain the transcendence of **nirvana.**

5

(© Ramesh C. Dhussa)

'Wagha' border between India and Pakistan. This is one of the most travelled borders between these two countries. Amritsar is located about 30 miles on the Indian side. One can clearly see the flag of Pakistan with crescent and star on the one side of the border, and the tri-colored Indian flag on the other side of the border.

The high point of Buddhist expansion came upon the conversion of the Mauryan emperor Asoka to the Buddha's Way in the third century B.C. In the eighth year of his reign, Asoka was so deeply moved by the devastation caused by warfare to conquer a neighboring kingdom, he decided to reject the use of military force to add to his kingdom. He would rule his realm rather by moral force. His new policy, which he proclaimed on a series of pillars erected throughout his kingdom, was to shun aggression and to seek "safety, control, justice and happiness for all beings." He thus gave a wide legitimacy across the span of his empire in the northern plains region to the Buddhist dhamma, upon which his policy was based.

Also during his reign, **Asoka** sent his son, Mahendra and daughter, Sanghamitra, to bring the teachings of the Buddha to Sri Lanka. Mahendra's arrival in 246 B.C. marks the beginning of the Theravada Buddhist tradition on that island.

Brahmin religious authority continued to spread through the northern plains and peninsular regions of South Asia. But its full cultural impact was not realized until the Gupta imperial dynasty in the fourth century A.D. Sanskrit, the sacred language of the priesthood, had by then become accepted as appropriate for the royal court and all of the intellectual and artistic endeavors that the court supported. The influence of other religious communities, especially Jains and Buddhists, led the Brahmins to become vegetarian in their diet. And a great surge of popular religious lore, long practiced but unrecognized in courtly circles, infused courtly life with new perspectives, enthusiasm, and theistic fervor. The

austere righteousness and the intricate, sacrificial purity of the earlier eras were augmented by a sense of divine playfulness spun out in recitations of exemplary cosmic exploits of unnumbered gods and goddesses, of heroes and heroines from a mythic past.

The Gupta Era, from A.D. 300 to 650, was a time of great creative activity, drawing upon and affirming enhanced Sanskritized models devised by the Brahmin priesthood. The poetic works of Kalidasa, the philosophical writings of Shankara, and the artistic creations found at Ajanta, Ellora, and Elephanta all portray the imaginative insight, excitement, and refinement achieved in that eclectic, yet highly disciplined and politically stable, era.

In the centuries following the Gupta era, the Brahmin community gained economic dominance in addition to their intellectual and religious authority. In reward for the Brahmins' courtly and religious services, they received land grants—even entire villages—as gifts from Hindu monarchs. Their increasing prominence in all of these aspects of courtly life established a pattern for social change in those regions of the subcontinent where Hindus predominated. Today, to achieve higher status in the hierarchical caste structure, other communities emulate the patterns of behavior practiced by high-caste Brahmins, a process called Sanskritization.

This label indicates how the pastoral religious traditions of the ancient Aryan cow herders in the central portion of the subcontinent have developed and gained stature and authority during the many centuries since the early Vedic Age.

The Mughal Empire

The second migration to have a major impact on the peoples of South Asia came 3,500 years later, and reveals a different pattern of acceptance. This migration was of militant Mughals, descendants of Mongols, who moved into South Asia by the Mongols' triumphant marches across Central Asia.

Babur was the first, when he established a tenuous foothold in 1504 with the capture of the city of Kabul, in what is now Afghanistan. Competition for control of the north-central plains was fierce; and not until the reign of his grandson, Akbar (1556–1605), did Mughal rule begin to establish firm imperial control in that commanding region of the subcontinent.

During his reign, Akbar established an extremely effective administrative network to maintain authority over the realms he conquered. He also maintained a luxurious court, which supported an extensive creativity in art, music, architecture, and literature. Akbar's rule was a magnificent time, driven by his own desire to absorb the best of the wealth of traditions—Persian, Indian, and even European—that he welcomed into his domain.

The fruits of Akbar's attempts to achieve cultural synthesis remain in the arts. The greatest triumph is architectural: the Taj Mahal. Shah Jahan, Akbar's grandson, built this exquisitely beautiful mausoleum in Agra, in memory of his beloved wife, Mumtaz Mahal, who died in 1631. Miniature painting and Hindustani music continue to reveal the integration of art forms introduced under Akbar's imperial patronage. And remnants of his administrative structure adopted by the British colonial government are also evident in village life today.

The Mughals were not the first Muslims to enter South Asia. Arab traders plying the coastal ports had introduced the new Islamic faith as early as the eighth century. They were followed by itinerant Sufi teachers, who settled in villages throughout the subcontinent. Their commitment to a religious life drew respect and veneration from a number of indigenous peoples receptive to spiritual insight and leadership. The more mystical quality of the faith of these masters converted large numbers to Islam, mostly in the northwest corner of the region, the **Punjab,** and the northeast, Bengal—areas where Buddhists had previously been the most numerous.

Further conversions took place during the militant rule of the Sultans, who dominated portions of the Gangetic plain for three centuries prior to the arrival of the Mughals. The mosque, the daily calls to prayer, Muslim festivals, and Islamic law became an authentic part of the social fabric of South Asian life. They were accepted, even though these Muslims were a small religious minority in the central regions of the subcontinent.

The imperial stature, administrative acumen, and grandeur of Mughal rule gave immense institutional status to Islam as a distinct religious faith and political legitimacy to an extensive Muslim community. Even today, Pakistan's aspiration to identify the nation as a modern Islamic Republic builds upon this heritage of that Mughal imperial presence.

But Mughal domination in the political realm did not lead to mass conversions among the much larger Hindu population who resided in the central and southern portions of their empire. Akbar tried to synthesize his refined, imperial Islamic faith within a common South Asian culture. His hope was that all his subjects might share in a single, universalist religion, which he

(Copyright © 2006 Glowimages, Inc./Punchstock (DAL gwt170007))

The Taj Mahal is one of the wonders of the world. This mausoleum was built in the 17th century by Mughal emperor Shah Jahan in the loving memory of his beloved wife, Mumtaz Mahal. Mumtaz, and later Shah Jahan, were buried inside this monument. The Taj Mahal is located about 120 miles south of the capital city, New Delhi, in Agra in Uttar Pradesh, India.

called "Divine Faith," Din-i-Ilahi. Inspired social reformer poet Kabir also sought a more inclusive religious perspective among followers.

Because of the structural integrity and diversity of the many religious communities that fell under the inclusive umbrella of Hinduism, their attempts to unify Islam and Hinduism were not successful. Under British colonial rule during the nineteenth century, the separate religious identities of Hindus and Muslims were affirmed. Their difference as religions became the basis for the division of Bengal in 1905, and the creation of Pakistan separate from India with the departure of the British Raj in 1947.

Religious identity has been at the heart of antagonism and warfare between Pakistan and India since their independence. It is the source of communal riots and terrorism throughout the subcontinent to this day.

After the Aryan invasion and before the Mughal migration, several other tribes and ethnic groups had migrated to South Asia from various regions of central Asia. These waves generally occurred between the 2nd century B.C. and 2nd century A.D. Prominent among them were Shakas, Huns, Parthians, and Kushans.

This is a scene in New Delhi, capital of India. Crowds, vehicles, litter, and various shops, are the typical street scene.

The Aryan and Mughal migrations reveal two very different experiences of incorporating foreign peoples into the social fabric of the subcontinent during the long course of its history. But they also identify a single pattern of cultural integration. The early Aryan culture, through continuing interaction and adaptation over a long period of time, came to dominate the social realm—not by political force but by intellectual and religious authority, which set the norms that define the culture. One of those norms is to maintain the integrity of differing linguistic, religious, and ethnic groups who live in the subcontinent by isolating them as discrete cultural units within an abstract, hierarchical framework called the caste system.

The Mughal migration reveals that even extensive political domination, both military and administrative, is not sufficient to create or coerce cultural assimilation in a social environment that accepts cultural pluralism as normal.

Both of these migrations contributed significantly to the development of South Asian civilization. They also demonstrate that the social diversity of language, religion, ethnic community, and social status is deeply rooted in South Asia. As celebrated in the creation hymn (10.90) in the Rg-Veda, social distinctions are a part of cosmic order, and not easily homogenized.

The British Raj

The British colonial Empire brought another significant impact on the evolution of the distinct culture of South Asia. It was not a migration; and, unlike the Mughal experience, it had little impact on the creative arts on the subcontinent. The British Raj was primarily political, imposing colonial rule over the subcontinent from the mid-nineteenth century until the 1940s. Its impact lies largely in the introduction of democracy, industrial development, technology, and westernization.

British presence on the subcontinent began in the early 1600s, when the East India Company, with head offices in London, England, established trading centers along the coast of India. In these activities, the British entrepreneurs were following a pattern of maritime commerce in this region that goes back to the Harappan cities in the third millennium B.C., during the earliest days of South Asia civilization.

This British commercial interest, which became dominant in South Asia during the eighteenth century, had no intention of establishing any political authority in the subcontinent. The British were there primarily for economic advantage, spending much of their time and effort with local rulers trying to gain favor and exclusive licenses for trade. But as they became more entangled with these authorities, especially as they struggled to diminish competing European interests in the region, they began to bring the peoples of the subcontinent increasingly under their own political control.

In the early 1800s, their greater political involvement stimulated a concern to bring social reform to the subcontinent as well. The character of their reform was most strikingly expressed in a famous "Minute on Education," written by an East India Company Supreme Council member, Thomas Macauly, in 1835.

Macauly urged that the British administrators create a special class of South Asian people who would be "Indian in blood and color, but English in taste, in opinions, in morals, and in intellect." These clerks of the company would be groomed to bring the new ideas of individualism, technology, democracy, and nationalism, which were then evolving in Europe and America, to usher South Asia into the modern world.

This energizing—but ethnocentric—reform movement received a resounding jolt in British India in 1857, when an isolated British Indian Army unit rebelled. Eighty-five soldiers were jailed for refusing to use ammunition greased with animal fat. Initially it was a minor incident. But among other things, it revealed a British insensitivity to Hindu religious attitudes toward the use of beef fat (for Hindus, the cow is sacred) and Muslim religious attitudes toward pork (that it is polluting). This minor rebellion became the stimulus for a popular uprising across the entire north-central region of the subcontinent. People took it as an opportunity to express a shared and growing sense of dissatisfaction with the British domination of their land. It grew into the "Great Mutiny" of 1857.

The spontaneity of this revolt contributed to its lack of organization and direction. It was soon subdued by British military might. But its widespread appeal revealed that, for all of the enthusiasm and good will that the British rulers felt toward their South Asian subjects, their intentions—which appeared appropriate in their Western context—were not going to be readily accepted. The cultural context of South Asia was too substantial, too complex, and too different to be easily reformed.

The reform movement of the early nineteenth century gave way to a more blatant colonial domination of the subcontinent during the second half-century. In 1858, the British Crown assumed direct control of British India. Queen Victoria became the first to bear the title "Empress of India."

The impact of the British Raj is still evident in the setting of the dividing lines that established the boundaries between the nations in Bhutan and Nepal with Tibet by a line drawn along the peaks of the Himalayan mountains—the McMahon Line. British authorities also secured the other borders of these two countries, which were determined before British rule by Gurkha and Tibetan conquests. The Raj used the existing natural and political realities to assert its own governing authority within them.

By contrast, the setting of the borders of Afghanistan did not appear to have recognized indigenous factors. The Durand Line between Afghanistan and Pakistan was first designated by Sir Mortimer Durand, the foreign secretary of the British Indian government in a treaty with Abdur Rahman Khan, the Emir of Kabul, in 1893, to recognize the limit of British administrative control after two unsuccessful Afghan wars. It was further established by a treaty between Czarist Russia and Great Britain in 1907, in response to British colonial interests to contain any Russian aspirations to gain access to the Arabian Sea. As a consequence, Pashto-speaking people, called **Pathans,** in the northwest corner of the subcontinent were divided.

In 1979, at the time of the Soviet invasion of Afghanistan, about 6 million—more than a third of the total population of that country—lived on the Afghan side. Another 16 million lived on the other side of the border, constituting the dominant population in the Northwest Frontier Province of Pakistan. A total today of about 40 million people, their separation as dominant minorities between two nationalities remains a significant contention in South Asian politics.

The border determination of greatest impact was the decision by the Raj in 1947 not only to grant independence to a large portion of British India to become a new republic, but also to establish a separate Islamic country, called Pakistan ("Land of the Pure"). At that time, those administrative districts under direct British control with a majority Muslim population were assigned to Pakistan, and those with a Hindu majority to India. The accession of the princely states that were not under direct British control—about 40 percent of the subcontinent—into either India or Pakistan, was to be based on the preference of the ruling maharajas of these states.

There were two large exceptions to this process of accession. The princely state of Hyderabad, in the Deccan, had a Muslim leader and a Hindu majority population. It was absorbed into India when Indian troops rushed into the state to quell riots that came in the wake of the partition of India and Pakistan in 1947. The princely state of Kashmir, on the other hand, had a majority Muslim population and a Hindu maharaja. It was nominally acceded to India by Maharajah Hari Singh in October 1947, as Pakistani forces had begun to enter Kashmir and were fast approaching the city of Srinagar.

The result of this process of border determination was a Pakistan divided into two sections, East and West, on the shoulders of the subcontinent, separated by 1,000 miles of India; and

(Copyright © Hitendra Sinkar Photography/Alamy Images)

This is the western gateway of Stupa No. 1 at Sanchi. Sanchi is situated in the state of Madhya Pradesh in India. It is located about 30 miles from the capital city of Bhopal. Sanchi has several Buddhist stupas, monasteries, and temples. These structures date back to between 3rd century B.C. and 12th century A.D. The Mauryan emperor, Ashoka founded all of the stupas in Sanchi. The most magnificent, and largest of these is the "Great Stupa of Sanchi." It is also among the oldest of the existing structures in India, dating back to the Buddhist period.

a Kashmir still divided between the unresolved claims of both India and Pakistan and a United Nations (UN) resolution to encourage the people of Kashmir to have a choice.

Even with the setback experienced in the Mutiny of 1857, Western political ideas of democracy, social reform, and freedom of expression continued to spread through South Asia. The Indian National Congress was formed in 1885 to seek opportunities for South Asians to shape and to participate in a growing body politic. In 1919, Mohandas Gandhi emerged as the leader of this movement. Through the power of his example and his great organizational skills, he was able to build grassroots support for the Congress throughout British India. Enlivened by a spirit of democracy and of political freedom, this movement first paralleled and then superseded British colonial rule.

The British imperial presence also brought to South Asia the concept of a modern nation. An independent, democratically elected government was the goal—certainly for those who were under foreign colonial domination; but also for those who had been under traditional, autocratic rule of hereditary maharajas, tribal leaders, and vestigial imperial domains. Upon achieving independence, South Asian peoples awoke from a long era of unrepresentative leadership. Forceful ideas began to take on relevance: liberty achieved through democracy, prosperity through economic growth, and individual human rights sustained by law. These have become the standards by which the success of a nation's quest for modernization is measured.

The British colonial government set these standards as its expectation of the countries to which it granted independence in the middle of the twentieth century—to India and Pakistan in 1947, and Sri Lanka in 1948. The other smaller nations—Afghanistan, Bhutan, Maldives, and Nepal—which trace the origin of their governments to more autocratic traditions of long standing in the subcontinent, are challenged to hold these same standards to their performance for recognition as modern states. They are all seeking new opportunities for expression, for economic growth, and for taking control of their destiny as politically free peoples among the nations of the world.

The British colonial interaction with South Asia is now over. Yet it continues, like the Aryan and Mughal experiences, to have a discernible impact in the subcontinent. Significant changes are occurring in the political and economic life because of the British Raj, just as the artistic and Islamic influences of the Mughal era are also evident in contemporary South Asia. And the religious and intellectual heritage shaped by the evolution of Aryan culture continues to be profoundly present.

All of these threads—Aryan Shak, Huns, Parlhians Kushans, Mughal, and British Raj—contribute to a unique and distinctive culture. They are intricately interwoven among themselves and with the many other influences both indigenous and brought by centuries of maritime commerce and arrival of Central Asian people to form the tapestry of the long, rich, and varied heritage of the peoples who belong to South Asia.

IMAGE 2: A DIVERSE SOCIAL ENVIRONMENT

It is the endurance of this civilization, despite its encounter with a host of other cultures and other political influences, that has led many observers to conclude that the Hindu style is absorptive, synthesizing, or tolerant. What they see is something quite different, namely, Indian civilization's ability to encapsulate other cultures and make it possible for many levels of civilization to live side by side. But encapsulation is neither toleration, absorption, nor synthesis.

—Ainslie T. Embree

Approximately 1.6 billion people in South Asia are more than five times the population of the United States living in half as much space. That is more than a fifth of the total population of the world, and increasing at an alarming pace. The World Bank projects that at the current rate of growth, the population of the subcontinent will exceed 1.8 billion by the year 2025.

Every country in South Asia is seeking to curb this rate, with varying success. Sri Lanka has been the most effective, where the annual growth rate is less than 1 percent. The education of women has been the key to limiting its population growth.

This large population is composed of many different ethnic, religious, linguistic and social groups, displaying a wide variety of beliefs and customs: Hindus, Muslims, Christians, Sikhs and Buddhists, Jains, and Zoroastrians (Parsees); Sherpas in the mountains and fishermen and pit weavers along the tropical shores of the coasts; elegant urban aristocrats and naked religious mendicants; tribal peoples and computer engineers; beggars, film stars, and Kathakali dancers; and many more interwoven into the multi-stranded fabric of South Asian life. It is a rich panoply of all sorts and conditions of humanity.

The persistence of caste communities vasnas (jatis) in a hierarchical social system that holds them together illustrates the encapsulation of this incredible mix of people that preserves side by side such a multitude of customs and traditions. The caste vasna (jati) into which one is born in India provides a great sense of social cohesion, of belonging, not assumed by individualism in the United States. American students are often troubled that their Indian hosts do not feel comfortable with them until they can identify them as another one of the students at the university. The students are doing their own thing by taking up studies in India, and want to be accepted as individuals. Their hosts feel more accepting of them when they can identify them as belonging to a recognized group.

There are hundreds of thousands of such kinship groups throughout the country, each with its own distinctive characteristics that places it in an encompassing hierarchical order. In a normal village setting, individuals will interact on a daily basis with others from about 20 different jatis. The locally accepted position of their jati in the social hierarchy of the caste system determines the expected norms of their daily interactions, which are careful to respect the distinctive characteristics of each. To the unfamiliar eye, individuals in these jati communities may look the same. In many instances, the distinguishing characteristics must be delineated by very fine strokes to convey the separation that preserves the distinctive character of each. Occupation and affinal relationships are two of the more obvious characteristics that define them.

Jatis are identified by a traditional occupation, from which each derives its name. The name dhobi (washerman) indicates one who belongs to a community of washermen, chamar to a community of shoe makers, or jat to a farmer family. Each jati has a traditional role in which it functions in the economy of the village as a whole, and also in the ceremonies of village festivals, which it has performed for generations. Settlement patterns uncovered in the ancient Harappan cities suggest that the separation of communities by task has been around for a long time. Accepting of different groups into a hierarchical rank in the total social fabric is a way for inclusion that preserves for each its own skills and cultural habits. This system of ranking by task is also of longstanding.

Endogamy also preserves the distinctive characteristics of a community by expecting every individual's marriage partner to be selected from their own jati. In a society where young adults are accustomed to having their marriages arranged by their parents, the unique characteristics of the jati are preserved from generation to generation.

With the introduction of democratic forms of government in contemporary South Asia, jati identification has been reaffirmed for those placed in the lower ranks of the caste system in two ways: by reserved electorates and affirmative action.

During the years leading up to India's independence, efforts were made to include a voice for "untouchable," oppressed (Dalit) communities, officially designated as Scheduled Castes by the British Raj census, by reserving a certain number of legislative seats in government for them. Mahatma Gandhi strongly opposed this initiative, asserting that the scourge of untouchability should be removed by social reform, not by instituting it into the structure of government. He was opposed by an articulate leader of the Scheduled Castes, Dr. Bhim Rao Ambedkar, who had studied jurisprudence at Columbia University, and later became Chairman of the drafting committee that wrote the Constitution of the Republic of India. Gandhi won that battle, by a fast-unto-death in Poona in 1932. But Dr. Ambedkar succeeded in including in India's Constitution, adopted in 1950, provision for the reservation of 15 percent of civil service jobs and 7.5 percent of schools for members of Scheduled Castes and Scheduled Tribes. Controversy and public demonstration have continued over the amount and the extent of this affirmative action reservation by the Kalelkar (1953) and **Mandal** (1979) Commissions. But the identification of its recipients by caste community (jati) identity continues.

The newly formed government of the Republic of Nepal provided for the election of 55 percent of its legislature by proportional representation for women and marginalized and oppressed caste communities to assure full participation in its first national elections on April 10, 2008.

The process of encapsulation as isolating and preserving discrete caste communities is also evident among the many different religious communities and linguistic groups in South Asia into which one is also born. But here the defining characteristics and the structural integrity which has kept them separate, even over long periods of familiarity and interaction, can be done in broader strokes.

KALEIDOSCOPE OF RELIGIONS

Hinduism and Islam—one indigenous, the other imported—are by far the largest of the world's religions on the subcontinent. Approximately 62 percent of the population is Hindu and about 31 percent Muslim. Hinduism is the dominant religion in India (80.3 percent of the population) and Nepal (80.6 percent). Islam is dominant in Pakistan (97 percent), Bangladesh (83 percent), Afghanistan (99 percent) and Maldives (100 percent). Buddhism, though started in India, is practiced by only 1.8 percent of the total population of the subcontinent. But it is the predominant religion in Sri Lanka (70 percent) and Bhutan (75 percent). Jains are an even smaller religious community that originated in the subcontinent. They trace their faith to Vardhamana Mahavira, a religious leader who lived in northern India at the same time as the Buddha, in the sixth century B.C. There are also Sikhs, whose religion was founded by Guru Nanak during the sixteenth century, A.D., in the northwestern part of South Asia known as the Punjab. Because religious minorities tend to concentrate in specific regions of the subcontinent, Sikhs, who represent only 1.9 percent of the population of India, are a majority of 62 percent in the State of Punjab.

Other religious communities, originating outside of the subcontinent, include Christians, Jews, and the Parsis, whose Zoroastrian faith had its origin in ancient Persia at the time of the Vedas, more than 3,500 years ago.

(Copyright © Guarav Sharma (DAL mhhe015304))

Buddha in the Buddha Golden Temple in the Namdroling Monastery (Little Tibet), Byalukuppe, Coorg, India. His Holiness, Pema Norbu Rinpoche, established Namdroling Monastery shortly after he came to India from Tibet. Now the Namdroling Nyingmapa Monastery is the largest teaching center of Nyingmapa; a lineage of Tibetan Buddhism in the world.

All of these religious communities, even when influencing each other, continue to reaffirm the structural integrity of their own faith as separate from the faiths of others. This persistence accounts for the immense variety of Hinduism, which is actually a composite term that includes a multitude of diverse religious groups. Hindus do share some common teachings and perspectives. They all, for example, affirm the transmigration of the soul after death to some other form of life. This belief they share with Buddhists and Jains, which is why many Hindus consider Buddhists and Jains to be within the inclusive umbrella of Hinduism. But the many different communities within Hinduism follow separate religious traditions in an immense variety of ways, each the result of an evolution over a distinct path during many centuries.

The earliest record of the Hindu religious tradition is the Rg-Veda, an anthology of 1,028 poems drawn together from the collections of several families of Vedic priests into its current form around the tenth century B.C. Many of the poems were composed earlier, and presuppose an even earlier history of religious belief and practice. Traditionally the sacred preserve of the Brahmin priesthood, the Veda is not widely known or understood among Hindus today. And the Vedic sacrifices around which the collection of sacred poems was initially created—and upon which the religious authority of the Brahmin priesthood was initially established—are rarely performed.

More characteristic of Hindu life today are the rituals, traditions, and festivals celebrated at the innumerable temples and shrines that dot the countryside, daily worship called puja, and the sanctity of an epic fragment called Bhagavad Gita ("The Song of the Lord"). All of these have been added to the religious practices of the Hindus after the Vedic period (1500 to 500 B.C.).

These later additions reveal that Hinduism has changed significantly since Vedic times. But it has not evolved as a single religious tradition. By incorporating and encompassing many diverse strands at different times in separate ways, it has become a vast array of schools and sects and disciplines, all encompassed within the Hindu fold today.

Among these sects are the Vaishnavites, who worship God as first revealed in the **Rg-Veda** as **Vishnu**. They recognize His manifestation in a number of avatars (incarnations) drawn from other and later traditions. These incarnations include Krishna, the Buddha, and Kalki (the "One who is to come"). Shaivites belong to a separate sect that traces the origin of its faith even farther back, to representations of **Shiva** as Pasupati ("Lord of animals"), found in the artifacts of the Harappan Civilization, and as Nataraj (the "Lord of the Cosmic Dance"). The gods of other regional religious traditions have been incorporated into the Shaivite fold as children of Shiva and his consort Parvati. Ganapati, the elephant-headed god, remover of obstacles, becomes one such deity, who remains the primary focus of worship in the Indian state of Maharashtra.

In addition, Hinduism includes worshipers of Krishna and Ram and of the Goddess in a variety of manifestations: in the Great Tradition as Kali, Durga, or Devi, but also among innumerable regional and local deities who benefit specific villages or protect against certain diseases. Their virtues and powers are enthusiastically celebrated throughout the country in an annual cycle of religious festivals unique to every village.

And there is yoga, a spiritual discipline that does not affirm the existence of any deity. Any description of Hinduism must attempt to contain this complete array of forms and practices, each with its own history, tradition, and authority, for a vast number of religious communities who consider themselves Hindu.

Buddhism also originated in South Asia and evolved as a separate religion since the sixth century B.C. Siddhartha Gautama, the founder of the faith, was born a prince in a remote north Indian kingdom not under the sway of a Brahmin priesthood. He renounced his royal inheritance to seek an ultimate meaning for his life. After many years of diligent search, he received the enlightenment of the "Four-fold Truth." His teaching to his disciples about the pervasive presence of misery *(dukha)*, of its cause and its removal, was the basis on which this religion developed and expanded throughout the subcontinent.

Buddhism was originally the faith of a monastic community, the **sangha.** It was composed of those who, attracted by the Buddha's example and teaching, abandoned their worldly activities to commit themselves to following his path, or *dhamma,* in communal and meditative isolation. The conversion of the Mauryan emperor Asoka to the Buddha's teaching in the third century B.C. brought about a significant change in the Buddhist tradition. His political authority gave greater currency to the Buddha's *dhamma* throughout the society. He also endowed the community with royal patronage, which encouraged not only its growth but also spawned a creative outburst of Buddhist art, literature, and philosophy. Tributes to this heritage have survived in the exuberant carvings and frescoes in the caves at Ajanta, and in the majestic tranquility of the sculpture of the Buddha teaching at Sarnath. It was this highly expressive and energetic Buddhism that, during the centuries following Asoka, burst forth into two traditions to the far reaches of Asia—the Theravada (teachings of the elders) to Sri Lanka and Southeast Asia, and the Mahayana (vast vessel) to China, Japan, Mongolia, and Tibet.

Buddhism, though indigenous, remained among a dominant Hindu society an encapsulated religious community, even when favored by imperial patronage for several centuries after Asoka. During that time it did manage to introduce vegetarianism as a social virtue to be observed by Brahmins among the Hindus. Unlike Hinduism, it declined dramatically in the north-central region of the subcontinent toward the end of the first millennium,

(Archeological Survey of India, Government of India)

This sculpture, dating from the fifth century A.D., is a majestic portrayal of the heavenly body (*sambhogakaya*) of the Buddha teaching at the deer park in Sarnath, soon after he had attained enlightenment. His earthly body is portrayed on the base by the wheel of dharma among his disciples. The content of his teaching is what remains on earth after his entering nirvana.

as many were drawn to the teachings of Sufi mystics. Beginning in the eleventh century A.D., that region was subjected to the military attacks and religious zeal of Islamic potentates from Central Asia.

Buddhism survives today in enclaves along the borders of South Asia: in Ladakh, the section of Kashmir closest to China; in Bhutan, also along the Himalayan border, next to Tibet; and in Sri Lanka, off the southeastern coast of peninsular India. It was revived in India among the **Mahar** community in Maharashtra under the leadership of Dr. Bhim Rao Ambedkar, the chairman of the committee that wrote the Constitution of the Republic of India. During the years leading up to India's independence he protested Hindu discrimination against communities designated as "untouchable," and advocated for the abolition of caste. As a final act of rejection of Hindu caste repression, he converted to Buddhism in 1956.

Christianity was first introduced to the subcontinent, according to legend, by the Apostle Thomas during the first century A.D. It was certainly known to silk traders from Egypt passing through Afghanistan to China during the second century. A small community of Syrian Christians known as the Mar Toma Church migrated to Kerala in the fourth century.

The Portuguese first brought Roman Catholicism to the western coast of India during the 1400s. The English East India Company did not permit Protestant missions to work in the subcontinent until the early 1800s.

Today, these Christian communities add up to less than 3 percent of the total population of South Asia. They have become a significant force in the political life of the subcontinent only in the state of Kerala, at the southwestern edge of the Indian peninsula, where they form nearly one third of the population.

Islam was brought initially to the subcontinent by Arab traders plying the coastal shores of peninsular India soon after the hegira, or flight of Mohammed from Mecca in A.D. 622. Recognition of the integrity of the many encapsulated religions in South Asia became the basis for the wide and rapid spread of the influence of Islamic mystics, called **Sufis,** during the early years of Islamic influence there. Where Sufi teaching and practice were consistent with the values and experience of the religious communities already there, they were readily venerated and even co-opted. People of many different faiths participated in worship at shrines honoring Sufi saints.

The Islamic faith of the Sultans who began to rule portions of the northern plains of South Asia during the eleventh century, was also recognized, but not so readily accepted. Through their political rule and adherence to the institutions of Islam, Muslims became more defined as a distinct religious community by the 5 pillars of Islamic faith, Shahada, prayer five times a day, alms giving, pilgrimages to Mecca, and fasting during the month of Ramadan.

The predominance of Muslims on the western and eastern ends of the north-central plains region led to the creation of the separate western and eastern arms of the original nation of Pakistan in 1947. Although nearly seven million Muslims migrated from India to Pakistan at the time of independence in 1947, 150 million still reside in India today, forming a significant religious minority (13.4 percent). The population of all Muslims in the subcontinent—close to 491 million—is more than three times the number of Muslims in the Arab world. Only Indonesia, with 205 million, has more Muslims in a single nation.

Most of the Muslims in South Asia belong to the **Sunni** tradition. In Maldives, one has to be Sunni as a requirement of citizenship. Significant minorities of Shi'ite Muslims live in Afghanistan, Bangladesh, and Pakistan, in which the Islamic faith is the predominant religion of the country, and are subjected to some discrimination. In Pakistan and Bangladesh, Sunnis also challenge the legitimacy of members of the Ahmadhiya sect of Islam.

Communal strife between religions does occur at times in a variety of forms throughout the subcontinent. The resistance of the people of Kashmir to the imposition of military repression by the government of India in 1982 was expressed in religious terms. Armed bands of Islamic militants ambushed, burned, and kidnapped throughout the mountain valleys and in the once placid Vale, all in the name of protecting their religion. The conflict killed many thousands. And thousands of Hindu families fled their homes in fear of this violence.

The military action of the Sikh Golden Temple complex in Amritsar in 1984 by the Indian Army to remove a Sikh nationalist leader led to the assassination of Prime Minister Indira Gandhi, followed by the killing of three thousand Sikhs in north India.

The demolition of the Babri Masjid, a mosque built for the Mughal Emperor Barbur in the sixteenth century in Ayodhya, led to communal rioting across India. More than 1,000 lost their lives in the 10 days of rioting that followed in Mumbai in January, 1993.

In 2002, communal violence broke out in the town of Godhra in Gujarat in response to the death of 58 Hindus, mostly women and children, in the burning of a railway car, while returning from a pilgrimage to Ayodhya. In reprisal, more than 1,200 Muslims in slum dwellings were killed, and many more left homeless. The state government, accused of not acting sufficiently to control the violence, used the event to gain support among the Hindu population for its reelection in December of that year. Terrorist bombings in Ahmedabad, Jaipur, and Delhi were carried out by a group of Islamic militants gaining support from the Students Islamic Movement of India (SIMI). Hindu extremists have been identified as those setting off bombs in the Muslim section of the city of Malegaon, not far from Mumbai, in September, 2006 and 2008.

Religious discrimination has also exacted a toll in South Asia. The comprehensive Sachar Committee Report, released in November 2006, shows that Muslims in India are significantly disadvantaged in education and government jobs. Experiencing this discrimination also contributed to the disaffection of the Students Islamic Movement of India. Discrimination against Nepali Hindus contributed to their expulsion as refugees from Buddhist Bhutan. And Dalit converts to Christianity in the Indian state of Orissa came under attack when a conservative Hindu community accused them of killing its leader.

Some of the greatest violence based on religious identity in South Asia has not been between religions, but within a single religious community. Muslims, as they have become modern and democratic in independent nations in South Asia, are pulled in opposite directions by two dynamic, opposing reform forces: secularism and fundamentalism.

Jinnah, the founder of Pakistan, a lawyer trained in England, did not consider himself a religious person, nor his country to be theocratic. He rather envisioned a secular, democratic state created to preserve the existence and culture of an Islamic people threatened by a dominating Hindu society in British India. In this he followed the example of Ataturk in Turkey.

This vision continued to be affirmed by Zulfikar Ali Bhutto, founder of the Pakistan People's Party in 1967, and by his daughter, Benazir Bhutto, the first woman to become prime minister of Pakistan in 1988. An enthusiastic majority of moderates, particularly lawyers and entrepreneurs, pushed for the return of democracy to Pakistan in the national elections that overthrew General Musharraf as president in February 2008.

During this same time an Islamic fundamentalist movement gained strength in the Islamic world in an atmosphere of fear and antipathy for Western ways, and of social disruption and disorientation. Old ways were changing, with nothing reassuring to take their place. The fundamentalist **Salafiya** movements latched onto a clear and assured set of prescriptions of a normative past that then became, for them, a sacred mission to replicate. This Islamist ideology found expression in political parties like the Muttahida Majlis-e-Amal (MMA), which required institution of theocratic law (Shariah) enforced by autocratic power (as in the example of **Wahabism** in Saudi Arabia).

The most far reaching impact of this fundamentalist reform has been in Afghanistan. The **Taliban** ("religious students") rose in 1993 amongst the Pashto-speaking peoples of southern Afghanistan in protest against the egregious immorality of the **Mujahideen** ("holy warriors"), who were fighting each other and ravaging the country after the Soviet withdrawal in 1989. Their reforming zeal swept across the country, and by 1999, forces allegiant to it controlled most of the country. They then imposed a harrowing rule of righteous repression, especially upon women, administered by its most conscientious administrative department, the Promotion of Virtue and Prevention of Vice.

Following the terrorist attacks in the United States on September 11, 2001, and the refusal of the Taliban leadership to extradite or exile Osama bin Laden, United States and coalition forces backed a residual, Tajik-led Northern Alliance force to recapture Kabul and bring about the collapse of the Taliban control of the country.

Hamid Karzai was elected president in national elections held in October, 2004. His support came only from Kabul and Pashto-speaking areas to the south of the city. The weakness of his government, rife with corruption, and the misguided use of force by U.S. and NATO units assigned to protect the country, allowed the Taliban resurgence from sanctuaries in Pakistan with a mission to rid their country of foreign military infidels. The strength of their cause, together with the creation of an indigenous Taliban in Pakistan has produced a reign of terror that threatens the democratically elected governments in both Afghanistan and Pakistan.

Islamist fundamentalism has not gained such support among Muslims in the rest of South Asia. But the vehemence and violence of their mission is dramatically visible in dramatic terrorist acts which occurred on August 17, 2006, when 500 bombs went off simultaneously in 63 of Bangladesh's 64 districts, and more recently, on September 19, 2008, in the bombing of the Marriott Hotel in Islamabad, Pakistan, and on November 26, 2008, in Mumbai, when a heavily armed band of militants attacked the railway station, a Jewish center, and two five star hotels, killing 172 people. All of these acts were done in the name of the Islamist **jihad;** religious sacrifices to assert the fundamentalist version of their faith.

The differences between and within religions are not always confrontational. Mutual respect is generally accepted in recognizing the integrity of the many religious communities that have been encapsulated. The daily interaction among peoples of different faiths tend to be accommodating and harmonious. But because of the prevalence and immediacy of religion in defining the distinctive character of the many social groups which live side by side throughout South Asia, that identity is readily invoked in conflicts. Even when disputes originate between individuals, they rapidly become characterized by any opposing

religious identity of the participants. The same dynamic occurs when people of the many different language groups of the subcontinent confront or threaten one another.

MANY LANGUAGES

Foreign visitors to the growing commercial city of Kolkata (Calcutta) during the late eighteenth century were struck by the immense diversity of languages encountered there. The language of the city marketplace was Portuguese, a vestige of the early domination of East Indian trade by Portugal. The language of government was Persian, also a vestige of the Mughal imperial past. By contrast, the languages of the courts were Sanskrit and Arabic (depending upon to which tradition of law those pursuing legal redress belonged). None of these languages was the common tongue, or vernacular, of the people who lived in Calcutta. But each had a specific place and context in which it was considered appropriate.

Had the visitors wandered into the streets or into homes, they would have discovered another variety of languages. Different tongues spoken by the common people reflected the places of origin of those who moved to Calcutta to take part in the growing activity and prosperity there. Because most of these people came from the immediately surrounding area, the most prevalent vernacular was Bengali.

Today, the English language has replaced the many foreign languages used in the more formal aspects of contemporary urban life, and Bengali remains the common language of the people. But many other languages are spoken in the streets and homes of the city.

Hundreds of vernaculars are spoken throughout South Asia today. In India alone, thirty-five different languages are spoken by more than a million people. These languages belong to four distinct language families broadly distributed across specific regions of the subcontinent. The major dialects in the northernmost, Himalayan region are Tibeto-Burmese, related to the languages across the northern and eastern borders of the subcontinent. Their presence reveals that those living in the remote valleys of that region had more extensive cultural interaction through the rugged and forbidding mountains and jungles along those borders than with the more settled plains to the south.

The prevalent languages of the northern plains region, southern Sri Lanka, and Maldives belong to the Indo-European family of languages, distant cousins of Latin, Greek, and the Germanic tongues of the West. The Aryans, migrating cattle herders from Central Asia who wandered into the subcontinent almost 3,500 years ago, introduced an earlier form of this language family, called Vedic or Sanskrit, to this part of the world.

A totally separate family of languages is spoken among the tribal peoples who still inhabit the remote hill regions of peninsular India. These are generally called Munda languages, and are related to those spoken by the Aboriginal peoples of Australia to the southeast. The Indo-European and tribal families of languages reveal far-reaching interconnections that existed thousands of years ago among peoples who are now widely separated.

Dravidian is yet another language family. Its roots can be traced only to the South Asian subcontinent itself. Today the Dravidian languages are spoken mostly in the south of India and the northern part of Sri Lanka, but they are not confined to the subcontinent. They have been carried to East Africa, Singapore, the Fiji Islands, and the West Indies by immigrants who continue to affirm their South Asian heritage in these many other parts of the world.

Each of the numerous languages that belong to these four families has a specific area in the subcontinent in which it is spoken by the vast majority of the people. It is easy to see where these languages predominate in India and Pakistan, because state borders within these countries have been drawn to enclose specific dominant-language groups. Afghanistan and Sri Lanka are also divided into language-area sections.

The integrity of these languages is retained even beyond the region where they are predominant as minority linguistic pockets in other language areas. Thus, a variety of languages may be found anywhere, especially in cities, where migrants from many parts of the country tend to settle in sections of the city with others who share their native language.

Some of these many languages have developed literary and classical forms of expression, but all are most widely familiar as colloquial dialects, which, like accents, reflect common usage among specific groups of people in particular places. Colloquial dialects would seem to be the form of language most subject to assimilation with other languages that are spoken around it. Because of the diverse social context in which they are spoken, these languages do interact and influence each other. But this interaction has not led to their becoming assimilated into a common tongue. That each continues distinct in its integrity as a separate language is a primary example of encapsulation as a way of describing the social dynamic of the people of South Asia.

The language one learns first in childhood is one's "mother tongue." This way of describing one's native language reveals that, for the people of South Asia, one is born into a language community which is intrinsic to one's identity as a person, even when residing in countries far away from the subcontinent. As is true for an individual's caste community and religion, one is born into them, and they remain inherently descriptive of who one is.

Even though the Muslim population of Pakistan is divided between Sunnis and Shi'ites (77 percent and 20 percent, respectively, of the total population), political identity based on language has played a much more important role than religion. During their early years of independence, the common Muslim faith of the peoples of East and West Pakistan did not override the ethnic and linguistic differences between the Bengali speaking peoples of the east and the Punjabi dominated western wing of the country. That opposition led to the break away and independence of Bangladesh as a separate country in 1971.

Even today, language identity is a vital factor in the distinction between the muhajirs—families who migrated at the time of Pakistan's independence in 1947—and the indigenous peoples of the country. The muhajirs retain and cultivate the use of Urdu, the mother tongue they brought with them from India. They are also primarily an urban community, living mostly in the city of Karachi.

To maintain their identity as a distinct community in the Islamic Republic of Pakistan, about 20 million muhajirs formed a political party, now called the Muttahida Quami Movement

(MQM), to represent their interests in the affairs of state. Members in this party have been subjected to severe harassment in Karachi, a city that recorded 1,800 people killed on its streets in 1995, most believed to be politically motivated. The imposition of federal rule and the creation of military courts in the city in November 1998 was understood by the MQM as an effort to destroy the movement as a political force. The leader of the party, Altef Hussain, now resides in self-imposed exile in London.

Sri Lanka is experiencing conflict where linguistic identity reinforces the separation between the regions of a country where different religions are predominant. The majority of Sri Lankans are Buddhists who speak the Sinhalese language. In the northeast region of the country, however, most of the people are Hindu, with significant Muslim enclaves, and are Tamil-speakers. The regional basis of this separation has allowed these communities to coexist for centuries. But the quest to achieve a single national identity since the independence of the country in 1948 has resulted in intense warfare between these two very different communities. Because of the importance of their language differences, these militant groups see the conflict more as cultural—as tigers against lions—rather than as religious.

A map which delineates the predominant language areas throughout the entire subcontinent, like a map of the religious communities described earlier, looks like an intricate patchwork quilt. The pattern of the language quilt, however, is not the same as for religions.

Generally speaking, people belonging to different religions in the same place speak the same language, but those belonging to the same religion speak many languages. Only in the smaller countries of the subcontinent—Bhutan, Maldives, and Sri Lanka—do religious identities and language identities tend to correspond. Only in Maldives, the smallest of the countries of the subcontinent, do these categories coincide with its national boundaries; only there does being a citizen of the country generally mean that one speaks the same language and worships in a common faith.

VAST SPECTRUM OF SOCIETY

The difference between urban and rural life in South Asia as defining the identity of a people is important because the total urban population is only 24 percent (vs. 74 percent in the United States). India will soon have the second-largest urban population in the world, but urban dwellers still constitute less than a quarter of the total population of the country. Rural ways and the rural voice still have a significant role, and, as recent national elections in India reveal, a significant voice in determining the priorities and direction of South Asian political life.

There is also a vast disparity between the wealthiest and the poorest of the poor. Recognition of these inequalities has led to the development of **SEWA (Self-Employed Women's Association)** in India and the Grameen Bank and BRAC (Bangladesh Rehabilitation Assistance Committee) in Bangladesh, institutions that have created effective methods for providing capitalization of assets among the poor. Cooperatives modeled on these programs have been set up throughout the subcontinent, primarily to help women develop self-supporting careers.

Religion, language, urban/rural difference, and wealth/poverty all reveal an immense diversity and variety in the social fabric of South Asia. The violence that often results from their interaction reveals the depth and the extent of these differences as establishing the unique identity of each of the many social groupings into which the nations of South Asia are divided.

Extended kinship groups (jatis), tribes, migrant peoples, religious communities, and even highly mobile urban classes are accepted as they are, as distinct communities within a stratified society. Social pressure toward bonding and conformity within these groups is so strong that they are not expected to assimilate or fit in with the distinguishing characteristics of others. They thus remain an encapsulated yet integral part within the whole fabric of South Asian society.

Although there have been periods of great confrontation, discrimination, and violence, the wide diversity among the many different peoples of South Asia is generally accepted as both inevitable and normal. Like the four-fold layering of humanity set forth in the Vedic hymn celebrating the sacrificial offering of primordial man in the creation of the universe, social diversity is a cosmic reality.

IMAGE 3: POST-COLONIAL SOUTH ASIA

On the balmy evening of August 15, 1947, Earl Mountbatten of Burma, the great-grandson of Queen Victoria and the last viceroy of India, gave a sumptuous party in the Mughal Gardens of Delhi to mark the end of the Indian Empire. Thousands of tiny lanterns hung from the bougainvillea and jacaranda trees as the great personalities of India—native princes and Maharajas in dazzling array, British colonial army officers, and Indian politicians—wandered among the fountains and rose beds, sipping champagne and eating canapés. Mountbatten moved among the throng with his vivacious wife, Edwina, whose close relationship with Jawaharlal Nehru, India's foremost statesman, was already the source of local gossip. India had been independent for less than 24 hours, and Pakistan was not yet a day old.

It was a surreal occasion—Britain renouncing and dividing up the jewel of the Empire; India and Pakistan applauding freedom. As night fell on Delhi, that night, the subcontinent was already in flame. Thousands had perished in an orgy of religious riots. Over the coming months the riots spread in a holocaust of communal violence in both newly independent India and Pakistan which challenged the governments of both countries. The break-up of Britain's Indian empire involved the movement of some 12 million people, uprooted, ordered out, or fleeing their homes and seeking safety. The violence polarized communities on the subcontinent as never before. It left two traumatized, injured nations—suspicious and fearful of one another even to this day—where once there had been one country of loosely interwoven peoples.

INDIA: AN EMERGING POWER

Soon after independence, India held great promise; its foreign reserves were among the world's largest, at $2.1 billion in 1950, and it accounted for 2.4 percent of global trade. Over the next 44 years, however, attempts to follow the Soviet model of self-sufficiency brought India to the verge of bankruptcy. Domestic savings failed to keep pace with the investment needed to contain unemployment, especially as India's working age population expanded. The crisis begged for drastic reform, and in 1991 the government delivered. A solid foundation for growth is now in place, backed by successive governments, has increased the country's foreign reserves and raised annual economic growth from an average of around 4 percent in the four decades before the reform to almost 8 percent today. Growth rates of 10 percent are within reach. The amount of foreign direct investment into the country has grown. As India's economic growth has accelerated significantly over the past two decades, so too, has the spending power of its citizen. Real average household disposable income has roughly doubled since 1985. With rising incomes, household consumption has soared and a new Indian middle class has emerged. Over the next two decades income levels will triple and India will climb from its position as the 12th-largest consumer market today to become the world's fifth-largest consumer market by 2025. Over 291 million people will move from desperate poverty to a more sustainable life, and India's middle class will swell to 583 million people. In order for India to achieve these positive results, the country must continue to reform and modernize the economy, as well as address significant shortfalls in its infrastructure and education system which have lagged behind in the postcolonial period. The growing openness and competitiveness of the Indian economy, and favorable demographic trends will help achieve the growth path.

India is expected to become the world's most populous country by 2035. It's already the youngest: one-fifth of the world's population under 24 years lives there. While this kind of population growth represents a huge opportunity, it also highlights the need to invest substantially in human-resources development, particularly in education and health-care, and to create adequate employment opportunities. India's educational attainment remains poor compared with that of other nations, including China: only 60 percent of Indians are literate, compared with 90 percent of Chinese. Reforms designed to improve literacy rates must begin at the elementary-school level. Experience around the world suggests that a good primary education in rural areas is critical. Indian states in general have failed to provide quality education to students in rural areas. Lifting literacy rates will be vital to shift a growing populace from agriculture to high value economic activity. In higher education, India must produce more graduates with the skills needed for employment in the global economy.

While state governments in western and southern states continue with the reform process, eastern states such as Bihar and Uttar Pradesh are lagging behind. Things have started moving in some eastern states like Bihar in recent years, but Jharkhand and Chhattisgarh were not showing any positive developments. Orissa has managed to carry out some of the most difficult reforms. Having also successfully implemented reforms, Orissa is now extremely well placed to fully exploit its large coal and iron-ore reserves; not surprisingly, Orissa attracts almost one-third of the net foreign direct investment to India. Political space and acceptance of reforms is expanding in postcolonial India. The poor are voting in larger numbers—a phenomenon that reflects their desire to participate in the Indian economic success story. That India has survived as the world's largest democracy and is now emerging, with over a billion people, as an economic giant, is one of the remarkable tales of modern times. Postcolonial India's strengths lie in its history of pluralism and

Karol Bagh is a middle class shopping area and is one of the busiest shopping centers in Delhi. People from all parts of the world come here to buy consumer goods, like cloths, gold ornaments, and other items. Perception is that in Karol Bagh one can find good quality merchandise at moderate prices.

the vibrancy of its democracy. Democracy is often portrayed as a handicap in India's drive for economic success and global stature because decision-making can be agonizingly slow. But besides offering a basic human right and dignity, it provides a stability and resilience that help India withstand internal strains.

Rapid, non-linear growth in a democratic environment; aspirations and promise of the world's youngest population; investment opportunities arising out of government's commitment to enable and sustain current levels of growth; market dynamics created by the world's youngest and fastest growing consumer base; the shared history that binds diverse cultures together as they script a prosperous future, are the features which characterize postcolonial India in 2011.

PAKISTAN: A COUNTRY IN TURMOIL

When it emerged as an independent state in 1947, Pakistan was considered a moderate Muslim nation that could serve as a model for other emerging independent Muslim states. Pakistan's founder, Muhammad Ali Jinnah, was a Shia Muslim. Its first law minister was a Hindu. Its foreign minister belonged to the Ahmadiyya sect, which opposes jihad. Although Pakistan's birth was accompanied by religious riots and communal violence, the country's founders clearly intended to create a nonsectarian state that would protect religious freedoms and provide the Muslims of South Asia an opportunity to live in a country where they constituted a majority.

Over the years, however, Pakistan became a major center of Islamic extremism. Pakistan's rulers played upon Islamic ideology as an instrument for strengthening Pakistan's identity.

Islamist militants were cultivated, armed and trained during the 1980s and 1990s in the Pakistani military's effort to seek strategic depth in Afghanistan and to put pressure on India for negotiations over the future of the Himalayan territory of Jammu and Kashmir. An environment dominated by Islamist and militarist ideologies created an ideal breeding ground for radicals and exportable radicalism. Islamic extremists have put down deep roots in society. This goes well beyond the mountainous regions that are the traditional home to religious warrior tribes. The country's largest city, Karachi, is a militant hotbed. Parts of all Pakistani provinces have been radicalized, including the most populous, Punjab. Terrorism now touches all Pakistanis. The country is becoming more like Afghanistan—only with nuclear weapons. The people who cross the porous border between Pakistan and Afghanistan, an arbitrary line drawn by the British in the 1890s—consider them the same country. Pakistan has yet to show that it wants to—or that it can—control the Islamist wave.

In 2011, Pakistan, with an economy hollowed out by bad management, official corruption, and rising Islamic religious fervor is facing a critical mass of despair among its 180 million people. The mixture of religious ideology and economic frustration is sweeping much of Pakistan. The return to civilian government after decades of military rule has meant little to the people because government has done little for the citizens. During more than 60 years of history, the government remains dominated by the families of a favored few wealthy Pakistanis. They maintain a system of corrupt patronage and protect the interests of their landed and industrial class. Parts of Pakistan's major cities—Karachi, Islamabad, and Lahore—have elegant multistory homes with shiny sport utility vehicles parked in gated driveways. But very few of these households pay income tax because the politicians who make the rules are also Pakistan's richest citizens who have found a way to exempt themselves. The overwhelming majority of the country's tax burden is carried by the manufacturing sector which makes up only 19 percent of the nation's economy but pays 51 percent of its taxes. Most economic activity takes place in the shadows. Merchants make up a fifth of the economy, but carry 6 percent of the tax burden. Agriculture which employs half of Pakistan's population pays no federal tax. Its profits go largely to the wealthy landowners. The government takes in little in taxes, and as a result provides little in services. There is a festering inequality in Pakistani society, where the wealth of its most powerful members is never redistributed or put to use for public good.

Poor economic conditions of ordinary people lie at the base of Pakistan's problem. The unemployment rate has soared to 34 percent. Many of the unemployed are young men who attended religious schools, known as madrasas, run by radical clerics who favor Islamist teachings and an anti-Western ideology. Many of them have been recruited by the Taliban, Lashkar-e-Taiba and other militant groups. In 2010 Pakistan was buffeted by major floods, a fresh wave of suicide bombings and the killing of a senior politician early in 2011 for his opposition to the nation's blasphemy laws. The elite security guard who shot the politician has been hailed as a hero by lawyers, politicians and religious leaders.

Yet postcolonial Pakistan with precarious economic and political outlook has continued to survive. It is a state that refuses to fail. A partial explanation for Pakistan's staying power is that it has become an extraordinary state that thrives on crisis. It is well versed in the art of prising cash out of donors by convincing them of abyss. It knows that the United States—which is now providing about $2 billion a year in assistance—will continue to bail it out. The United States approved a $7.5 billion five year assistance package in 2009. The aid program to Pakistan, the second largest recipient of U.S. civilian aid after Afghanistan, is designed to help stabilize the fragile country. The Islamic insurgency has made it dangerous for the U.S. aid personnel to operate in some parts of Pakistan. In addition, the United States remains deeply unpopular in Pakistan, in part due to strikes by unmanned drones against Taliban militants on the border with Afghanistan.

BANGLADESH: LAND OF GREEN AND WATER

Not long ago, when you thought of a South Asian country ravaged by floods and natural disasters, poorly governed and not on the brink of chaos, Bangladesh came to mind. Former U.S. Secretary of State Henry Kissinger called the country a "basket case" at its birth in 1971. Much of the country's post colonial history can be summed up as a blur of political protests and natural disasters punctuated by outbursts of jihadist violence, the occasional military coup, and the long running feud between Prime Minister Wajed and her main rival, Bangladesh Nationalist Party leader Khaleda Zia.

No longer. In 2010 Bangladesh was one of the six countries in Asia and Africa feted by the United Nations for its progress toward achieving its Millennium Development Goals, a set of targets that seek to eradicate extreme poverty and boost health, education and the status of women world-wide by 2015.

Bangladesh has achieved a great deal with its economy growing at nearly 6 percent a year. It exported $12.3 billion worth of garments in 2009. It has curbed population growth with the average Bangladeshi woman having fewer than three children in her lifetime, down from more than six in the 1970s. It has confronted both terrorism and Islamic ideology; the government has arrested local members of the Pakistani terrorist group Lashkar-e-Taiba, and Jamaat-ul-Mujahideen, a domestic outfit responsible for a wave of bombings in 2005.

Politically secular, religiously Muslim, and culturally Bengali, Bangladesh is now relatively stable and prosperous with a higher growth rate and lower birth rate as compared to Pakistan. Both Pakistan and Bangladesh have alternated between civilian and military rule. With 171 million people in Pakistan and 164 million in Bangladesh, they are the world's sixth and seventh most populous countries. But Pakistan houses a vast religious and military establishment that seeks to hold the country together by using Islam and animosity towards India as glue. As a percentage of gross domestic product Pakistan spends more on its soldiers than on its school teachers; Bangladesh does the opposite. In foreign policy, Pakistan seeks to maintain its influence in Afghanistan and wrest control of Indian Kashmir. Bangladesh prefers cooperation to confrontation with its neighbors.

Of course, it will take more before Bangladesh turns the corner for good. Bangladeshi garment workers, who make clothes for western brands such as Gap, Marks and Spencer are among the world's lowest paid garment workers with pay raises in November 2010 ranging from $23 to $43 a month. It was their first pay rise in four years, a period of soaring food and fuel prices. While starting from a cheaper base than China, Bangladeshi industrial hubs are facing mounting labor unrest and intense upward pressure on wages. However, Bangladesh government is sensitive to the interests of garment factory owners, of whom 29 sit in the 300-seat parliament, while many other lawmakers have stakes in garment factories. Those interests leave government unwilling genuinely to engage with labor groups such as the Bangladesh National Garment Workers Federation which has about 23,000 members.

SRI LANKA: A LUSH TROPICAL ISLAND NATION

For a quarter century, postcolonial Sri Lanka seems to have been plagued by misfortune, including a brutal civil war between the Sinhalese majority and Tamil minority. But the conflict finally ended in May 2009, ushering in a more peaceful era for this island off India's coast. Fresh investments and consumer optimism spurred by the end of the war are helping the economy. Expatriates are sending more money home, foreign investors are expanding operations, government is in the middle of an infrastructure push. Victory over the Tamil Tiger separatists has opened the north and east of the country to more development by investing in the area and integrating it with the rest of the island nation's economy. The government is hoping that those regions will make ideal destinations for eco-tourists. Before the conflict started in 1982, Sri Lanka used to attract about half as many tourists as Thailand. In 2009, it attracted less than one-twentieth of the number of tourists who visited Thailand. While tourism accounts for only around 1 percent of the gross domestic product, it could climb as high as 6 percent.

As Sri Lanka recovers from a decades-long civil war, one of its brightest business prospects came as a result of the civil war. With a population of 20 million, Sri Lanka has an estimated 10,000 certified accountants, and an additional 30,000 students are enrolled in accounting programs. Sri Lanka's accounting speciality is rooted in the country's history of colonialism and conflict. As qualified students could not find a place in public universities, many enrolled in private accounting schools with British origins. During the civil war period Sri Lankan accountants sought jobs overseas. But now the government hopes that young Sri Lankan financial experts will stay at home instead. With widespread use of English and a literacy rate of over 80 percent, along with lower wages, Sri Lanka hopes to transform its postwar economy from tea and textiles to a high end outsourcing powerhouse. Offices in Sri Lanka are doing financial work for some of the world's biggest companies such as HSBS and Aviva. It is not simply payroll and bookkeeping, the outsourced work includes derivatives pricing and risk management for money manager and hedge funds, stock research for investment banks and underwriting for insurance companies. The wage differences between Sri Lanka and the United States, and even Sri Lanka and India, are a major factor in attracting global accounting business to Sri Lanka. In 2008 the median annual wage for accountants was $59,430 according to the Bureau of Labor Statistics. Sri Lankan accounting professionals receive an annual pay package of $5,900, according to a 2010 survey by the Chartered Institute of Management Accountants. Wages in Sri Lanka for financial outsourcing are about one-third less than in neighboring India. It appears technology, not textiles, is in Sri Lanka's future.

NEPAL: IN THE SHADOW OF MT. EVEREST

Nestled between emerging nuclear superpowers China and India, Nepal is a country most people think of—if they think of it at all—as the home of the tallest mountain in the world, the mythical yeti monster, the birthplace of Buddha, copious marijuana and plenty of hippie travelers to smoke it. It is still that place for many visitors. But it is also a state teetering on the brink of collapse. The country's present political and economic situation is unstable. Once a monarchy, Nepal is now a fragile democracy.

BHUTAN: KINGDOM IN THE CLOUD

Bhutan. Bhutan is a tiny country wedged between Tibet and India and famous for its national philosophy of "gross national happiness." Unlike the gross national product, gross national happiness is based more on Buddhist spiritual values and cultural traditions than on modern measures of economic success. Bhutan is a modern day Shangri-La in South Asia. Its isolation is more than geographic and applies to many other aspects of life in the country. Television and the Internet did not reach the country until 1999 and even today do not extend to every corner of this largely agrarian country. Bhutanese are required by law to wear national dress in public settings. Men wear a kind of knee-length robe known as the gho, and women wear a full-length dress called the kira. The country has diplomatic relations with only a handful of nations that does not include

the United States. The Bhutanese government sharply limits the number of tourists who may visit—and requires a minimum expenditure of at least $250 a day per person. This way it attracts only well-heeled tourists, in contrast to the backpack crowds that frequent Nepal.

The 21st century is slowly creeping upon Bhutan. The country's revered monarchy engineered a peaceful transition to parliamentary democracy in 2008. Many residents are migrating from rural areas to urban centers like Thimphu. Its population has increased to about 100,000 from 45,000 a decade ago; land values have climbed 150 percent over the past few years. With an economy dominated by agriculture and government work, government is planning development programs to create jobs, and pushing an array of projects, including a new domestic airline, an information technology park, and a $1 billion plus "education city" they hope will attract satellite campuses from major universities in India and abroad. However, the new projects are stirring anxiety among some residents who believe Bhutan's peace and stability may be jeopardized if it opens much further.

THE MALDIVES: PEARL IN THE SEA

Eighty percent of the Maldives, a chain of about 1,200 islands in the Indian Ocean southwest of India, lies no more than about three feet above sea level. The nation's highest point is six feet above the ocean. Threatened with the possibility of becoming the first nation submerged under the sea, the Maldives has championed the cause of reducing industrial greenhouse gases to slow the gradual warming of the Earth's atmosphere.

Since the late 1980s, the Maldives has experienced side effects of global warming: beaches eroded and an increase in severe storms accompanied by tidal swells and floods that have affected a third of its islands. As a small, isolated country, the Maldives has difficulty getting other nations to take seriously the environmental threat to its existence. Government policies have cost the Maldives some of its natural protection from the sea. Around its heavily promoted beach resorts, careless snorkelers, divers and swimmers have killed some coral reefs. Other reefs have been destroyed by islanders who mine them for sand and construction material as their only source of income.

Postcolonial South Asia as a region is going to remain volatile in the coming years and India will have to deal with the developments in Pakistan and Bangladesh. In the coming years, both China and the United States will be assisting Pakistan, militarily as well as economically. However, there has been a growing recognition in the United States and the West about India as a factor of stability in South Asia. This is a major paradigm shift in the Western approach to India.

India has developed greater linkages with Iran, Afghanistan, Gulf States, Myanmar and Southeast Asian countries. India's strategic economic aid to link Herat in Afghanistan with Jawahar port in Iran has removed Afghanistan's complete dependency on Pakistan for its access to the sea. There have been close historical ties between India's western states and the Gulf Region, and today, India's stakes in this region are higher than ever. Indian workers living in the Gulf region, who number 3.8 million, remit US$15–20 billion to India. Over 70 percent of India's oil imports come from Iran and the Gulf and Kerala's economy would suffer if there were any political and economic stability in the region. In Southeast Asia, India has benefited

Aerial view of one of the Maldives Islands, south Asia.

from the substantial level of discomfort and fear with regard to China owing to its big size and domineering economic and military image, and Japan for its World War II colonization campaign. India's benign image and its growth potential is welcomed in Southeast Asia, but the level and range of cooperation will depend considerably on how India engages with China. Road and rail connectivity projects are underway with Myanmar such as the road project connecting Tam with Kalemyo. The viability of a railway project extending up to Hanoi is being discussed. India is developing a hydroelectric power plant on river Kalemyo in Myanmar, through which electricity will be provided to India's northeastern states.

IMAGE 4: DEMOCRACY IN SOUTH ASIA

The spirit of democracy is not a mechanical thing to be adjusted by the abolition of forms. It requires a change of the heart.

—Mohandas K. Gandhi

The nations of South Asia have faced many obstacles in their quest for modern democratic governments.

First of all, the ideology of nationalism based on the will of the people established by adult franchise came from the west through British colonial rule. The formation of such nations evolved over several centuries in western Europe and America among dominant groups of culturally homogeneous people. Those of different cultural backgrounds, those who spoke different languages, and even women, were simply ignored in this process. Because this assumption of a dominant male ethnicity was unchallenged, it was taken for granted that the male citizens' shared sense of identity as a nation would take precedence over any cultural differences among residual minority groups within the nation. All participants in the political process would blend into the culture of the politically dominant.

The assumption that dominant ethnicity determines the distinctive character of a nation could not be easily transposed into the diverse cultural environment of the peoples of South Asia. They are so accustomed to living in what Shashi Tharoor calls "a singular land of the plural," in which no ethnic nor linguistic group is in a majority, that they do not understand common citizenship to be something that would demand greater allegiance than the community identities that separate them from all other linguistic, religious, and social groups among whom they live. They were not prepared to think of themselves as having a shared political identity as a nation.

The idea of modern democracy introduced by colonial rule also did not enter a political vacuum. Traditional sources of honor, allegiance, and identity based on patriarchal structures within the family, in the villages, and among petty kingdoms continued to dominate public life. The Great Mutiny of 1857 in British India demonstrated widespread resistance to British colonial attempts to enlighten its South Asian subjects. The British recognized this indigenous authority when they invited the maharajas who fled during the Mutiny to return to administer their former kingdoms. It is also recognized by those who seek to work with the "warlords" in Afghanistan today.

Efforts in the twentieth century to encourage public participation in the political process, to realize a government of the people, reveal the adaptability of village level, caste community, and language area institutions. Established patterns of grass-roots governance continue to be significant factors in implementing and shaping the transition from traditional power structures into democratic forms.

(United Nations Photo 382236 BP/b)

A group of distinct, hardy people from the province called Baluchistsan, in southwestern Pakistan. They are called 'Baluchis' and noted as the brave 'fighter race'. The wearing style of turbans among these people is different and unique from others.

India, Bangladesh, and Nepal have adopted policies that reserve public offices for women. Even there, those women elected to responsible positions still meet strong resistance to their authority from entrenched patriarchal power elites.

Sirimavo Bandaranaike and Chandrika Kumaratunga, who served as prime ministers and presidents in Sri Lanka, Prime Ministers Indira Gandhi in India, Khaleda Zia and Hasina Wajed in Bangladesh, and Benazir Bhutto in Pakistan are all remarkable women who have served their countries with distinction. Yet, each of them has gained prominence in national political life because of the dominant roles of their fathers or husbands. Traditional power structures do not relinquish their authority easily, if at all.

Religion and National Identity

Because language, religion, and nationality affirm self-authenticating corporate identities, political leaders have drawn upon established languages and religions to create national allegiances and encourage participation in the public domain. The traditional affiliations of dominant religious groups are especially convenient for this purpose.

The division of that portion of British India under the colonial government's direct control into India and Pakistan in 1947 deliberately used religious identity to create new nations. It assigned those districts in which the majority of the population was Muslim to Pakistan, and Hindu-majority districts to India.

Muhammad Ali Jinnah, in his appeal for the founding of Pakistan, claimed the uniqueness of their identity to be based on cultural rather than religious difference. More recently, the Bharatiya Janata Party, the ruling party in India from 1999 to 2004, similarly framed its quest for a policy of Hindu nationalism as cultural, as **Hindutva** (Hindu-ness). They both wanted to avoid the appearance of religious discrimination, even though religious identity was the determining factor.

The use of a religious community's bonding dynamic for political ends changes the relationship it affirms among the people. It reduces religious identity from a symbolic expression of ultimate truth, a *mythos,* to an ideology that is historically concrete, literally true, and both socially and geographically exclusive. At its worst, the political use of religious symbols has led to absolutizing the nation-state itself.

The reduction of religious identity to national identity is pervasive throughout our world today. The fervor created by appealing to people's religious allegiances to promote a political cause or ideology has led to communal rioting, terrorism, and terrible bloodshed. It has left a trail of human misery in the Middle East, Africa, Northern Ireland, the former Yugoslavia, and in South Asia.

The Partition of British India in 1947

The ethnic, linguistic, and religious groupings used in Western Europe to build the political identity of nations became especially divisive in South Asia's pluralistic social environment. The creation of the new nations of India and Pakistan out of the British Indian Empire isolated vast numbers of people not included in the dominant religious identity around which the national borders were drawn. Millions of Hindus and Sikhs living in areas of the subcontinent that became Pakistan, and Muslims finding themselves in an independent India, felt threatened as minorities in these newly established nations. Communal violence erupted across the subcontinent.

Children of many faiths and backgrounds who had grown up together, had learned and played together in the same classes in school for years, suddenly, on the day of independence of their country, became enemies. Dazed and mystified, those of minority faiths were whisked away during the night to seek asylum across the border. Many did not make it.

Fourteen million people fled, the largest refugee migration ever experienced in the world. Homeless and threatened in their own lands, they were forced to flee in haste, destitute of any possessions, to cross the new national borders in a quest for survival. As Hindus and Sikhs moved toward India and Muslims toward Pakistan in opposite directions across the border drawn between the two countries, many thousands were abducted and raped, hundreds of thousands senselessly killed.

Kushwant Singh writes of the devastating impact of that violent confrontation on a Sikh village near the border, in his novel *Train to Pakistan:*

Early in September the time schedule in Mano Majra started going wrong. Goods trains had stopped running altogether, so there was no lullaby to lull them to sleep . . . All trains (now crowded with refugees) coming from Delhi stopped and changed their drivers and guards before moving on to Pakistan.

One morning, a train from Pakistan halted at Mano Majra railway station. At first glance it had the look of trains in the days of peace. No one sat on the roof. No one clung between the bogies. No one was balanced on the foot-boards. But somehow it was different. There was something uneasy about it. It had a ghostly quality.

(That evening) the northern horizon, which had turned a bluish gray, showed orange again. The orange turned into copper and then into luminous russet. Red tongues of flame leaped into the black sky. A soft breeze began to blow towards the village. It brought the smell of burning kerosene, then of wood. And then—a faint acrid smell of searing flesh.

The village was stilled in deathly silence. No one asked anyone else what the odour was. They all knew. They had known it all the time. The answer was implicit in the fact that the train had come from Pakistan.

That evening, for the first time in the memory of Mano Majra, Imam Baksh's sonorous cry did not rise to the heavens to proclaim the glory of God.

Those who survived this massive migration did not experience the exhilaration of political freedom. They found themselves bewildered refugees, homeless in the lands of their birth, unwelcome in the lands to which they fled. The Partition of British India led to a human catastrophe that has left an abiding scar on the subcontinent.

The Independence of Bangladesh in 1971

A further consequence of the 1947 partition of British India was the separation in 1971 of East Pakistan to form the independent country of Bangladesh. The ethnic and linguistic identity of the Bengali Muslims, which they share with the people of West Bengal in India, proved stronger than their religious identity as Muslims in a Pakistan dominated by the ethnically and linguistically different, and financially advantaged, Muslim population of West Pakistan.

The Pakistan government, then under the martial rule of General Yahya Khan, sought to preserve its union by military force. It subjected the Bengali freedom fighters movement to an intense military assault from West Pakistan in a desperate attempt to hold the country together. According to a *New York Times* report at that time (June 7, 1971):

People have killed each other because of race, politics, and religion; no community is entirely free of guilt. But the principal agent of death and hatred has been the Pakistani Army. And its killing has been selective. According to reliable reports from inside East Pakistan, the Army's particular targets have been intellectuals and leaders of opinion—doctors, professors, students, writers.

That reign of terror caused over 200,000 deaths. And eight million people fled across the East Pakistan border into the squalor of refugee camps in the neighboring states of India. That number included over 1,500 physicians and 10,000 teachers. The International Rescue Committee reported in 1971:

With the closure of the borders by the Pakistani military, large numbers are continuing to infiltrate through the 1,300-mile border with India through forest and swamps. These groups, with numbers sometimes up to 50,000 in a 24-hour period, have for the most part settled along major routes in India. They are found wherever there is a combination of available ground and minimal water supply. . . . The refugee camps may vary in size from small groups to upwards of 50,000. There has been an extraordinary effort on the part of the West Bengal and Indian governments to organize these camps and supply them with at least minimal amounts of food and water.

The refugee diet . . . consists of rice boiled in open clay pots, some powdered milk which is occasionally available, and dall, which is a lentil type of bean used for a thin soup . . . At this point the diet would be classified as barely adequate.

Political turmoil along with annual heavy flooding of its many rivers has sustained the flow of refugees out of the country. It is estimated that anywhere from 7 million to 12 million Bangladeshis are living in India today. Lack of documentation and of will has hampered sporadic attempts to repatriate these refugees to their homeland.

A military coup killed the leader of the freedom movement, Prime Minister Mujibur Rahman, in 1975, just four years after independence. And a second coup killed his successor, General Ziaur Rahman in 1981. Their deaths initiated an intense rivalry between Mujibur Rahman's daughter, Sheikh Hasina, as head of his Awami League, and Begum Khaleda Zia, the widow of General Zia, head of his Bangladesh National Party. As leaders of the country's two largest political parties, their opposition has denied the country political stability for almost twenty-three years.

Islamist militancy and terrorism have grown during this time of political turmoil, particularly on a wave of fundamentalist Islamist fervor throughout the Muslim world following the 9/11 terrorist attacks in the United States. Begum Zia's Bangladesh National Party (BNP) defeated Sheikh Hasina's Awami League government in October, 2001, with the support of the Jamaat-e-Islami. That radical Islamist party had sided with the Pakistani army during the quest for Bangladesh independence in 1971, and has continued to push its agenda for a fundamentalist religious identity for both Bangladesh and Pakistan.

Terrorist incidents rose from sixty in 2004 to ninety in 2005, in which 396 people died. Notable among these incidents were grenade attacks at Awami League political rallies, in Dhaka on August 21, 2004, which killed 22 party members, and in Habiganj on January 27, 2005. The deaths of five Awami League activists there included Shah A. M. S. Kibria, former Finance Minister, Foreign Secretary, and Executive Secretary of the United Nations Economic and Social Commission for Asia and the Pacific. Sheikh Hasina received injuries during those attacks, for which she received treatment in the United States in the summer of 2008.

A dramatic sequel of terrorism happened seven months later. As described by Haroon Habib in *The Hindu,* August 23:

> August 17, 2005, will go down in the annals of Bangladesh history. In an unprecedented act of terror, nearly 500 bombs went off simultaneously in 63 of Bangladesh's 64 districts killing 2 people and injuring at least 200. The targets were government and semi-government establishments, especially the offices of local bodies and court buildings.

The Zia government did little to investigate attacks on its political opposition, and to check the rise of further terrorist acts. Public opinion attributes this reluctance to the need of support from the Islamic fundamentalist parties to retain its tenuous control of power.

Begum Zia's government did make a claim to "successfully combat terrorism in the name of Islam" by high profile arrests in March, 2006, of two terrorist group leaders who had close links with, and the protection of, the Jamaat-e-Islami party, a fundamentalist coalition member in her government. Their capture in anticipation of national elections expected to be held in January 2007, suggested that the ruling Bangladesh National Party acknowledged that popular support for religious extremists, never great, was declining, and their support might become a political liability.

Mob demonstrations leading up to the January election caused its suspension and the imposition of a military-backed caretaker government. During its rule, in an attempt to defuse their political antagonism, both Sheikh Hasina and Begum Zia and some 200 other political leaders from both of their parties were placed in jail on charges of graft and corruption. In a further move toward normalcy, the interim government set December 29, 2008, for national elections for a new government. Under political pressure to assure the participation of both of their parties in these elections, both leaders were released from jail on bail.

With a strong showing in local elections held on August 4, and the triumphant return of Sheikh Hasina from her medical treatment in the United States on November 6, the Awami League did extremely well, winning 230 of 299 seats in the National Legislature in the December 29 national elections. With its commitment to secular government and its more conciliatory stance toward India, the country can look forward to greater control over terrorist activity in its midst.

Continuing Kashmir Problem

The large number of refugees and continuing incidents of terrorism in South Asia since 1947 reveal the heavy toll in human displacement and suffering caused by religious nationalism in seeking political identity among the culturally diverse peoples of the subcontinent.

When India and Pakistan became independent in 1947, forty percent of British India was under the direct control of independent Maharajas. In recognition of their sovereignty, it was determined that they should decide to which country they should accede, to either India or Pakistan. In most cases, as they were not given any other choice, that was an easy decision. The state of Jammu and Kashmir was unusual in that it had a Muslim majority under the rule of a wavering Hindu Maharaja, Hari Singh. He was already facing an indigenous independence movement closely tied to the **Indian National Congress,** lead by Sheikh Abdullah, the "Lion of Kashmir."

For Pakistan, Kashmir's accession was an issue of their religious identity as an Islamic state. Because the majority of the population of the state was Muslim, under the rules set by the British Raj for partition, it should be part of Pakistan. India illegally invaded Kashmir in 1947, and has been forcefully occupying that portion of the former princely state that was not liberated by Pakistan in 1948 and by treaty in 1965. Because Pakistan became a separate country to protect the freedom and the cultural integrity of the Islamic peoples in the subcontinent, its support for the freedom of the Kashmiri people from Hindu India's oppression is integral to its identity as an Islamic state. Pakistan has been eager to engage international support to implement 1948 UN resolutions for a plebiscite to let the people of Kashmir decide to which country they want to belong.

For India, it is an issue of the sovereignty of a secular nation. It asserts that Kashmir became an integral part of the country when the Maharajah of Jammu and Kashmir, even under duress, acceded it to India in 1947, according to those terms of the partition of India and Pakistan. Only in the Vale of Kashmir do Muslims outnumber Hindus, who predominate in the Jammu section of the state, as do Buddhists in Ladakh. Because of this diversity of religious groups, India's response is framed in its constitutional commitment to secularism. In Kashmir, as in the nation, the religious identity of any segment of the population should not determine the political status of the whole.

Its claim to sovereignty has been validated, India contends, by elections held for public office in their portion of the state since 1952, although sporadically between 1980 and 2002, and again in 2008. They obviate the need for a UN plebiscite. Such elections, it also points out, have never been held in Pakistan occupied Kashmir, which is ruled by a governor appointed by the central government in Islamabad.

The people of Kashmir are caught in this dispute between India's claim of secular identity and Pakistan's religious nationalism. It led to outright warfare between the two countries, in 1948 and in 1965, when the state was divided along a Line of Control. On either side of this line, both India and Pakistan describe the other's portion as foreign occupied.

The hope of those living in the Vale of Kashmir to preserve their own independent, more accepting, traditional life has been jolted first by heavy handed Indian administration in the name of making them part of India. But even more devastating has been the rise of terrorism as an instrument of opposition to Indian subjection and humiliation of Kashmir's Muslim population. The military occupation and the insurgency in Kashmir have accounted for more than 45,000 deaths there since 1989.

The level of violence also drove some 300,000 Hindu pandits from their ancient homes in the Vale of Kashmir, many as refugees into Jammu. Life in the Vale became for them a living hell.

Salmon Rushdie describes a Pandit's loss of harmony and the peaceful beauty of the sonorous mountains of Kashmir in his novel *Shalimar the Clown*.

[Pandit Pyarelal Kaul] closed his eyes and pictured his Kashmir. He conjured up its crystal lakes, Shishnag, Walur, Nagin, Dal; its trees, the walnut, the poplar, the chinar, the apple, the peach; its mighty peaks, Nanga, Parbat, Rakaposhi, Harmukh. *The pandits Sanskritized the Himalayas.* He saw the boats like little fingers tracing lines in the surface of the waters and the flowers too numerous to name, ablaze with bright perfume. He saw the beauty of the golden children, the beauty of the green- and blue-eyed women, the beauty of the green- and blue-eyed men. He stood atop Mount Shankaracharya which the Muslims called Takht-e-Sulaiman and spoke aloud the famous old verse concerning the earthly paradise. *It is this, it is this, it is this.* Spread out below him like a feast he saw gentleness and time and love. He considered getting out his bicycle and setting forth into the valley, bicycling until he fell, on and on into the beauty. *O! Those days of peace when we all were in love and the rain was in our hands wherever we went.* No, he would not ride out into Kashmir, did not want to see her scarred face, the lines of burning oil drums across the roads, the wrecked vehicles, the smoke of explosions, the broken houses, the broken people, the tanks, the anger and fear in every eye. *Everyone carries his address in his pocket so that at least his body will reach home.*

Afghanistan: Soviets, Taliban, and Terrorism

Terrorist attacks against innocent people in response to competing ideologies and military oppression have been a part of the South Asian landscape for many years. Afghanistan began to experience the severe devastation of warfare and terrorism in 1979, when the Soviet Union sent troops into Afghanistan to suppress those opposed to the Afghan People's Democratic (Communist) Party rule. The military might of the Soviet army forced some 400,000 Afghan Pashtuns to flee into Pakistan, to live in refugee camps among the 16 million Pashtuns who live on the other side of the Durand Line that divides them between two countries. The Soviet's devastating scorched earth policy over the next decade forced many more across the borders into refugee camps in Pakistan and Iran. By 1989, the number of refugees rose to six million, more than one-third of the country's total population.

Most came across in groups of fifty or one hundred, villages or nomad clans led by maliks, the local tribal chieftains. They brought more than 2 million animals with them—goats, sheep, buffaloes and camels. It was a timeless sight. The men in turbans or woolen or embroidered caps, baggy pants and vests or robes like academic gowns, bandoliers of cartridges across their chests, old rifles or new machine guns on one shoulder. Their sons

were dressed the same way, miniatures of their fathers. The animals and the women walked behind. When they stopped, they sometimes took the tents offered by the United Nations or, sometimes, just recreated their katchi villages on the other side of the mountains. Then the men, many of them, went back to kill Russians.

—Richard Reeves, *Passage to Peshawar*

The Pakistan government aided especially those refugees who belonged to conservative religious groups called the mujahideen (holy warriors), who had been engaged in opposing social and political reform in their country even before the Soviet incursion. Finding support for his own military rule by assisting the United States in resisting Soviet expansion into the region, General Zia al-Haq contributed not only advanced military weapons, but also medical assistance, terrorist training, and encouragement to those who fled the devastation of Soviet attacks on their lands. Iran and Saudi Arabia also made significant contributions to the Afghan cause. As a result, the refugee camps became not just places of refuge for those displaced from Afghanistan, but also staging and rehabilitation areas for the mujahideen returning to fight against Soviet occupation in their country.

The success of this insurgency led to the withdrawal of the Soviet army in 1989, and consequently of U.S. support to Afghanistan. Their withdrawal created space for intense internal fighting among rival mujahideen leaders, who were united only to oppose Communist rule in their country. Their warfare for control of Kabul caused immense destruction to the city. Hundreds of thousands fled, reducing by half its prewar population of close to 1 million. Countless others abandoned their blown-out villages.

In 1993, the Taliban, a militant Islamic revolutionary movement, arose amidst the country's political chaos, violence, and corruption with an urgent call for fundamentalist religious reform. With Pakistani and Al Qaeda support, it was able to capture Kabul in 1996, and, by 1999, to dominate some 90 percent of the country. It imposed upon the lands it controlled a welcome sense of peace, together with an extremely oppressive social order based on a religious ideology which asserted strict adherence to Islamic law and rejected democracy as an assault on God's sovereignty over all aspects of human life.

During the years of occupation, internal conflict, and Taliban domination any semblance of civic order and public services simply disappeared. In the solemn words of Barnett R. Rubin, "Afghanistan has been ruled, in whole or in part, at times badly and at times atrociously, but it has not been governed."

Hazardous also were land mines planted through wide, unmapped areas of the country. Reports in the fall of 2002 recorded over 300 land mine injuries a month throughout the country. And then came the intensive bombing by U.S. forces to destroy Al Qaeda and Taliban in response to the terrorist attacks in the United States on 9/11/2001. All of these offered small inducement for the refugees to return to their former homes. Refugee camps, with strong international support, provided some opportunities for education, social reform, health care, and employment not available under Taliban domination in their homelands, especially to women.

By the end of 2001, 12 years after the Soviet withdrawal, 2.2 million refugees were still in Pakistan, 2.4 million in Iran and around 1 million in refugee camps in Afghanistan itself.

Two million refugees returned in 2002, overwhelming the meager resources available in Afghanistan. In January 2003, the UN High Commission on Refugees recommended that no more return because of the lack of security, facilities, and humanitarian aid to support them.

In December 2001, a UN-sponsored Bonn Agreement provided for a provisional government, with a U.S. endorsed Pashtun, Hamid Karzai, elected its leader. Steps toward a permanent government began with preparations for a national election for president in October 2004. Karzai won 55 percent of the vote, and became president for a five-year term. Elections for Parliament and 34 provincial assemblies were held in September 2005.

The results of these elections reaffirmed the religiously conservative bases of power among the clan and tribal leaders in the countryside. Their fundamentalist ideology and militant opposition to foreign intervention was revealed in the resurgence of the Taliban among Pashtuns on both sides of the Durand Line, supported by the illicit wealth of opium production. Increasing acts of terrorism, and devastating military battles between the Taliban and U.S. and NATO forces assigned to suppress them are creating havoc and destruction among the civilian population, particularly among the Pashtuns.

Without an effective response to the Taliban's terrorist violence in support of religious fundamentalism and in opposition to foreign military occupation, Afghanistan will remain a battered and impoverished nation. Inefficiency and corruption in government is also slowing meager attempts at reconstruction and rehabilitation among a people too long punished by opposing regional, ethnic, and religious forces within and international competition from outside.

Terrorism in Pakistan

The encouragement of the mujahideen in response to the Soviet occupation of Afghanistan in 1979, together with General Zia al-Haq's policy of Islamization to gain popular support for his despotic rule, gave impetus to Islamist militancy in Pakistan. And concern to maintain influence in Afghanistan as a policy of "strategic depth" to protect its own safety, led Pakistan to support the expansion of the Taliban as it grew to assert its fundamentalist religious agenda across most of Afghanistan during the 1990s.

The shared religious fervor of the Pashtuns on both sides of the border intensified with the destruction of the twin towers of the World Trade Center in New York on September 11, 2001. The 9/11 attacks confirmed for all Islamist militants the symbolic power of terrorism, even against overwhelming economic and military odds, as it had also overcome the Soviet military occupation in Afghanistan.

Muslims throughout South Asia saw the American "war on terror" in response to 9/11, particularly the invasion of Iraq, as an attack on their faith. Such an assault legitimized the violence of the extremists' jihad (holy war) to protect Islam. Such was evident in the extensive violent protests in Pakistan depicted in a cartoon of Mohammad in a Danish newspaper, which was offensive even to the more numerous but unheard moderate Muslims in the country opposed to violence.

The "war on terror" also presented President Musharraf with a demand to choose whether Pakistan was going to continue to support the Taliban or withdraw it to provide the United States with a base to attack the Taliban and Al Qaeda in Afghanistan. His commitment to join the United States in the "war on terror" contained several ambiguities that continued to complicate this new relationship.

First of all, it did not acknowledge Pakistan's need for its own security to maintain "strategic depth" in Afghanistan by retaining what vestige it could of influence that had, before 9/11, been the charge of Pakistan's military intelligence (ISI). Particularly unsettled by India's increasing diplomatic and rehabilitation activity with the Karzai government in Kabul, the role of ISI in Afghanistan has not been clear.

Pakistan's commitment to the "war on terror" also assumed that General Musharraf, as president, had control over the rugged, mountainous Federally Administered Tribal Areas (FATA) along the border with Afghanistan, into which the Al Qaeda leadership and the Taliban insurgency in Afghanistan escaped during U.S. military engagement in the fall of 2001. Since Pakistan's independence, this area had been loosely administered among autonomous, isolated tribes outside of the jurisdiction of the national government and courts. Fiercely independent, the tribal leaders did not recognize any institution of the government, and particularly the army, as its own.

More complex was Musharraf's assertion that he alone could control the threat of terrorist activity emanating from this area, a conceit that he exploited to garner financial support from the United States to sustain his military government.

A final ambiguity in General Musharraf's commitment of Pakistan to the American "war on terror" was the assumption that use of military force is an effective response to terrorism. Because it is a response to the symptoms of terrorist violence throughout South Asia, military intervention has served more as a stimulant to more violence than a solution to the ideological issues from which it stems.

In reality, rather than suppressing Taliban insurgency in Afghanistan, the "war on terror" created an indigenous Taliban movement in FATA for jihad (holy war) against not only the American "war on terror" but also Pakistan's complicity in it. The Pakistani Taliban soon developed sufficient strength to challenge the tribal leaders in FATA, and to threaten the entire country. Musharraf's attack to remove militant Islamists from the Lal Masjid (Red Mosque) in Islamabad in July, 2007, was a critical step toward his resignation as president on August 18, 2008. By the time of his declaration of a state of emergency on November 3, 2007, he had effectively lost control of everything in the country. The assassination of Benizer Bhutto on December 27, and the results of the parliamentary elections on February 18, 2008, drove home this reality,

The subsequent bombing of the Marriott Hotel in Islamabad on September 20, 2008, was a vivid awakening to Islamist terrorism in the most secure center of the nation. It was becoming a threat to the very survival of Pakistan itself.

Terrorism in India

Terrorist groups in Pakistan that had taken up the cause of Muslims in Kashmir were also energized by the success of the jihad (holy war) in Afghanistan during the 1980s. Following the withdrawal of the Soviet army from Afghanistan in 1989, India identified large numbers of Islamic militants trained in camps set up by the **Lashkar-e-Taiba, Jaish-e-Mohammad,** and

Hizbul Mujahideen, terrorist organizations with purported contacts with Pakistan's intelligence agency (ISI), to train jihadis to infiltrate into Kashmir to fight with local insurgents and to organize terrorist cells there.

Following 9/11, President General Musharraf of Pakistan sought to use his prominence as a critical ally in the effort to rout **Al Qaeda** and the Taliban out of Afghanistan to bring his country's claim for Kashmir to the international community for resolution.

Because both India and Pakistan accepted Taliban accountability for terrorism for harboring Al Qaeda terrorists in Afghanistan, India thought that the United States should hold President Musharraf to the same standard for his government's support for those committing terrorist acts in India. After numerous diplomatic encounters to improve relations between the United States and India, the American government applied strong diplomatic pressure on President Musharraf to rein in recognized terrorist groups in Pakistan, and to limit infiltrators and support from them to the insurgency. This he agreed to do in January 2002, and the number of terrorist incidents in Kashmir began to diminish.

Secret negotiations to find a solution to the Kashmir dispute have intensified among private parties and public officials. At the meeting of the Non-Aligned Nations in Havana in September 2006, Prime Minister Manmohan Singh and President Musharraf initiated a framework toward resolving their differences over terrorism and other issues of the Kashmir conflict. Asif Ali Zardari, upon his election as president of Pakistan on September 11, 2008, announced that resolution of this conflict was high on the agenda for his new administration.

But even with this improving environment, terrorist activities in India have not ceased. A series of bomb explosions in a number of cities outside of Kashmir began in 1993, at the same time when Islamist terrorists made their first attempt to blow up the World Trade Center in New York City. Twelve bombs exploded in Bombay, one near the Stock Exchange, killing 287 and wounding 713. On October 29, 2005, an explosion in the Sarojini Nagar Bazaar in New Delhi, killed 62 people, and injured 155 more. A sniper killed an Indian Institute of Technology professor in Bangalore on December 27, 2005. Bombs were set off in a railway station and a Hindu temple in Varanasi on March 7, 2006, killing 21 and wounding 62. More dramatic in this series was another set of bombs set in seven commuter trains leaving Mumbai on July 11, 2006, exploding within a span of 11 minutes, killing 187, and injuring over 700. And even more recently, terrorists carried out a blatant military raid on several high profile hotels, the railway terminal, a hospital, Jewish center, and restaurant in the center of Mumbai's financial district on November 26, 2008. Indian authorities trace these incidents to militant cells, some based in Kashmir, with ties to terrorist groups in Pakistan. Police and covert services have not been adequate to anticipate and avert these devastating attacks.

As in Pakistan, terrorism based on religious ideology is also coming from different indigenous sources. Alleged state government complicity in the mob devastation of the Muslim community in Godhra, Gujarat, following the death of 58 Hindu pilgrims in a train fire on February 27, 2002, radicalized an indigenous protest movement called the Students Islamic Movement of India (SIMI). An offshoot of this group, calling itself the Indian Mujahideen, claimed responsibility for a series of terrorist bomb attacks in a number of cities, including Jaipur on May 13, Ahmedabad on July 26, and Delhi on September 13, 2008.

A similar form of terrorist act occurred on September 8, 2006, near a mosque in Malegaon, in northern Maharashtra, killing 31 people, and injuring over 200 others. A sequel bombing on September 29, 2008, identified the perpetrators as members of a Hindu extremist group, and other sources of terrorist attacks in India.

These bombings are not the only source of terrorist activity in India. Nor are they all conducted by religious extremists. A violent peasants revolt in the village of Naxalbari, West Bengal started the Naxalite Maoists revolutionary movement in eastern India in 1967. Today, the movement is conducting a terrorist insurgency against the government and civil militias in the mineral rich forests of eastern India, causing havoc, mostly among tribal peoples. A humanitarian doctor, Dr. Binayak Sen, who set up a hospital for the poor in Chhattisgarh, has been imprisoned for alleged links with the Maoists since May 14, 2007. His imprisonment has provided him opportunity to formulate thoughtful, nonviolent steps toward resolution of this conflict in his October 21, 2008, Letter from the Raipur Jail.

Separatist insurgents in the northeastern states north of Bangladesh have sporadically carried out deadly attacks on the civilian population. On October 30, 2008, three car bombings in Assam killed 77 people. Although there was an initial attempt to place blame for this act on a Bangladesh based Islamist terrorist group (HuJI), evidence of the purchase of the cars used for the bombing identified the National Democratic Front of Bodoland as responsible. The NDFB was formed in 1986 to agitate for a separate state for the Bodo people. Its terrorist activity had been seriously limited by the destruction of its training camps in Bhutan by the Bhutan Royal Army in 2004. This attack also came as a surprise.

With so much terrorist activity going on in India, Prime Minister Manmohan Singh proclaimed at a police academy graduation ceremony on October 27, 2006: "Terrorism is the most dangerous threat today and it has become a hydra-headed monster."

This sentiment was repeated by Maulana Mansoorpuri at a gathering of 6,000 Muslim religious leaders from all over India at the Darul Uloom Deoband in Hyderabad on November 8, 2008 to ratify a fatwa against terrorism. The fatwa asserts emphatically "There is no relation whatsoever between Islam and terrorism. . . . Islam rejects all kinds of unjust violence, breach of peace, bloodshed, murder and plunder and does not allow it in any form."

The use of religious identity for ideological objectives has contributed to much of the terrorist violence in South Asia. Large numbers of civilians have also been killed or become refugees as the result of communal violence in both Sri Lanka and Bhutan, where the overwhelming majority of their populations are Buddhist. That those belonging to religious minorities also speak a different language adds to their separation from the dominant religious majorities in both of these countries. But the source of this violence is more in the quest for national identity than religious ascendancy, in the name of ideology rather than of truth.

The Sri Lankan Scene

Despite its many achievements in democracy, economics, and human development, Sri Lanka has been entangled since 1983 in devastating communal warfare between the government and a militant faction of Tamil-speaking Hindus called the Liberation Tigers for Tamil Eelam (Nation), the LTTE. This dispute has caused over 65,000 deaths and displaced as refugees more than a million people.

Tamil speakers make up about 18 percent of the total population of the country. They live mostly in the northern and eastern part of the island, which has been a Tamil homeland for more than 2,000 years. There they constitute a plurality if not an outright majority in the political districts of that region.

The example of the creation of India and Pakistan would have suggested the division of the island into two countries, based on the majority populations in each of the districts of the British Crown colony, then called Ceylon. But in 1948, it was hoped that the political identity of a unified island nation would take precedence over the religious and linguistic identities of its constituent regions. It was also hoped that such a unifying political identity would prevail over any cultural and linguistic affinity of the Tamil population in northern Sri Lanka with the larger neighboring state of Tamil Nadu, across the Palk Strait in south India.

At the time of independence, there were an additional 800,000 Indian Tamils in Ceylon. They were distinct from the indigenous Tamil community of the north, imported by the British from Tamil-speaking south India during the nineteenth century to work on the coffee, rubber, and tea plantations in the southern hills of the colony. The new Ceylonese government declared these Tamils stateless and pushed for their repatriation to India. In 1964, and again in 1974, the government of India agreed to receive 600,000 "plantation Tamils" back into India. The Ceylonese Tamils saw these deportations as ominous.

Tensions between the Sinhalese majority and Tamil minority increased during a period of uneasy accommodation. In 1956, which marked the 2,500th anniversary of the Buddha's attaining *nirvana,* the newly-elected Sri Lanka Freedom Party passed the "Sinhala Only" act to make the language of the Buddhist majority the one official language of the country. In response to Tamil protests, originally non-violent, communal riots broke out, leading up to 1983, when anti-Tamil riots throughout the country killed over a thousand people. The LTTE, a small, militant separatist group, then rose with a vengeance to defend the linguistic identity and political freedom of the Tamil people. Guerrilla warfare broke out in the predominantly Tamil-speaking areas of the north and east.

The devastation caused by this violent insurgency and the Sinhalese Army response to put it down forced many Tamils to flee the country. By May 1991, some 210,000 refugees were reported to have made it to south India. Another 200,000 sought asylum in Europe. But most displaced by warfare have continued to suffer the ravages of civil conflict in Sri Lanka, dependent upon relief efforts set up within the country itself. They became refugees in their own land.

In 1987, the Sri Lankan government invited India to send a "Peace Keeping Force" to attempt to suppress the LTTE. But the deployment of the Indian army was not able to bring the two sides together, and the invitation was withdrawn in 1990.

Between 1983 and 2002, in spite of two brief cease-fires and talks between the LTTE and the Sri Lanka government, warfare increased in intensity and devastation.

With encouragement from the Norwegian government, both sides of the conflict agreed to a cease-fire in 2002, and entered into negotiations toward a political settlement of their dispute. Displaced persons from the northeast region of the country began to return to their homes.

There was little progress in negotiations during a period of military restraint. The LTTE strengthened its forces, abducting children into its military according to UNICEF reports. It also established de-facto administrative control in the north and east region. Because of bickering over control of relief and rehabilitation efforts, even the shared catastrophic impact of the Indian Ocean **tsunami** in 2004 did not bring the opposing forces any closer together. Military encounters, with increasing intensity, broke down the cease-fire agreement during 2006. The Sri Lanka army then undertook a costly major offensive against the LTTE, driving its forces during the fall of 2008 into its fortified bases along the northeast coast of the country.

In response to a plea from the government of India over the plight of Tamil civilians endangered by this intensified fighting, President Rajapaksa assured that he was "clear that there are no military solutions to political questions. I am committed to political solution and ending Tamil civilian hardships."

Despair in the lives of the Tamil people and a compassionate resolution of their civil conflict is summarized in the plain words of Jagan, recorded by Nirupama Subramanian in *Sri Lanka, Voices from a War Zone:* "We carry a double burden now. We have to fight the Sinhalese racism and the tyranny of the Tigers, both together."

Bhutan's Refugee Problem

Even the small country of Bhutan, tucked away in the high Himalayan mountains, has not been immune from an ideological crisis and violence in shaping its path to representative democracy. The shape of the issue appears discouragingly familiar: Can the identity of the nation include as citizens all those living within its borders who belong to distinct ethnic, religious, and linguistic minorities?

The gradual move toward modernization in this mountain kingdom has led to the migration of laborers, some from India, but in greater numbers from Nepal. The Nepali immigrants have settled almost entirely in the more productive southern part of the country, where they live as a distinct minority called Lhotshampas. In 1988 they were estimated to constitute as much as 42 percent of the population of Bhutan.

This migration challenged the traditional way of life of the Bhutanese people. To meet this challenge, the government of Bhutan took a number of actions to create a national identity based upon its Buddhist heritage. These actions included the adoption of Dzongkha as the national language and the mandating of a national dress for formal occasions. These actions were not specifically aimed at the Nepali population though. However, actions were reflective of the agitation brought on by Nepalis living in the neighboring former kingdom of Sikkim that became part of India in 1974.

In 1985, the government passed a Citizenship Act, which allowed citizenship only to those Nepalis who could claim residency before 1958. In 1988, this act was enforced by a census in southern Bhutan, to identify those immigrants who could not claim legal residency. The rigor of this census became a direct assault on the Nepalis. The deportations, social unrest, and terrorist acts which followed led to the flight of many Nepalis from the country. By July, 1993, 85,000 had made their way into refugee camps set up by the United Nations High Commission for Refugees in eastern Nepal.

The governments of Nepal and Bhutan have met 16 times to seek a solution to the plight of these refugees. In 2001, the Bhutan government offered a process for selecting those eligible for repatriation. But its terms were so restrictive that little was accomplished.

There is hope that international pressure can encourage an early and just solution. In September 2008, the United States agreed to admit 4,833 as a first installment of resettling 60,000 of these refugees. Militant factions in Bhutan oppose this resettlement option, convinced that only restoration to full citizenship in Bhutan is an acceptable solution for all refugees now living in deteriorating conditions in the UNHCR camps in Nepal. They also launched terrorist bombing in Thimpu on January 20, 2008, to protest the exclusiveness of the country's first national elections.

The basic issue remains: how can Lhotshampas be accepted and protected as full citizens in Bhutan's new constitutional monarchy if the nation's identity is defined exclusively by religion and language?

Terrorism in Nepal

Nepal, by contrast, experienced a dramatic change in terrorist activity in 2006. Seventy-seven terrorist incidents occurred in the first three months. Then they suddenly dropped to almost none.

Maoist militants had ravaged the country since 1996, an insurgency against the "feudal autocracy" of the king that has claimed more than 13,000 lives. But in May 2006, the Maoists decided to abandon armed struggle to remove the oppression of monarchy in Nepal by joining in a cease-fire with a recently empowered Seven Party Alliance. To participate in a democratic republic free of royal interference became for them a more promising way to achieve their revolutionary goals.

Many were skeptical, but the leaders of the Maoists and the Seven Party Alliance agreed on November 21, 2006, to a UN supervised disarmament of both Maoist and Royal Nepali Army forces and a government run by a Council of Ministers, with the king deprived of all power during the interim period.

The immense significance of this Comprehensive Peace Agreement was proclaimed by Girija Prasad Koirala, the leader of the Seven Party Alliance, at the time of signing: "This has given a message to the international community and terrorists all over the world that no conflict can be resolved by guns. It can be done by dialogue."

Further negotiations became necessary to overcome opposition to elections for a national Constituent Assembly from separatist groups, especially among the Madhesi people who live in the southern, Hindi speaking Terai. These discussions led to a dual ballot system to provide proportional representation for women and oppressed and marginalized groups, and constituency level voting for political parties in the Constituent Assembly. Elections were held on April 10, 2008, which provided the Maoist Party with 220 of 601 seats. A coalition of the other major parties led to the election of president Ram Baran Yadav, and the first vice president Parmananda Jha, both of whom are Madhesis. The president, in turn, appointed Pushpa Kamal Dahal, known as Prachanda, the leader of the Maoist insurgency, as prime minister. The Assembly voted (560–4) to depose King Gyanendra on May 28, 2008, to bring a peaceful end to 240 years of monarchy in Nepal.

Strides toward Democracy

Newly elected governments with high voter participation in Nepal, Pakistan, Bangladesh, Bhutan, and the Maldives (which ended 30 years of rule by a benevolent despot without violence in a run-off election for president on October 29, 2008), indicate that the nations of South Asia are making strides toward democracy. But they still face many political and economic challenges. As the diversity among them might suggest, none of them has responded to these challenges in the same way. How each is progressing on its separate path is discussed in each of the country reports that follow.

A common thread among these varied responses has been the attempt to achieve a political solution to adversarial relations among peoples that are based on more traditional and profound expressions of human identity than that of the nation-state. A political solution to human strife was the assumption and the promise in the formation of nations in Western Europe during the eighteenth and nineteenth centuries. But the experience of two world wars in the twentieth century and the continuing presence of terrorist violence and of refugees throughout the world suggest the inadequacy of nationalism based on self-determination as a way to achieve lasting unity and peace.

The independence of nations and freedom of the individual are worthy political goals. But the South Asia experience reveals to us that they are not ends in themselves. Nor can they be imposed. It has to evolve from within.

Alexis de Tocqueville observed in the early years of the nineteenth century that the long-term success of democracy in the United States depends not upon the structure and institutions of the government, but upon the habits of the heart of the American people. Mahatma Gandhi, on the threshold of political independence for the people of India, also realized that democracy was not just a matter of form. It is a matter of the heart and soul of a people.

IMAGE 5: MAHATMA GANDHI

Generations to come, it may be, will scarce believe that such a one as this ever in flesh and blood walked upon this earth.

—Albert Einstein

The name of Mahatma Gandhi comes up in a number of contexts in looking at the uniqueness of South Asia. His role in shaping the freedom movement on the subcontinent was immense. He identified himself with the common people, adopted their dress and simplicity of life, and traveled from village to village to spread his message of reform. He encouraged everyone to use the spinning wheel and to wear clothes made of the hand-spun cloth called khadi. He called for national boycotts. And he fasted. In these many ways, he managed to get everyone involved in the political process of becoming a new nation.

In this way he was able to restructure the Indian National Congress as the instrument for India's freedom. The power base of this movement had resided in an intellectual elite, who had shaped its policies for achieving independence since 1885. Gandhi, building on a large number of grassroots initiatives, brought the power base to the village level. Under his leadership, removing the oppression of colonial rule was something that was happening to everyone, in every corner of the land.

Of greater international significance is the method of nonviolent protest against social injustice that Gandhi developed during his years in South Africa. He applied this method with confounding consistency in leading the peoples of British India to freedom in 1947. Its effectiveness was partly the result of his ability to discipline people in the deployment of his method. He was also able to command accountability from those who were the oppressors. In this way he established a viable alternative to power politics to achieve historic goals. Gandhi called this method **satyagraha,** or Soul Force. And he encouraged its use to empower all who are oppressed and powerless to gain the courage, the discipline, and the vision to become free.

In the time since his death in 1948, a number of important events have changed the course of history. The rise of the Solidarity movement in Poland initiated the crumbling of the Soviet Union and its grasp on Central/Eastern Europe. The civil rights movement in the United States, under the leadership of Dr. Martin Luther King, Jr., initiated a national policy on race relations to correct historic injustices to minority students and workers. The election of Nelson Mandela and his African National Congress to political leadership in 1994 brought the end of Apartheid in South Africa. These events released new energy and a vision of hope for positive change in the world. All traced their inspiration for how to disarm oppressive political power with nonviolent public protest to Mohandas Karamchand Gandhi, the man who came to be called the Mahatma.

> Woman is the companion of man, gifted with equal mental capacities. She has the right to participate in the minutest details in the activities of man, and she has an equal right of freedom and liberty with him.
> —Mahatma Gandhi, 1917

Early Years

Gandhi was born in Porbandar, a small seaport town on the western coast of the Kathiawar peninsula in western India, on October 2, 1869. His father was a diwan, or prime minister, in the employ of maharajas in that region. Although Mohandas was the youngest, the fourth child of his father's fourth wife, he was expected to continue his father's and grandfather's political careers. He was groomed from an early age for leadership.

Yet Gandhi proved to be an indifferent student. He found mathematics particularly difficult. When he was 13, his parents

arranged for his marriage to Kasturbai, a young woman six months older than him. In spite of her gentle and accepting nature, he accounted himself an immature, jealous, and domineering husband. He was later to credit her example as a patient and devoted wife in leading him to see the virtues of a life committed to nonviolence.

Gandhi's mother also had a deep influence on his life. A devout Hindu, she revealed to him, by her life of devotion, the power of religious faith and fasting. When, at 18, Gandhi went to England to study law, he vowed to her that he would abstain from meat and wine while away. His determination to honor this vow set a pattern of discipline in keeping commitments for the rest of his life.

Gandhi stayed in England for just three years. He proved himself an able enough student to pass the London Matriculation examinations in Latin, French, and chemistry, and, a year later, his law examinations. He was admitted to the Bar on June 10, 1891, enrolled in the High Court on June 11, and sailed for India on June 12.

Shy and sensitive, Gandhi was not able to establish a law practice in Bombay, nor with his brother back in Porbandar. So he leapt at an opportunity with a local firm of Muslim merchants to work on a case in South Africa. The original assignment was for one year. In the course of that year he became so involved in the plight of Indians living in that country that he stayed for more than 20 years—and changed the course of history on two continents.

In South Africa

Gandhi's first encounter with discrimination against Indians in South Africa came in 1893, when he was thrown out of a first-class compartment of the train he was taking to Johannesburg. His enraged reaction to this affront convinced him that an appropriate response would be to encourage the diffuse group of Indians living there to work together to protest the many abuses they all experienced as non-whites in that country. He became engrossed in organizing campaigns and demonstrations for Indian rights. Finding this work demanding and effective, he decided to stay on in Africa. He established a law practice in Johannesburg to support his reform efforts and his family, whom he called from India. He also set up a weekly newspaper, *Indian Opinion,* and purchased a farm on which to set up a commune to maintain the paper's publication.

As the South African government imposed more and more restraints on the Indian people living in the country, Gandhi orchestrated a series of nonviolent protest demonstrations that engaged increasing numbers of Indians. His last protest march recruited more than 2,000 men, women, and children, and was joined in sympathy by 50,000 miners and indentured laborers. Such wide participation led the government to reconsider its policy and enact a law in 1914 to prohibit offensive discriminatory practices against all Indians living in South Africa. This movement was so ordered and disciplined by his commitment to nonviolent resistance that Gandhi emerged from this experience a leader of immense stature. He was someone to be reckoned with in South Africa—an achievement that was noticed in England and in India.

> Non-violence is the greatest force at the disposal of mankind. It is mightier than the mightiest weapon of destruction devised by the ingenuity of man.
> —Mahatma Gandhi, 1935

Mahatma Gandhi spent time every day spinning as an act of self discipline and meditation. He encouraged his followers to do the same and to wear home spun khadi garments as symbolic acts of self reliance expressive of the freedom from British rule he sought for his people. "Be the change you wish to see in the world."

The direction of Gandhi's growth in South Africa was, in a significant way, thrust upon him. He could have been treated there with polite respect, done his job, and returned to India unnoticed. Being thrown out of a railway car because of his color and national origin was something Gandhi neither anticipated nor felt he deserved. In responding to this immediate experience of social injustice, he gained a sense of something much greater than just what was happening to him. He discovered a personal mission that he felt compelled to fulfill: to bring together an oppressed people in a quest for social justice.

Being by temperament introspective, deliberate, even fastidious, Gandhi searched within himself for resources to meet this challenge. This quest brought him to affirm intuitively (for he had no formal training in its conceptual intricacies) two precepts drawn from the classical heritage of South Asia. First, and more consciously, Gandhi identified his mission with the ancient concept of **dharma**, of cosmic moral order. This concept was set forward in the early Sanskrit epics, the Mahabharata and the Ramayana, as the proper behavior for ruling princes—not only as the moral foundation of their authority to rule, but also as the source of the well-being of their subjects.

Gandhi pursued the private aspect of dharma (the moral foundation for leadership) with determination. His autobiography, *The Story of My Experiments with Truth,* written mostly in 1926, is replete with descriptions of his attempts to discipline his personal life around issues of celibacy, vegetarianism, puri-

fication, and self-control. He continued this pattern of moral exploration and testing throughout his life, always seeking to be better prepared (by which he meant morally adequate) to undertake the public tasks he felt compelled to perform. Even toward the end of the long struggle for national independence, the primary issue was not whether the British would grant freedom to the people of the subcontinent. His greatest concern was whether he, personally, was morally pure enough to lead the people of India to this goal.

Equally important to Gandhi was the public aspect of dharma—that it was to be realized for everyone's benefit. The cosmic dimension of dharma is realized not in the abstract, nor just in one's personal life, but in the public affairs of humanity. This awareness made his personal experience of discrimination in South Africa a public offense that would be righted only when discrimination would not be practiced against any Indian residing there. Gandhi's awareness of the epic precept of dharma made him sensitive not only to the stringent moral demands of his mission, but also to the magnitude of its objective. He ultimately sought to liberate a people not just from the injustice of colonial rule, but from all oppression, to allow them to become truly free.

The second precept of the classical heritage which Gandhi affirmed by his experience in South Africa was an awareness of a truer, deeper reality of "self" than he normally experienced in the everyday world. He experienced glimpses of a more ultimate reality of being, what in the classical heritage of South Asia was called atma. In his quest for this higher being of self, Gandhi intuited that a vital quality that distinguishes it from the ordinary experience of self is that it is by nature nonviolent:

> Non-violence is not a garment to be put on and off at will. Its seat is in the heart, and it must be an inseparable part of our very being.

It was this deeper, more refined self that was to define the distinctive character of the mission to which he had been called—that only the means could justify the end. Above all else, the means must be nonviolent.

Gandhi's concern for reducing the level of violence in our everyday lives and in the world around us reinforced his moral image of dharma. Joined with an intimation of the atma, nonviolence requires a discipline that identifies and refines our awareness of our true self.

> The acquisition of the spirit of non-violence is a matter of long training in self-denial and appreciation of the hidden forces within ourselves. It changes one's outlook on life . . . It is the greatest force because it is the highest expression of the soul.

Gandhi's living out of these important concepts of dharma and atma identified him on a profound level with the people from India then living in South Africa. He spoke to them out of a context to which they were uniquely prepared to respond as a distinct group of people. It is also significant that his initial steps to leadership took place far from India. Author V. S. Naipaul, recalling his own upbringing as an Indian in Trinidad, describes an important social dimension to Indian life that Gandhi would have only experienced outside of India.

> These overseas Indian groups were mixed. They were miniature Indias, with Hindus and Muslims, and people of different castes. They were disadvantaged, without representation, and without a political tradition. They were isolated by language and culture from the people they found themselves among; they were isolated from India itself. In these special circumstances they developed something they never would have known in India: a sense of belonging to an Indian community. This feeling of community could override religion and caste.

Naipaul added that it was essential for Gandhi to have begun his freedom movement for the Indian peoples in South Africa. "It is during his . . . years in South Africa that intimations came to Gandhi of an all-India religious-political mission." Had he begun in India, he would not have known for whom he was seeking independence. In South Africa, Gandhi discovered a destiny for a people to become a free nation. As in the case of his own sense of mission, Gandhi returned to India with the conviction that this free nation could not be born until the people of India had discovered their soul.

Return to India

Gandhi returned to India in 1915, at the age of 45. By then he was recognized as a leader of people and proponent of "Ahimsa" (non-violence). Soon, he was widely acclaimed as the Mahatma, the "Great Souled One." The title of 'Mahatma' was given to him by India's Nobel Prize winner in 1913, Rabindra Nath Tagore.

Gandhi worked toward the removal of British colonial domination in India much as he had worked to overcome discrimination in South Africa: by addressing particular instances of oppression. Initially these did not involve the government. Gandhi first addressed the inequities between English plantation owners and peasants in the eastern province of Bihar, and Indian mill owners and mill workers in the western city, Ahmedabad. Feeling that Indian independence from British colonial rule should not replace one oppression with another, he attacked the subservient role imposed upon women in Indian society. He also took up the plight of "untouchable" communities—what he called "the ulcer of untouchability" in Indian life. Between 1915 and 1948, Gandhi initiated hundreds of nonviolent protest actions against a wide range of social injustices and abuses throughout the country.

One of Gandhi's most important achievements in the independence movement of India was his ability to lead the diverse people of the subcontinent to a shared vision of what it meant to be free. Drawing upon the importance of symbolic thought as developed in the classical heritage of his people, he insisted that people of all stations and walks of life take on the daily discipline of spinning thread for their clothing on a spinning wheel. This action not only freed them from the economic tyranny of dependence upon cloth manufactured in England; more important, spinning encouraged them to be self-reliant even while living under the burden of British colonial rule.

Gandhi's most dramatic act of satyagraha was in 1930, when he led his followers from Ahmedabad on a 200-mile walk to collect salt from the sea, in protest against the salt tax imposed by the British government. What began as a march of 78 men and boys, specially trained to undertake the journey, gathered more and more people as it made its way through the Gujarati countryside. When the column reached Dandi on the shore, the company had grown to thousands. The Oscar-winning film *Gandhi* gives a vivid picture not only of the energetic figure of Gandhi himself leading the march, but also of the dramatic swelling of the crowds who joined behind him to make the salt march a powerful expression of public support. Gandhi compared the march to the Boston Tea Party, which anticipated the war for independence in America. It was the culminating act of a series of nonviolent protests against British rule that led to the beginning of home rule in 1937 and the total withdrawal of British colonial government in 1947.

These examples reveal Gandhi's immense power to draw people into the modern political process by creating powerful symbolic actions. In performing them, people in all reaches of British India began to assert and discover the qualities of freedom among some of the simplest, most immediate elements of their lives: their clothing and food. These simple acts were symbolic in the classical sense in pointing beyond themselves to express what it is to be truly free.

GANDHI AND FASTING

Fasting became another aspect of Gandhi's leadership role during his years in India. He conducted 17 fasts "to the death." The first happened soon after his return from South Africa, as a part of his efforts to resolve the dispute over wages between

GANDHI'S MESSAGE OF LOVE, NONVIOLENCE STILL TIMELY

BULLETIN OF ASIAN GEOGRAPHY
Summer 2005
Volume 29, Issue 1
PP. 3-4
By Pradyumna P. Karan
Professor of geography
University of Kentucky

At a time when the world is witnessing mounting violence, terrorism and natural hazards partly due to our refusal to live in harmony with nature, it is appropriate to remember that October 2 will mark the 136th birth anniversary of Mohandas Gandhi, also called Mahatma Gandhi, whose teachings on nonviolence and living in harmony with the environment have been powerful forces.

That doctrine of nonviolence does not mean a passive submission to terror and aggression, but is based on the principle that the human spirit is more powerful than tanks and aircraft.

Gandhi proposed nonviolence as an affirmative force for a peaceful solution of differences, and as respect for environment and a sustainable nature society relationship.

I visited him at a prayer meeting in March 1947. Each day at sunset, Gandhi held a public prayer meeting no matter where he was, reading passages from the Gita, Koran, and Bible and ending in community singing, sometimes with his favorite Christian hymn, *When I Survey the Wondrous Cross*.

The dusty air filtered the crimson glow of the setting sun on the large lawn in central Patna, a city in the middle Ganges valley of north India. The scarlet-purple tentacles of the bougainvillea bush climbed tenaciously up the surrounding fence. There, in such tranquil beauty, was the spot for Gandhi's prayer meeting in Patna.

The multitudes came on foot from the far-flung countryside to see and listen to him. Darshan, which means to see and feel, is a deep-rooted Indian psyche, a sort of mystic rite. A Hindu would walk barefoot hundreds of miles to touch the sacred waters of the Holy Ganges, or visit a mountain shrine, or listen to a political leader, or be blessed by a holy man.

At the Central Lawn (now renamed Gandhi Maidan), when I was ushered into his presence, the streaks of sunlight glowed on the frail brown figure of Mahatma Gandhi. He sat silent, cross-legged, and smiling. He was of medium build, pleasant personality, weighing about 115 pounds, with prominent ears, sparse white moustache and full lips.

His beaming eyes peered at me above the steel-rimmed glasses. His face radiated a peculiar beauty; it was constantly animated, reflecting his changing moods and impish humor. He was the spirit of India as antique as its saints and faiths.

Wrapped in a cotton sheet, preaching the message of love, Gandhi became a fascinating and vaguely disturbing figure for imperial Britain. This one-time Inner Temple lawyer, dubbed as "seditious" and a "half-naked fakir," had been invited to Buckingham Palace for tea with the King Emperor. And there, dressed only in his loincloth and sandals, Gandhi appeared a true portrayal of Kipling's Gunga Din. Later, when questioned on the appropriateness of his apparel, Gandhi replied with a smile, "The king was wearing enough for both of us."

His voluntary poverty, simplicity, asceticism, humility and saintly figure made him a kind of holy man emerging from the mists of India's past to generate a new India. He had become a legend—the very incarnation of compassion, a beacon of religious tolerance, champion of the poor, on whom he bestowed a sense of self respect.

To a world engulfed in violence then as now, Gandhi offered an alternative, the doctrine of ahimsa—nonviolence—a moral crusade instead of an armed rebellion. Gandhi inculcated faith in spirit and the way to explore the heart of man.

Yet for all his adoration by the masses and the nobility of his purpose, Gandhi was not a deity or a saint, but a human being who had his full share of the tears and foibles in the world around. Once he studied law in London as a shy, melancholy youth, seeking to turn himself into a proper Englishman. He tried elocution, studied French, learned violin and practiced the waltz on dance floors.

"So you are studying geography and economics?" Thus the Mahatma greeted me during my visit. I stammered: "Indian economics and geography." Our brief conversation diverted to India's vernacular regions and languages, and English as a unifying factor. The interview was over, and as I was leaving the Mahatma muttered: "Go and work hard, not hardly."

Fifty-eight years after the meeting, this little encounter with the Mahatma still lingers fresh in my memory. On May 26, along with a colleague and his wife, I visited Rajghat, the place of Gandhi's cremation in Delhi. There on a broad expanse of lawn is a low concrete memorial surrounded by an iron rail where people come by the thousands from dawn to dusk to pray and pay homage. We took off our shoes and walked a few steps to pay our homage.

On the memorial are printed Gandhi's last words: Hai Ram [God be praised]. Gandhi's message of nonviolence, tolerance, and living in harmony with nature are perhaps more significant in the 21st century than they were decades ago.

the mill workers and the mill owners in Ahmedabad in 1918. Like his earlier actions, it was not premeditated, but grew out of the circumstances in which he found himself. The strike that he was urging the workers to sustain was exhausting their resourc-

es and their resolve. To encourage them to continue, he decided to subject himself to the same threat of starvation that the prolonged strike was imposing upon them. He could not demand of the striking workers more than he would demand of himself. So

(Copyright © 2006 Glowimages, Inc./Punchstock (DAL gwt170027))

One can see Mahatma Gandhi's statue almost in all cities and towns in India. This is one of the ways people pay their respect and homage to the "Father of the Nation." Mahatma Gandhi is also called by a nickname "Bapu." Bapu in Hindi means "Father." This picture shows a close up view of the statue of Mahatma Gandhi in the city of Jaipur in Rajasthan, India.

from the Indian community as a whole the need to reform itself by eliminating the scourge of discrimination and oppression based on caste. Dr. Ambedkar saw Gandhi's objection as an attempt to keep untouchables under Hindu oppression. But Gandhi was adamant, and on September 20, he began a fast to raise Hindu consciousness about the evils of caste discrimination and to alter the British proposal. Resolutions against discrimination and intense discussions with the untouchable leaders immediately ensued. Five days later, a compromise pact was achieved and sent to London, where it was accepted by the Prime Minister. By this fast, Gandhi made a significant impact, for the first time, on a specific British government policy in India. And, as fate would have it, all of this happened while he was imprisoned by the Colonial Government in Yeravda Prison in Pune, Mahara-Shtra, under a century-old regulation which allowed the government to hold him for suspected sedition without sentence or trial.

During the spring of 1933, Gandhi fasted again on behalf of the untouchable communities as an act of purification. He described it as "an uninterrupted twenty-one days' prayer."

Gandhi fasted twice during the final year of his life, in Calcutta from September 1 to 5, 1947; and in New Delhi, beginning on January 13, 1948. In both instances he was responding to the communal rioting between Hindus and Muslims following the partition of British India and the independence of India and Pakistan on August 15, 1947. By this time, as Gandhi entered his 78th year, people throughout the subcontinent were caught up in daily reports on the state of his health during the fasts. And they were stirred to meet his expectations of amity between the two new countries and among the religious communities which resided in both. In January, Gandhi specifically demanded as a condition of ending his fast the reparation to Pakistan of its share of British India's assets retained by the Indian Government. When that was done, the Pakistan foreign minister before the United Nations Security Council directly attributed to Gandhi's fast a "new and tremendous wave of feeling and desire for friendship between the two Dominions."

By his many and creative acts for freedom and by his fasting, Gandhi was able to command enormous authority among the people—all without the benefit of holding any political office. During his many years of leadership in the independence movement, he held only one elective position. He was elected president of the Indian National Congress in 1925. But he held the office for only one year. He stepped down to give a place to Sarojini Naidu, the first woman to be elected to that office.

Being out of political office seemed to increase the impact of his singular, moral basis for authority. It was even more commanding when he took moral positions in direct confrontation with the authority structures of his time. For his opposition to the colonial rule of the British Raj, he spent 2,049 of his most politically active days (more than five years) in jail. His self-affirming authority as a political figure and his commitment to nonviolence as the guiding principle for political action won for Gandhi universal recognition as the conscience of an empire and the "Father of the Republic of India."

Any sense of achievement that Gandhi might have felt because of India's independence in 1947 was negated by the scourge of communal rioting and bloodshed which swept across

he began a fast that would continue until the workers received the wage they were demanding from the mill owners.

Unlike later fasts, this gesture prompted neither wide public awareness nor concern. And Gandhi himself was not entirely comfortable about the coercive elements of his action. But the mill owners were moved by this dramatic placing of himself on the line. After the third day of his fast, they agreed to a compromise in which all parties could feel some gain. Of more lasting significance, Gandhi's action and resolution did not allow the workers to abandon their commitment to improve their lot. He taught them by example to become empowered by their own inner strength.

In 1932, Gandhi began a series of fasts based on his concern for the plight of the "untouchable" communities in India. His initial protest was against the attempt on the part of the British Government to set up separate untouchable electorates in a provisional government in British India, a policy that was supported by Dr. B.R.Ambedkar and other leaders of the untouchable communities. Gandhi's objection was that giving the untouchable communities separate political status removed the subcontinent as the specter of partition of British India into two separate nations loomed. As the time of independence approached, Gandhi did not go to the capital to see the reins of power passed. Instead, he walked from village to village in the Noakhali district of East Bengal, seeking to quench the flames of violence that scorched that land. Gandhi was deeply shaken, doubting his effectiveness to bring the message of nonviolence to the people. But Lord Mountbatten, who was in New Delhi as the governor-general of newly independent India, described Gandhi's effectiveness in a very different way: "In the Punjab we have 55,000 soldiers and large scale rioting is on our hands. In Bengal our forces consist of one man, and there is no rioting."

Though we may know Him by a thousand names, He is one and the same to us all.

—Mahatma Gandhi, 1926

The Light Endures

Gandhi remained convinced that Muslims and Hindus could live at peace together in a single, secular nation. For Gandhi, truth was not the exclusive possession of any religious community but, rather, what revealed the transcendent unity of all people. This conviction was to cost him his life.

A young Hindu, passionately afraid that Gandhi was threatening Hinduism by being too accommodating to Muslims, assassinated him at his evening prayer meeting on January 30, 1948. That evening, Gandhi's longtime friend and protégé, the prime minister of the newly formed government of India, Jawaharlal Nehru, announced his death over the radio:

Our beloved leader, Bapu, as we call him, the father of our nation is no more. . . . The light has gone out, I said, and yet I was wrong. For the light that shone in this country was no ordinary light. The light that has illumined this country for these many years will illumine this country for many more years . . . and the world will see it and it will give solace to innumerable hearts.

In leading the vastly diverse peoples of India to their independence through the first half of the twentieth century, Mahatma Gandhi learned that political power is normally based on oppression and the use of force. But that coercive power leads only to bondage, violence, and suffering. He became convinced that political freedom cannot be achieved by force. It can be realized only in discovering within ourselves a more profound and demanding quality of human identity and relationship, a quality that is characterized by nonviolence. Only when we become genuinely nonviolent in ourselves and in our relationships with others can we become truly ourselves. Nations also must become genuinely nonviolent. Then they, too, will discover an identity as a people which is inclusive of all who live within their borders. Only then can we begin to think about achieving peace among nations.

Eric Ericson, in his perceptive biography, *Gandhi's Truth*, describes this insight as a profound source of hope for the survival of the human race:

To have faced mankind with nonviolence as the alternative to [such policing activities as the British massacre in Amritsar] marks the Mahatma's deed in 1919. In a period when proud statesmen could speak of a "war to end war"; when the superpolicemen of Versailles could bathe in the glory of a peace that would make "the world safe for democracy"; when the revolutionaries in Russia could entertain the belief that terror could initiate an eventual "withering away of the State"—during that same period, one man in India confronted the world with the strong suggestion that a new political instrument, endowed with a new kind of religious fervor, may yet provide mankind with a choice. And the "instrument" is "Ahimsa"—non-violence.

India (Republic of India)

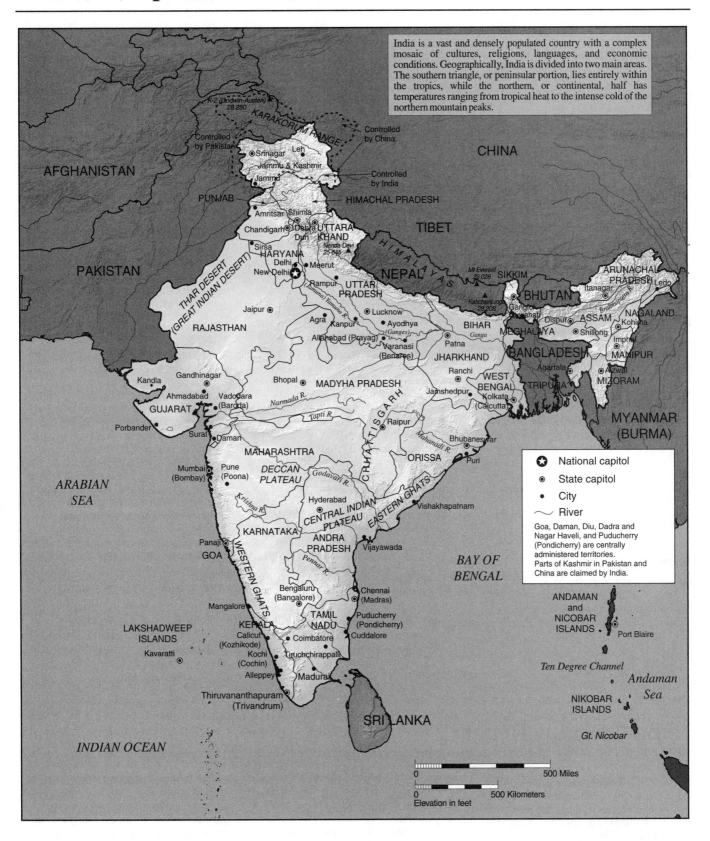

India is a vast and densely populated country with a complex mosaic of cultures, religions, languages, and economic conditions. Geographically, India is divided into two main areas. The southern triangle, or peninsular portion, lies entirely within the tropics, while the northern, or continental, half has temperatures ranging from tropical heat to the intense cold of the northern mountain peaks.

CHINA

AFGHANISTAN

K-2 (Godwin-Austen) 28 250

KARAKORUM RANGE

Controlled by China

Controlled by Pakistan

Srinagar   Leh

Jammu & Kashmir

Jammu

Controlled by India

PAKISTAN

PUNJAB

HIMACHAL PRADESH

Amritsar   Shimla

Chandigarh   Dehra Dun   UTTARA KHAND

Sirsa   Nanda Devi 25 645

HARYANA

TIBET

HIMALAYAS

Mt Everest 29 028

SIKKIM

Delhi   Meerut

New Delhi

Rampur

THAR DESERT (GREAT INDIAN DESERT)

Jaipur

RAJASTHAN

Jumna/Yamuna R.

UTTAR PRADESH

Agra   Kanpur

Lucknow

Ayodhya

Allahabad (Prayag)   (Ganges)

Varanasi (Benares)

NEPAL

Kahchenjunga 28 208

Gangtok   Guwahati

BHUTAN

Itanagar

ARUNACHAL PRADESH   Ledo

Brahmaputra R.

Dispur   ASSAM   NAGALAND

Shillong   Kohima

MEGHALAYA

Imphal

BIHAR

Ganga

Patna

JHARKHAND

Ranchi

Kandla

Gandhinagar

Ahmadabad   Vadodara (Baroda)

GUJARAT

Porbander

Surat   Daman

Bhopal

MADYHA PRADESH

Narmada R.

Tapti R.

CHHATTISGARH

Raipur

Jamshedpur

WEST BENGAL

Kolkata (Calcutta)

Agartala   TRIPURA

BANGLADESH

Mahanadi R.

Bhubaneswar

ORISSA

Puri

MAHARASHTRA

Mumbai (Bombay)

Pune (Poona)

DECCAN PLATEAU

Godavari R.

Krishna R.

Hyderabad

CENTRAL INDIAN PLATEAU

Aizwal

MIZORAM

MYANMAR (BURMA)

ARABIAN SEA

EASTERN GHATS

Vishakhapatnam

★ National capitol
◉ State capitol
• City
〰 River

Goa, Daman, Diu, Dadra and Nagar Haveli, and Puducherry (Pondicherry) are centrally administered territories.
Parts of Kashmir in Pakistan and China are claimed by India.

KARNATAKA

ANDRA PRADESH

Vijayawada

Pennar R.

BAY OF BENGAL

Panaji   GOA

WESTERN GHATS

Bengaluru (Bangalore)

Mangalore

Chennai (Madras)

TAMIL NADU

Puducherry (Pondicherry)

Cuddalore

ANDAMAN and NICOBAR ISLANDS

Port Blaire

LAKSHADWEEP ISLANDS

Kavaratti

KERALA

Calicut (Kozhikode)

Kochi (Cochin)

Alleppey   Madurai

Coimbatore

Tiruchchirappalli

Ten Degree Channel

Andaman Sea

NIKOBAR ISLANDS

Thiruvananthapuram (Trivandrum)

SRI LANKA

Gt. Nicobar

INDIAN OCEAN

0   500 Miles

0   500 Kilometers

Elevation in feet

India Statistics

GEOGRAPHY

Area in Square Miles (Kilometers): 1,296,010 (3,287,590) (about 1/3 the size of the United States

Capital (Population): New Delhi 21.72 million, 2009

Environmental Concerns: deforestation; soil erosion; overgrazing; desertification; air and water pollution; lack of potable water; overpopulation

Geographical Features: upland plain (Deccan Plateau) in south, flat to rolling plain along the Ganges, deserts in west, Himalaya Mountains in the north

Climate: varies from tropical monsoon in south to temperate in north, to arctic in the Himalayas

PEOPLE

Population

Total: 1,189,172,906 (July, 2011 est.)
Annual Growth Rate: 1.344% (2011 est.)
Rural/Urban Population Ratio: 70/30 (2010)
Major Languages: 41% Hindi, 8.1% Bengali, 7.2% Telugu, 7% Marathi, 5.9% Tamil, 5% Urdu, others; 24 languages spoken by 1 million or more persons; 324 distinct languages (Peoples of India 2000)
Ethnic Makeup: 72% Indo-Aryan, 25% Dravidian, 3% Mongoloid and other (2000)
Religions: 80.5% Hindu; 13.4% Muslim; 2.3% Christian; 1.9% Sikh; 1.9% other. (2001 Census)

Health

Life Expectancy at Birth: 65.77 years (male); 67.95 years (female) (2011 est.)
Infant Mortality: 47.57/1000 live births (2011 est.)
Per Capita Total Expenditure on Health: $100 (WHO 2005)
HIV/AIDS Rate in Adults: 0.3% (2.4 million) (2009 est.)

Education

Adult Literacy Rate: 61% (47.8% female) (2001 census)
Compulsory: in 23 states to age 14

COMMUNICATION

Telephones: 35.77 million main lines (2010)
Cell Phones: 670 million (2010)
Internet Users: 61.338 million (2009)

TRANSPORTATION

Highways in Miles (Kilometers): 1,991,786 (3,320,410 km.) (2009)
Railroads in Miles (Kilometers): (64,015 km.) (2009)
Usable Airfields: 352 (2010)

GOVERNMENT

Type: federal republic
Independence Date: August 15, 1947
Head of State/Government: President Pratibha Patil / Prime Minister Manmohan Singh
Political Parties: Bahujan Samaj Party or BSP; Bharatiya Janata Party or BJP; Biju Janata Dal or BJD; Communist Party of India or CPI; Communist Party of India-Marxist or CPI-M; Dravida Munnetra Kazagham or DMK; Indian National Congress or INC; Janata Dal (United) or JD(U); Jharkhand Mukti Morcha or JMM; Left Front (an alliance of Indian leftist parties); Lok Jan Shakti Party or LJSP; Nationalist Congress Party or NCP; Pattali Makkal Katchi or PMK; Rashtriya Janata Dal or RJD; Samajwadi Party or SP; Shiromani Akali Dal or SAD; Shiv Sena or SS; note—India has dozens of national and regional political parties; only parties or coalitions with four or more seats in the People's Assembly are listed
Suffrage: universal at 18

MILITARY

Military Expenditures: 25% of GDP
Current Disputes: with Pakistan and insurgents in the state of Jammu Kashmir; with Naxalites in eastern India, independence movements in northeastern India, and terrorist bombings throughout India; border disputes with China; distribution of river waters with Pakistan, Nepal, and Bangladesh

ECONOMY

Currency ($ U.S. Equivalent): 46.163 rupees = $1 U.S. (2010)
Per Capita Income/GDP: $3,400 / purchasing power parity $4.046 trillion (2010 est.)
GDP Growth Rate: 8.3% (2010 est.)
Inflation Rate: 11.7% (2010 est.)
Unemployment Rate: 10.8% (2010 est)
Population Below Poverty Line: 25% (2007 est.)
Labor Force by Occupation: 52% agriculture; 14% industry; 34% services; (2009)
Natural Resources: coal (fourth-largest reserves in the world), iron ore, manganese, mica, bauxite, titanium ore, chromite, natural gas, diamonds, petroleum, limestone, arable land
Agricultural: rice, wheat, oilseed, cotton, jute, tea, sugarcane, lentils, onions, potatoes, dairy, sheep, goats, poultry, fish
Industry: textiles, chemicals, food processing, steel, transportation equipment, cement, mining, petroleum, machinery, software, pharmaceuticals
Exports: $1201 billion f.o.b. (2010 est.) (primary partners United States, UAE, China) (2009)
Imports: $327 billion (2010 est.) (primary partners China, United States, Saudi Arabia, UAE, Australia, Germany, Singapore) (2009)
Human Development Index (ranking): 119 (UNDP 2010)

India Country Report

India is the largest and most varied of the countries of South Asia. It is the only one to extend through all the subcontinent's geographical regions, from the snowy peaks of the Himalayas, more than 25,000 feet high, to the tropical beaches of the Malabar Coast on the Laccadive Sea. And its population is very diverse, divided by languages, religions, and cultures, by cities and villages, by extremes of poverty and wealth. It is a land of many contrasts.

India is also crowded, and getting more so every day. On May 11, 2000, the government of India officially recognized the birth of the child that extended its population to one billion. Now 1.189 billion people, about 17 percent of the world's population, are living on approximately 2.3 percent of its total landmass. Almost four times more people than are living in the United States occupy one-third the amount of space. And their numbers are growing at an annual rate of 1.344 percent.

(Copyright © Parvinder Sethi (DAL mhhe009000))

Indian streets are good examples of democracy and freedom. Here, on a New Delhi street, people, cows, bicycles, automobiles, and cart vendors, all coexist and are free to stay or move as they choose.

India reaches farthest to the north among the high peaks of the Karakoram Range in the western Himalayan Mountains, beyond the glacial plateau of Ladakh. There, west of Tibet, India shares a disputed border with China. This boundary extends east through the high ridges of the Himalayas, skirting the mountainous kingdoms of Nepal and Bhutan to the hill country of the northeast frontier. There it encounters another portion of its 2,000-mile contested border with China. It then swings south along the western edge of Myanmar (Burma) and back around Bangladesh to the Bay of Bengal.

Because of the unrelenting arctic cold of the barren glaciers coursing the steep, southern slopes of the Himalayas, much of the northern border area of India is uninhabitable. The average population density is a sparse 70 people per square mile, interspersed in protected gorges and fertile valleys that sustain isolated settlements. Most of the Himalayan peoples tend flocks of sheep, yak, and goats, or work the tea plantations and orchards on the lower foothills. In warmer seasons they form small bands of traders and bearers making arduous, heavy-laden treks through snow-clad passes over the divide into Tibet. The extreme height, isolation, and breathtaking beauty of this region have found expression in distinctive folk traditions of colorful art, music, and dance. Numerous Buddhist monasteries and an occasional Hindu shrine dot the rugged mountain landscape.

DEVELOPMENT

With a growing middle class and economic reforms in 1991, India has a near developed economy. It leads in Intelligence Technology, has a large, young labor force, and a GDP approaching 10% annual growth. But it is lagging in employment growth and infrastructure, and slowing with the global economic recession in 2008. Two thirds of the work force is in agriculture, which produces less than one fourth of the GDP. Almost 30 percent of the population lives in poverty, not sharing in the new wealth.

This remote Himalayan region is the source of a great river system, the Jumna-(Ganga). These rivers provide an uneven but unbroken flow of life-sustaining water down the mountain valleys and into the great northern plains, the breadbasket of northern India. The cultivation of grains and rice is the main economic activity on these plains by peoples who live closer and closer together as these rivers, joined at Allahabad, extend to the east toward the Bay of Bengal. The density of the rural population rises to over 2,000 people per square mile in the delta of the (Ganga) River.

This great central plain is the most arable, irrigated, and populated region of India. Historically, it was the home of its great empires—the Mauryan (320–125 B.C.), Gupta (300–650 A.D.), and Moghul (1526–1857 A.D.) Dynasties. New Delhi, the capitol of India,

lies at the upper end of this region, on the Jumna River. Although it became the capitol of British India only in 1911, it is from this site that the Islamic Sultans of the thirteenth century and the Moghul kings in the sixteenth century controlled the plains to the east and the Deccan plateau to the south.

Farther east along the Ganges River are the even more ancient cities of Varanasi and Patna, known before the time of the Buddha in the sixth century B.C. as Kasi and Pataliputra, renowned for their commerce and learning. Much of India's wondrous classical tradition in art, literature, music, and philosophy evolved in this region during the times of imperial dominance and patronage. Even today, the Gangetic plain retains its traditional importance in the political and cultural life of India.*

Rising to the south of the Gangetic plain, in peninsular India, is a wide plateau flanked by two mountain ranges. They are older, smaller, and warmer than the Himalayas, but are also sparsely populated. They have long provided refuge for renegade princes, slopes for coffee and tea plantations, shelter for wild game, and homes for most of India's tribal populations.

As in the central plain, most of the people in the Deccan live in small villages and depend upon agriculture for their subsistence. Because the only sources of water for farming are the unpredictable seasonal rains brought by the southwest monsoon, this region has not had the economic base for the political domination experienced in the Gangetic plain. Only when the great empires of the north have swept south has this region shared in a common history with the rest of the country. Otherwise, separated by geography and language, the Deccan has supported many local kingdoms and developed its own traditions and cultures.

Three of India's larger industrial cities—Hyderabad, Ahmedabad, and Bangalore—are in the Deccan region. Ahmedabad, long known for its textile mills, is today the capitol of India's fastest-growing industrial state. Bangalore has become the center of the nation's high-technology industries—telephones, jet engines, and computers. Hyderabad is also rapidly developing its own high-tech industries and is the base for Microsoft operations in India.

The fourth region of India is the coastal plain, a narrow strip of low-lying, tropical land around the edge of the Indian peninsula. During the monsoon seasons, this plain is filled with luxuriant growth, especially along the southwest Malabar

---

*Joshua Hammer, *A Prayer for the Ganges,* Smithsonian, November, 2007.

Coast. Its rich harvests of rice and fruits support the highest rural population density in the country—more than 4,000 people per square mile. This region also experienced the devastating impact of recent natural disasters. The official death toll of the Indian Ocean tsunami on December 26, 2004, on the Andaman and Nicobar Islands just north of Sumatra, Indonesia, and the coastlands of Tamil Nadu approached 11,000. That is comparable with the tolls caused by the earthquake in Gujarat in 2001, and by the cyclone in Orissa in 1999.

India's two largest urban centers, the port cities of Mumbai (Bombay) and Kolkata (Calcutta), and its fourth-largest city, Chennai (Madras), are in this coastal region. These cities were built during the expansion of European commerce in the sixteenth and seventeenth centuries and became thriving hubs of commerce under British colonial rule. Today, they are the most important centers for banking, investment capital, and international trade for all of India.

The growth of the population in all of the cities of India is immense. In the metropolitan region of Mumbai (Bombay), India's largest city, the population rose from 9.9 million in 1991 to 16.4 million in 2001, and to 20 million in 2008. By 2015, Mumbai will be the world's second largest city. And India will have the largest urban population in the world.

This increase is due as much to in-migration from the villages with the lure of urban opportunity as to the birth rate and increasing life expectancy of the urban population itself. With this dramatic increase, the pressure on urban lands and services is staggering, the ability to cope near—many would say past—its limit.

This limit was certainly passed by an outburst of urban rioting that erupted in Mumbai for 10 days in January 1993. It began in a climate of communal tension between Hindus and Muslims throughout India following the destruction of a Muslim mosque in Ayodhya in the north-central region of the country on Dec. 6, 1992. Mobs swept through the slums of the city, burning, stabbing, and looting. According to Human Rights Watch, more than 1,000 people were killed and thousands more wounded. Many more fled, homeless, to other parts of the country in the wake of this devastation. Although based on tensions of national scope, the Mumbai riots revealed the latent social unrest and uncontrollable violence that lurk amid the increasing poverty and oppression of a fast-growing urban population.

Even with this staggering urban growth over the next decade, India's cities will still hold less than 35 percent of its total population. Today, about 70 percent of the population lives in small, agricultural villages, tied to the traditional patterns of a rural countryside. India will be for the foreseeable future a nation of villages.

Control of population growth in India follows a pattern of uneven, but significant change. Nine of the states and Union territories, mostly in the south of India, who govern about 12 percent of the total population, have made remarkable progress in reducing their annual rate of growth in recent years to less than 1.3 percent. Two states, Maharashtra and Punjab, according to the 2006 National Family Health Survey, have achieved a "replacement level" of population, producing an average of two children per family. These states demonstrate that family-planning policies can control population growth. Twelve states, with 55 percent of the population, still have growth rates close to 2 percent. It is their lack of progress toward limiting growth that places the national average at 1.344 percent.

In response to this imbalance, the national government adopted, for the first time, in February, 2000, a 10-year "population policy" encouraging all states to work toward replacement levels of growth. It also proposed not to change the number of representatives from each state in the national legislature for the next 25 years, so that no state would be penalized politically for reducing its proportion of the nation's population.

THE SOCIETY

The differences between the geographic regions of India contribute to, but do not account for, the complex mingling of culture and societies that are found in such wide array within each region. The people are divided in many other ways—by language, religion, and complex social groupings called castes.

Language

The original linguistic survey of British India in 1898 identified 188 languages and 544 dialects. A more recent comprehensive ethnographic study, "Peoples of India," identified 324 distinct languages in the country. Hindi is the most prevalent among the major languages in the northern plains region and central India. Others that belong to the Indo-European family of languages include Bengali, Punjabi, languages of Bihar, and Urdu. Oriya, Marathi, and

Gujarati extend beyond the northern plain region into the northern parts of the Deccan and the coastal plains. Tamil, Telugu, Kanarese, and Malayalam are the major languages in the southern part of peninsular India. They belong to a totally different family of languages, called Dravidian.

The Constitution of the Republic of India recognizes 17 Indo-European and Dravidian languages. This list does not include English, which is still the link language, the language of higher education, the professions, and national business and government in most parts of the country. Nor does it include the many tongues spoken by the mountain and tribal peoples who live in the remote parts of the north, east, and peninsular India. These languages belong to very different families of languages which are spoken by Tibetans, Burmese (people of Myanmar), and even by the Aboriginal peoples of Australia.

The government of India recognized the importance of language identity in 1956, soon after the country's independence, when it established new state boundaries. One was drawn to divide the old British province of Bombay between those who speak the Marathi language and those for whom Gujarati is the mother tongue. This division created the states of Maharashtra and Gujarat. The Presidency of Madras was divided into Tamil Nadu for Tamil speakers, and Andhra Pradesh for those who speak Telegu.

Identification with a particular language is through the family into which one is born, by one's mother, not by one's location. Adjusting the boundaries of the new states to coincide with the predominance of a language group did not change the linguistic identity of those who spoke other mother tongues in that state. Other-language-speakers live as minority groups, many times in enclaves, to preserve the distinctive ethos of their linguistic identities. These different linguistic groups stand out in the cities, where Bengalis and Tamils live in Mumbai (Bombay), for example, and Malayalis and Telugus in Chennai (Madras).

No single language is spoken or understood by more than 41 percent of the people. There have been attempts to establish Hindi, the most prevalent language among the states in the north-central region of India, as the national language. The states of the other regions of the country have resisted this status for any language, particularly one that is not their own. They cannot easily accept having their political identity defined, nor their primary education taught, in any other language than their own mother tongue.

(Copyright © Guarav Sharma (DAL mhhe015310))

This shore temple is located in Mahabalipuram, about 40 miles south of Chennai, India. The Shore Temple (700–728 BC) is so named because it overlooks the Bay of Bengal. It is built with blocks of granite, dating from the 8th century AD. The Mahabalipuram village was once a busy port during the 7th and 8th century reign of the Pallava dynasty during the reign of Narasimhavarman.

Religion

India is also divided by religions, but in a different pattern. Whereas Hindi is nationally a minority language, Hindus are 80 percent of the total population, and live in every region of the country. Islam is the largest of the minority religions. The practitioners total close to 150 million, slightly less than the total population of Muslims in Pakistan, and more than in Bangladesh. But they are just 13.4 percent of the total population of India. All other religious minorities—Sikhs, Jains, Christians, Buddhists, Zoroastrians and others—together make up only 6.6 percent.

The minority religions tend to concentrate in specific regions of the country in large enough numbers to become politically significant. Muslims are an overwhelming majority in Kashmir, and they are a sizable minority in the north-central state of Uttar Pradesh. Sikhs are close to 62 percent of the population of the state of Punjab. And Jains are in large enough numbers in Gujarat, and Christians in Kerala, along the southwest coast, to have an impact on the cultural, educational, and political aspects of life in those states.

With so many differences, one wonders how India holds together. From the day of its independence as a nation, it has been challenged to find its identity as a multi-ethnic, multi-religious, multi-language country.

Economic Disparity

A four-year-old girl with her legs crippled by polio drags herself to the nearest open drain in Bombay's shantytown Dharavi. She cups the foul-smelling water and pours it on

(Copyright © Tim Gainey/Alamy RF (DAL AYFBPF))

Although India as a whole is not noted for the production of natural rubber, rubber tree plantations are vividly seen in the southern state of Kerala. The rainy, tropical climate is suitable for rubber plantations in this part of the country.

her body. That is her daily morning bath, a ritual repeated by children in thousands of slums across the country.

Some 15 miles south of Dharavi in the expensive neighborhood of Altamount Road, the six-year-old son of a wealthy businessman has a massive birthday bash on the manicured lawns of his father's palatial villa as similar rich children from the neighborhood ride around on camels and ponies supplied for the occasion.

What bonds these two children are the extremes of life that India's 350 million children face every day. By all accounts, the children in the condition that the Dharavi girl finds herself grossly outnumber those who can afford the lifestyle of the boy on Altamount Road.

—Neelish Misra, *India Abroad*
(November 1, 1996)

Another challenge in modern India is the extent and the visibility of poverty. Meager subsistence is the rule for the more than 200 million people in rural areas who live below the poverty line. Because village economy is based upon the production and distribution of food in exchange for craft services or labor—the **jajmani** system—low income

(Copyright © Digital Vision/PunchStock (DAL 064037))

This group of Indian men and women, sitting at a workstation, is busy polishing electronic parts in an Indian electronic factory. This manufacturing industry aspect is growing in this country. In addition, Indian women, like in other developed countries, work side by side with men

means barely above starvation. Seventy-three million people live in urban slums, living on less than $1 a day. In Kolkata (Calcutta), beyond the slum-dwellers, many thousands of homeless sleep on the streets each night.

The scope of India's urban poverty is hard to imagine. V. S. Naipaul gives this vivid description of his visit to the largest slum in Mumbai (Bombay) called Dharavi:

Back-to-back and side-to-side shacks and shelters, a general impression of blackness and grayness and mud, narrow ragged lanes curving out of view; then a side of the main road dug up; then black mud, with men and women and children defecating on the edge of a black lake, swamp and sewage, with hellish oily iridescence . . . [It] was also an industrial area of sorts, with many unauthorized businesses, leather works and chemical works among them which wouldn't have been permitted in a better-regulated city area. . . . Petrol and kerosene fumes added to the stench. In this stench, many bare-armed people were at work: gathering or unpacking cloth waste and cardboard waste, working in gray-white dust that banked up on the ground like snow and stifled the sounds of hands and feet, working beside the road itself or in small shanties: large scale rag-picking.*

—*India, A Million Mutinies Now*

---

*"Urban Poverty in India: A flourishing slum," *The Economist*, Dec 19, 2007; "Dharavi, India's largest Slum, eyed by Mumbai Developers," *Los Angeles Times* Sept 8, 2008; Matias Echanove and Rahul Srivastava, "Taking the Slum out of 'Slumdog,'" *New York Times*, February 21, 2009.

The Green Revolution in the late 1950s introduced new, hybrid strains of rice and wheat, and grain production has increased dramatically. Since 1970, India has imported grains only once, in 1987, when lack of monsoon rains diminished the yields enough to create a national shortage. Other times of famine have occurred in different regions when drought, earthquakes, storms, and political unrest have left large numbers of people in both cities and villages with barely enough to eat. Without further reduction in India's birth rate and an increase in urban development, it is hard to imagine how the nation's economic progress will be able to reduce the anguish of poverty and environmental decay for an increasing population. All of the gains now have to be distributed among too many needy people.

Remarkable in this context has been the emergence of a significant middle class, of households that are earning more than necessary for simple survival: food, clothing, and housing. A report to the Millennium Conference held in New Delhi in February, 2000, estimated that 25 percent of the total population in India is affluent and upper middle class, with sufficient income to stimulate a market economy as consumers. This class almost equals the population of the United States. Another 40 percent of the population is identified as lower middle class. They have risen for the most part out of the throes of subsistence and are increasing the level of household incomes at impressive rates. These new incomes created new markets and opportunities for a population long characterized as impoverished, austere, and protected by restrictive economic planning and import controls.

The emergence of the middle class was stimulated by reforms to liberalize India's economy initiated by then Finance Minister Manmohan Singh in 1991. They divested some of the government's public sector industries, reduced government red tape, and decreased restrictions on foreign investment. All of these reforms led to a spurt of an average annual real growth rate in the gross domestic product (GDP) of more than six percent. Impressive growth in the steel, textile, and automotive parts industries culminated in an ambitious plan by Tata Motors to mass produce a $2,500 car. With a growing young labor force to employ in this sector as it expands, (a resource not so available to China) the industrial sector is expected to continue improving.

An even more stimulating part of India's economic development is in its service sector of information technology (IT) and information technology enabled services (ITES), especially since the Y2K crisis. In a more globalized economy, India has taken the lead in software creation, professional-service consulting, and setting up call centers to provide a myriad of financial and support services to companies around the world. Business process outsourcing (BPO) in the IT sector of India's economy grew at an annual rate of 29 percent in 2002, to command 80 percent of the world market, making it the fastest growing industry in India. Exports in the IT sector were worth $36 billion in 2005—one quarter of India's total exports.

This phenomenal growth was built upon a young, educated, two-million strong elite. Although they represent but a small portion of India's labor pool of 464 million, their success and new incomes are producing a ripple effect on the entire economy. They are also producing a new class of "zippies," young adults looking for designer products in high-rise malls around the centers of IT activity in cities across the country.*

Among the number of complex challenges to India's economic development is the global financial crisis that is generating massive recession everywhere. Because India's banks, both nationalized and private, have been under greater regulation, and are less exposed to highly leveraged speculation, the government anticipates a less debilitating impact of this crisis on the Indian economy. Looking to the indigenous base of India's economy, and as national elections approach, it exudes optimism about continuing GDP growth, at least to 7 percent, in spite of the economic slowdown in international markets.

FREEDOM

The world's largest democracy, India has maintained stable parliamentary and local government through free elections and rule of law since the adoption of its constitution in 1950. Terrorist acts by Pakistani and indigenous Jihadis, Naxalites in east central, and separatist groups in northeast India continue to threaten the civilian population.

Even without the challenge of the global crisis, India has development problems of its own. It does not have adequate infrastructure investment to provide necessary transportation and energy for its industrial expansion. Its labor laws, some of which go back to 1947, discourage increasing and seasonal adjustments in employment, and are overly restrictive and protected by political populism. And consumer demand,

*Rashmi Bansal, "India's Remix Generation," *Current History,* April 2007.

growing four times faster than the economy, is outstripping the production that generated it. The global recession is, ironically, having an impact on the imbalance in imports and inflationary pressure created by this consumer demand. India will just have to produce more on its own, and has developed the entrepreneurial skills to generate the capital resources to do so.

The agricultural sector has its own set of challenges. It employs two thirds of the labor market, but produces less than a quarter of the GNP. It is growing at only 3 percent, and rural unemployment is increasing, to over 8% in 2005. Globalization and decreasing water supply are increasing stress and indebtedness for farm communities, leading to an increasing number of suicides. Six hundred million people in 600,000 villages across the country are largely untouched by the benefits of the new prosperity. The 73 million who live in urban slums are also excluded by the unequal distribution of new wealth.

Since the election in 2004, the Congress Party's United Progressive Alliance has introduced a number of populist reforms to generate inclusive growth. In a "New Deal for Rural India," it has increased expenditures for debt relief, irrigation, health, and education. Most ambitious is a National Rural Employment Guarantee Scheme, to provide minimum wage for at least 100 days of work to one member of every unemployed household, initially in 200 rural districts. In April 2008, it was extended to all rural districts in the country. The wages are supplied 90 percent by the central government and the work projects are administered by local governments to develop local infrastructure. Although uneven in its implementation, this initiative has provided significant benefit to masses of unskilled, landless workers. Even more important, it has increased family stability and given a sense of empowerment to an impoverished people.**

The economic future of India is tempered by the overwhelming demands of teeming population and extensive poverty in both cities and villages, of environmental degradation, corruption, and strife. But aiming at a balance of productive activities which maintain a continuing growth in GDP and a more equitable distribution of the wealth it creates holds the possibility for India of sustaining a healthy democracy.***

**Jean Dreze, "NREGA: ship without rudder?" *The Hindu,* July 19, 2008.
***Sadanand Dhume, "Is India an Ally?" *Commentary,* January, 2008; Tarun Khanna, "China + India, The Power of Two," *Harvard Business Review,* December 2007.

(United Nations Photo Library PH #86277/pcd)

First Indian Prime Minister Jawarhalal Nehru, tours the first penicillin factory at Pimpri, India, with his daughter, Mrs. Indira Gandhi, on August 2, 1956.

INDIA SINCE INDEPENDENCE

The substantial economic development and control of population growth in India have happened in the context of an even greater affirmation in the lives of the Indian people. With the achievement of independence in 1947, India pulled itself together as a unified, national federation in which every adult citizen has the right to vote.

As a new nation, India had first to establish an independent, sovereign government, free of colonial domination and holding the allegiance of its vast and diverse population. This task was achieved by the transition of the Indian National Congress, which since 1885 had led the movement for India's political freedom, to the majority political party in a Constituent Assembly set up by the British Raj in 1935. At the time of independence, the Congress Party formed an interim government, with its leader, Jawaharlal Nehru, serving as prime minister. With the adoption of its Constitution on January 26, 1950, the Republic of India became a democratic, secular federation of what is now 28 states and 7 union territories.

The Constitution established a parliamentary bicameral national Legislature: the Lok Sabha (House of the People), with 545 members serving five year terms, and the Rajya Sabha (Council of States), with 12 members appointed by the president and 238 members elected proportionately by the legislative assemblies in each of the states and union territories. Executive leadership is provided by the prime minister, appointed by the president, with the support of a majority of the Lok Sabha. The president is elected to a five year term by a majority of all of the elected and appointed members of the two houses of parliament. The role is severely limited by the Constitution, so that the president serves mostly

as a symbolic head of state. But he or she can, upon the advice of the prime minister, suspend both national and state governments. This President's Rule provision has been used in recent times far more frequently than the framers of the Constitution envisioned.

Five uninterrupted years in office was the rule during the early years of the Republic, when the government was firmly under the control of Prime Minister Jawaharlal Nehru. Nehru's charismatic leadership and commitment to democracy brought together many disparate interests into the Congress Party. Since his death in 1964, many of the country's social and regional factions have become more politically savvy in gaining representation for their own interests in the national legislature. The Lok Sabha has thus become more representative of the diversity of the country. But with regional, ethnic, and special interests more dominant, its institutional authority and its ability to achieve a national political agenda have diminished.

The Congress Party began to win less than a majority of seats in the Legislature in the 1970s. Selecting a prime minister became a more complex and tenuous process of forming coalitions than of single party leadership.

By the elections in the spring of 1996, the Bharatiya Janata Party (BJP) became the first party to compete with the Congress Party on the national level. It won 186 seats, mostly from the north-central plains states. The Congress Party came in a distant second, with 136 seats. The president invited Atal Behari Vajpayee, leader of the BJP, to become prime minister, but he could not garner the support of a 273-seat majority needed to gain the confidence of the Lok Sabha. He resigned even before the newly elected legislature convened.

In the 1998 elections, the BJP again won the most legislative seats, but still fell short of commanding a majority. This time Vajpayee was able to bring together a coalition of 19 parties. The vote to install his government was 274 seats in favor. His victory was achieved only through the last-minute support of a regional party from the state of Andhra Pradesh.

Vajpayee managed to hold this coalition together to remain in office as prime minister for a little more than a year. Then the leader of another coalition party from Tamil Nadu, withdrew her party's support. Without it, Vajpayee lost his majority, and was forced to resign. With no alternative leadership able to achieve a majority, new elections were held in the fall of 1999. The BJP won 183 seats and returned to power in a newly formed coalition of 24 parties, called the National Democratic Alliance.

Vajpayee remained in power for almost five full years. Feeling confident of his party's success based upon their Hindu nationalist platform and economic reforms, he called for elections in April 2004.

Much to everyone's surprise, the BJP was defeated in the polls. The Congress Party eked out a plurality. With a coalition of 15 other parties to form the United Progressive Alliance, and the support of the communist parties, CP-M and CPI, it was able to form a government. On the urging of Sonia Gandhi, leader of the Congress Party, Dr. Manmohan Singh, a Sikh and former finance minister, became prime minister. He immediately set forward a "Common Minimum Programme" to establish a political agenda acceptable to all members of the coalition and the communist parties needed to hold a majority of the Lok Sabha.

Other political parties that represent specific minority interests in the political spectrum have gained strength. The Bahujan Samaj Party (BSP) and the Samajwadi Party (SP), represent Dalits (traditional untouchable communities, 16 percent of the nation's population) and Muslims (13 percent). Though these parties were aligned in opposition to each other, they won increasing numbers of legislative seats in both national and state by-elections. Based on its victories in the 1996 state election, the BSP joined forces with the Bharatiya Janata Party in Uttar Pradesh. Its leader, Mayawati, became the first woman Dalit to hold the office of chief minister of an Indian state.

The Samajwadi Party won the second largest number of votes in the 1998 national elections in Uttar Pradesh, reducing the BJP's dominance in that state and preventing it from winning a majority in the Lok Sabha. The election results suggest that, if the BSP and the SP had joined together, they might have routed the BJP in its greatest stronghold in India. In the 2002 state by-elections, the SP and the BSP won more seats than the ruling BJP, which fell from 158 seats in 1999 to 88. The BJP remained in power in Uttar Pradesh only by joining again with the BSP to form a majority in the state Legislative Assembly.

The success of these parties representing the "underclasses" reveals a growing awareness on the part of the disadvantaged communities of how democracy can work to their advantage. Such recognition can only strengthen the role of democratic government to address the needs of all of the people in the nation.

Parliamentary democracy founded in the Constitution of the Republic of India has worked well. Political parties and the ballot box have identified the public will and determined the direction of policy in the Lok Sabha, even for some of the most secessionist-minded groups in the country. The unexpected defeat of the Bharatiya Janata Party (BJP) in the elections of 2004, and the continuing rise of the Bahujan Samaj Party (BSP) and Samajwadi Party (SP) give dramatic witness to the power of the voice of the people.

The ballot box has also worked to determine the membership and agendas of the similarly structured, though less orderly, legislative assemblies on the state and municipal levels of government.

Elections have become an important part of Indian life. Among the many villages in the country, they are taking on the character of a festival, as reported under the headline "Joy and Order as India's Voting Starts:"

What seemed important was not so much which of the dozens of political parties was up or down, or which local candidate from among the 15,000 running across India was likely to win. What permeated the mood was something as old as independent India itself: the sheer pleasure of taking part in a basic democratic rite, the business of appointing and dismissing governments, that has survived all of the disappointments that Indians have endured in the past half-century. In a troubled land, democracy means there is hope.

—*The New York Times*
(April 18, 1996)

CHALLENGES TO DEMOCRACY

Many factors have contributed to the success of democracy in India. Some will point to the example and the many years of preparation promoted by British colonial rule. Others look to the inspiration of Mahatma Gandhi and his leadership of the Indian National Congress, which brought the independence movement to the people of the subcontinent. Also important has been the Constitution and the vital leadership and vision of Jawaharlal Nehru and the Congress Party in implementing its guarantees. Other factors include the remarkable restraint of the Indian army, the dedicated service of the Indian Administrative Service, and an enlightened press. Yet with all of their important contributions, democracy still faces many challenges in India today.

An unusual challenge came in 1975, unusual because it arose totally in the context of constitutional government itself.

And it was quickly met by the power of the ballot box.

In 1975, Prime Minister Indira Gandhi, to protect herself from a legal challenge to her office, asked President Ahmad to declare a "National Emergency," under the "President's Rule" provision in the Constitution. That act suspended for two years the normal function of government and the civil liberties protected by the Constitution. National elections were postponed, opposition leaders were put in prison, and press censorship was imposed. But when national elections were reinstated in 1977, the people of India voted her and the Congress Party out of office. They were not going to have their political freedom eroded. And their's was the final say.

Indira Gandhi had gained prominence as the only child and home provider of Jawaharlal Nehru. She became a widow in 1960, upon the death of her husband Feroze Gandhi, a Parsi journalist, and no relation to the Mahatma. That she became prime minister of India in 1966, and was reappointed in 1980, is itself remarkable because the Indian cultural environment assigns a more subservient role to women, and especially to widows. Her achievement underscores another, more far-reaching challenge to democratic government in India: that the institutions of government, not indigenous to India, function somewhat like a superstructure imposed upon traditional patterns and mores that are both substantial and persistent even as the Indian people become more modern.

HEALTH/WELFARE

India's commitment to village development and universal education has improved diet, hygiene, medical services, and literacy. Birth control policies are implemented unevenly, and poverty is extensive, especially in urban slums. The National Rural Employment Scheme adopted in 2005 intends to alleviate rural poverty.

Laws, for example, have been enacted to protect women against abuses sanctioned by traditional practices. Dowry has long been expected to be paid by a bride's family to her prospective in-laws as an inducement and condition of marriage. It was outlawed by the Dowry Prohibition Act, enacted in 1961 and strengthened by amendments in the 1980s. The government of India also, in 1993, ratified the International Convention on the Elimination of All Forms of Discrimination Against Women. The practice of dowry nevertheless continues unabated, sanctioning instances of manslaughter or suicide, excused as

"dowry death" or "bride-burning," when subsequent dowry demands by the groom's family are not met or issues of incompatibility surface. Dowry demands have increased and spread more widely across India as the society has become more consumer conscious. And the incidence of "accidental" death has increased to 7,000 per year among newlywed women.

With more recent policies to limit population growth and with advanced gender detection technology, India is recording a significant decline in the ratio of girls to boys in the population less than six years old. The national average of sex ratio in the 2001 census was 927 girls to 1000 boys, with many states falling below 800. Government laws in 1994 to prohibit the use of technology for prenatal sex determination have had limited or no impact on the traditional preference for a male heir sustained by the patriarchal structure of the family. Discrimination against women has increased in these and many other ways, even as India adjusts to more modern economic conditions.

Equality for all citizens is another example of an issue affirmed by the Constitution of India, but not fully observed in practice. The framers of the Constitution even included affirmative action provisions to reserve places for those of traditionally untouchable castes in education and government. Yet many belonging to lower castes who have benefited by affirmative action in education are not able to get jobs upon graduating from college because of continuing discrimination in the marketplace. This discrimination functions openly in the daily lives of villagers throughout India, and even among Indian nationals who have moved to other, more socially liberal parts of the world, but not at the same rigidness.

The Challenge of Caste

Because of its hierarchical structure, the caste system is by definition inequitable, and thus a contradiction to the equality presupposed by democracy. Particularly, those who are of lower rank feel the tremendous weight of its oppression. Those with higher or improving rank are not so troubled by this inherent inequality. One's attitude toward the caste system may depend largely on one's place in the system.

To many the caste system is a rigid structure that divides people into distinct social groups that are ranked in a fixed hierarchy. For others, the system is seen not as separating basically similar people into isolated groups, but rather, as a structure that holds very diverse groups of people together. And its hierarchical structure, rather than fix-

India is modernizing and industries are flourishing, but at the same time, mechanization of manual labor has not become a common scene in the Indian construction industry. Presented here is a common sight in the housing construction industry. Heavy loads of brick are carried by women laborers on their heads from the stock site to the construction site.

ing people into permanent levels, provides them with some opportunity for social mobility. As with so much about India, the caste system is more complex and more flexible than appears on the surface.

The caste system is based upon a social group for which Westerners do not have a counterpart. In the north of India, the caste community is generally called a jati (a word based on a verbal root meaning "to be born"). It is an extended kinship group whose perimeters extend beyond the natural family. The jati is also endogamous, which means that it provides the pool of acceptable marriage partners. Natural family members are excluded from this pool by generally accepted rules of incest. A jati thus extends the idea of a family to a larger social group made up of extensive cousins and potential in-laws.

Jati is important to an Indian's self-identity. Whereas Westerners tend to think of themselves in society primarily as individuals, in India, one is more apt to think of oneself primarily as belonging to one's jati. It provides a context for all of one's interactions with others, with respect to working, socializing, eating, and especially as regards marriage. In India, where marriages are mostly arranged by parents, the expectation to marry someone of one's own jati is generally the rule.

The jati is further defined by a traditional occupation, passed on from generation to generation, which gives each jati its name. There are many thousands of jati caste communities throughout India, most of them confined to a single linguistic region. There may be as few as two or three jatis in the remote mountain valleys of the Himalayas. Generally, in the more densely populated areas of India, a villager will interact with about 20 different such caste groups in his normal daily life.

The jati is the social unit that is placed in the hierarchical ranking of the caste system. Here is where the possibility of flexibility, or mobility, arises. That one belongs to a certain jati is fixed by birth. Where that jati is ranked in the hierarchical caste order is not. Its rank is based on some general rules that are accepted by almost everyone. For example, **Brahmin** jatis of traditional priests are placed at the top of the caste hierarchy. That they are expected to abjure wealth, practice asceticism, and revere learning is a significant feature of this system. It does not hold a high esteem for those who hold political power, are famous, or pursue money and become conspicuous spenders.

The hierarchical ranking of this system demeans in rank jatis that perform menial tasks such as cleaning latrines, sweeping streets, and removing the carcasses of dead animals. People belonging to these jatis are called "untouchables," a designation which reveals the ancient priestly caste's understanding of its own supremacy in rank. Brahmins as a community had to remain ritually pure in order to retain the efficacy and respect for their priestly functions. Those who performed "polluting" functions in the society—those dealing with human waste and animals—had to be avoided for fear of their diminishing the priests' sacred power. They were thus placed lowest on the hierarchical scale and declared "outcastes."

Mahatma Gandhi, in his crusade to remove the scourge of the demeaning term "untouchable," called them Harijans, "children of God," and encouraged members of his religious community to perform the "polluting" functions for themselves. In many parts of India today people in these jatis prefer to be called Dalits (the "oppressed"), and are seeking recognition as equal members of Indian society. Their quest, however, still meets a great deal of resistance throughout the country.

For those jatis that fall between the high-ranked Brahmins and the low-ranked Dalits, though every jati has its own rank, the basis of ranking is not so clear or consistent. Some occupations, such as land cultivators or carpenters, are generally accepted as higher than potters, herders, and washermen. Land or industrial ownership, and thus control over production in a village, called dominance, is an important determinant in caste rank. Social practices, such as ritual observance, dress, vegetarian diet, and with whom one eats, may also determine rank. Different rules apply in different situations. As norms and conditions change, so is the rank of one's jati open to change.

Many examples illustrate this fluidity of ranking. The jati names of several ancient emperors betray an absence of royal blood, or, at least, of earlier royal rank for their caste. Such did not prevent them from becoming kings. A striking, more contemporary example is the Nadar community in south India. It was considered an untouchable community in the nineteenth century, but is now accepted as a merchant caste. K. Kamaraj, a Congress Party member in the Lok Sabha, led the syndicate that first proposed Indira Gandhi to be the Congress Party's candidate for prime minister in 1966, following the death of her father. Kamaraj was a Nadar.

Even Mahatma Gandhi's family was not fixed in jati rank. The family name (*gandhi* means "grocer") identifies a bania, merchant, background. Both Gandhi's grandfather and father served as chief ministers for maharajas of small Indian states, a role traditionally reserved for Brahmins. Gandhi was himself thrown out of his jati by the elders of his community when he went to England to study law. He stepped out of the caste system altogether when he was accepted as a person committed to a religious life, when he became the Mahatma.

The position of any specific jati in the social hierarchy is based primarily on the acceptance of its claim to rank by members of the other jatis with which it interacts. Because mobility is open only to the entire jati, and not to individuals within it, and members of other jatis need to agree, change in rank does not happen quickly. Nevertheless a social dynamic extends through the system that asserts a claim to higher rank and encourages others to accept that claim.

The Caste System and Political Change

Democracy as a form of government does not happen in a social vacuum. In India, the pervasive tenacity of the caste system has contributed a stabilizing context in which democracy has been able to take hold. And its cohesion and flexibility has provided a dynamic within a traditional social context for democracy to work. The right of all adults to vote to determine who will represent them is new to India. In a system that combines diverse peoples, in which every jati has a place, and rules of ascendancy are continually being worked out, the role of the vote in which everyone participates to grant political power emerged as an acceptable way to affirm rank status that already existed within the village hierarchy. The system does not have to change; it simply has to adapt itself to an additional way to assert ascendancy.

Winning of elections by commanding votes has found a place in the traditional caste structure in two important ways. First, because jatis extend through many villages within a linguistic region, they provide cohesive units for regional associations formed to promote political causes important to their jati members as voting blocks in elections. They also function as lobbies in the halls of government between elections. Such blocks have led to the rise of political parties to assert the rights of the Dalits in northern India.

Within a single village, the traditional caste structure adapts to democratic elections by creating voting blocks out of the local authority structures, called factions, already in place in the villages. The power of higher castes in a village faction is based on the control of production and distribution of food that is harvested from village lands. Those who dominate these village resources are quick to convert into votes for their chosen candidates the allegiances created by the dependency of those of lower jati rank in the village who serve and get food from them. Thus democracy is co-opted to support traditional patterns of social life rather than to reform them.

The slow pace of land reform in India, in contrast to the rapid acceptance of new methods of agriculture that produced an abundance of grain in the Green Revolution, is evidence of this adaptation of democracy to traditional sources of power. New laws have broken up large land estates and reduced absentee landlordism. But politically active, regional landholder jati associations have been able to block legislative action on some of the most difficult village problems: landlessness and underemployment, the inequities of wealth and privilege, and landowner-laborer relations. Disputes between landowners and their laborers are still mostly resolved by force, with little interference by the police or protection from the courts.

This amazing, and sometimes horrifying, capacity for persistence and adaptation of India's traditional social institutions is a basis for concern. But they may also provide the multicultural context in which

(© Ramesh C. Dhussa)

'Harmandir Sahib', popularly known as the 'Golden Temple', is located in the city of Amritsar, Punjab in India. This bird's-eye view vividly presents a panoramic scene of the complex of the Golden Temple. This 'Gurudwara' (Sikh temples are called 'Gurudwara') is considered the holiest Sikh pilgrimage place. The main temple is decorated and walls are covered with gold plates. Pilgrims bathe in the holy pond surrounding the temple.

the liberating force of democracy may be achieved without the need for violent revolution.

ACHIEVEMENTS

Through the Green Revolution, India has been self-sufficient in grains since 1970. Technology and a growing middle class have attracted increasing direct investment in the economy. The impact of Indian Americans and popular artists like musician Ravi Shankar reveal the vitality of India's heritage of creativity in language, art, and human relations.

The Challenge of Religious Nationalism

Another persistent challenge to India's democracy as its people have become more politically conscious has been to hold itself together as a nation in the face of many competing and divisive forces for greater religious, linguistic, or ethnic autonomy. Insurgencies and the recent proliferation of terrorist acts throughout South Asia have been pursued in the name of more exclusive political identities.

The writer V. S. Naipaul assumed from his childhood in Trinidad that immigrants from India of many different backgrounds shared a cultural identity as Indians. When he visited India he was surprised to dis-

cover that this was not true for the same diversity of people who lived in India itself:

> When I got there I found [the idea of being an Indian] had no meaning in India. In the torrent of India, with its hundreds of millions, that continental idea was no comfort at all. People needed to hold on to smaller ideas of who and what they were; they found stability in the smaller groupings of region, clan, caste, family.
>
> —*India: A Million Mutinies Now*

None of these smaller ideas of identity are based on political associations. They are, rather, linguistic, religious, and social, such as caste, into which the people of India are grouped not by events, but by birth.

Because 80 percent of the people of India are Hindu, their religion is readily available to create an exclusive national identity. Their overwhelming number is a source of great concern to those who are in a religious minority: Muslims, Sikhs, (Zoroastrians), Buddhists, Jains, Christians, and Jews. The call for the separate nation of Pakistan was in response to this anxiety among the Muslim community in British India. How could a predominantly Hindu society, determined to meet its own objectives in a democracy, not discriminate

(United Nations Photo Library PH #433984/Eskinder Debebe)

UN Secretary-General Ban Ki-moon (left), and Indian Prime Minister Manmohan Singh: Nuclear Security Summit, Washington DC, April 10, 2010

against, if not actually oppress, people of other religions?

The Indian National Congress, which for 60 years worked constructively and diligently for the independence of India from British rule, was committed to realizing a free India as a secular state. Mahatma Gandhi's vision of a universal religious identity and the democratic idealism of India's leaders in its early years as a republic held to the goal that the government must recognize the presence and the integrity of its many different religious communities. In the words of India's Constitution, "all persons are equally entitled to freedom of conscience and the right freely to profess, practice, and propagate religion." Freedom for all religions prohibits the domination of any religion over any of the others.

The separation between the secular identity of the nation-state and the religious identities of its peoples has not, however, always been clear.

Three specific movements have challenged the commitment to political secularism in India. First is the outright demand by a militant wing of the Sikh community for an independent state, called Khalistan, to be established in the current state of Punjab, in northwest India.

To quell the violence of this nationalist demand in its frequent, random terrorist attacks and kidnappings, the Indian army went into the Golden Temple in Amritsar to rout out of the temple's protective walls a militant Sikh separatist leader who had sought sanctuary there. The outrage felt by the Sikh community over this assault on

the sacred shrine of the entire Sikh community led to the assassination of Prime Minister Indira Gandhi later that year by two Sikh members of her bodyguard. Her death stirred reprisals against Sikhs, killing 3,000 in riots across the north of India.

Continuing violence caused the suspension of the 1991 elections in Punjab. After political order was restored, they were held in February 1992, and a moderate Sikh, Prakash Singh Badal, was elected chief minister of the state. His assassination in August 1995, revealed that tension still existed among Sikhs and with surrounding Hindu communities. Yet, the 1996 and all subsequent elections in Punjab have been conducted with a remarkable reduction of violence.

Indira Gandhi's response to Sikh militancy was secular in intent: to hold India, with all of its religious differences, together as one nation. But religious rather than political identities defined the participants in this confrontation. The drastic consequences were the result of Sikhs and Hindus having greater allegiance to the exclusiveness of their religion than to the inclusiveness of the nation.

The second recent challenge to political secularism in India has been the rise of religious nationalism as a political movement. The man who assassinated Mahatma Gandhi in 1948 did so in the name of Hindu nationalism. He felt that Gandhi's attempts to accommodate the Muslim communities into an independent India were compromising his Hindu faith too much. By this action, he affirmed the greatest fears of those advocating an independent Pakistan:

that they would not receive equal status as a religious minority in the new nation of India. As a consequence of Mahatma Gandhi's example and his death, the quest to achieve a truly secular nation took on great urgency during the early years of India's independence.

As political awareness and participation increased among India's peoples, their religious identity has also been stimulated. One impetus was a television extravaganza. In 1987, a film producer, at the invitation of the national government, created a television series based on the Ramayana, a classical Indian epic.

The original Sanskrit account of the ideal Indian prince, Rama, recognized by Hindus as an incarnation of the Supreme God Vishnu, was composed 2,000 years ago. The story is more popularly known and celebrated among the Hindi-speaking population in a translation of this epic done by a religious poet, Tulsidas, in the sixteenth century A.D. Doordarshan, the national television channel, broadcast the modern television serial, described as "a mixture of soap opera and national mythology," on Sunday mornings in 104 half-hour episodes.

During its broadcast, almost all of India came to a halt. More than 100 million viewers were glued to any television set (some 25 million of them) they could find. The serial was an immense success, both in telling the story and in spreading the virtues of television among millions of new viewers.

The intent of the government and the serial's producers had been to extol India's ancient, albeit Hindu, heritage as a way of encouraging a greater sense of national pride. The serial actually stirred up religious sentiments of both Hindus and the minorities who had reason to fear the arousal of such passion.

The television serial also coincided with the rise of a new political party committed to Hindu nationalism, the **Bharatiya** Janata Party (BJP). In a country where many have risen to political prominence through the film industry, it is not difficult to ascribe increasing popularity of this new party directly to the broadcast of the Ramayana. Even more did the BJP gain from a sequel television serial. India's other, older and longer epic, the Mahabharata, was presented in 93 hourlong episodes from October 1988 to July 1990. Like the Ramayana, this epic extols the virtues of an ancient Hindu past. And it includes the original recitation of the most revered text of contemporary Hinduism, Bhagavad Gita, "The Song of the Lord."

The Bharatiya Janata Party had won only two seats in Parliament in the elections of 1984. In 1989, its holdings jumped

(Copyright © Parvinder Sethi (DAL mhhe009010))

Even in today's modern India, most rural dwellers cook their food with wood and clay ovens. Here a kitchen in rural restaurant is depicted in the northwestern desert to semi-desert region of India, near the city of Jaipur.

(© Ramesh C. Dhussa)

Kashmir Valley is famous for its natural beauty including snow capped mountain ranges and colorful fragrant flowers. The valley of Kashmir is also famous for ornamental glittery attire for women. Here, two tourists clad in Kashmiri traditional dress.

to 89. In the 1991 elections, they won 118 seats, then second only to the Congress Party, which won 225 seats, briefly diminishing that party's hopes for a majority in the Lok Sabha. The BJP won a slim majority that year in the legislative assembly of India's largest state, Uttar Pradesh, a long-time Congress Party stronghold.

In this rise to political prominence, the Bharatiya Janata Party tied its fortunes directly to another incident which is also related to Rama, the hero of the Ramayana, and that also received extensive television viewing attention, but this time as national news. The BJP leadership became actively involved in a campaign to build a temple to Rama on the site of his legendary birthplace in the city of **Ayodhya,** in eastern Uttar Pradesh. Through a number of public demonstrations, including a chariot procession across northern India, the party was able to rouse a large amount of public support for the building project and for its leadership as a political force. Such a mingling of religion and politics was effective, but potentially dangerous.

What made the building campaign particularly volatile was that the location for the temple to Rama was on the site of the Babri Masjid, a historic, but unused, Muslim house of prayer. This mosque was built in 1528 (purportedly on the site of a temple that had been destroyed) for **Babur,** the first of the Islamic Moghul Emperors in India. Because the Muslim community was equally eager to preserve the vestiges of its own glorious past in India, the project placed the BJP in direct conflict with the Indian Muslim minority. In hopes of working out a political compromise that would not stimulate further religious antagonism between Hindus and Muslims, Prime Min-

ister Narasimha Rao placed the dispute over the ownership of this land in the hands of the Supreme Court of India.

The BJP, in control of the Uttar Pradesh government, became impatient with the maneuvering by the prime minister. It supported a rally on Dec. 6, 1992, at the Babri mosque/proposed Rama temple site in Ayodhya. The BJP's aim was to keep national attention on its objective to promote the interests of Hindus, and to urge approval to build the temple. A crowd of over 700,000 people from across the country gathered for the rally in that city of some 70,000 residents. Even though the national government had assigned 15,000 troops there to maintain order, the situation got out of control, and a small group of enthusiasts scaled the Babri mosque and pulled it apart.

The response throughout the country was immediate and devastating. Dormant feelings of anger, fear, frustration, and hatred erupted into communal riots across India. Hundreds of people were killed, and vast numbers of shops and homes destroyed, from Assam to Kashmir to Kerala. The violence quickly spread into neighboring Pakistan and Bangladesh, where Hindu temples and homes were destroyed in reprisal. A tinderbox of communal resentment based on religion had exploded.

These outbursts of communal rioting and the increasing strength of the BJP as a political party both suggested that the Hindu religious identity of the majority of the Indian people was defining their national character more powerfully than the political institutions that were established by the Constitution in 1950. The dawn of Ram Raj, an idyllic age of government led by the power of God, was proclaimed, and the specter of Hindu religious fundamentalism was on the rise.

The BJP continued to increase in political strength. The party's greatest appeal was among an emerging rural middle class throughout north India. This more traditional support suggests that the real power of the BJP was not religious, but rather, the conservative forces of the privileged who dominate India's agrarian society. Even though this political base built on communal sentiment that identifies India as exclusively a Hindu nation, it never got wider support.

To gain a majority in the Lok Sabha, the BJP had to form coalitions with other parties, which caused it to temper some of its extremist Hindu positions. It continued to rewrite India's history in school textbooks and to permit attacks against Christian missionaries and converts. But its assertions of Hindutva (Hinduness) were presented as cultural, not religious. Its main concern was to be a national political party, not to establish a national religious identity.

The BJP, under the leadership of Prime Minister Atal Bihari Vajpayee, in a 24-party coalition called the National Democratic Alliance, stayed in power from 1999 until the elections in 2004 on the national level. But during this time it lost control of legislatures in seven states, retaining its power in only four others. An important exception was in Gujarat, where the BJP survived a challenge in by-elections held in December 2002, in response to communal violence that broke out on February 27, 2002.

That violence began when 58 passengers, mostly women and children, were killed in a train in which they were returning from a pilgrimage to Ayodhya to visit the Ram temple site. The train was allegedly set on fire by a band of Muslim slum dwellers from the town of

(United Nations Photo Library PH #204462/Mark Garten)

Secretary-General Ban Ki-moon lays a wreath at Raj Ghat, site of cremation of the remains of Mahatma Gandhi.

Godhra, in eastern Gujarat. Attacks in reprisal against Muslim communities in the state led to the destruction of many homes and the death of more than 1,000 people.

Accusations were made that the BJP government in Gujarat did not act to contain the violence against the Muslim population. It was suspended by President's Rule and by-elections were set to be held after a cooling-off period. The party used this episode of communal violence, and a terrorist attack on a Hindu temple in September, to generate political support among the Hindu majority in the state. In the December by-election, the BJP won a commanding majority, 117 out of 182 seats in the state Assembly.

Nationally, however, the violence against Muslims in Gujarat stirred a reaction against Hindu nationalist sentiment. Prime Minister Vajpayee felt called upon to stress the need for a more balanced, secular approach to government. In the elections in the spring of 2004, the BJP won only 138 of the 543 seats in the Lok Sabha.

Their defeat suggested that their religious agenda had played itself out in Indian national politics. Shashi Tharoor expressed a more respectful understanding of the religious integrity of Hinduism than its reduction to political identity when he wrote in response to the communal violence that followed the Ayodhya temple episode:

It pains me to read in the American newspapers of "Hindu fundamentalism," when Hinduism is a religion without compulsory fundamentals. That devotees of this essentially tolerant faith are desecrating a place of worship and assaulting Muslims in its name is a source of both sorrow and shame. India has survived the Aryans, the Mughals, the British; it has taken from each—language, art, food, learning—and outlasted them all. The Hinduism that I know understands that faith is a matter of hearts and minds, not bricks and stone.

—*Indian Express*
(January 20, 1993)

The third challenge to political secularism is in the state of Jammu and Kashmir, the one state in India where Muslims are an overall majority. The Congress Party first attempted to suppress an independence movement in Kashmir by successively courting and jailing Sheikh Abdullah, whose initial quest for Kashmiri freedom was from Maharajah Hari Singh before the independence of India in 1947.

After Abdullah's death in 1982, Prime Minister Indira Gandhi, upset by initiatives by his son, Farooq Abdullah, to obtain greater autonomy for Kashmir, appointed a dedicated civil servant, Jagmohan, as governor of the state. He dismissed the state legislature under the "President's Rule" provision in the Constitution, and instituted severely aggressive measures by India's military to enforce his control.

The Muslim separatist movement, energized by this repression, received additional religious fervor and support from militant Muslims, *jihadis,* mostly from Pakistan, who had been fighting in Afghanistan during the 1980s to free that country from Soviet military occupation. Using the weaponry and terrorist tactics learned to overcome the massive strength of the Soviet army, the insurgents attacked the Indian military and many civilians with deadly force. More than 45,000 people were to die in this conflict.

During this time of violence, India's military presence, mismanagement of elections, and human rights abuses continued to erode public support. But the government of India still asserted its claim to sovereignty granted by Maharajah Hari Singh in 1947, by calling for legislative elections in the fall of 2002 and, again, in 2008. It attempted to encourage the All Parties Hurriyat Conference, a conglomerate of 23 separatist parties in Kashmir, to participate in these elections. The Hurriyat declined, stating that a dialogue between India and Pakistan about their rival claims for Kashmir should occur before any elections that presuppose India's sovereignty over them. Even though many believed that the 2002 elections would not be possible because of the anticipated violence, 44 percent of the electorate voted. They defeated the incumbent National Conference. A coalition of the Peoples Democratic Party, the Congress Party, and the Peoples Democratic Forum, a Communist party, gained a slim majority to form a new government. The new chief minister, Mufti Mohammad Sayeed, head of the PDP, promised to "heal the wounds of militancy" in this terribly ravaged state.

General Musharraf's commitment in January 2002 to stop the infiltration of Pakistani militants into Kashmir led to a considerable reduction of violence in the Valley. And the joint leadership of the PDP and Congress Party was able to restore confidence of the Kashmiri people in their government. A dispute over the use of land by a Hindu religious group in Kashmir during the summer of 2008 led to large demonstrations of young protesters against Indian military occupation in Kashmir and calls by separatist groups to boycott the fall elections. But turnout at the polls, under extensive police protection, was over 60 percent. Omar, Sheikh Abdullah's grandson, and his National Conference were returned to power with a plurality of 28 of 87 seats in the state legislature.

Hope for a resolution of the Kashmir issue is increasing with a more conciliatory attitude of Pakistan's new President Zardari. The Mumbai terrorist attack on November 26, 2008, is making it even more urgent and no less elusive. The Kashmiri remain caught between the conflicting national ideologies of India's need to affirm its commitment to an inclusive, secular state and Pakistan's claim that it is the only legitimate government for Muslims in the northwestern portion of the subcontinent.*

Although jihadi violence has diminished in Kashmir, Islamist terrorism has increased in other parts of India. A deadly bombing in Mumbai took place in 1993, and again in 2006. Random bombs have also been detonated in a number of other Indian cities. Most devastating, armed militants invaded the financial district of Mumbai, on November 26, 2008, killing 172 in the railway station, a Jewish center, and two of the city's most exclusive hotels. These acts have been traced to terrorist organizations in Pakistan. This support suggests that militant elements in Pakistan remain convinced that the tension created by terrorist attacks throughout the country to destabilize India is the best means to obtain security for Pakistan as well as push their fundamentalist agenda in this volatile region of the world.

Other bomb incidents in Jaipur, Ahmedabad, and Delhi have been traced to indigenous Muslim groups radicalized by the violence against Muslims in Gujurat in 2002. They identify themselves as the Indian Mujahideen. Radical Hindu groups perpetrated terrorist bombings of Muslims in Malegaon, and in Orissa, Hindu extremists torment Christians among the Dalit population there.**

Religious ideology is not the only source of terrorist activity in India. Separatist groups have been selectively bombing in the northeast region of India since 1979, in quest of greater autonomy if not outright independence for the Assamese and Bodo people. And Maoist groups and countering Salwa Judum militias have been spreading violent destruction across the tribal areas of eastern India.*

Terrorism has become an unsettling force in the quest for economic growth and peaceful democracy in India, and it is taking a heavy toll.

REGIONAL POLITICAL CONCERNS

As India becomes more economically productive, it enters into a global arena with both the United States and China to find more sources of energy. Its economy at

*Steve Coll. "The Backchannel," *The New Yorker,* March 2, 2009.
**Somini Sengupta, "Hindu Threat to Christians: Convert or Flee," *NY Times,* Oct 13, 2008.

Timeline: PAST

3000–1500 B.C.
Harappan city culture

1500–500 B.C.
Aryan Vedic culture

500 B.C.–A.D. 300
Buddhist philosophy

A.D. 200–1000
Classical Hindu culture

1200–1857
Medieval Islamic influence

1602–1857
British East India Company

1857–1947
The British Raj era

1885
The founding of the Indian National Congress, start of the independence movement

1915
Mohandas Gandhi returns to India from South Africa

1930
Gandhi conducts the Salt March

1935
The Government of India Act provides limited self-government

1947
Independence

1947–1964
The Jawaharlal Nehru era

1950
The Constitution establishes India as a democratic, secular, sovereign nation

1965–1984
The Indira Gandhi era

1975
National emergency was declared and led to the suspension of civil liberties

1984
Operation Blue-star attack on the Golden Temple, Amritsar; the assassination of Indira Gandhi

1984–1991
The Rajiv Gandhi era

1990s
Rajiv Gandhi is assassinated; the Babri Masjd is destroyed and leads to riots nationwide; nuclear tests startle the world; rise to power of the BJP, a Hindu nationalist party

PRESENT

2000s
India expands its role in regional and global political and economic organizations

Communal violence in Gujarat leads to state elections

The Kashmir dispute remains intractable and dangerous

2004
Congress Party defeats BJP in national elections

Manmohan Singh becomes Prime Minister

Tsunami devastates Andaman and Nicobar Islands, coast of Tamil Nadu, causing 10,000–20,000 deaths

2006
Terrorism accounted for over 2000 deaths, over half by Kashmiri cells supported by Pakistan based groups in Kashmir and throughout India, notably in Mumbai on July 11, and another 600 by Naxalites in east central India.

2008
Terrorist bombings in Jaipur, Ahmedabad, and New Delhi are traced to indigenous Islamists radicalized by discrimination against Muslims. Armed attack by 10 terrorists on central railway station, a Jewish center, and two 5-star hotels in Mumbai kills 172, strains relations with Pakistan.

2009
National elections for Lok Sabha

2011
India and Pakistan agree to continue talks to normalize relations as their prime ministers meet at the World Cup cricket match between the two countries in Mohali, India

the present rate of growth will demand, in twenty years, double what it uses today. India has significant coal reserves, but 90 percent of its oil is imported. That India looks to Iran as a major supplier places it in an adverse relationship with the United States politically as well.

India's quest to be recognized as a nuclear power made nuclear proliferation another major issue in its relations on the world scene. The world was shocked when India tested nuclear bombs in May 1998, and Pakistan followed with tests of its own two weeks later.

Pakistan, because it recognizes India as a continuing threat to its existence, does not feel secure with India's overwhelming nuclear advantage. The rise to power of the Bharatiya Janata Party as a Hindu nationalist party added to Pakistan's apprehensions. It felt compelled to answer India's test.

India did not react to Pakistan's tests. Nor did it respond to Pakistan's nuclear threats during the Kargil incursion in the summer of 1999, which it repulsed with conventional arms. And it did not assert its nuclear capability in its military build-up in 2002 to stop further terrorist acts following the attempt to blow up the Parliament Buildings in New Delhi on December 13, 2001. Both countries recognize the power of the rhetoric of nuclear deterrence, particularly in getting America's attention.

(© Ramesh C. Dhussa)

Note the ornamental detailed carving in this turret. This is one of many in the Jaisalmer fort in the city of Jaisalmer in western Rajasthan. This fort is called 'The Golden Fort'. The city of Jaisalmer is also known as 'The Golden City'. These names originated from the fact that the fort and also a large number of buildings in the city are built of locally available yellow sandstone. The yellow color of sandstone imparts a golden hue to the fort and other edifices.

But they also avoid any circumstance for the actual use of nuclear weapons. Both realize that nuclear warfare in South Asia would be a catastrophic end for both countries. India's need for nuclear deterrence, ever since 1971, has been to defend itself not from Pakistan, but from other atomic powers, especially China.

Ironically, the American response to India's nuclear tests did not acknowledge that U.S. policy itself contributed to India's need to acquire what its strategic planners call "credible minimum nuclear deterrence." In the absence of binding international disarmament or control over nuclear weapons development, India's security depends upon its developing sufficient second-strike capability to have a credible response to a threat of nuclear attack.

India's one attempt to confront its large Asian neighbor, China, with conventional arms was to settle a border dispute in 1962. This confrontation led to a humiliating rout of India's border forces. Relations with China since have been formal, and inconsequential, due in large part to a lack of interest on China's part. India cannot help feeling that its nuclear capability has been an important protection, and is reluctant to participate in any regional nuclear agreement that excludes China. Its preference would be to have all the major powers, including the United States, join in an enforceable nuclear disarmament treaty.

India is concerned that U.S. nuclear policy is not committed to a workable timetable to eliminate all nuclear weapons in compliance with the Nuclear Non-Proliferation Treaty, which the United States signed in 1968. It does not have any confidence that the U.S. can restrain, specifically, China's ability to destabilize South Asia by providing nuclear materials to Pakistan. And U.S. policy did not prevent Pakistan from providing nuclear know-how to other countries. In the absence of such assurance, India, for its own security, requires that it retain its nuclear testing option. In spite of immense diplomatic pressure, India, like the United States, has not signed the Comprehensive (Nuclear) Test Ban Treaty.

India has combined its policy of credible deterrence with a unilateral commitment not to make a first-strike use of nuclear arms. It has signed a no-first-strike agreement with China. And Pakistan's President Zardari has offered to join in a similar agreement with India.

The most recent step in India and the United States' dance on nuclear capability came with an agreement for the United States to provide India with nuclear fuel and technology, with certain restrictions on its use and an attempt to restrict any further testing of nuclear weapons by India. It was initiated at a joint meeting of Prime Minister Manmohan Singh and President George W. Bush at the White House on July 18, 2005 and finally accepted by a confidence vote in the Indian Lok Sabha on July 22, 2008, approved by a waiver of the Nuclear Suppliers Group (NSG) on September 6, and ratified by the U.S. Congress on December 8, 2006.

This agreement passed in the Lok Sabha over strong opposition to India's becoming entangled in any subservient relationship with the United States. It passed in Congress partly because the United States does not see India's nuclear arms capability as a threat because of its history of stable, civilian government. Also significant was the influence of the India lobby in the United States, reflecting an increasing population, now some 2 million, of students and professionals who have migrated from India to form the wealthiest ethnic minority in the United States. But the strongest incentive was the hope that a democratic and economically expanding India would become a strategic security partner in future engagement with China. The achievement of this important agreement has not only increased India's nuclear energy potential. It has also recognized India as a legitimate nuclear power.*

Because of its overwhelming size, and now with its increasing economic clout, India remains dominant in relation to the other countries of South Asia.

Bhutan's economy is, for example, totally dependent upon Indian investment, and its foreign relations are, by longstanding treaty, handled by the government of India. Though the issue of terrorism in India is most seriously emanating from jihadis trained in Pakistan and infiltrating through Kashmir, Bangladesh, and Nepal, Bhutan acted quickly to India's request to eliminate hideouts and training camps for militant insurgent groups active in Assam and Nagaland in northeastern India.

Because of the terrorism issue, relations with Pakistan and Bangladesh have been more contentious. They are both aware that India, by attacking Pakistan in 1971, determined that they are two nations instead of one. Also important, the rivers that represent the major source of water for irrigation in both of these countries, unlike Bhutan and Nepal, originate in and are controlled by their powerful neighbor.

*Pavel Podvig, "A Silver Lining to the US-India Nuclear Deal," *Bulletin of the Atomic Scientists,* 21 October 2008.

India supported the Sri Lankan government in its protracted war against the Tamil separatist LTTE, but has been wary of the dangers to an increasing number of internally displaced Tamil civilians in the intensifying conflict. India was the first to send naval ships for relief work in Sri Lanka, and to the Maldives and Sumatra, following the tsunami disaster in December, 2004.

India continues to pursue avenues of wider economic and diplomatic cooperation. It maintains an active role in the 113-nation Non-Aligned Movement, which met in Havana, Cuba, in September 2006. It also became a full dialogue partner in the Association of Southeast Asian Nations (ASEAN) in January 1997. This status in ASEAN is shared with the United States, the European Union, Australia, Japan, and South Korea. India's admission overcame the concerns of Southeast Asian leaders that they not be drawn into such South Asian issues as the Kashmir dispute.

India is seeking greater recognition in the world. As its nuclear deal with the United States brought acceptance of it as a nuclear power, it also appreciates the opportunity to contribute to solving the global economic crisis as a developing nation in the G20 deliberations. And it aspires to become a permanent member of an expanded United Nations Security Council.

Even with such substantial gains and aspirations, V. S. Naipaul aptly does not use the word "success" to describe what is happening in India. There is too much poverty, inequality, disparity, conflict, and violence. But he recognizes that much of this condition is the result of an awakening of a new political consciousness in the country. "A million mutinies supported by twenty kinds of group excess, sectarian excess, religious excess, regional excess."

And he finds in this awakening a vision of hope: "the beginnings of self-awareness . . . the beginning of a new way for the millions, part of India's growth, part of its restoration."

Afghanistan (Islamic Republic of Afghanistan)

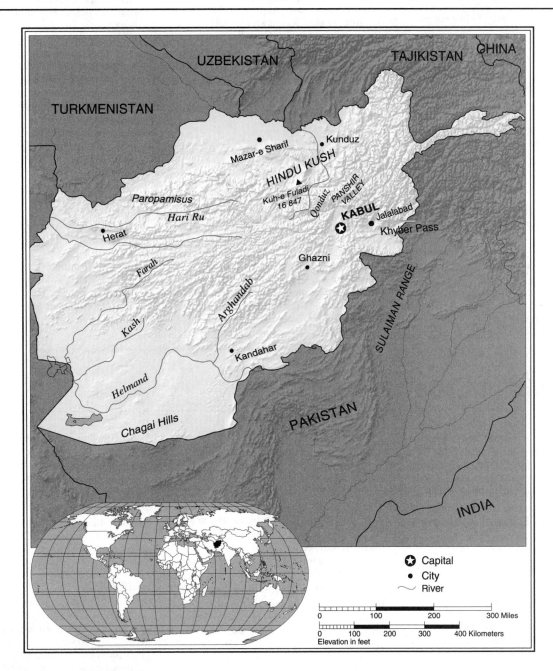

Afghanistan Statistics

GEOGRAPHY

Area in Square Miles (Kilometers):
251,827 sq mi (652,230 sq km) (about
the size of Texas)

Capital (Population): Kabul 3.573 million
(2009)

Environmental Concerns: limited fresh
water sources; soil degradation;
overgrazing; deforestation;
inadequate supply of potable water.

desertification; air and water pollution

Geographical Features: mostly rugged
mountains; valleys in the north and
southwest

Climate: arid to semiarid; cold winters
and hot summers

PEOPLE

Population

Total: 29,835,392 (2011)

Annual Growth Rate: 2.375% (2011 est.)

Rural/Urban Population Ratio: 77/23
(WHO 2006)

Major Languages: 50% Afghan Persian
or Dari; 35% Pashto; 11% Turkic; 30
minor languages; much bilingualism

Ethnic Makeup: 42% Pushtun; 27% Tajik;
9% Hazara; 9% Uzbec; 4% Aimak;
3% Turkman; 2% Baloch; 4% other

Religions: 80% Sunni Muslim; 19% Shi'a
Muslim; 1% other

Health

Life Expectancy at Birth: 44.79 years (male);
45.25 years (female) (2008 est.)
Infant Mortality: 149.2/1000 live births
(2008 est.)
Per Capita Total Expenditure on Health:
$26 (WHO 2005)
HIV/AIDS Rate in Adults: 0.01% (2001 est.)
(N/A WHO 2005 est.)

Education

Adult Literacy Rate: 28.1%;
(12.6% females) (2000 est.)
Compulsory (Ages): 7–14

COMMUNICATION

Telephones: 129,300 main lines (2009)
Cell Phones: 12 million (2009)
Internet Users: 1 million (2009)

TRANSPORTATION

Highways in Miles (Kilometers):
(42,150 km.)
Usable Airfields: 53 (2010)

GOVERNMENT

Type: Islamic Republic
Independence Date: August 19, 1919
(from United Kingdom control)
Head of State/Government: President
Hamid Karzai is Chief of State, Head
of Government
Political Parties: 43 parties approved by
Ministry of Justice
Suffrage: 18 years of age, universal

MILITARY

Military Expenditures: 1.9%
Current Disputes: severe internal conflicts
with Taliban

ECONOMY

Currency ($ U.S. Equivalent): .45
afghanis = $1 U.S. (2010)
Per Capita Income/GDP: $1,000
(2010 est.)
GDP Growth Rate: 8.9% (2010 est.)
Inflation Rate: 13.3% (2009 est.)
Unemployment Rate: 35% (2008 est.)

Labor Force by Occupation:
78.6% agriculture; 5.7% industry;
15.7% services
Population Below Poverty Line: 36%
(2008–09)
Natural Resources: natural gas;
petroleum; coal; copper; talc; barite;
sulfur; lead; zinc; iron ore; salt;
precious and semiprecious stones
Agriculture: opium poppies; wheat;
fruits; nuts; wool; mutton; sheep skins;
lambskins
Industry: small-scale production of
textiles, soap, furniture, shoes;
fertilizer; apparel, food products, non-
alcoholic beverages, mineral water,
cement; handwoven carpets; natural
gas, coal, copper
Exports: $547 million (not including
illicit exports) (primary partners
United States, India, Pakistan,
TajiKistan) (2009 est.)
Imports: $5.3 billion (primary partners
United States, Pakistan, Tajikistan,
India, China, Germany, Russia) (2009)
Human Development Index (ranking):
155 (UNDP 2010)

Afghanistan Country Report

Afghanistan is a rugged and mountainous country, nearly the size of Texas. It is
divided through its center by the western
extension of the high Himalayan mountain
range known as the Hindu Kush. The land
slopes away from this range in three different directions into jagged foothills and
stark river valleys.

DEVELOPMENT

Thirty years of warfare and
religious repression have
devastated the economy
and welfare of the people.
Continuing Taliban insurgency, terrorism,
and corruption have hindered reconstruction.
Poppy cultivation for heroin is the primary
source of wealth.

Only 12 percent of this rugged land is
arable; and it receives an average rainfall of
less than 12 inches a year. Severe drought
conditions throughout the country from
1999 to 2006 drastically reduced even that
rainfall for agricultural production and deci-
mated the livestock of the Kuchi people,
Afghanistan's nomadic herders. Toward
the south, the land becomes inhospitable
desert, racked by seasonal sandstorms that
have been known to bury entire villages.
The mountainous terrain in the north has

mineral resources, primarily iron ore and
natural gas, which are unexploited but hard
to obtain. This part of the country experienced a severe earthquake in February 1998,
which destroyed more than 20 villages, killing several thousand people. The country,
once celebrated for lush oases and luxuriant gardens of fruit, can nowhere today be
characterized as naturally comfortable or
abundant, except in the growing of poppies.

The three-way slope of the landscape
from the high ridge of the Hindu Kush
divides Afghanistan into three distinct ethnic and linguistic regions. Northern Afghans
are predominately Uzbeks and Turkmen,
who share a strong sense of identity as well
as the Turkic language with the peoples
who live across their northern border in
Turkmenistan, and Uzbekistan—former
republics of the Soviet Union.

The Tajik and Hazara peoples, who are
27 and 9 percent of the population respectively, live in the central section on the western slope of the Hindu Kush toward Iran.
The Tajik, of ancient Persian origin, are primarily Sunni Muslim. The Hazara are Shi'a
Muslims who trace their descent from the
invaders of Genghis Khan from Mongolia
in the thirteenth century A.D. They share a
common language, Dari, which is a dialect
of Farsi, the language of Iran (where Shi'a
Muslims are predominant).

The Pashtuns (also called Pathans or
Pushtuns), are the largest ethnic group,
14 million strong, about 42 percent of the
total population. They live on the southeastern slope of the country, and are themselves divided into tribal groups, such as
the Durrani and the Ghilzai. The Durrani
Pashtuns have been politically the most
dominant during the past 300 years.

FREEDOM

National elections for president
were held in 2004, and for
national legislature in 2005. But
public life is still controlled by
local and regional clan leaders, warlords,
and drug dealers. U.S. and NATO forces are
assigned to restore order and security, but
the Taliban insurgency continues to grow in
strength.

The Pashtuns are mostly Sunni Muslims, but they speak a different language,
Pashto. They share this language and ethnic identity with some 26 million Pashtuns, who live across the Durand Line,
established as the boundary between them
by the British in 1893. The Pakistani Pushtuns provided shelter to more than three
million Afghan Pashtun refugees during
the Soviet occupation of Afghanistan from

(Photo by Historicus, Inc. (DAL 4093))

An Afghan girl writes on a chalkboard during class in Rukhshana School, March 11, 2002. Afghanistan

American and Soviet aid, he improved agriculture, by the use of irrigation, and health services, and encouraged an industrial sector to increase the country's wealth. In 1977, he promulgated a new Constitution that outlawed all political parties except his own, including the largely urban and intellectual Communist party. A new assembly then elected Daoud President of the Republic of Afghanistan.

The Soviet Occupation

Resistance to Daoud's nationalist reform program came from both sides of the political spectrum. From the more conservative elements in the countryside, a zealous group of militant clan leaders, armed and trained by Pakistan, arose to harass his government. Strengthened by a rising Islamic-fundamentalist zeal, they called themselves mujahideen—fighters for the faith. But Daoud was more concerned about the growing influence, encouraged by the Soviets, of the leftist, modernizing groups in Kabul. He began to purge suspected Communists from the military and the bureaucracy. Within a year, army officers, threatened by this purge, assassinated him. Nur Mohammed Taraki, leader of the Peoples Democratic (Communist) Party, took over the reins of government.

President Taraki was assassinated in 1979, to be followed by an arch-rival, Hafizullah Amin.

Both leaders had adopted vigorous campaigns to break up the landholdings of the local chieftains and increase literacy among the people. Mujahideen resistance intensified to a point where President Amin sought Soviet aid to protect his government. The Soviet government, fearing that continuing civil strife would diminish its influence and investment, and threaten the security of the adjoining Soviet states to the north, sent 85,000 troops in December 1979. They deposed Amin and his radical faction of the Communist Party, and installed Babrak Karmal to undertake a more moderate approach to socialist reform.

Forces of resistance in the countryside intensified in their opposition to foreign intervention in addition to the reforms seeking centralization, industrialization, and modernization. In the face of Soviet military repression, more than 3 million Pashtuns crossed the border into Pakistan. The affluent established residences in Peshawar and Quetta. The vast majority moved into hastily constructed refugee camps. Another 2 million fled across the western border into Iran. Having gathered their families into the safety of camps across the border, supplied by Pakistani,

---

1979 to 1989, and to unnumbered Taliban insurgents since their defeat in 2001. Their common identity also sustains a latent aspiration for a single Pashtun nation. This aspiration is a source of genuine threat to the unity of Pakistan, which has given it urgency to be involved in Afghan affairs.

Emperors briefly united Afghan lands in the twelfth and eighteenth centuries, but neither empire lasted more than a generation. Fiercely independent local chieftains and clan leaders, sometimes called warlords, have been the most powerful political force in the country. They have, for generations, been the bearers of a clan's or tribe's sense of identity, allegiance, and honor.

Afghanistan's traditional wealth was based on its position along the silk route between China and Europe. The petty chiefs extracted from travelers significant bounty in custom fees, commissions for protection, or loot. The prominent role of drug trafficking and arms dealing in Afghan life today draws on this heritage. According to United Nations reports, Afghanistan produces over 90 percent of the world's supply of heroin, worth billions of dollars from 8,200 tons of poppy harvested in 2007, and 7,700 tons in 2008.

MODERN HISTORY

British Indian forces marched into Afghan territory twice during the late nineteenth century, but soon withdrew. In 1893, they left the country in the hands of Abdur Rahman Khan, the Emir of Kabul. During his reign, he hoped to "break down the feudal and tribal system and substitute one grand community under one law and one rule." But

the many local chieftains and clan leaders, claiming independent authority, resisted. They did participate in a succession of national councils, called loya jirga, to legitimize royal claims for ceremonial leadership.

In 1953, Sadar (Prince) Mohammed Daoud Khan, then commander of the Afghan army, seized the authority of prime minister to the then Emir of Kabul, Zahir Shah. He instituted many economic and social reforms, leading up to the adoption of a constitutional monarchy with a nationally elected legislative assembly in 1964. His reforming zeal allowed women to remove the chadri (the traditional heavy veil worn in public), and to participate for the first time in that election. Also participating was a newly formed, but already fractious, Communist Party.

Elections were held again in 1969, but this time the religiously and socially conservative clan leaders better understood the electoral process. They gained control of the Assembly in order to preserve their traditional authority, and effectively limited further reform.

Impatient with this resistance, Sadar Daoud overthrew the government in 1973. He sent Zahir Shah into exile and set himself up as military dictator. With both

---

HEALTH/WELFARE

Even with significant foreign aid, because of corruption, warfare, and insurgency, public services are very limited. The traditional repression of women also contributes to the lack of human resource development in health and education.

(UN Human Rights Council UNHCR PH#16045/A. Hollman, Photographer)

Millions of refugees who fled to Pakistan and Iran during the Soviet occupation of Afghanistan were reluctant to return to Afghanistan. This was due, in no small part, to the constant fighting among the mujahideen and then to problems with the Taliban. Women and children are particularly vulnerable groups of refugees.

Iranian, Saudi, and U.S. military and logistical support, they formed a fighting force of mujahideen to conduct an insurgency in their home country.

This incursion of Soviet military forces in 1979 also intensified the Cold War competition between the United States and the Soviet Union, which transformed Afghanistan into a proxy international battlefield. During the years of occupation, Soviet military strength increased to 120,000 troops. With both sides armed with advanced weaponry, warfare ravaged the countryside.

ACHIEVEMENTS

The government continues to seek avenues for peace. Given the continuing devastation and lack of security, the greatest achievement may simply be their survival.

Twelve thousand of 22,000 villages and more than 2,000 schools were destroyed, and 1 million Afghans and 13,000 Soviet soldiers were killed.

The Soviet Withdrawal

In 1986, Dr. Muhammed Najibullah replaced Babrak Karmal as president. In 1988, the leaders of seven mujahideen groups joined in Pakistan to form an interim government in exile. Faced with this resistance, the Soviet Union became unwilling to sustain

the losses of an intensifying military stalemate. In 1989, it withdrew its forces, and in 1991, agreed with the United States that both would stop arming the warring factions in Afghanistan.

Lack of cohesion—religious, ethnic, and military—among the mujahideen hampered their attempts to overthrow the Kabul government for three years after the Soviet troops departed. President Najibullah offered to form a joint government with them, but they could only agree that they did not want to share any part of a new government with the Communists.

In March 1992, Najibullah's army overthrew him, and mujahideen forces, under the command of Ahmad Shah Masood, a Tajik from Panshir, overtook the city of Kabul. Their victory was followed by a loya jirga, "national council," to elect Burhanuddin Rabbani, a Tajik, as interim president and draw up a new Constitution. But the rivalry among the mujahideen leaders, particularly between Rabbani and Gulbuddin Hekmatyar, a Ghilzai Pashtun, led to intense fighting in Kabul and a further collapse of civil order throughout the country. The periodic assaults and bombings among rival mujahideen parties seeking control of the city reduced much of it to rubble.

In 1993, a group of Pashtun religious students called the Taliban ("seekers of religious knowledge") from the southern city of Kandahar rose up in indignation against the militancy and corruption of the mujahideen. Their reforming fervor spread

rapidly among a people weary of uncontrolled violence, fear, and destruction.

The Taliban became a formidable force, supplied by arms and logistics from Pakistan, manpower from local clan militias, war orphans from Islamic parochial schools called madrasas, religious volunteers (jihadis) from many countries, and financial support and training from Al Qaeda. By the fall of 1996, they controlled the southern two thirds of the country and drove the mujahideen out of Kabul. They established a reign of reactionary religious terror in a city that had aspired for so long to become modern.

Their reforming zeal countenanced many human rights abuses. Most oppressed were women, particularly widows, who were deprived of jobs, humanitarian aid, and education. By 1999, Taliban forces controlled 95 percent of the country. Only a small vestige of the anti-Soviet resistance called the Northern Alliance held out in the northeastern corner of the country.

The Soviet incursion, the deadly fighting among the mujahideen and the rise of the Taliban subjected the Afghan people to the ravages and repression of more than twenty years of war. Many who became refugees during the Soviet occupation, because of the destruction of their homes, the depletion and mining of their fields, and, after October 7, 2001, fear of American bombing, remained in their squalid refugee camps. Women especially hesitated to return, because of fear of repression in their homelands by the fundamentalist fervor of both the mujahideen and Taliban leaders. By the end of 2001, there were still 2.2 million refugees in Pakistan, 2.4 million in Iran and around 1 million in refugee camps in Afghanistan itself.

Restoration

Following the terrorist attacks in the United States on September 11, 2001, an international coalition led by the United States joined forces with the Northern Alliance to destroy Al Qaeda and punish the Taliban for its role in the 9/11 assault on the United States. In a dramatic reversal, Pakistan withdrew its support from the Taliban and it collapsed. Kabul was soon recaptured and Al Qaeda training camps were dismantled.

The coalition victory created a new opportunity for political stability and reconstruction in the country. An impressive list of regional leaders emerged to take part in this effort. Some had joined the mujahideen in opposition to Sadar Daoud's reforms in the 1970s. All had a part in the violent infighting following the Soviet withdrawal, based on their leadership of the many diverse ethnic and tribal groups in the country. Many of them retained their own private militias, and were sustained by foreign aid and a flourishing trade in heroin production. The Tajik leaders of the Northern Alliance were initially the strongest: former president Burhanuddin Rabbani, and Muhammad Fahim and Yunus Qanuni, both successors to Ahmad Shah Masood, military commander of the Northern Alliance, who was assassinated on September 10, 2001.

The United Nations initiated the rebuilding of Afghanistan by gathering representative leadership from across the country in Bonn, Germany, in December 2001. Its intent was to establish institutions of government with authority separate from that of the indigenous leaders. Despite the good intentions, the Afghan government created at Bonn remained on the traditional power base of the so-called warlords.

An international peacekeeping force (ISAF) was also set up to establish security. It began with 8,000 soldiers from over 30 countries. But it had limited reach outside the capital city.

In June 2002, on terms set under United Nations auspices in Bonn, a follow-up council of 1,500 selected leaders convened in Kabul to create a transitional government. It elected as interim president, Hamid Karzai, a Pashtun with strong American support. Because he did not have an indigenous political base, he seemed most suited to hold the office above the taint and fray of traditional clan power struggles and to attract international contributions for rehabilitation.

Steps toward a permanent government began with preparations for national elections for president to be held in October 2004. These included more than 1,600 polling stations set up by the International Organization for Migration in Pakistan for 738,000 refugees still in that country who registered to vote. Eighty percent of them voted. About half of the 500,000 refugees who registered in seven offices in Iran also voted. The IOM achieved the largest refugee participation ever in a national election. Over all, Hamid Karzai received 55.4 percent of the vote.

Karzai's largest support came mostly from Kabul, where the evidence of foreign investment was most visible, particularly in the person of the U.S. ambassador, Zalmay Khalilzad (known in Kabul as "the Viceroy"). He also had some support from Pashtun regions to the south, where local leaders and the Taliban still retained control. Yunus Qanuni, a Tajik, briefly interior minister and head of intelligence in the interim government, won 16.3 percent of the vote, mostly from his ethnic base in the north-central region of the country. He

was subsequently elected Speaker of the Afghan Parliament. Mohammad Mohaqiq, the Hazara leader, received 11 percent from Hazara dominant districts, and 10 percent voted for Rashid Dostum, an Uzbek from the northern region. President Karzai did not appoint any of them to his cabinet.

Parliamentary elections for the Wolesi Jirga, or lower house, and provincial elections were finally held on September 18, 2005. With the Taliban calling for a boycott, 53 percent of 12 million registered voters cast their ballot. The results included 68 seats, 27 percent, for women. But overall they reinstituted the traditional bases of power in the country. Such did not hold out much promise for institutional independence and reform.*

A survey conducted in 2006 by the Post-Conflict Reconstruction Project of the Center for Strategic and International Studies found the people disappointed in four categories of their public life: security, justice, social well-being, and economic opportunity. That survey concludes:

"Gains have been made in education, communication, government processes, institutional capacity, roads and the private sector. Yet, the big issues from the beginning of the intervention remain: how to manage warlords and continued impunity, how to decrease poppy and drug trafficking, how to stop support for the Taliban, how to deliver electricity and revitalize the judiciary, and how to provide economic development in areas with limited access and infrastructure and serious security constraints."

With the people not convinced of improvement in their lives, and with the Taliban finding safe haven in Pakistan, its insurgency gained in strength. The force used by the American and NATO troops to suppress it, taking an intolerable toll of civilian casualties, made their presence equally burdensome. Increasing recognition that a military solution to this conflict is not possible has led to calls for dialogue with militant Islamist groups not only in Afghanistan, but also in Pakistan, which has its own Taliban terrorist groups. The Saudi government is attempting to initiate talks between President Karzai and Taliban leaders.

Effective counterinsurgency will not be easy. Afghanistan has for too long been torn asunder internally by so many levels of conflict: opposition between traditional lifestyles in the countryside and the cosmopolitan urban society in Kabul, and between fundamentalism and reform in Islam played out within longstanding ani-

*Carlotta Gall, "In Poverty and Strife, Women Test Limits," *New York Times,* October 6, 2008.

Timeline: PAST

A.D. 1747–1973
Loose tribal federation

1907
The British and Russians establish the boundaries of modern Afghanistan

1973–1978
Military dictatorship

1978–1992
Communist Party rule

1979–1989
Soviet military occupation

1980s
A mujahideen resistance is formed in Pakistan

1990s
Communist government overthrown, Mujahideen leaders compete for control

Taliban emerges in protest, captures Kabul and dominates most of the country

PRESENT

2000s
Deeming them "un-Islamic," Taliban destroys ancient Bamiyan Buddhist statues. U.S. led coalition in "war against terror" to destroy Al Qaeda joins Northern Alliance to recapture Kabul.

2002
Provisional government set up under UN initiated Bonn Agreement. Hamid Karzai elected interim president.

2004–2005
Presidential and National Assembly elections held. Hamid Karzai elected president.

2005–2009
Taliban insurgency increases against U.S. and NATO forces sent to secure country. Poppy cultivation remains a large percentage of GDP and world heroin market, supports local clan leaders and insurgency.

2009
Election for president

2011
President Karzai makes first official state visit to Russia by an Afghan leader since the end of the Soviet invasion in 1989.

mosities among different ethnic and linguistic groups, and rivalries among tribes, clans, and religious sects.

The country has also to deal with the conflicting interests of neighboring Iran, India, and Pakistan. And major powers have introduced a whole new scale of mass destruction, arms trading, international drug dealing, and terrorist training.

War-ravaged and impoverished for years, the people of Afghanistan need substantial, regionally focused assistance and cooperation to achieve some semblance of sustainable governance and social welfare.

Bangladesh (People's Republic of Bangladesh)

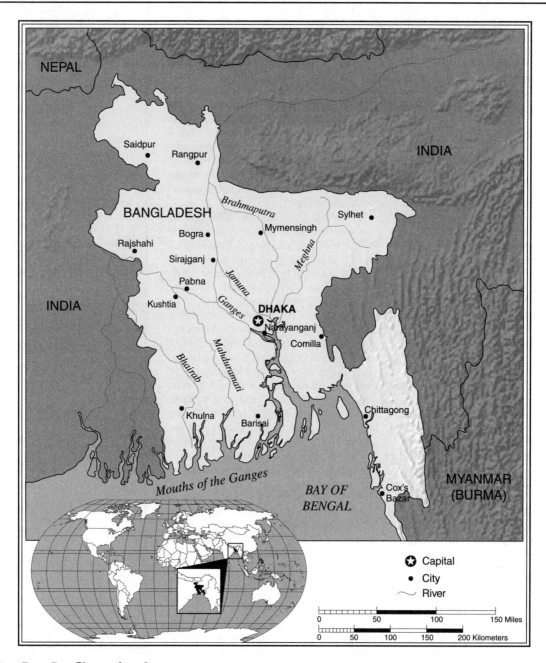

Bangladesh Statistics

GEOGRAPHY

Area in Square Miles (Kilometers):
55,597 (143,998 sq km) (about the size of Wisconsin)

Capital (Population): Dhaka (14.251 million) (2009 est.)

Environmental Concerns: water pollution; soil degradation; deforestation; severe overpopulation

Geographical features: mostly flat alluvial plain; hilly in the southeast

Climate: tropical; monsoon; mild winter, hot, humid summer

PEOPLE

Population

Total: 158,570,535 (2011 est.)

Annual Growth Rate: 1.5662% (2011 est.)

Rural/Urban Population Ratio: 72/28 (2010)

Major Languages: Bangla; English

Ethnic Makeup: 98% Bengali, 2% tribal groups and non Bengali Muslims (1998)

Religions: 89.5% Muslim, 9.6% Hindu, 0.9% other (2004)

Health

Life Expectancy at Birth: 67.93 years (male); 71.65 (2011 est.) years (female)

Infant Mortality: 50.73/1000 live births (2011 est.)

Per Capita Total Expenditure on Health: $57 (WHO 2005)

HIV/AIDS Rate in Adults: less than 0.1% (2009 est.)

Education

Adult Literacy Rate: 43.1%; (31.8% female) (2003 est.)
Compulsory (Ages) 6–11; free

COMMUNICATION

Telephones: 1.522 million main lines (2009)
Cell Phones: 50.4 million (2009)
Internet Users: 617,300 (2009)

TRANSPORTATION

Highways in Miles (Kilometers): 128,926 (239,226 km.) (2003)
Railroads in Miles (Kilometers): 1,681 (2,622 km.) (2006)
Usable Airfields: 17 (2010)

GOVERNMENT

Type: parliamentary democracy
Independence Date: December 16, 1971 (from West Paskistan)

Chief of State: President Zillur Rahman
Head of Government: Prime Minister Sheikh Hasina Wajed (since January, 2009)
Political Parties: Bangladesh Nationalist Party, Awami League, Islami Oikya Jote, Jamaat-e-Islami, Jatiya Party (Ershad), Jatiya Party (Manzur).
Suffrage: universal at 18

MILITARY

Military Expenditures (1.3% of GDP): (2009) (SIPRI)
Current Disputes: boundary disputes with India and Myanmar, illegal trade, migration, violence, transit of terrorists across porous borders

ECONOMY

Currency ($ U.S. Equivalent): 70.59 taka = 1$ U.S. (2010)
Per Capita Income/GDP: $1,700 (2010 est.)/$259.3 billion

GDP Growth Rate: 6% (2010 est.)
Inflation Rate: 8.1% (2010 est.)
Unemployment Rate: 4.8% (2010 est.)
Labor Force by Occupation: 45% agriculture, 25% services, 30% industry (FY 2008)
Population Below Poverty Line: 40% (2010 est.)
Natural Resources: natural gas; arable land; timber
Agriculture: rice, jute, tea, wheat, sugarcane, potatoes, tobacco, pulses, oilseeds, spices, fruit, beef, milk, poultry
Industry: jute, garments, cotton textiles, tea processing, newsprint, cement, light engineering, chemical fertilizer, sugar
Exports: $16.24 billion (2010 est.) (primary partners United States, Germany, United Kingdom, France, Netherlands)
Imports: $21.34 billion (2010 est.) (primary partners China, India, Singapore, Japan, Malaysia)
Human Development Index (ranking): 129 (UNDP 2010)

Bangladesh Country Report

Bangladesh, the youngest nation of South Asia, won its independence from Pakistan in 1971. It is also the most densely populated. More than 153 million people, half the population of the United States, live in an area smaller than the state of Wisconsin, at an average rural density of 2,600 per square mile.

Bangladesh is a fertile delta country fed by three major rivers, the Brahmaputra, the Ganga (Ganges) and the Maghna. They expand into 700 rivers to flow in intricate and shifting channels into the Sundarbans—tide country—leading into the Bay of Bengal. The Sundarbans is a land of sandbars and great reefs, many of which are submerged at high tide, with only tree-tops standing above the water. Its marshy thickets are also the home of crocodiles and the Royal Bengal Tiger.

In the monsoon season, flooding waters frequently overflow the embankments surrounding settlements along these many rivers. The worst flood of the last century, in 1988, paralyzed the central part of the country, killing 800 people and leaving almost 30 million homeless. A single cyclone in May 1991 killed 130,000 people. Devastating flooding occurred again in 1998. In 2004, thirty-nine of the country's 64 districts where overrun with water, leaving 35 million with severe losses estimated

at $7 billion. And in November, 2007, 150 mph Tropical Cyclone Sidr hit the south coast, forcing 1.5 million to flee their homes, destroying crops on 77,450 acres and leaving 1,723 dead. Natural disasters remain a constant threat to all aspects of life in Bangladesh.

It remains one of the poorest countries in the world; 61 percent of the urban population is below the poverty line, according to a recent Asian Development Bank survey, and over half of the total population lives on less than $1 a day. Among the poor are almost 300,000 tribal peoples, along with some 280,000 refugees from Myanmar, isolated among the hills and jungles in the eastern regions of the country. The Lushai, Murung, and Kuki subsist as they have for thousands of years, practicing slash-and-burn agriculture and the rite of bride capture.

DEVELOPMENT

Primarily an agricultural country subject to natural disasters, political instability, and unemployment, Bangladesh has made remarkable progress in human resource development by its many NGOs. Natural gas and textiles have become the greatest producers of wealth.

Independence

The origin of Bangladesh as an independent nation began in 1905, when Lord Curzon, the British viceroy in India, attempted to divide the Colonial Province of Bengal into a predominantly Muslim East Bengal (which then included Assam) and a Hindu West Bengal. In the 1947 partition, when Pakistan became independent, a truncated yet predominantly Muslim province of East Bengal became the eastern wing of Pakistan.

East Pakistan had the larger population, but economic and political power resided in the western wing. Attempts to impose Urdu as the national language of Pakistan, and favoritism toward the western wing in economic development, led to student demonstrations in East Pakistan in 1952.

In 1970, in Pakistan's first popular national elections, the Awami League in East Pakistan, led by Sheikh Mujibur Rahman, won a majority of seats in the national legislature. Because he had long been an advocate for greater Bengali autonomy, the political leaders in West Pakistan refused to accept him as prime minister. In response to this stalemate, President Yahya Khan suspended

Bicycle rickshaw, a mode of transportation, plays a very significant role within the city limits. This is an easily available and relatively inexpensive mode of transportation for populated areas. It is powered by human labor riding the bicycle and pulling the passenger.

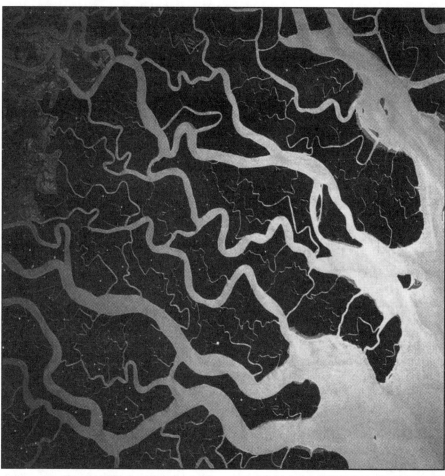

The southern half of Bangladesh is characterized by the true delta formed by the silt deposits brought down by the river's Ganga (Ganges) and the river Brahmaputra. The elevation of this delta from sea level is very low. Here, many distributaries of Ganga and Brahmaputra rivers can be seen.

the Assembly. The people of East Bengal rioted in protest. President Yahya Khan tried to suppress this public outcry by military force.

During eight months of military repression, the Pakistan army killed many hundreds of thousands, and eight million people fled as refugees into India.

In December 1971, India attacked Pakistan in support of the Bengali resistance movement to free the people of East Bengal from Pakistan's military rule. Mujibur Rahman became president, then prime minister of the new nation.

Almost all citizens of Bangladesh share a common Bengali ethnic and language identity, and most are Sunni Muslims. With so much upon which to build a democratic nation—language, religion, culture, and a successful fight for its independence—the country still struggles to achieve political stability.

Although he was a popular leader, Mujibur Rahman did not prove an effective administrator in the face of severe overpopulation, poverty, famine, and natural disasters. His increasingly authoritarian rule led to a military coup in 1975, in which he and most of his family were killed.

FREEDOM

Elections are held on a regular basis and 30 percent of local government offices are reserved for women. Rivalry between the two major parties, corruption, and license for terrorism have led to instability on the national level. Due to public unrest, elections were suspended in January, 2007, and were reinstated in December, 2008.

General Ziaur Rahman, army chief of staff, took over as martial-law administrator with the intent to lead the country back to democracy. He created his own political party, the Bangladesh Nationalist Party (BNP), and encouraged others to participate in national elections to elect 300 members to the national Legislature. (Thirty women members were subsequently to be elected by vote of the Legislature under a constitutional provision that expired in 2001). He also developed an economic policy to increase agricultural production, education, and health care.

Ziaur restored an independent executive presidency, and won the election in 1978. In the legislative elections in 1979, his BNP won two-thirds of the seats in the national Legislature.

In 1981, dissident military officers assassinated General Zia. The political chaos following his death again led to martial law in 1982, under General Hussain Muhammed Ershad, chief of staff of the army.

Ershad continued General Zia's policies of economic development and social reform. He also instituted a National Security Advisory Council to increase military participation in government. This move caused political unrest that led to his downfall. Although he won the presidential election in 1986, his party won only a very slim and widely questioned majority in the legislative elections that followed.

Two new leaders, each related to Ershad's more charismatic predecessors, came onto the national scene in protest against the 1986 election. Begum Khaleda Zia, the widow of General Zia, became

(Copyright © 1997 IMS Communications Ltd/
Capstone Design/FlatEarth Images (DAL 011EN1))
Bangladesh is a very densely populated country.
Per capita income of this country is low, and a
large number of people hardly earn enough to
meet their daily needs. The overall condition of
houses reveals poor living environments.

head of the Bangladesh National Party
(BNP) after her husband's death. Sheikh
Hasina Wajed, the eldest of only two surviving daughters of Mujibur Rahman, led
the Awami League (AWL). The rivalry and
mistrust between these two has denied the
country political stability ever since.

President Ershad first attempted to suppress their protest. Then, in December 1987,
he dissolved the Legislature and called for
new elections. The BNP and the Awami
League both boycotted, and public opinion
turned against him. In 1990, he resigned, and
Justice Shahabuddin Ahmed of the Supreme
Court was appointed acting president.

National elections to restore the government were held in February 1991. Begum
Zia was elected president, and her BNP,
polling 31 percent of the votes, won 140 seats
in the 300-member legislature. The Awami
League, although gaining almost the same
percentage of the popular vote, came in a
distant second, with 84 seats.

A national referendum in September
1991, supported by both the BNP and the
Awami League, placed executive power
in the hands of the prime minister of the
national legislature. Begum Zia then
stepped down as president. Because her
party did not command a majority of Legislature seats, she accepted the support of

the Jamaat-e-Islami, a conservative Islamic
party, to win the prime minister's office.
Though a small minority, it persuaded
Begum Zia's government to condemn a
young doctor-turned-author, Dr. Taslima
Nasreen, for alleged "blasphemy" in
her popular novel, *Lajja.* The government arrested Nasreen for "outrage[ing]
the religious feelings" of the people of
Bangladesh. Having posted bail, Dr. Nasreen escaped to live in exile in Sweden,
Germany, the United States, and ultimately
in India. This episode raised international
concern, not only for the right of freedom
of expression, but also as an indicator of
the political strength of religious fundamentalism in Bangladesh.

HEALTH/WELFARE

In the absence of stable
government, many NGOs have
evolved to provide extensive
disaster relief, job opportunities,
education, and environmental protection. The
country has made significant gains in literacy,
health care, and reduction in birth rate from
3.3 percent to 1.566 percent since 1971.

The close split of the popular vote
between the two leading parties in the
1991 elections led Sheikh Hasina's Awami
League to protest the outcome, and call for
new elections. In 1994, her party's boycott
stymied legislative activity. New elections were held in June 1996. The BNP's
standing was reduced to 116 seats, and
the Jamaat-e-Islami to three seats. With
the support of what remained of General
Ershad's party, Sheikh Hasina garnered the
votes to become prime minister. This time
it became the BNP's turn to boycott the
Legislature.

The new Legislature still enacted an
important initiative for women in government. This law reserves for them three of
the 10 directly elected seats in the 4,298
local councils that form the lowest tier of
government in Bangladesh. Elections for
these councils started in December 1997.
This was an important step toward increasing the place of women in a country where
traditional religious teachings and social
custom have accepted their repression.

Sheikh Hasina's Awami League government was able to complete a full
five-year term in control of the national
legislature. But her liberalizing initiatives
to establish modern secular rule in Bangladesh and build its relationship with India
came to a sudden and surprising end in the
elections of October 2001. Begum Zia's

Timeline: PAST

A.D. 1757–1947
British control over Bengal

1947–1971
East Pakistan

1971
The birth of Bangladesh

1972–1975
Mujibur Rahman's presidential rule

1974
Severe flooding causes 400,000 deaths

1975–1989
Following assassinations of national
leaders, Military Chiefs of Staff work to
sustain institutions of democracy.

1990s
1991 cyclone causes 130,000 deaths;
1998 flooding kills 800, leaves 30 million
homeless

Parliamentary government re-established,
enacts legislation to reserve 3 of 10 local
council seats for women.

1991 Begum Khaleda Zia becomes
prime minister.

1996 Sheikh Hasina Wajed becomes
prime minister.

PRESENT

2000s
Women seek more reserved seats in the
national Legislature

Bangladeshis continue to seek grassroot
solutions to their country's severe
economic and social problems

2001
National elections, Begum Zia again
becomes prime minister

2004
Almost 2/3 of country flooded by
monsoon, causing $7 billion in damage

2006
Professor Muhammad Yunus awarded
Nobel Peace Prize for providing
microcredit to the poor.

National elections postponed and then
cancelled due to public demonstrations
led by Awami League.

2007
A caretaker government, with military
support, installed.

2008
Elections for National Assembly held.

Awami League scores major victory in
National Assembly elections held on
December 29

2009
Sheikh Hasina Wajed becomes prime
minister

2011
Minorities Minister Shahbaz Bhatti is
assassinated. The only Christian in the
cabinet, he had received death threats
for urging reform to the blasphemy laws.

BNP campaigned on a pro-Islamic and isolationist platform, in alliance with three other conservative parties in order not to split their votes. Their alliance came to power in a landslide victory with 191 seats for the BNP, with 46 percent of the popular vote, and 18 for the Jamaat-e-Islami. The Awami League, with 42 percent of the vote, won only 62 seats. There were many indigenous causes for the rout of the Awami League. But the terrorist attacks in the United States the month before stirred Islamic fundamentalist fervor in Bangladesh, as they did in many places in the Islamic world.

ACHIEVEMENTS

The success of BRAC, Proshika, and the Grameen Bank as NGOs to provide health, education, and financial opportunities for the poor. Professor Yunus, founder of the Grameen Bank, received the Nobel Peace Prize in 2006.

Islamist militancy increased in the country. Sixteen major terrorist incidents led up to grenade attacks on Awami League political rallies in Dhaka on August 21, 2004, and in Habiganj on January 27, 2005. On August 17, 2005, five hundred bombs exploded simultaneously across the country. Rioting broke out in the streets, followed by strikes in protest called by the Awami League. The BNP denied any involvement in any of these incidents. It did arrest two high profile terrorists in March 2006. But it continued to appear restrained in reining in the forces of religious and sectarian violence as it sought continuing Islamic fundamentalist support in the next national election.

The election was set for January 21, 2007, with a caretaker government installed 90 days prior, in October, to assure free and fair voting. The Awami League, now part of a 14-party alliance, immediately protested the composition of the interim government as being pro-BNP and contested some 14 million false names that appeared on the voter rolls. Their alliance carried out a series of crippling transportation strikes throughout the country. As a result, the election was cancelled, and an interim caretaker government, with military support, was installed.

In hopes of overcoming the impasse of their political rivalry, the interim government incarcerated both Khaleda Zia and Sheikh Hasina on charges of graft. In response to public concern about its extending rule, the interim government set new elections for December 29, 2008. With extended negotiations to assure the participation of both parties, voter rolls were corrected, and the two leaders were released on bail.

These elections were won overwhelmingly by the Awami League, taking 230 of 299 seats in the National Legislature. The BNP won 27 and the Jamaat-e-Islami only 2 seats. These results promise a more productive future for the national government under the leadership of Sheikh Hasina.

Outside of government channels, the picture has been more positive. The people have shown outstanding initiative in human development from the ground up to meet the challenges of population growth, rural poverty, and disaster relief through grassroots, voluntary, non-government organizations (NGOs). The Bangladesh Rehabilitation Assistance Committee (BRAC), with a staff of 108,000, provides health services to more than 100 million people every year, educates 1.5 million children in 52,000 schools, and creates job opportunities for the landless poor. It has become so large that it functions like a parallel state.

Proshika is another large NGO that does environmentally sensitive human development among the extremely poor, with emphasis on organic sustainable farming, planting trees, and installing SONO filters to remove arsenic from well water.

The Grameen Bank, founded by economics Professor Muhammad Yunus, provides small loans to poor people in five-member groups without collateral. It has been successful in creating credit for more than 7.3 million borrowers, 97 percent of whom are women, and recovers more than $5.87 billion a year. The bank also trains its borrowers through its Sixteen Decisions around nutrition, home repair, management skills, and public health. Its effectiveness among the impoverished in Bangladesh has established it as a model for economic empowerment of the poor in more than 43 other countries. Professor Yunus was awarded the Nobel Peace Prize in 2006 for his work to alleviate poverty with the Grameen Bank microcredit initiative.

CHALLENGES

Because of its large and growing population, its limited resources, unemployment, corruption, and a succession of natural disasters, Bangladesh has struggled since its independence to achieve prosperity for its people. Cyclones and floods severely reduce agricultural production, which is barely sufficient to feed Bangladesh's population even in good times.

Many skilled workers found jobs in the Persian Gulf region. In 1998–9, they sent back to Bangladesh $1.71 billion in remittances. But recent unrest there has led to their return to flood the country's already overcrowded job market.

Natural gas is the country's greatest potential resource, with reserves sufficient to provide for its energy needs. But without other natural resources to broaden its industrial base and create new employment, with a decline in the world market for their burlap (jute) and textiles, the country's largest exports, and with the global economic crisis, a sustained GDP growth of 5.6 percent will be difficult to maintain.

With hopes for continuing international support and a stable, democratically elected leadership, a resilient and responsive people remain committed to providing education, health care, meaningful employment, and prosperity for all in their nation.

Bhutan (Kingdom of Bhutan)

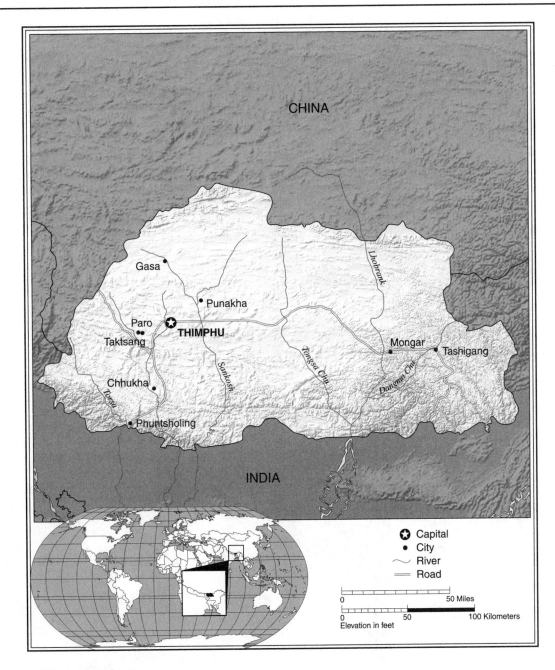

Bhutan Statistics

GEOGRAPHY

Area in Square Miles (Kilometers): 14,824 (38,394 sq km)
Capital (Population): Thimphu (89,000) (2009)
Environmental Concerns: soil erosion; limited access to potable water
Geographical Features: mostly mountainous with some fertile valleys and savanna

Climate: tropical in southern plains; cool winters and hot summers in central valleys; severe winters and cool summers in the Himalayas

PEOPLE

Population

Total: 708,427 (July, 2011 est.)
Annual Growth Rate: 1.201% (2011 est.)

Rural/Urban Population Ratio: 35% of total population (2010)
Major Languages: Dzongkha; various Tibetan dialects; Nepalese dialects
Ethnic Makeup: 50% Bhote; 35% Ethnic Nepalese; 15% indigenous and migrant tribes
Religions: 75% Buddhist; 25% Indian- and Nepalese influenced Hinduism

Health

Life Expectancy at Birth: 66.46 years
(male); 68.19 years (female) (2011 est.)
Infant Mortality: 44.48/1000 live births
(2011 est.)
Per Capita Total Expenditure on Health:
$85 (WHO 2005)
HIV/AIDS Rate in Adults: 0.2%
(2009 est.)

Education

Adult Literacy Rate: 47% (2003 est.)

COMMUNICATION

Telephones: 26,300 main lines (2009)
Cell Phones: 327,100 (2009)
Internet Users: 50,000 (2009)

TRANSPORTATION

Highways in Miles (Kilometers): 2,292
(8,050 km.) (2003)
Useable Airports: 2 (2010)

GOVERNMENT

Type: to constitutional monarchy
Independence Date: December 17, 1907
Chief of State: King Jigme Khesar
Namgyel Wangchuk
Head of Government : Prime Minister
Jigme Thinley
Political Parties: Bhutan Peace and
Prosperity Party, DTP; and People's
Democratic Party, PDP
Suffrage: 18 years of age, universal

MILITARY

Military Expenditures: 1% of GDP
(2005 est.)
Current Disputes: territorial disputes with
China

ECONOMY

Currency ($ U.S. Equivalent):
46.6 ngultrum = $1 U.S. (2009)

Per Capita Income/GDP: $5,000/
$3,526 billion (2010 est.)
GDP Growth Rate: 6.8% (2010 est.)
Inflation Rate: 4.3% (2008 est.)
Labor Force by Occupation: 43.7%
agriculture, 17.2% services, 39.1%
industry (2004 est.)
Population below Poverty Line: 23.2%
(2008)
Natural Resources: Timber, hydropower,
gypsum, calcium carbide
Agriculture: rice, corn, root crops,
citrus, foodgrains, dairy
products, eggs
Industry: cement, wood products,
processed fruits, alcoholic beverages,
calcium carbide, tourism
Exports: $513 million (primary
partners India, Bangladesh, Italy)
(2008)
Imports: $533 million (primary partners
India, Japan, China) (2008)
Human Development Index (ranking):
n.a. (UNDP 2010)

Bhutan Country Report

Bhutan is a small Himalayan country,
about the size of Vermont and New Hamp-
shire combined. Its highest point reaches
24,783 feet along the border with Tibet.
The land falls through a series of cascading
river valleys down the southern slopes toward Assam, on the eastern side of the subcontinent. Its southern border—barely 100
miles away, yet more than 24,000 feet below—touches the edge of the Brahmaputra
River plain, through narrow, humid, gorge-
like valleys of bamboo jungle.

Most of the 708,427 people in the country (2011 estimate) live in the broader,
fertile, pine-filled valleys of the central
region, from 5,000 to 9,000 feet above sea
level. Isolated by its terrain and eager to
preserve its Mahayana Buddhist heritage,
the country has moved very cautiously into
the modern world.

DEVELOPMENT

Ninety-three percent of Bhutan's
labor force is in self-sufficient
agriculture. Concerned to
preserve its Buddhist heritage,
it is cautiously developing a tourist industry
and, with India's help, expanding its vast
hydroelectric potential.

Culturally, religiously, and linguistically, 50 percent of the people of Bhutan are
closely related to Tibet. Dzongkha, the most

Many religious sites and sacred locations are situated in the Himalayan mountain ranges from
Kashmir in the west to Arunachal Pradesh in the east. These include primarily Hindu shrines,
Buddhist stupas and temples, and Sikh gurudwaras. Depicted here is a Buddhist religious place
and community in the Eastern Himalayan region.

common language spoken in the northern
and western regions, is the official language of the country. Other Tibetan dialects
are spoken in the eastern regions, where
the people are more closely related by

custom to Assam. The remaining 35 percent are Nepali and Hindi-speaking peoples, most of whom have recently migrated
into the country as laborers, and have
settled in the southern region closest to

India. Several thousand Tibetans fled into Bhutan following the Chinese takeover of their country and subsequent repressions during the 1950s.

The Mahayana Buddhist religion in Bhutan—as distinct from the Theravada Buddhism of Sri Lanka and Southeast Asia—also traces its origin to Tibet: to the Nyingmapa school of the Red Hat sect. Important monasteries, as at Taktsang (the Tiger's Lair), celebrate the teachings of the learned Indian monk Padma Sambhava, who introduced Buddhism into Tibet in the eighth century. He is described as the heroic Guru Rimpoche ("Precious Teacher") coming on a flying tiger to drive the forces of evil out of Druk Yul, "Land of the Thunder Dragon."

A Tibetan lama, Shabdrung Ngawang Namgyal, brought the isolated valley peoples under a single authority in the 1600s. He also established a tradition of religious leadership sustained by identifying the embodiment of his mind reincarnation (Dharma Raja) through successive generations. The religious authority of his Dharma Raja was subsumed during the 1930s under the temporal authority of a dynastic monarchy that was established in 1907 under British colonial rule.

THE MONARCHY

British military forces advanced into Bhutan in 1864 to repel Tibetan and Chinese claims of control over the Himalayan Mountains. In gratitude for his help in their successful attack of Tibet in 1903, the British rewarded Ugyen Wangchuk, then feudal lord (Penlop) of the north-central district of Tongsa, by assisting him to become Druk Gyalpo, the hereditary "Dragon King" of Bhutan, in 1907.

The British continued to oversee the external affairs of the country, but allowed the new king to rule independently in domestic matters. In 1949, with the end of the British Raj in 1947, Bhutan extended this agreement "to be guided in regard to

(Courtesy of BhutanNewsOnline.com)

Former King Jigme Singye Wangchuck with his four wives, Queens Ashi Tshering Yangdon Wangchuck, Ashi Tshering Pem Wangchuck, Ashi Dorji Wangmo Wangchuck, and Ashi Sangay Choden Wangchuck, all sisters.

(Kaptan/courtesy Bhutan Majestic Travell)

His Royal Highness Dasho Jigme Khesar Namgyel Wangchuck, consecrated King of Bhutan on November 6, 2008. He studied at Magdelen College, Oxford University, from which he was awarded M Phil in politics.

its foreign relations" to the government of India. India has allowed Bhutan latitude in establishing international agreements, including support of Bhutan's admission to the United Nations in 1971.

Jigme Dorji Wangchuk, grandson of Ugyen Wangchuk, instituted a number of reforms to bring his country cautiously into the modern era. To encourage more participation in government, in 1952, he established a National Assembly, the Tshoghdu. The Assembly had 151 members, 31 of whom were appointed by the king. The rest were elected by hereditary village headmen in the districts. They also served as local judges in a judicial system in which the king was the chief justice. As king, he also remained the religious head and chief executive of the country.

In 1968, the king granted the Assembly powers to limit his absolute authority. He could no longer veto legislation passed by majority vote of the Assembly. Also, by a two-thirds vote, the Assembly could force the king to abdicate. But in that case, only the next claimant in his hereditary line could succeed him. This provision reproduces on the national level the traditional family expectation that a landholder will pass on his lands to his eldest son as soon as the heir comes of age.

Jigme Dorji Wangchuk's reforms also included the elimination of serfdom by granting public lands to landless servants. But in order not to disrupt traditional social patterns and create unemployment, he did not break up large private landholdings.

Jigme Singye Wangchuk, then 17 years old, succeeded Jigme Dorji Wangchuk upon his death in 1972. He continued his father's policies of gradual reform. During the summer of 1998, he expanded

the powers of the National Assembly by replacing his royal Council of Ministers with a cabinet elected by the Assembly. It was to be "vested with full executive powers to provide efficient and effective governance of our country." The Assembly, with some reluctance, carried out his wishes by electing a cabinet from a list of candidates that he provided.

In 2002, the government began a process to elect its village headmen by popular vote rather than hereditary appointment. In 2005, in his National Day Address, King Jigme Singye Wangchuk announced "that the first national election to elect a government under a system of parliamentary democracy will take place in 2008." At the same time, he announced that he would delegate his kingship to his eldest son, Jigme Khesar Namgyel Wangshuk. The 28-year-old King was crowned by his father at 8:31 A.M. on November 6, 2008, a time designated as most auspicious by royal astrologers. A draft constitution was prepared in 2007, in anticipation of the first national elections, which were held on March 24, 2008. Its provisions require all candidates for the 47 seats in the new National Assembly to have both parents be Bhutanese-born and to hold a graduate degree. Almost 75 percent of the registered voters participated to elect an overwhelming majority of 45 seats to the Bhutan Peace and Prosperity Party (DPT). Its leader, Jigme Thinley, was elected prime minister on April 9, 2008. The justices of the High Court are still appointed by the king. King Jigme Singye Wangchuk thus led his country toward the beginnings of democracy, while at the same time assuring stability of the government through elite representation.

ECONOMIC DEVELOPMENT

India has been the largest investor in the development of Bhutan's economy. In the face of Chinese threats of invasion over border disputes during the 1950s, the Indian government built a road from Bhutan's southern border to the capital, Thimphu. It took 112 miles of winding roadway to cover a straight-line distance of 45 miles. In 1996, India began a project to extend this roadway into eastern Bhutan.

With India's help, Bhutan has also increased the country's energy potential. The first of six hydroelectric projects, the 336-megawatt Chuka Hydroelectric Project, financed by the Indian government, was completed in 1987, to export electricity to India. The 1,020-megawatt Tala Hydroelectric Project, started in 1997, began production in 2006. India provided 60 percent of the cost and technical assistance for this project. These two, together with the 60-megawatt Kurichhu project (2002) in eastern Bhutan, produce over 40 percent of Bhutan's annual revenue. An even larger joint India project, the Sunkosh 4,060-megawatt project, which would also provide water for irrigation to India, is expected to be completed by 2020.

The importance of this relationship with India was affirmed by Bhutan's response to India's request in 2004 to remove camps set up within its borders by insurgents from Assam and Nagaland. The Royal Bhutan Army destroyed 30 camps in a swift military operation.

THE CHALLENGE OF MODERNIZATION

Bhutan has extensive forestry reserves that remain virtually unexploited. Twenty percent of the country has been set aside for preservation. The Royal Manas National Park, a 165-square-mile sanctuary established along its southern border, is designed to protect the natural wildlife of South Asia. Many of the species there are endangered.

Tourism in this incredibly beautiful natural environment is being developed on a "low volume and high value" policy to develop its economic potential so as not to undermine the traditional Buddhist life of its people, and to maintain its natural preserve.

The development of the human resources of the country has also taken a measured pace. Canadian Jesuit Father William Mackey has led the development of the nation's educational system to provide 180 schools and a national college. Still,

Timeline: PAST

A.D. 1616–1930s
Dharma Raja of Tibetan lamas

1907
Tongsa Penlop becomes hereditary king

1910–1947
British control over Bhutan's external affairs

1949
Indian control over Bhutan's external affairs begins

1953
A constitutional monarchy is established; the National Assembly has power to limit authority of king

1972
Jigme Singye Wangchuck becomes king

1980s
The Citizenship Act was enacted to limit citizenship to Nepali migrants. Unrest led to flight and deportation of 85,000 refugees to camps in eastern Nepal.

Building of hydroelectric power and limited tourism begin to contribute to country's economic growth.

1990s
Many Nepali immigrants are denied citizenship; demonstrators protest government policies toward Nepalis

PRESENT

2000s
Gradual government reforms leading to a parliamentary democracy begin.

Attempts to repatriate Nepali refugees from camps in eastern Nepal stall.

2008
National Assembly elections held on March 24; Jigme Khesar Namgyel Wangchuck installed as King.

Initial 5,000 of Nepali refugees resettled under United Nations High Commission on Refugees plan to resettle 60,000 in the United States.

2011
The notes verbales and the joint communique on the establishment of diplomatic relations was signed and exchanged between ambassador and permanent representative of Bhutan to the United Nations in New York, Lhatu Wangchuk, and ambassador and permanent representative of Spain to the UN in New York, Juan Pablo de Laiglesia.

only a small percentage of school-age children attend, and the adult literacy rate is estimated at 47 percent, among the lowest in Asia.

Health services are also meager; the expectation is that the family unit will remain the primary source of social welfare. The annual birth rate is a significant

2 percent, but the level of infant mortality is also high. The large number who become Buddhist monks also restrains population growth. The average life expectancy among the Bhutanese people is estimated to be 65.53 years.

HEALTH/WELFARE

The family and the village have the primary responsibility for the welfare of the people. In the 1950s the king instituted a program for social work for monks living in the state-supported monasteries. The government has also initiated an education program, but the literacy rate remains one of the lowest in South Asia.

Immigration has presented another challenge of modernization to the values of its rich natural and religious heritage. Most of the work force of Bhutan is employed in subsistence farming on the 16 percent of the land that is available for cultivation and pasture. Because this sector is self-sufficient, the country has had to import workers from neighboring Nepal and India to provide the labor needed to develop its industry. Their migration has challenged the country's efforts to preserve a national identity out of the exclusive culture of the dominant Buddhist community. To protect this identity, the government passed a law in 1985 to deny citizenship to all who could not claim legal residency before 1958.

A census taken in 1987 to enforce this exclusive nationalistic policy stirred political unrest among the Nepalis living in the southern part of the country, which led to terrorist attacks on schools and other public buildings. Government deportations in response moved eighty-five thousand people out of Bhutan into refugee camps set up by the United Nations High Commission on Refugees in the eastern part of Nepal.

After thirteen futile attempts to resolve the issue, in 2001, the governments of Bhutan and Nepal agreed to conduct a pilot screening of 12,000 refugees residing in one of the camps in Nepal. The Bhutan representatives divided these refugees into four categories. Only 2.5 percent of them were determined to be bona fide citizens eligible for repatriation to Bhutan. Those assigned to Category II (70 percent) were described as "voluntarily" migrated from Bhutan more than a decade ago. In order to return, they would be required to apply for citizenship. The requirements for readmission include a two-year probationary delay and proof of fluency in the Dzongkha language of northern Bhutan. Screening began in a second refugee camp. But bilateral talks in 2003 failed to resolve issues of screening and of the rights and security of those readmitted.*

In response to the plight of the discouraged and restive 105,000 refugees remaining in seven camps in Nepal, the International Organization for Migration is preparing for the migration of 60,000 of them to resettle in the United States.

---

*Brad Adams, "Letter to Prime Minister of Bhutan regarding discrimination against ethnic Nepalis," *Human Rights Watch,* April 16, 2008.

According to the UN High Commission on Refugees, 5,000 will be resettled in the United States, Australia, and New Zealand in 2008.

Within Bhutan, increasing interaction with western life styles introduced by satellite television and the Internet is also changing attitudes and expectations among the youth. A youth-led Communist Party of Bhutan-Maoists is initiating agitation for a more inclusive government and the return of the Nepali refugees to Bhutan. As a traditional and cautious Bhutan seeks to become more democratic and developed, an enlightened role of the monarchy

appears to hold the greatest promise for resolving peacefully the cultural and political tensions created by the modernization of the country.

ACHIEVEMENTS

Twenty percent of the country has been set aside for the preservation of its vast forest and wildlife reserves. In keeping with its Buddhist heritage, it seeks to achieve, as a nation, an increase in Gross Domestic Happiness, rather than GDProductivity.

Maldives (Republic of Maldives)

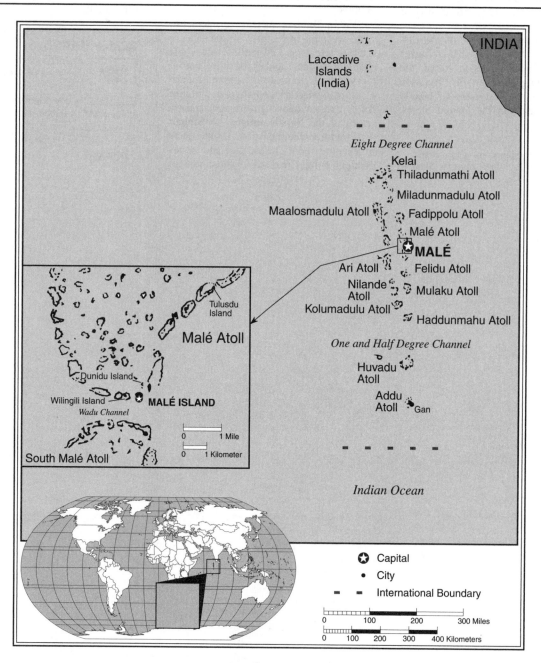

Maldives Statistics

GEOGRAPHY

Area in Square Miles (Kilometers):
115,058 (298) (about 1.7 times the size of Washington D.C. in land mass, but stretched as islands over 510 miles of the Indian Ocean)

Capital (Population): Malé (120,000) (2009) living on 7/10 square mile island (1.813 sq km)

Environmental Concerns: depletion of freshwater aquifers; global warming and sea level rise; coral-reef bleaching

Geographical Features: flat, with white sandy beaches

Climate: tropical; hot; humid; monsoon

PEOPLE

Population

Total: 94,999 (July, 2011 est.)

Annual Growth Rate: −0.151% (2011 est.)

Rural/Urban Population Ratio: 60/40 (2010)

Major Languages: Maldivian Dhivehi; English is spoken by most government officials

Ethnic Makeup: South Indians, Sinhalese, Arabs

Religion: Sunni Muslim

HEALTH

Life Expectancy at Birth: 74.45 years; (72.22 years male; 76.8 years female)

Infant Mortality: 27.45/1000 live births (2011 est.)

Per Capita Total Expenditure on Health: $878 (WHO 2005)
HIV/AIDS Rate in Adults: less than 0.1% (2009 est.)

Education

Adult Literacy Rate: 93.8%
Education: 12 years

COMMUNICATION

Telephones: 49,913 main lines (2009)
Cell Phones: 461,149 (2009)
Internet Users: 86,400 (2009)

TRANSPORTATION

Airports: 5
Highways in Miles (Kilometers): (88 km.; 66 km in Malé)

GOVERNMENT

Type: republic

Independence Date: July 26, 1965 (from the United Kingdom)
Head of State/Government:
   President Mohamed Nasheed
Political Parties: registered in June, 2005: Adhaalath (Justice) Party AP, Dhivehi Rayyithunge Party DRP, Islamic Democracy Party IDP, Maldivian Democratic Party MPD.
Suffrage: universal at 21

MILITARY

Military Expenditures: 5.5% of GDP 2005 est.
Current Disputes: none

ECONOMY

Currency ($ U.S. Equivalent):
   12.8 *rufiyaa* = $1 U.S. (2010)
Per Capita Income/GDP: $4,600/$1.776 billion (2010 est.)

GDP Growth Rate: 4% (2010 est.)
Inflation Rate: 6% (2010 est.)
Labor Force by Occupation: 65% services, 11% agriculture, 23% industry (2006 est.)
Natural Resource: fish
Agriculture: fish, corn, coconuts, sweet potatoes
Industry: tourism; fish processing, shipping, boat building, coconut processing, garments, woven mats, rope, handicrafts, coral and sand mining
Exports: $163 million f.o.b. (2009 est.) (primary partners France, Thailand, Italy, United Kingdom, Sri Lanka) (2009)
Imports: $967 million f.o.b. (2009 est.) (primary partners Singapore, UAE, India, Malaysia, Sri Lanka, Thailand) (2009)
Human Development Index (ranking): 107 (UNDP 2010)

Maldives Country Report

Maldives is a string of 1,192 tiny tropical islands grouped into 26 atolls in the Indian Ocean about 400 miles southwest of India. The island chain stretches 510 miles north to south across the equator. Most of the islands are small, the largest being less than five square miles in area. The highest elevation is only 8 feet above sea level, with many rising barely six feet above the ocean waters. They were easily submerged under the fourteen-foot high Indian Ocean tsunami wave on December 26, 2004, and more frequently by storm swells. They are fragile, remote, but enticingly beautiful.

DEVELOPMENT

Fishing and tourism are the major industries of this nation of islands. Both were severely damaged by the 2004 tsunami. Tourism is recovering rapidly, while fishing boats and housing remain restoration issues.

(Copyright © Peter Cade/Getty Images (DAL 200158457-001_20))

Maldives is a country of archipelago. The average elevation of these islands is hardly a few feet above sea level. Palm trees are the most common natural vegetation of this island country. Here groves of palm trees line the shore of Kuredu Island, Maldives.

Most of the islands are covered with lush scrub growth, some have coconut-palm groves, and all are surrounded with coral reefs and clear waters abundant with fish. The mean daily temperature remains at a humid 80°F year-round, especially during the monsoon season from June to August. Because of a shortage of fresh water and arable land on most of the islands, only 200 of them are inhabited. Almost 30 percent of the total population of 94,999 lives in the capital city on the island of Male, which is just 7/10 of a square mile.

The earliest inhabitants of Maldives came from south India and Sri Lanka. Remains of shrines indicate the migration of Buddhists around the second century B.C. Dhivehi, the prevailing language of the islands, is further evidence of early Buddhist settlement. It is derived from Pali, the classical language of Buddhism in India, from which the Sinhalese language of Sri Lanka also comes.

Because the Maldive islands lie across the maritime trade route between Africa and East Asia, Arab traders often stopped there. The arrival of an Islamic Sufi saint in 1153 A.D. led to the conversion of the people to Islam. Since then Dhivehi is written in Arabic script, with the addition of many Arabic and Urdu words. The Moroccan explorer Ibn Battuta visited Male in the fourteenth century, during his extensive travels through North Africa and Asia. Because of his Islamic scholarship, he was invited to stay on Male as a judge. His accounts give a colorful description of island life at that time. Today, citizenship is restricted to Sunni Muslims, and the country's legal system is based on Shari'a, Islamic law.

Two immense global currents challenge the Maldives today: the revolution of self-determination through democracy and the rise of ocean waters by global warming.

FREEDOM

Rights of citizenship are restricted to Sunni Muslims. Although declared a democratic republic in 1968, it has slowly moved toward legislative reforms and an independent judiciary. Political parties became legal in 2005, the first national election for president was held in October, 2008, and national legislative elections in 2009.

THE BEGINNINGS OF REPRESENTATIVE GOVERNMENT

Strongly united under the authority of a sultan (an Islamic monarch), the Maldivians have remained fiercely independent since the twelfth century. A local leader, Bodu Muhammad Takurufanu, repulsed a brief Portuguese colonial intrusion in 1573. Maldives became a protectorate under the British crown in 1887. Even then, the Maldivian leaders did not permit British interference in local governance.

The British established a military base on the southern island of Gan during World War II and an air base in 1956. But strong anti-foreign sentiment forced the closing of the base in 1976, 14 years before the end of a 30-year lease with the British. The following year, Maldives rejected a Soviet offer to lease the base for $1 million per year.

In 1953, the sultan, Muhammad Amin Didi, declared Maldives a democratic republic, with himself as president. But the power of governance remained with an appointed "Regency Committee." In 1968, Amin Ibrahim Nasir, who had served since 1957 as prime minister in the Committee, instituted a new Constitution with an elected legislature (Majlis). This body selected him as its nominee to become president of the country. The Constitution prohibited political parties to form any opposition.

During his tenure as president, Ibrahim Nasir abolished the post of prime minister and increased his presidency

to quasi-sultan status. He won a second five-year term in 1973. He did not seek reelection in 1978, and was succeeded by Maumoon Abdul Gayoom.

President Gayoom was elected for six terms; the only candidate in the national referendum to have his nomination approved by a majority vote of the 42-member Citizen's Majlis. Each time he received more than 90 percent of the popular vote. His 30-year rule came to an end on October 28, 2008, when, under an amended Constitution, he was defeated in a run-off in the country's first multi-party, direct election for president. Mohamed Nasheed, a long-time political activist and leader of the Maldivian Democratic Party, became his successor.

HEALTH/WELFARE

The government developed an emergency rescue service able to reach 97 percent of the population widely dispersed among the habitable islands of the country. Its literacy (293.8 percent) is the highest in South Asia.

ECONOMIC DEVELOPMENT

President Gayoom's enlightened economic policies encouraged significant growth in the fishing and tourism industries. Almost half of the country's workforce is employed in fishing, mostly using traditional craft called dhonis. In the 1980s, government funds helped to construct canning and cold-storage facilities, as well as more than 200 modern fishing boats, to expand the catch—and the markets—for this valuable resource.

ACHIEVEMENTS

With substantial international help, the country has made substantive recovery from the tsunami damage. To preserve its fragile environment and its peace-loving character, it is a strong advocate for reducing global warming and making the Indian Ocean a nuclear-free zone.

In 1981, an international airport was constructed on an island near Male to serve with airports on the islands of Hulule and Gan. This facilitated increases in the number of tourists. In 2004, 615,000 came to vacation in 87 resort zones on isolated

---

*Raquel Rolnik, "UN Special Rapporteur on Adequate Housing," *UN News Centre,* February 26, 2009.

atolls. With continuing foreign aid, the country sustained an impressive growth rate, around 7 percent from 1995 to 2004, and the second highest per capita income in South Asia.

These industries, together with a reviving coconut crop and a modest shipping fleet, did not balance the import needs of the country, especially for food. The country received more than 20 percent of its revenue as foreign aid, and it continued to accumulate debt.

Then on December 26, 2004, came the devastating tsunami. Although only 108 were drowned, it destroyed 120 fishing vessels and twenty-one of the tourist zones, and left 29,000 homeless. Tourist visitors dropped by 36 percent in 2005. Total damage to the islands was estimated at $470 million, more than 62 percent of its GDP. Impressive international support has helped the country to recover. Tourist centers have been rapidly rebuilt. But it will take years to restore the homes and trades of an impoverished population spread among the inhabited islands.*

Maldives has no institutions of higher learning, and medical facilities are limited. There are only four hospitals. But extended restoration and education programs and an emergency medical rescue service among the outlying islands rank Maldives just below Sri Lanka in South Asia in the UN Human Resources Development Index. Adult literacy has grown to 293.8 percent, and the government continues to work to improve water supplies and to eliminate water-borne diseases through water purification, desalinization, and other public-health measures.

PUBLIC PROTEST FOR DEMOCRACY

For all of the benefits of economic growth and human services, their fruits were distributed unevenly among the population. In response to this inequality under Gayoom's despotic rule, an increasing cadre of political activists sought greater democracy. The initial government response was suppression. An opposition candidate for president in 1993 was banished from the country for 15 years. Five others, including Mohamed Nasheed, were detained for circulating articles critical of the government. He was designated an Amnesty International Prisoner of Conscience in 1996. On September 20, 2003, while Nasheed was in exile in Sri Lanka, Evan Naseem, a political prisoner, was beaten to death in jail. That same year, the Majlis established a Human Rights Commission to look into reports of increasing prison abuses.

In August 2004, Nasheed helped to organize public demonstrations to protest

Malé, the capital of Maldives, where more than 100,000 live on the 7/10 square mile island.

the killing of Naseem, the detention of other political dissidents, and to call for democratic reforms. The government responded by declaring a state of emergency and arrested Nasheed and hundreds of other protesters, including several members of the Majlis advocating for political parties. A year later, on June 3, 2005, the Majlis amended the Constitution to allow political opposition. Three parties, Gayoom's own Dhivehi Rayyithunge Party (MPP), the Islamic Democracy Party (IDP), and Nasheed's Maldivian Democratic Party (MDP) quickly registered. They were later joined by the religiously conservative Adhaalath (Justice) Party (AP).

These steps were not sufficient for a country impatient for political freedom. The Maldivian Democratic Party organized a political rally for November 10, 2006, to push for further constitutional reforms. It was cancelled when the government threatened to punish any who took part.

In response to increasing public pressure, President Gayoom considered further constitutional amendments he hoped could be accepted in a deliberate and orderly manner. His proposal included limited terms for the presidency, a strengthened parliamentary form of government, and an independent Supreme Court. He finally ratified them to establish a new Constitutional

Timeline: PAST

300 B.C.
The earliest evidence of Indian Buddhist civilization

A.D. 1153
Conversion to Islam in Maldives

1153–1968
Maldives is an Islamic sultanate; Bodu Muhammad Takurufanu repulses brief Portuguese intrusion to the islands in 1573

1300s The famous Moroccan explorer, Ibn Battuta, was invited and appointed a judge in Maldives.

1887–1968
Maldives is a British protectorate

1968
Maldives becomes an independent democratic republic without political parties

1988
An attempted coup is put down by the Indian Army

1990s
The government seeks to improve social services, incurring substantial debt in the process. Maldives agitates for global environmental responsibility

PRESENT

2000s
At the Coral Reef Symposium in October 2000, Maldives' marine environment is cited as heavily damaged by global warming

2004
Public protest for greater democracy leads to declaration of a state of emergency

Tsunami kills 82, causes extensive damage to tourist and fishing industries

2005
Constitution is amended to allow for political parties. Tourist industry quickly restored after tsunami damage. Restoration of fishing fleet and housing remain to be done

2008
Mohamed Nasheed elected in first national democratic elections for president

2009
First election for the Majlis contested by political parties

2011
Minorities still face repression and marginalization, says London-based Minority Rights Group International.

order in August, 2008, that anticipated multi-party presidential elections to be held in October.

In the election on October 8, Gayoom won only 41 percent of the vote, to

Mohamed Nasheed's 25 percent. Against the combined effort of the opposition parties, he lost to Nasheed's 54 percent tally in the run-off on October 28. As a primary, if reluctant, participant in the turbulent process toward greater democracy, he graciously accepted this end to his 30-year rule.

Multi-party elections for the Majlis for the first time were set for February, 2009.

THE RISE OF THE OCEAN

The islands offered little resistance to the tsunami in 2004. The force of the wave inundated most of the islands, submerging two-thirds of the capital city Male. And it contaminated most of the islands' groves and fresh water supplies.

But increasing population and a developing economy are having a longer-term impact on the islands' limited resources and fragile environment. The daily use of fresh water is drawing upon the aquifers faster than the annual rainfall replenishes them. And increasing human contamination threatens what water is available.

More critical is saltwater intrusion due to the breakdown of the protective coral reefs and the rise in the level of the ocean due to global warming. To restrain the short-term impact, the government built an expensive, six-foot retaining wall around parts of the island of Male, paid for by the Japanese government, with expensive restoration costs attached. The long-term outlook is overwhelming.

Newly elected Mohamed Nasheed faces many immediate problems of declining tourism, population growth, high unemployment, and a growing drug culture. Also recognizing the threat of the ocean's rise to the islands' future, he has called for the creation of a sovereign wealth fund, drawn from the country's tourist receipts, to be able, when necessary, to purchase a new homeland for the Maldivian people.

Nepal (Federal Democratic Republic of Nepal)

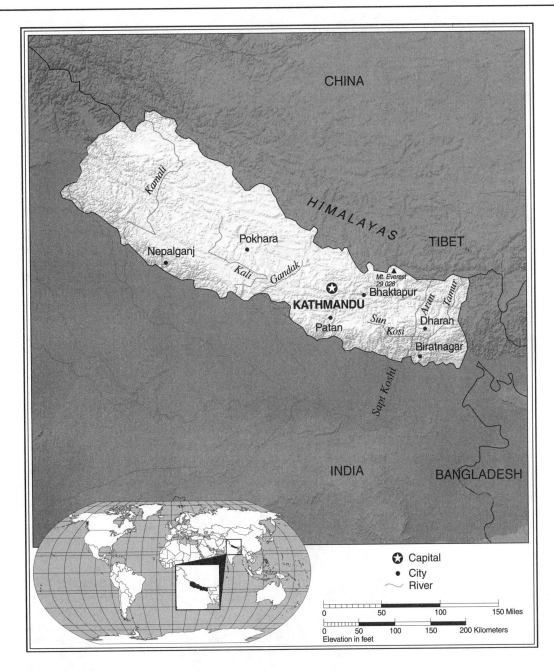

Nepal Statistics

GEOGRAPHY

Area in Square Miles (Kilometers):
56,812 sq. mi. (147,181 sq. km.)
Capital (Population): Kathmandu
(990,000) (2009 est.)
Environmental Concerns: widespread
deforestation, wildlife conservation;
water and air pollution
Geographical Features: Terai, flat river
plain in south; central hills; rugged
Himalaya Mountains in north;
landlocked
Climate: cool summers and severe winters in
the north; subtropical in the south (Terai)

PEOPLE

Population

Total: 29,391,883 (2011 est.)
Annual Growth Rate: 1.596% (2011 est.)

Rural/Urban Population Ratio: 19% of
total population (2010)
Major Languages: 47.8% Nepali;
12.1 Maithali; .4% Bhojpuri; numerous
other languages and dialects; English
link language in government and
business (2001 est.)
Ethnic Makeup: 15.5% Chhettri,
12.5% Brahman-Hill, 7% Magar,
6.6% Tharu, 5.5% Tamang,
5.4% Newar, 4.2% Muslim,

3.9% Kami, 3.9% Yadav, 32.7% other (Gurung, Rai, Lumbu, Sherpa, and many smaller groups) (2001 census)
Religions: 80.6% Hindu, 10.7% Buddhist, 4.2% Muslim. 3.6% Kirant, other 0.9% (2001 census)

Health

Life Expectancy at Birth: 64.94 years (male), 67.44 years (female) (2011 est.)
Infant Mortality: 44.54/1000 live births (2011 est.)
Per Capita Total Expenditure on Health: $76 (WHO 2005)
HIV/AIDS Rate in Adults: 0.4% (2009 est.)

Education

Adult Literacy Rate: 48.6% (34.9% female) (2001 census)
Education: male 10 years, female 8 years (2003)

COMMUNICATION

Telephones: 820,500 main lines (2009)
Cell Phones: 7.618 million (2009)
Internet Users: 577,800 (2009)

TRANSPORTATION

Highways in Miles (Kilometers): (17,282 km.) (2007)
Railroads in Miles (Kilometers): 36 (59 km.) (2008)
Usable Airfields: 47 (2010)

GOVERNMENT

Type: federal democratic republic
Independence Date: 1768 (unified)
Chief of State: President Ram Baran Yadav
Head of Government: Prime Minister Jhala Nath Khanal
Political Parties: Communist Party of Nepal (Maoist), Communist Party of Nepal (United Marxist-Leninist), Nepali Congress Party, Madhesi Jana Adhikar Forum, Terai Madhesi Democratic Party/Nepal Sadbhawana Party, other smaller parties
Suffrage: universal at 18

MILITARY

Military Expenditures: 1.6% of GDP (2006)
Current Disputes: boundary with India (dispute over source of the Kalapani River), refugees, illicit drug smuggling

ECONOMY

Currency ($ U.S. Equivalent): 72.56 *rupees* = $1 U.S. (2010)
Per Capita Income/GDP: $1,200/ $35.31 billion (2010 est.)
GDP Growth Rate: 3.5% (2010 est.)
Inflation Rate: 8.6% (2010 est.)
Unemployment Rate: 46% (2008 est.)
Labor Force by Occupation: 75% agriculture, 18% services, 7% industry (2010 est.)
Population Below Poverty Line: 24.7% (2008)
Natural Resources: quartz, timber, water, scenic beauty, hydropower, lignite, copper, cobalt, iron ore
Agriculture: pulses, rice, corn, wheat, sugarcane, jute; root crops, milk, water buffalo meat
Industry: tourism; carpets, textiles, small rice, jute, sugar and oilseed mills, cigarettes, cement and brick production
Exports: $849 million (2009) (primary partners India, United States, Bangladesh, Germany)
Imports: $5.26 billion (2009) (primary partners India, China, Indonesia)
Human Development Index (ranking): 138 (UNDP 2010)

Nepal Country Report

Nepal is like a Tantric mandala: colorful and intense, leading to unexpected levels of awareness. The country is breathtaking, like the magnificent Mount Everest's peak, the highest in the world, which dominates a majestic row of 10 Himalayan Mountains over 26,000 feet high that mark the formidable boundary between Nepal and Tibet. The land falls steeply from this arctic height into the lush Kathmandu Valley, some 20,000 feet below. It then rises again over the smaller, barren Mahabharat range, up to 11,000 feet, and drops once more through the foothills into a marshy plain, called the Terai, along the Ganga (Ganges) River, about 900 feet above sea level. Nepal is a land of immense natural contrast, with habitat for a wide variety of species, from the elusive snow leopards in the mountains to elephants, monkeys, tigers, and crocodiles in the Terai.

Nepal is also home to a wide variety of people. Almost 30 million are broadly divided by region, religion, and language into three distinct groups.

The mountainous region to the north is sparsely inhabited, mostly by those of Tibetan descent and language who follow the Lamaist, or Tibetan, Buddhist tradition. Their dress and many customs are from Tibet. Some, for example, practice

(Copyright © The McGraw-Hill Companies, Inc./Barry Barker, photographer (DAL mhhe016159))

Sadhu in traditional ochre-colored dress, beaded necklaces, and traditional religious face paint, at temple in Kathmandu, Nepal.

polyandrous marriage, wherein the wife of the eldest son is also married to his younger brothers. In such families, their lands are not usually subdivided. The brothers also share in the few seasonal occupations that the frigid terrain allows: cultivating in spring, herding in summer, and trading in winter.

DEVELOPMENT

 Most of Nepal's economy relies on subsistence agriculture and diminishing trade between Tibet and India. The successful ascent of Mt. Everest introduced a thriving tourist trade that persisted through the ravages of a militant Maoist insurrection from 1996 to 2006. It remains among the poorest nations in the world.

Even though arable land is scarce and trade has been drastically reduced by the Chinese takeover of Tibet, the people of this region are more prosperous than those living in the more fertile valleys to the south. The alternative to family life presented by the Buddhist monastic tradition also restrains population growth. Although their small, isolated communities span almost half of the total land area, they constitute only 3 percent of the total population of Nepal.

"Swayambhunath Stupa," (Swayambhu, meaning "Self-Created or Self-Existent," and "Almighty," one meaning of Nath) as this religious place is called, is the most ancient and enigmatic of all the holy shrines in Kathmandu valley, Nepal. Its lofty white dome and glittering golden spire are visible for many miles and from various directions. Historical inscriptions describe that this Stupa had become an important Buddhist pilgrimage place by the 5th century AD. It is believed that its origins date back to an earlier time, long before the arrival of Buddhism into this region.

Almost a third of the population lives in the Terai, the low-lying, southernmost region of the country in the Ganga (Ganges) plain. These Madeshi are mostly Hindu, although some are Muslim. They speak dialects of Hindi and are ethnically and culturally very close to their Indian neighbors. Because the land is flat, fertile, and nurtured by the snow-fed rivers flowing out of the mountains, agriculture is the primary activity. Although it is a narrow strip of land, only about 20 miles wide, and occupying 17 percent of the country, it produces more than 60 percent of Nepal's gross domestic product (GDP).

Two thirds of the population of Nepal, the Pahari, live in the interlying hill region. It is also predominantly agricultural. Arable lands are scarcer than in the Terai and are terraced for farming. Because of the altitude, the growing season is also shorter and the yields lower. At the center of this region is the Kathmandu Valley, a lush alluvial plain 15 miles long and 12 miles wide. Nepal's three largest cities: Kathmandu, Patan, and Bhaktapur are in this valley, absorbing more of its land as they continue to expand. Wide arrays of ethnic and cultural identities co-mingle here, interacting with the many

Spinning a prayer wheel is an important religious ritual in Buddhism.

surrounding cultures to create a distinctive artistic style and to fuse an overwhelming multiplicity of religious expression. Their Nepali language is based on the Indo-European languages of India, infused with extensive Tibeto-Burman borrowings.

SOCIAL DIVERSITY

Nepali social diversity is partly due to the rugged terrain, which has kept many small groups isolated east to west in the several river valleys that descend down the steep southern slopes of the mountains. Also important, Nepal has long provided extensive trade routes from India north up the river valleys, through the high mountain passes into Tibet, and on into China. Nepali traders along these routes have maintained distinct ethnic identities, whether their primary interaction has been with the Tibetan culture to the north or with the Hindu culture to the south. The success of their mercantile activity with such distinct partners has reinforced the cultural contrasts between Tibet and India within the central region of Nepal itself.

The hierarchical social structure known as the caste system in India also contributes to Nepal's social diversity. This system, ranking rather than assimilating, maintains the distinctive customs and traditions of different communities. The Nepalese criteria for ranking appear more flexible than in India. The Gurkhas, for example, famous for their military prowess and courage, are recruited from three different Tibeto-Burman language communities from different parts of Nepal. They join together because of the opportunity for military employment that a shared identity as

Gurkhas affords. Similarly, several distinct tribal groups in the Terai have claimed a single ethnic identity as Tharus in order to gain strength as a political force not available to them as separate minorities. In contrast, Thaksatae villagers have distanced themselves from other Thakalis, with whom they share ethnic, linguistic, and religious identities, in order to maintain the trading privileges that they have achieved as a distinct community within that group.

POLITICS

Prithvi Narayan Shah, king of the western province of Gorkha forged the unity of present-day Nepal in the eighteenth century A.D. He conquered the surrounding kingdoms and established his dynasty in Kathmandu, the capital of a defeated Newar ruler. His family's reign was circumscribed first by the British East India Company in 1815, and later, in 1845, by the Kathmandu Rana family, which established a powerful and hereditary prime ministry to rule the Shah domain.

In 1950, with the departure of the British Raj from the subcontinent, a national movement, modeled on the independence movement in India and led by the Nepali Congress Party (NCP), overthrew the Rana family. King Tribhuvan Vir Vikram Shah supported the anti-Rana movement and became a national hero. Upon his reinstitution as full monarch in February 1951, he worked to bring constitutional democracy to Nepal. Although his son, Mahendra, who succeeded him in 1955, was less sympathetic, his initiatives still led to national

(United Nations Photo Library #380286 /Ray Witlin)

The geographic contrast in Nepal is dramatic. The Himalayas are the highest mountains in the world and act as an impressive backdrop for many of the populated areas.

elections in 1959, under a new Constitution that established a Parliament with powers that limited the role of the king. The NCP won a majority in the new Parliament.

A year later, King Mahendra, asserting himself as an absolute monarch, dismissed the NCP government and banned all political parties. In 1962, he introduced a tiered election system, starting on the local level with elections to choose a village council (panchayat). Members of the local panchayats elected representatives to an 11-member district panchayat, which in turn elected members to the National Panchayat. The National Panchayat elected its own prime minister. But the king reserved the power to appoint all of the Council of Ministers, who ran the government. This structure reinforced the traditional political power of the local landlords throughout the country. The landlords, in turn, reaffirmed the authority of the king.

King Mahendra died in 1972. His son Birendra succeeded him. In 1980, in response to growing public agitation, King Birendra held a referendum to see whether the people wanted to continue the party-banned, tiered election for membership in the National Panchayat or return to a multi-party, national election. The tiered system won by a small margin. Ironically, the majority of those elected to the National Panchayat in 1986 favored limiting the power of the king.

Encouraged by this result, leaders of the banned political parties organized public demonstrations to return to universal suffrage. A growing middle class, disaffected by economic hardship and the bungling, opportunistic leadership of the tier-elected Panchayats, supported this initiative. In response to the popular outcry, King Birendra worked out with the party leaders a new Constitution that limited his absolute sovereign power and established a multi-party, democratically elected, parliamentary government.

National democratic elections—the first since 1959—were held in 1991. The Nepali Congress Party again won a majority. But the leadership could not hold the allegiance of its members, leading to a no-confidence vote in Parliament, its dissolution, and new elections.

FREEDOM

The kingdom of Nepal became a constitutional monarchy in 1959, but parliamentary rule had limited success in meeting the country's many needs. The Maoist insurgency increasingly ravaged and dominated the country until 2006, when it agreed to join in a nationally elected constituent assembly freed of royal interference. National elections were held on April 10, 2008, and the monarchy was abolished on May 28, 2008.

In the 1994 elections, no party won a majority. The Unified Marxist-Leninist Party (UMLP) put together a fragile coalition that lasted for less than a year. The NCP then formed a coalition to gain a majority. Two years later, this coalition also fell apart. Not wishing to face a new general election, the UMLP gave its support to a monarchist who harked back to the days of King Mahendra, even though his party held only 10 seats in Parliament. Six months later, he was ousted by members of his own party. They formed a new coalition with the NCP. After a stormy six months, Girija Prasad Koirala, a longtime leader in the NCP, became the fifth prime minister in the four years since the 1994 elections.

In the 1999 elections, the Nepali Congress Party won enough seats to form a government of its own under new leadership. But a revolt within the party a year later led to Girija Prasad Koirala becoming prime minister again.

Two crises during this time of political volatility and corruption in Parliament unsettled the country even more.

On July 1, 2001, Crown Prince Dipendra brutally murdered his father. Not permitted by his mother to marry the woman of his choice, the distraught prince dressed in fatigues, grabbed an M-16 rifle, and shot his parents, his younger brother and sister, and an uncle and two aunts, before taking his own life. This episode shocked the country. The king's brother, Gyanendra, with a temperment ill suited to a country struggling with democracy, was hastily installed as king in his place.

HEALTH/WELFARE

In education and social services, the country struggles with limited resources, isolation, diversity, and insurgency. Adult literacy and life expectancy are both low. Malnutrition caused by a limited growing season and urban expansion has led to high levels of retardation and blindness.

A greater challenge to the government came from a dissident group of militant communist Maoists, strongly opposed to monarchy, corruption, and the oppression of the country's many poor. They drew their revolutionary inspiration from Mao's revolution in China, from the Naxalite movement in India, and the Shining Path, an extremist militant group in Peru. Their guerrilla agitation started in 1996, with the splintering of the communist parties in Parliament. They began by recruiting support among villagers in the remote and disadvantaged regions in the western part of the country, and demanding "fees" from trekking tourists for "protecting" them. As their movement grew, a reign of terror ensued against those who resisted their cause. Abductions, maiming, and killing, matched in too many instances by abuses by the Royal Nepali Army, increased in intensity and violence throughout the countryside.

A month after the regicide, when a Royal Army unit refused to fight against the Maoist insurgents, Prime Minister Koirala resigned. He was replaced by a rival Congress Party leader, who attempted a truce with the Maoists. But it lasted only a few short months.

In November, 2001, King Gyanendra asserted his royal prerogative by declaring a state of emergency. On October 4, 2002, he dismissed the elected government and took over by royal decree. With foreign aid support, he mobilized the Royal Army of 95,000 to enforce his rule. Then, in hopes of placating the Maoists, he appointed directly a series of prime ministers, none of whom could function because they were opposed by a strong coalition of legislators who objected to the king's dissolution of Parliament. With increasing student activist support, they continued to call for the restoration of parliamentary government.

The conflict brought untold misery to a people already burdened with poverty, high population growth, and illiteracy. The Maoist insurgency cut deeply into tourist revenues and displaced more than 100,000 from their homes. More than 12,000 had been killed. Caught in a deadly battle between monarchy and anarchy, the government, debilitated by continuing political struggles with the king and with itself, was unable to respond.

ACHIEVEMENTS

A cease-fire and election agreement between the Maoist insurgents and the Seven Party Alliance in November, 2006, acknowledged democracy rather than war as the path to peace. Democratic election of a Constituent Assembly in April 2008 to abolish monarchy and create a new constitution is promising for effective governance.

In June 2004, responding to a sense of conflict fatigue on the part of his people, the king tried once again to initiate discussions with the Maoists. But with continuing political infighting in Kathmandu, and with the Maoists now effectively in control of 68 of the 75 districts in the country, they were not interested, particularly not to give any legitimacy to the king, whose rule they saw as evil.

Things began to change dramatically in April, 2006. Mass protests in the streets of Kathmandu forced King Gyanendra to reopen Parliament, under the leadership of a Seven Party Alliance. Even more dramatic, with the king's despotic power diminished, the Maoists realized that the path of violence was no longer an effective way to achieve their revolutionary objectives. They agreed to a cease-fire in May, and entered into negotiations with the Seven Party Alliance to create a

Timeline: PAST

A.D. **1742–1814**
The Shah dynasty's expansion of the Kingdom of Gorkha

1815
The British East India Company reduces the Gorkha domain to the kingdom of Nepal

1845–1950
Rana family domination of the Shah dynasty

1949
The founding of the Nepal Congress Party

1959–1960
Constitutional monarchy

1960–1991
Absolute monarchy with tiered panchayat election of national legislature

1991
Constitutional monarchy established with a multi-party democratically elected parliament. First national democratic elections held in 32 years

1990s
Fragile governments rule in rapid succession. Rise of the Maoist insurgency that increases terror and control of the country

PRESENT

2000–2005
Crown Prince Dipendra murdered King Birendra, succeeded by his brother Gyanendra. Country continues to struggle with widespread and severe poverty

2006
Maoists agree to cease-fire, disarmament, and participation in parliamentary government free of royal interference.

2008
Constituent Assembly elections held. By vote of Assembly, monarchy is abolished. Prachanda, leader of the Maoist Party, elected prime minister.

2011
Bangladesh and Sri Lanka signed five memorandums of understanding (MoUs) for cooperation in different fields including trade, agriculture, vocational education, and science and culture.

representative government that would eliminate the monarchy.

On November 22, 2006, after intense negotiations, and with UN help to neutralize the opposing armies, Pushpa Kamal Dahal, known as Prachanda, the fierce leader of the Maoist insurgency, and the venerable Girija Prasad Koirala, head of the Seven Party Alliance, signed a Comprehensive Peace Agreement that resolved many thorny issues to establish peace and set up steps toward electing a Constituent Assembly to create a constitution for a new republic. Such an accord between a terrorist group that was used to forcing its own way and an elitist clan of squabbling politicians in Kathmandu was an incredible achievement.

The accord was soon tested by some 24 militant separatist groups among the Madhesi, the native population of the Terai, who had long felt rejected when not neglected by the central government in the valley. The Democratic Madhesi Front (UDMF) led a crippling 16-day strike in the Terai region to press its demands for more representation if it was to participate in the Constituent Assembly elections. To honor its objective of a truly inclusive government, the Seven Party Alliance and Maoist leaders met with the UDMF and agreed to provide proportional representation for the Madhesis, aboriginal people, indigenous nationals, Dalits, and backward communities in all government services and to commit the Constituent Assembly to decide how the autonomous regions of the country would be structured. They further devised a dual voting system that would elect 240 members of the 601 seats in the Assembly directly;

335 members would be elected on a proportional representation of women (50 percent), and marginalized and oppressed communities (31.2 percent Madhesis, 13 percent Dalits); and 26 members would be nominated by the prime minister to assure representation from excluded groups.

The elections were held successfully on April 10, 2008, with the Maoists winning a plurality of 220 seats. At its first meeting on May 28, it voted (560–4) to abolish the monarchy and declare Nepal a democratic republic. On July 21, in a run-off election, it voted Ram Baran Yadav president and Parmananda Jha as vice president, both Madhesis from the Terai. In August, President Yadav appointed Prachanda, leader of the Maoist Party, prime minister of the Constituent Assembly.

CHALLENGES

Nepal's industrial potential has long been restrained by trade agreements that tie the country's economy to India's development policies. And its commerce has been severely limited by the difficulty in

traversing the trade routes to Tibet. According to the United Nations, 75 percent of the labor force is in agriculture, placing it among the least of the least-developed countries (LDCs). Unemployment is at 46 percent. According to a recent World Bank report, 24.7 percent of the people live in absolute poverty. The incidence of malnutrition-related retardation and blindness is high. Five thousand girls have been trafficked to India every year. HIV/AIDS is beginning to take its toll. In education and medical and social services, the country struggles with limited resources and isolation among its diverse population.

Prachanda, whose triumphant, nonviolent journey away from terrorist insurgency to head an inclusive, democratically elected government, must now seek to provide leadership to confront an array of difficult problems. With such overwhelmingly weak economic and human development conditions among such an awesome diversity of peoples in such a rugged, breathtaking landscape, even the effort to grasp such an incredible array of challenges leaves one with a sense of wonder.

Pakistan (Islamic Republic of Pakistan)

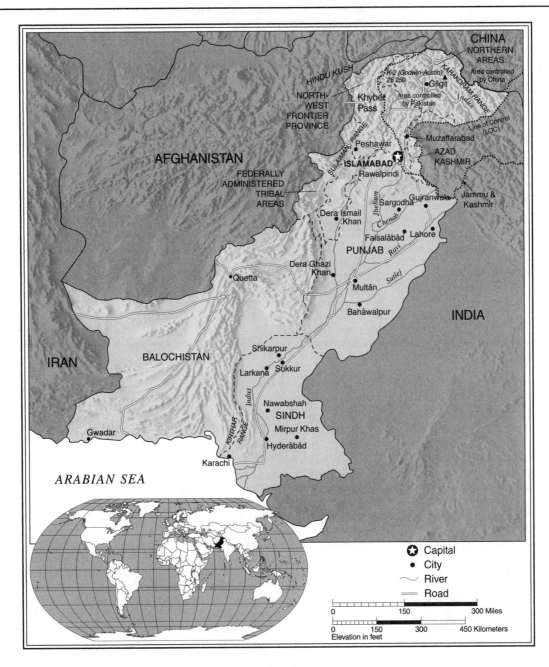

Pakistan Statistics

GEOGRAPHY

Area in Square Miles (Kilometers):
307,373 sq. mi. (796,095 sq. km.)
Capital (Population): Islamabad
(832,000) (2006)
Environmental Concerns: water
pollution, deforestation, soil erosion,
desertification, limited water supplies
Geographical Features: Flat Indus
plain in east; mountains in north and
northwest; Balochistan plateau in west

Climate: mostly hot, dry desert, temperate
in northwest, arctic in north

PEOPLE

Population

Total: 187,342,721 (2011)
Annual Growth Rate: 1.573% (2011 est.)
Rural/Urban Population Ratio: 36% of
total population (2010)
Major Languages: 48% Punjabi, 12%
Sindhi, 10% Siraiki (a Punjabi variant),

8% Pashtu, 8% Urdu (official), 3%
Balochi, 2% Hindko, 1% Brahui, 8% other
Ethnic Makeup: 44.68% Punjabi; 15.42%
Pashtun, 14.1% Sindhi, 8.38% Siraiki;
7.75% Muhajirs; 3.57% Balochi;
6.28% other
Religions: 95% Muslims (75% Sunni,
20% Shia), 5% other

Health

Life Expectancy at Birth: 64.18 years
(male); 67.9 years (female) (2011 est.)

GLOBAL STUDIES

Infant Mortality: 63.26/1000 live births
(2011 est.)
Per Capita Total Expenditure on Health:
$49 (WHO 2005)
HIV/AIDS Rate in Adults: 0.1%
(2009 est.)

Education

Adult Literacy Rate: 49.9% (36% female)
(2005 est.)

COMMUNICATION

Telephones: 4.058 million (2009)
Cell Phones: 103 million (2009)
Internet Users: 20.431 million (2009)

TRANSPORTATION

Highways in Miles (Kilometers):
(259,197 km.) (2007)
Railroads in Miles (Kilometers):
(7,791 km.) (2007)
Usable Airfields: 148 (2010)

GOVERNMENT

Type: federal republic
Independence Date: August 14, 1947
Chief of State: President Asif Ali Zardari

Head of Government: Prime Minister
Syed Yousuf Raza Gilani
Political Parties: Awami National Party,
ANP, Pakistan Muslim League PML,
PML/N (Nawaz Sharif faction),
Muttahida Majlis-e-Amal, MMA,
Pakistan Peoples Party, PPP, Muttahida
Qaumi Movement, MQM, many
smaller parties

MILITARY

Military Expenditures (3% of GDP):
(2007 est.)
Current Disputes: territorial disputes with
China and India, refugees, illicit drug
smuggling

ECONOMY

Currency ($ U.S. Equivalent): Rupees
85.27 = $1 U.S. (2010)
Per Capita Income/GDP: $2,400/$451.2
billion (2010 est.)
GDP Growth Rate: 2.7% (2010 est.)
Inflation Rate: 13.4% (2010 est.)
Unemployment Rate: 15%
(2010 est.)

Labor Force by Occupation: 43%
agriculture, 36.6% services, 20.3%
industry (2005 est.)
Population Below Poverty Line: 24%
(FY 2005–06 est.)
Natural Resources: land, extensive natural
gas reserves, limited petroleum, poor
quality coal, iron ore, copper, salt,
limestone
Agriculture: cotton, wheat, rice,
sugarcane, fruits, vegetables, milk,
beef, mutton, eggs
Industry: textiles and apparel, food
processing, pharmaceuticals,
construction materials, paper products,
fertilizer, shrimp
Exports: $20.29 billion (2010 est.)
(primary partners United States, UAE,
Afghanistan, United Kingdom, China)
(2009)
Imports: $32.71 billion (2010 est.)
(primary partners China, Saudi
Arabia, UAE, United States, Kuwait,
Malaysia, India) (2009)
Human Development Index (ranking): 125
(UNDP 2010)

Pakistan Country Report

Pakistan is the second largest nation in South Asia, about one-fourth the size of India, with less than one-seventh of India's population. It lies in the Indus River Valley, between the mountainous border with Afghanistan through which comes the famous Khyber Pass to the northwest, and the Great Indian Desert, and the Rann of Kutch, to the southeast. Long a land of transition between the rugged steppes of Inner Asia and the plains of India, it is today a new nation caught between the heritage of a glorious imperial past and the poetic image of an ideal theocratic future. The name, Pakistan, given by the Muslim poet Muhammed Iqbal in 1930, means "Land of the Pure."

The heritage of the people of Pakistan goes back to the earliest-known urban culture in South Asia. Excavations of the ancient cities of Harappa and Mohenjodaro, discovered in 1922, reveal an impressive civilization that dates from 3000 to 1500 B.C. Distinctive are its knowledge of hydrology and its use of irrigation to cultivate the valley with the rich waters of the Indus River. Surplus agricultural production led to extensive commerce in cotton and grains throughout the ancient world.

Islam is a religious faith based upon the teachings of the prophet Muhammad revealed in the Koran in Arabia during the

seventh century A.D. Arab traders and wandering Sufi mystics were the first to bring the religion into South Asia. The Sufis' spiritual discipline and religious teaching drew large numbers of indigenous peoples to submission to the will of Allah (God) as early as the eighth century. The spread of this vibrant faith and subsequent rule of Islamic sultans and emperors led to the creation of Pakistan as an Islamic Republic in 1947. Today, 95 percent of the 187 million people in the country are Muslim. Of these, 75 percent belong to the Sunni tradition. There are also small minorities of Hindus, Christians, and members of the Ahmadiya Sect of Islam, whose faith is considered heretical by the orthodox.

DEVELOPMENT

Extensive investment in the cotton textile and food processing industries has kept Pakistan's economy growing. But it has not been matched by human resource development. Agriculture still employs half of the labor force, but contributes less to the GDP. Earthquakes in October 2005 and 2008 and a growing indigenous Taliban insurgency impose a devastating impact on human life and development.

Mughals were militant Turks refined by the elegance of Persia and energized by their Islamic faith. The march of their conquering forces across the northern plains of South Asia to the Bay of Bengal in the sixteenth century marked the period of greatest glory in the heritage of the Pakistani people. Akbar (1556–1605), the greatest of them, is remembered for the opulence and splendor of his court, for the far-reaching administrative control of his empire, and for his elaborate building projects which still stand as massive tribute to his commanding wealth and intellect.

Pakistan became independent at the departure of the British Raj in 1947, created especially for the 7.2 million people (*mohajirs*) who migrated from India to preserve their culture and religion of a staunch Islamic and impressive imperial past. This heritage has been both an asset and an obstacle to its evolution as a modern nation state.

INDEPENDENCE MOVEMENT

The Muslim League was formed in India in 1906 to represent the interests of the Muslim minority under the British Raj. In the movement for freedom from imperial domination, they became convinced that they would be oppressed, perhaps even eliminated, in an independent India dominated by Hindus. In 1940, the League voted to demand a separate state for the Muslim population of British India.

The British Raj rewarded the persistence of the Muslim League's leader, Muhammad Ali Jinnah, by granting independence in 1947 to two nations instead of one. Its scheme to partition British India created a smaller, more populous East Pakistan, and a dominant West Pakistan, separated by nearly 1,000 miles of India.

This partition was disastrous. The Muslims in British India who most feared Hindu oppression were not those who had the security of living in Muslim majority districts, but those who lived in the Hindu-majority districts in north central India. They felt endangered in their own lands. Hindu and Sikh minorities in districts where the Muslims were in a majority also feared for their lives. This mutual fear caused the migration of 14 million people, Hindus, Sikhs and Muslims moving in opposite directions. Clashes in the border areas, especially in the Punjab, which was split in half between Muslim and Hindu districts, led to the killing of hundreds of thousands of bewildered, anxious people. The consequences of this human catastrophe are still felt among the families that survived.

FREEDOM

Since independence the country has been under martial law longer than democratically elected government. Popular elections were first held in 1971, and then suspended until 1988. National elections in February 2008 reaffirmed Pakistan's commitment to democracy, but the army is still a dominant force in the nation. Women are held to their traditionally subservient role in Islamic society, even after the reform of the Hadood Ordinance in 2006.

QUEST FOR POLITICAL STABILITY

The new Pakistan lacked adequate administrative services to cope with the disruption and bloodshed of the partition. Muhammad Ali Jinnah took upon himself the chief executive duties of governor general in the interim government. In ill health at the time, he died 13 months later.

Liaquat Ali Khan, his successor as prime minister, was assassinated in 1951. The Muslim League, imported from India, lost control of a unifying national agenda to the indigenous sources of provincial power: wealthy landowners and tribal leaders in the five distinct provinces in the country, each divided from the others by ethos and language.

The textile industry is a major foreign exchange earner of Pakistan. Cotton is a major agricultural product of this country. Here a worker is engaged with a spinning machine in a textile factory.

The provincial identities of the people in the new nation accentuated rather than mitigated their differences on the national level. The political solidarity of the Bengali people in the province of East Pakistan was first realized by their opposition to accept Urdu, the language of the *mohajirs,* immigrants from north central India, as the national language of Pakistan. This opposition led to their split from Pakistan to form an independent nation, Bangladesh, in 1971.

Distinct languages in each of the four remaining states in West Pakistan also take precedence over Urdu, which is spoken by 8 percent of the population. In the early years of independence, Urdu speaking immigrants made up 46 percent of the urban population in the country. Today, the Muttahida Quami movement (until recently the Mohajir Quami movement and now divided into two hostile camps), although limited to Karachi for its political base, is the fourth-largest political party in the country.

HEALTH/WELFARE

Emphasis on the military budget has slighted government attention to human resource development in education and social services. The birth rate remains high, and infant mortality at birth is among the highest in South Asia. Adult literacy is low. Among women it is little more than half that of the male population.

Punjabi speakers are more than half of the population. Punjab is the granary of the

country, with the most heavily irrigated and productive lands. Industrial development and wealth are also concentrated there. Lahore, its capitol city, was the administrative center for the region under the British Raj. All of these factors contribute to Punjabi domination in the ranks of the army and the civil services.

Sindh is the next-most-important state, sharing with Punjab about 90 percent of the industrial production of the country. Karachi, capital of the state, with a population of over 9 million, is Pakistan's largest city and commercial center, and to date its only seaport. Yet only 12 percent of Pakistanis are Sindhi speakers.

Ten percent of the population lives in the North-West Frontier Provinces, and the Federally Administered Tribal Areas (FATA), which lie along the rugged mountainous border with Afghanistan. The number of Pashtuns, who speak Pashto, increased by the influx of more than 3 million Afghan Pashtuns as refugees during the Soviet occupation of Afghanistan during the 1980s. Many of them who remain continue to cross the porous Durand Line. Pashtuns, some 40 million strong in this region, do not recognize it as a border between the two countries.

Balochistan, in the arid lands which border Iran and the Arabian Sea, is the largest state (40%) and the richest in natural resources. A seaport is being built with Chinese financing and labor at Gwadar on the coast. Yet the people who speak Balochi are less than 3 percent of Pakistan's population. A separatist movement started in 1973, based on many of the same issues that led to the break away of Bangladesh.

It has been suppressed by military force, which killed a respected tribal leader, Nawab Akbar Bugti, in August 2006.

Pakistani Muslims are also significantly divided between a majority who seek a modern Islamic identity, and the more traditional Islamists, who have long felt their commitment to exclusive, coercive theocracy challenged by the quest for modern democracy. With the departure of Soviet forces from Afghanistan in 1989, the jihadis—ones who struggle for the faith—turned to free the Muslims in Kashmir from Indian military occupation. With the intrusion of western values by the defeat of the Taliban in Afghanistan in 2001, their cause took on a new sense of urgency. For the 2003 parliamentary elections, fundamentalist parties formed a coalition called the Muttahida Majlis-e-Amal (MMA), representing Balochistan and the North-West Frontier Provinces, bordering Afghanistan. In the National Assembly, it became a significant force in promoting Islamist causes in this region and in the nation as a whole. With its influence greatly reduced in the 2008 elections, terrorism has become an increasing, destructive, alternative path to promote the Islamists' fundamentalist ideology. It is especially attractive among a disillusioned and impoverished youth in a country where those under 24 years old are 47 percent of the total population.

ACHIEVEMENTS

Industrial growth and political stability has been achieved, largely through military domination. Pakistan demonstrated its nuclear capability in tests in 1998.

Another challenge to a stable, democratically elected government in Pakistan is the wide division between the rich and the poor. A 1970 World Bank study found that 80 percent of the capital wealth in Pakistan was concentrated in just 22 families. A subsequent study in 1998 found 42.3 percent of the nation's wealth held by the top 20 percent of the population, with the lowest 10 percent having but 3.7 percent. The disparity between the industrial rich and the slum-dwelling poor in the cities continues to grow.

New wealth and a new class were created in Pakistan during the 1980s by jobs in the Persian Gulf oil fields. More than 2 million young people from all parts of the country sent home more than $4 billion a year, or about 10 percent of the country's gross domestic product. These monies stimulated conspicuous consumer buying, which led to a number of local enterprises using pickup trucks and video equipment. The loss of jobs during the Persian Gulf Wars had a doubly adverse impact on Pakistan's economy, cutting in half the remittances from overseas while increasing the number of unemployed within the country.

Amid all of these challenges to the formation of a single body politic, the Pakistan army has been the strongest force to unite a disparate and disengaged people under the fear of an imminent threat of war with India. Ironically, because of its dominant role to maintain unity and stability, the military has also impeded the growth of democracy in Pakistan. A diplomat recently characterized Pakistan as different from most countries, which, when they become independent, look for an army to protect it. Pakistan is an army looking for a country to defend.

A constitution to establish a national parliamentary government was finally adopted in 1956, affirming the common sovereign identity of the two wings of Pakistan as an Islamic Republic. Yet this and each of the successive attempts to establish democratic rule—in 1971 and in 1988—occurred under the watchful eye of the military, and ended in a takeover: by General Ayub Khan in 1958, by General Yahya Khan in 1969, by General Zia-ul-Haq in 1977, and by General Pervez Musharraf in 1999. In all, the country has been under martial law for 34 of its 62 years as an independent nation.

MARTIAL LAW: 1958–1971

General Mohammad Ayub Khan, commander-in-chief of the Pakistan army, became martial-law administrator in 1958, in hopes of stimulating economic growth among a people "not yet ready for democracy." He replaced the 1956 Constitution with a new Constitution, delegating extensive executive power to a president who would be elected only by those elected to local political offices. They also determined who would be elected to the National Assembly. In 1965, a limited electorate of "Basic Democrats," the 80,000 locally elected council members whom Ayub Khan accepted as prepared to vote, elected him president.

In the same year he was elected president, war broke out with India over their competing claims for the former princely state of Jammu and Kashmir, which has been partly occupied by India and partly by Pakistan since 1947. This war ended in military stalemate and a UN-observed cease-fire. An unfavorable peace settlement with India in the Tashkent Agreement of 1966 cost Ayub Khan his popular support.

Growing discontent over military rule during those years spawned two new political leaders, one in each of the wings of Pakistan. Mujibur Rahman, leader of the Awami League in East Pakistan, capitalized on the perception among the Bengalis that they were second-class citizens. His charismatic leadership won immense popular support for greater regional autonomy.

At the same time, Zulfikar Ali Bhutto, a Western-educated diplomat from a large landholding family in the province of Sindh, formed the Pakistan People's Party. Adopting the campaign slogan *Roti, Kapra aur Makon* ("Bread, clothes and shelter"), he mobilized a wide popular following in the western wing of the country toward a policy of democratic socialism. He did not attempt to generate a following of his own in East Pakistan.

President Ayub Khan was not able to contain either the Bhutto or the Rahman initiatives, and, in 1969, was forced to resign. General Yahya Khan, his successor, in a quest to bring order, declared the first popular national elections to be held in Pakistan since its independence, on December 7, 1970. In this election the Awami League won 160 of the 162 seats in the National Assembly assigned to the more populous East Pakistan. Bhutto's Pakistan People's Party won 81 seats of the 132 assigned to West Pakistan.

Bhutto felt that by winning a majority in West Pakistan, he was the rightful leader of the country. When he was not assured that position, he boycotted the new Assembly. In response, President Yahya Khan suspended the legislature, which led to a vehement cry for independence in East Pakistan. Yahya Khan sought to suppress this freedom movement by military force. Millions fled across the border for refuge in India. After several months of unrelenting bloodshed, the Indian government launched a military attack in support of the Bengali rebels. They won independence for a separate Bangladesh on December 17, 1971.

DEMOCRACY: 1971–1977

The freedom of Bangladesh left the Pakistan People's Party with a majority in the National Assembly, and Bhutto became the president of Pakistan. He led what was left of the country toward a socialist state by nationalizing banking and such major industries as steel, chemicals, and cement. His policy created employment opportunities in an already cumbersome civil-service bureaucracy, but discouraged investment and led to a decline in industrial production.

Bhutto was more successful in restoring parliamentary government. He created a new Constitution—the third in 26 years—that was adopted in 1973. It established a National Assembly of 207 members, all of them elected directly for five-year terms. Bhutto then became prime minister, elected by a majority of the legislature.

Bhutto called for elections in 1977 in hopes of getting endorsement for his leadership and his socialist economic policies. This call spurred an unexpected and virulent opposition of nine parties, which united to form the Pakistan National Alliance (PNA). Bhutto's Pakistan People's Party won the election. But the PNA, which won only 36 of 207 seats in the Assembly, charged that the elections had been rigged and took to the streets in protest. Bhutto called in the army to restore order and sought to negotiate with the PNA to hold new elections. Before any agreement was reached, Mohammad Zia-ul-Haq, chief of staff of the army, seized control of the government.

General Zia-ul-Haq promised to hold elections within 90 days, but then canceled them. He continued to hold out the promise of elections for the following 11 years, during which time he maintained firm military control. Part of that control was to bring charges against Bhutto of complicity in a political murder, which led to Bhutto's trial and execution on April 4, 1979.

MARTIAL LAW: 1977–1988

In the fall of 1979, Zia banned all political parties and imposed censorship on the press. The following year he removed from judicial review any actions of his government and decisions of the military courts. Many of these measures were cloaked in a policy of "Islamization," through which his military regime sought to gain public support by an appeal to traditional laws and teachings of Sunni Islam. Once again, entrenched divisions and political turmoil in the country led to repression more reminiscent of Medieval Muslim Sultanate imperialism than the workings of modern representative government.

Zia's consolidation of power in Pakistan coincided with the collapse of the Shah of Iran, the rise of Saudi Arabia as a power in the Middle East, and the Soviet invasion of Afghanistan. The response of the United States to these developments gave Pakistan a strategic role in protecting western sources of oil and containing Soviet expansion. U.S. support for his repressive military rule not only set back the quest for democracy, but also substantially weakened the authority of the Zia government itself.

DEMOCRACY: 1988–1999

A spirit of democracy did survive, if only partially, in a hasty referendum called by General Zia in 1985 to affirm his policy of Islamization, which elected him executive president for a five-year term. The Constitution of 1973 also survived, though altered by General Zia in an Eighth Amendment, to give the president power to dismiss the prime minister. He then called for legislative elections to be held in November, 1988. Before that date, Zia was killed in a helicopter crash and the Supreme Court quickly removed the ban on political parties. The elections were held as scheduled.

Bhutto's Pakistan People's Party, led by his daughter, Benazir Bhutto, won a plurality of 93 seats in the 217-member National Assembly, and she was invited to become prime minister. Then just 35 years old, she was the youngest person and the first woman to lead an Islamic nation.

Benazir Bhutto's tenure was based on an uneasy balance within the legislature itself. It was further complicated by competing claims outside the legislature by the other large power brokers in the nation—the army and the president. Even though General Beg, appointed army chief of staff in 1985, advocated restraint from involvement, the army remained a political presence.

In 1989, Benazir Bhutto tried to restore the full authority of the prime minister's office by having the Eighth Amendment of the Constitution repealed, but failed to get the necessary two-thirds vote. In the summer of 1990, her opposition in the National Assembly tried to defeat her, but could not get enough votes. President Ghulam Ishaq Khan then asserted his authority under the Eighth Amendment to dismiss her government with charges of corruption and nepotism.

In the elections which followed her dismissal, Mian Nawaz Sharif, chief minister of Punjab and head of the Islami Jamhorri Ittehad (IJI), or Islamic Democratic Alliance, brought his conservative party together with the communist-leaning Awami National party, dominant in the North-West Frontier Province, and the fundamentalist Jamiat-Ulema-i-Islam party. Their coalition won 105 seats in the 217-member National Assembly by winning 36.86 percent of the popular vote. Benazir Bhutto's People's Democratic Alliance (PDA) was reduced from 93 to 45 seats, even though it won 36.84 percent of the popular vote. Sharif, a member of a successful industrial family who migrated from Amritsar in East Punjab to Pakistan in 1947, became prime minister.

To fulfill a promise made during the campaign to form a coalition with the fundamentalist Islamic groups, Prime Minister Sharif introduced a law to make the Islamic code of Shari'a the supreme law of Pakistan. At the same time, he asserted that his Shari'a bill would not stand in the path to modernization. The Jamiat-Ulema-i-Islam party withdrew from the ruling coalition, objecting that Sharif's Shari'a bill was too vaguely worded and not being implemented.

Even without their support, Sharif still called upon Islam as a unifying force in holding the country together and in harmony with its neighboring countries to the west. His government enacted blasphemy laws and pushed to amend the Constitution to make the Koran "the supreme law of land." These acts were understood as efforts not only to divert attention from increasing economic woes and other political issues, but also to contain the potentially volatile force of religious fundamentalism as a threat to stability in the country.

Mian Nawaz Sharif also tried to repeal the Eighth Amendment to the Constitution that granted the president the powers of dismissal. President Ghulam Ishaq Khan then invoked it, for a second time, and in April 1993, dismissed the Sharif government, also on charges of corruption and nepotism.

This time, the Supreme Court overruled the president and reinstated the Sharif government. The army chief of staff, General Abdul Waheed, then brokered the resignation of both the prime minister and the president. The National Assembly and state legislatures were then dissolved, and new elections set for October.

In the 1993 elections, Benazir Bhutto's Pakistan People's Party won 86 seats, to 72 for Sharif's party. Her position was strengthened by the election a month later of Farooq Leghari, deputy leader of the PPP, to the office of president.

In her second term as prime minister, Benazir Bhutto pursued policies that destabilized the nation's economy, compromised foreign investment, and drove the inflation rate to 20 percent. In response, she imposed a sales tax that proved very unpopular. An image of rampant corruption in government, together with an attempt to appoint sympathetic judges to the high courts, also eroded her popular support. President Leghari dismissed her on charges of corruption and nepotism under the Eighth Amendment in November, 1996, and new elections were called for February 3, 1997. To avoid any legal action against her, Benazir Bhutto fled the country.

Even though voter turnout was low, Mian Nawaz Sharif and his Pakistan Muslim League Party won a two-thirds majority in the National Assembly. Benazir Bhutto's opposition party then joined his government to repeal the Eighth Amendment to the Constitution.

(Copyright © 1997 IMS Communications Ltd/Capstone Design/FlatEarth Images (DAL 007BI2))

A trading room in a bank, Karachi, Pakistan. Pakistan is also gradually adopting modern technology for everyday activity, especially in urban areas.

Reducing the power of the president did not place any restraint on the third element of political power in Pakistan, the military. Its dominance required the testing of Pakistan's nuclear capability immediately following India's nuclear tests in May 1998, even at the high cost of international disapproval and U.S. economic sanctions. And when Prime Minister Sharif repudiated the military attack into the Kargil District of Kashmir in the summer of 1999, the army chief of staff, General Pervez Musharraf, staged a coup in October. He then brought charges against Sharif for treason and attempted murder. The courts found Sharif guilty, and sentenced him to life in prison, which General Musharraf commuted to a life in exile.

MARTIAL RULE: SINCE 1999

General Musharraf's coup dismissed the parliamentary government elected in 1997. In June 2001, he took over the title of president to establish legitimacy for his martial rule.

Following the terrorist attacks in the United States on 9/11, the United States began military operations in Afghanistan to destroy Osama bin Laden and his Al Qaeda bases there. Pakistan became a necessary ally to provide bases and logistical support. Under strong American pressure, President Musharraf courageously withdrew support for the Taliban, which had been providing this fundamentalist movement with the infrastructure needed to control most of Afghanistan.

By November, 2001, the Al Qaeda had escaped to Pakistan's Federally Administered Tribal Areas (FATA) adjacent to Afghanistan. As the Taliban also began to

use this area as sanctuary for its insurrection against the American and NATO forces, Musharraf came under U.S. pressure to seal Pakistan's border with Afghanistan. Eager to maintain U.S. support for his military rule, President Musharraf set up military posts along the border, pursued Al Qaeda fugitives in the country, and disclaimed any continuing support to the Taliban.

Pointing to a significant loss of Pakistani soldiers in attempts to confront Afghan Taliban fighters, in September 2006, he made an agreement with some tribal leaders in Waziristan in FATA not to bring military force into the region if they restricted Taliban cross border activity. This agreement may have reflected the reality of his lack of control in that area. But as the tribal leaders could themselves do little to restrain a resurgent Taliban, his agreement did little to assure the Afghan government and U.S. and NATO forces assigned to fight the Taliban insurgency that Pakistan was an effective ally in this effort. He managed to reassure the American government sufficiently that he alone was capable of restraining terrorism in his country, while at the same time it was recognized that its presence as a threat was essential to his garnering American support for his rule.

Musharraf did not anticipate that his commitment to the "war on terror" would stir up a vigorous and determined, youthful Taliban movement in FATA itself. Pakistani Islamist militants grew in opposition not only to foreign military presence in Afghanistan and deadly U.S. air strikes into Pakistan, but also to the tribal leaders in FATA, and ultimately to the Pakistan army itself for complicity in America's

war. This indigenous terrorist movement, growing to a force of 30,000 fighters under the command of Baitullah Mehsud in South Waziristan alone, became sufficiently bold and strong enough to threaten the survival of Pakistan itself.*

President Musharraf managed also to distance his government from any involvement in the proliferation of nuclear technology conducted by A. Q. Khan, the founder of Pakistan's nuclear weapons program. In exchange for a pardon by the president, Mr. Khan took full responsibility for the illicit transfer of nuclear capability to other countries out of his research laboratories without authorization by the government. Musharraf then assured the world that as long as he was in power in Pakistan, its nuclear arsenal would not get into the hands of terrorists, nor into the hands of an anti-American opposition in Pakistan itself.

During the time of this buildup of terrorist activity which Musharraf was supposed to contain, he was also under considerable international pressure to return Pakistan to a democratic form of government. His ambivalent dealings with both Islamist terrorism and with democracy were to become his undoing.

In response to the international call for democracy, General Musharraf set elections for a new national legislature for the fall of 2002. To assure his control in this process, he called for and won a national referendum on April 30 to extend his presidency for another five years, regardless of the outcome of the legislative elections. He then proposed amendments to the constitution, which included restoring to the president the power to dismiss the prime minister, the cabinet, and even the legislature by decree.

The election results in October did not yield the popular support that Musharraf had sought. A pro-Taliban, anti-American coalition of Islamic fundamentalist parties, called the Muttahida Majlis-e-Amal (MMA), won sufficient support in Balochistan and the North-West Frontier Province, closest to Afghanistan, to gain 60 of 342 seats in the National Assembly. Benazir Bhutto's PPP, with her in exile, won 81 seats. Musharraf's own PML(Q) won a plurality of 118 seats. He was not able to form a government for six weeks, until he had enticed enough members away from the PPP to gain majority support. He still did not have enough votes to get the legislature to approve his constitutional amendments. Nevertheless, he closely oversaw the activity of the Assembly under the leadership of his designated prime minister.

*Dexter Filkins, "Right at the Edge," *New York Times Magazine,* September 7, 2008.

Through political maneuvering with the MMA, he got the Assembly to accept his presidency and constitutional changes, with the understanding that he would step down as chief of staff of the army by the end of 2004. Later he tried to remove constitutional constraints to his serving as both president and army chief of staff, but found himself in a confrontation with the Chief Justice of the Supreme Court, whom he suspended for misuse of judicial authority on March 4, 2007. A public protest, led by the country's lawyers, closed down the courts.

Thus began a series of steps to diminish his power, starting with a heavily boycotted election in the national legislature and provincial assemblies to re-elect him president on October 6. When the Supreme Court threatened to question the constitutionality of his election, he declared a state of emergency on November 3. He then placed those judges who did not support the emergency under house arrest. To resolve the issue of his joint tenure, he resigned as army chief of staff on November 28. The state of emergency was lifted on December 15, with parliamentary elections called for January 8, 2008. On December 27, former Prime Minister Benazir Bhutto, who had returned to Pakistan on October 18 in an American brokered deal that intended to have her appointed prime minister by President Musharraf after the elections, was assassinated while campaigning in Rawalpindi. The elections, postponed because of her death until February 18, marked an enthusiastic return toward democratically elected, parliamentary government.

Benazir Bhutto's PPP and its allies won control of the National Assembly and all of the Provincial Assemblies except Punjab, which was divided among three parties. Musharraf's party was resoundingly defeated throughout the country. Under threat of impeachment, he resigned as president on August 18, 2008.

After six months of political positioning, on September 11, 2008, the national and provincial legislatures elected Asif Ali Zardari, Bhutto's husband, president of Pakistan. Nine days later, on the eve of his first address to a plenary session of the National Assembly, a deadly bomb exploded in the nearby Islamabad Marriott Hotel. It was a dramatic reminder of the extent of bold and destructive terrorist acts coming to the very center of the country. In recognition of the serious nature of the threat of terrorism, the prime minister convened a special session of the National Assembly to explore how to deal with it. Though inconclusive, it rejected pursuing a military solution in favor of seeking avenues of dialogue.**

Pakistan's economic health, which improved modestly during the Musharraf years, is now confronted with severe deficien-

Timeline: PAST

3000–1500 B.C.
Harappan city culture

A.D. 1526–1857
The Moghul empire

1907
The founding of the Muslim League

1940
The Muslim League adopts the demand for the separate state of Pakistan

1947
The partition of British India; the creation of Pakistan

1948
War with India over Kashmir

1956
The first Constitution establishing Pakistan as an Islamic republic

1958–1969
Military rule of Ayub Khan

1965
War with India over Kashmir

1969–1971
Military rule of Yahya Khan

1970
First national popular elections: Mujibar Rahman's Awami League wins majority of National Assembly; Zulfikar Ali Bhutto's Pakistan People's Party wins West Pakistan majority

1971
War with India, the breakaway of East Pakistan to become Bangladesh, Bhutto becomes president of Pakistan

1973
A Constitution establishing parliamentary democracy is adopted; Bhutto becomes prime minister

1977–1988
Military rule of Zia-ul-Haq; national elections set; helicopter accident kills Zia; Benazir Bhutto becomes prime minister

1990s
Parliamentary democracy is restored, Pakistan tests its nuclear capability in the wake of Indian tests

1999
General Pervez Musharraf, army chief of staff, takes over government.

PRESENT

2000s
Military rule of General Pervez Musharraf Lack of human resource development and growing financial problems threaten the nation's economy.

2001
Pakistan becomes ally of the United States in "war on terror"

2002
Parliamentary elections restored, but President and General Musharraf remains firmly in control of the government.

2005
Deadly earthquake kills 87,000, leaves 3 million homeless in northern part of country.

2006
Nawab Akbar Bugti is killed in military repression of Balochistan insurgency

Government withdraws military from Waziristan tribal areas in agreement for tribal leaders to stop support for Taliban insurgency in Afghanistan.

2007
Lawyers protest President Musharraf's suspension of Supreme Court Chief Justice in March

Benazir Bhutto returns to Pakistan in October to take part in national elections, is assassinated on December 27.

President Musharraf declares national emergency on November 4, lifted December 15

2008
National elections held in February, Bhutto's PPP wins control of National Assembly and all province Assemblies but Punjab.

President Musharraf resigns in August.

Asif Ali Zardari, Bhutto's husband, elected president on September 11.

Islamabad Marriott Hotel damaged by terrorist bomb on September 20.

Pakistan receives $7.6 billion loan from the International Monetary Fund.

Pakistan agrees to bring to justice any Pakistanis responsible for November 26 terrorist attack on Mumbai, India.

2011
Introducing a new constitution for Nepal

cies enhanced by the world economic crisis. Early attempts by President Zardari to find international support achieved only an IMF loan of $7.6 billion on November 15, 2008, to meet the nation's foreign debt obligations. Longer term solutions to provide both economic health and security from Islamist terrorism continue to challenge Pakistan's fledgling parliamentary government.***

**Cristina Otten, "The Mumbai massacres and Pakistan's new nightmares," *The Hindu*, 15/12/2008 URL: www.thehindu.com/2008/12/15/stories/2008121556691100.htm.
***Adrian Levy and Cathy Scott-Clark, "On the Trail of Pakistan's Taliban," *The Guardian*, January 10, 2009.

To add to Pakistan's instability, a massive, deadly earthquake shook the mountains of northern Pakistan on October 8, 2005, killing more than 87,000 people. It took army units three days to cover 20 miles to get relief to Balakot, at the edge of the epicenter of the 7.6 quake. They found the town flattened, including 200 students crushed in their school building. Volunteers rushed to rescue the survivors before lack of food and medical care, and the onset of the arctic winter months, threatened to add to the quake's toll.

The international community responded generously to the country's call for help, pledging $6.5 billion to meet the rescue and reconstruction costs. And private donations added another $200 million. Of the more than 600,000 housing units needed by the 3 million made homeless by the quake, a third have yet to be built. A second major (6.5) earthquake in a remote region (NE of Quetta) in Baluchistan on October 29, 2008, destroyed 2,000 homes, adding to the country's relief burden.

INTERNAL CHALLENGES

The failures of America's "war on terror" and weakness of the government in Afghanistan, the rise of an indigenous Taliban terrorist offensive, the global economic crisis, and damaging earthquakes in Pakistan have all contributed to instability and insecurity in Pakistan.

Other challenges have long existed within the governance of Pakistan itself. Sporadic martial rule and a continuing disproportionately high defense budget ($4.517 billion, near 20 percent of the 2007 federal budget), a high rate of population growth (2.1 percent), corruption, the loss of human rights through the imposition of religious blasphemy laws, and, most significantly, the lack of human resources development have long had an impact on the well-being of the country.

Human development factors such as poor working conditions, low wages, especially for women, lack of job security, lack of skill training, and not keeping abreast of fashion trends have contributed to the decline in Pakistan's substantial textile industry. Even with significant investments in production technology and textile machinery and indigenous cotton production, its exports dropped 10 percent in 2006. In tightening world markets Pakistan is not able to compete with Bangladesh, which does not grow cotton.

A lack in human resource development is also evident in the limited—and elitist—opportunity for education in Pakistan. Literacy in the country is now at 49.9 percent, small improvement over the level, according to UNICEF, when Pakistan received its independence in 1947. Half of all secondary level students are educated in private schools, the only place they can get instruction in English, still the language of opportunity in the professions, technology, and trade.

Women are excluded even more from education: Their literacy is little more than half that of the men (36 percent to 63 percent). Girls represent only a third of the student population. This lack of education opportunity for women reflects the traditional expectation of their subservience and seclusion in Islamic society.

General Zia-ul-Haq affirmed this attitude as national policy when he enacted the Hudood Ordinance in 1979, which places particularly poor and illiterate women in danger of being jailed when accused of adultery or if they report being raped. In 2006 General Musharraf introduced a Women's Protection Bill, which attempted to qualify some of the more blatant discrimination against women in the Ordinance. It transfers issues of rape from Islamic law to Pakistan's penal code and makes accusations of adultery more stringent. The bill passed in the National Assembly over the strong objection of the fundamentalist Islamic parties. It was also opposed by human and women's rights groups, who wanted the Ordinance, which they claim has no basis in the Koran, repealed in its entirety. The admonition of the sixth Five Year Plan proposed during General Zia's reign still holds true: "In all societies, women's development is a prerequisite for overall national development; indeed no society can ever develop half-liberted and half-shackled."

Pakistan is committed to its survival as a unified, sovereign state, even though threatened by divisive political, social, and religious forces, and by substantive economic and human development challenges. Affirming its integrity as an Islamic republic, its greatest challenge is to become a fully developed modern nation while remaining faithful to the teachings of Islam.

Sri Lanka (Democratic Socialist Republic of Sri Lanka)

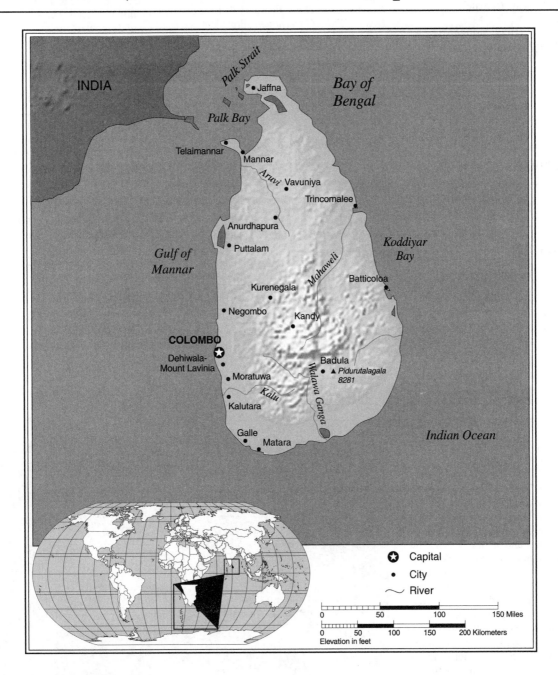

Sri Lanka Statistics

GEOGRAPHY

Area in Square Miles (Kilometers):
25,332 (65,610 km) (about the size
of West Virginia)
Capital (Population): Colombo, 681,000
(2009)
Environmental Concerns:
deforestation; soil erosion;
poaching; coastal degradation;
water and air pollution; waste
disposal

Geographical Features: mostly plain,
mountains in the interior
Climate: tropical monsoons

PEOPLE

Population

Total: 21,283,913 (2011 est.)
Annual Growth Rate: 0.934% (2011 est.)
Rural/Urban Population Ratio: 86/14
(2010)

Major Languages: 74% Sinhala
(Official Language), 18% Tamil,
8% other. English is commonly used in
government and is spoken competently
by about 10% of the population.
Ethnic Makeup: 73.8% Sinhalese,
7.2% Sri Lankan Moors, 4.6% Indian
Tamils, 3.9% Sri Lankan Tamils,
10.5% other (2001 Census provisional data)
Religions: 69.1% Buddhist, 7.6% Muslim,
7.1% Hindu, 6.2% Christian, 10% other
(2001 Census provisional data)

GLOBAL STUDIES

Health

Life Expectancy at Birth: 72.21 years (male), 79.38 years (female) (2011 est.)
Infant Mortality: 9.7/1000 births (2011 est.)
Per Capita Total Expenditure on Health: $189 (WHO 2005)
HIV/AIDS Rate in Adults: less than 0.1% (2009 est.)

Education

Adult Literacy Rate: 90.7 (2001 census)

COMMUNICATION

Telephones: 3.523 million (2010)
Cell Phones: 15.868 million (2010)
Internet Users: 1.777 million (2009)

TRANSPORTATION

Highways in Miles (Kilometers): (91,907 km.) (2008)
Railroads in Miles (Kilometers): (1,449 km.) (2007)
Usable Airfields: 18 (2010)

GOVERNMENT

Type: republic
Independence Date: February 4, 1948
Head of State/Government: President Mahinda Rajapaksa is both head of state and head of government.
Political Parties: Democratic National Alliance, United National Front, Tamil National Alliance, age; universal

MILITARY

Military Expenditures: 2.6% of GDP *(2006)* Refugees, human trafficking

ECONOMY

Currency ($ U.S. Equivalent): 113.36 *rupees* = $1 U.S. (2010)
Per Capita Income/GDP: $4,900/$104.7 billion (2010 est.)
GDP Growth Rate: 6.9% (2010 est.)
Inflation Rate: 5.6% (2010 est.)
Unemployment Rate: 5.4% (2010 est.)
Labor Force by Occupation: 41% Services, 26.3% Industry, 32.7% Agriculture (2008 est.)

Population below Poverty Line: 23% (2002 est.)
Natural Resources: limestone, graphite, mineral sands, gems, phosphates, clay, hydropower
Agriculture: rice, sugarcane, grains, pulses, oilseed, spices, tea, coconuts, rubber, milk, eggs, hides, beef, fish
Industry: processing of rubber, tea, coconuts, tobacco, and other agricultural commodities; telecommunications, insurance, banking; tourism, shipping, clothing, textiles, cement, petroleum refining, information technology services, construction
Exports: $7.908 billion (2010 est.) (primary partners United States, United Kingdom, India, Belgium, Germany, Italy) (2009)
Imports: $111.6 billion (2010 est.) (primary partners India, China, Singapore, Iran, South Korea (2009)
Human Development Index (ranking): 91 (UNDP 2010)

Sri Lanka Country Report

Sri Lanka is a small island nation that hangs like a pendant off the southeast coast of India. Extending 270 miles from north to south, and expanding to 140 miles in width toward its southern end, it occupies just 1.5 percent of the total landmass of the subcontinent. It was once renowned for its pleasant tropical climate and natural beauty. The Indian Ocean tsunami hit Sri Lanka with devastating impact on December 26, 2004. But even more, for the past 25 years, it has been ravaged by civil conflict. The country, once known as the "Pearl of the Orient," has become the "Lebanon of South Asia."

Sri Lanka is divided into two regions: a low-lying dry zone to the north and a mountainous wet zone to the south. At the center of the southern zone are the lush Kandyan Highlands, whose extensive tea and rubber plantations are watered by abundant rainfall, especially during the southwest monsoon season. Ceylonese tea, considered among the finest in the world, has recently been replaced by textiles as the country's leading export.

The northern plains are devoted mostly to rice cultivation for domestic consumption. Irrigation systems, necessary to support agriculture in this region, date from the earliest record of settlers from India, in the fifth century B.C. Marauding forces

(Copyright © Alasdair Drysdale (DAL mhhe010376))

Sri Lanka is famous for good quality tea. Tea plants are grown on hill slopes and need constant rainfall. Unlike rice paddies, water should not sit stagnant around tea plants. Thus, the rainy hill slopes are ideal for tea plantations.

from south India, which destroyed the city of Anuradhapura in the tenth century A.D., and malaria, borne by mosquitoes bred in the still waters of the irrigation lakes, drove

the population of the north-central region to the coastlands. Redevelopment of the blighted north-central region started during the British colonial period.

DEVELOPMENT

Human resource development and land and water reclamation for agriculture and energy have contributed most to Sri Lanka's economic health. In spite of a decline in the world tea market and, even more, the devastation of civil war since 1983 and the 2004 tsunami, the country's largely agricultural economy remains healthy.

In 1968 Sri Lanka undertook the Mahaweli River Project to build five major dams and irrigation works along the 207-mile course of Sri Lanka's longest river, from the central highlands to Koddiyar Bay on the east coast. This development cleared, resettled, and irrigated 900,000 acres. With substantial foreign investment, it was completed in 1983. The project now produces 20 percent of the country's rice and 45 percent of its power generation.

The Sri Lankan people are also divided, north and south. Seventy-four percent of Sri Lanka's population speak Sinhalese, 93 percent of whom are Theravada Buddhists. Eighteen percent of the population is Tamil speaking, two-thirds of whom are Hindu.

The Sinhalese trace their origin to fifth-century B.C. settlers from India. Legend describes their leader, Prince Vijaya, as of the race of the lion, a Sinhal, a symbol of royalty adopted from ancient Persian culture. Sent from north India by his father, he arrived on Sri Lanka on the day of the Buddha's death, in 483 B.C. and established his kingdom in the city of Anuradhapura in the north-central region of the country.

Tradition also traces the origin of Buddhism on the island to Mahendra, the son and his daughter Sangha-mitra and emissary of the Indian emperor **Asoka,** in the third century B.C. This Theravada tradition reveres the teachings of the earliest disciples of the Buddha—the elders (thera)—as contained in the Pali Canon. Itinerant monks from India carried these sacred texts throughout South and Southeast Asia during the early years of expansion of the Buddhist faith.

Portuguese, who arrived on the south coast of Sri Lanka in the early 1500s, drove many of the Sinhalese people of the south into the mountains. There they established a kingdom around the city of Kandy. Sinhalese Buddhists are divided today between the Kandyans, who live in the Highlands, and the "Low Country" people on the coastlands. The latter are more numerous (60 percent) and more prosperous, living in the more urban, coastal rim of the south.

The Tamils are also divided into two groups: the Sri Lankan Tamils (70 per-

cent) and the Indian Tamils (30 percent). The Sri Lankan Tamils are found mostly on the north and east coastlands. Almost half of this Tamil community lives in the northernmost district of Jaffna, representing 95 percent of the district population. They share a long history on the island with the Kandyan Sinhalese, with whom they have the most in common culturally and ethnically.

FREEDOM

Since 1983, the country has been torn apart by civil war between the Sri Lanka government and the militant LTTE, seeking independence for the Tamil speaking minority. This conflict has caused 70,000 deaths, and made many hundreds of thousands homeless as Internally Displaced Persons. International assistance to bring relief was withdrawn during intense fighting in 2008.

The Indian Tamils were brought to Sri Lanka in the nineteenth century to work as field laborers on plantations set up by the British in the Kandyan Highlands. Their number was greatly reduced during the 1960s and 1970s by their repatriation to India. Those who remained, about 5 percent of the population of Sri Lanka, eventually received status as citizens of Sri Lanka.

Significant Christian and Muslim communities (8 percent and 7 percent), belong to both language groups. The Tamil-speaking Muslims live mostly along the east coast; a minority caught between the northern Tamils and Kandyan Sinhalese.

INDEPENDENCE

The British were the first to unify these peoples under a single government administration, in 1815. They introduced the rudiments of a national government in the port city of Colombo, on the southwest coast, and democratic institutions throughout the country. The first general elections were held in 1931, to select representatives to a National Assembly by universal suffrage under strict colonial control.

On February 4, 1948, Sri Lanka, then called Ceylon, received its independence as a parliamentary dominion in the British Commonwealth. In 1972, the government adopted a new Constitution as an independent republic, with a single legislature of 168 elected members. A further constitutional change, in 1978, endowed the presidency with extensive, independent executive authority. Junius Jayewardene, who had been appointed prime minister in

(Copyright © Iconotec/Alamy Images (DAL AHBCXD))

Fishing is an important economic activity of Sri Lanka. Besides boat fishing," Chinese net" fishing is also practiced by fishermen. This fisherman is holding a Chinese net standing on the stilt.

1978 after a sweeping victory of his United National party (UNP) in 1977, was elected president in separate national elections held in 1982.

His victory occurred at a time of great social unrest in the country. The vigorous pursuit of development, resettlement, and land reform projects had the unanticipated consequence of making many Kandy Sinhalese homeless. Their restlessness was expressed by a militant, Marxist youth group called the People's Liberation Front (JVP), which began devastating attacks on villages throughout the south in 1971. These activities fed into an underlying conflict between the Tamil and Sinhalese populations that broke out into civil war in 1983.

CIVIL WAR

Soon after the independence of Sri Lanka, political leaders from the dominant Sinhalese community began to exploit a popular "Sinhala only" movement to eliminate advantages achieved by the Tamils during the Colonial period. S. W. R. D. Bandaranaike and his Sri Lanka Freedom Party, a coalition of leftist, pro-Sinhala groups, won the elections in 1956. He then introduced a bill to make Sinhalese the only official language of the country. The Tamil leaders responded with a nonviolent demonstration. Their protest incited an unchecked violent response by Sin-

(Courtesy of TamilNet)

Everyone standing around waiting at a distribution center in Jaffina for scarce food during the summer of 2006, when the Sri Lanka army cut off access to the city. This action caused the collapse of the Norwegian sponsored peace talks with the LTTE in Geneva in October 2006.

hala extremists. Bandaranaike's attempt to restrain the anti-Tamil violence, and to find some accommodation for Tamil interests, led to his assassination in 1959 by an extremist Buddhist monk.

HEALTH/WELFARE

The government provides national health care and extensive education, as well as extensive relief and rebuilding for victims of the war and the tsunami. International relief workers and many civilians have been displaced and killed in the crossfire during the wind down of 35 years of civil war.

Adding fuel to the fire, the new constitution, adopted in 1972, eliminated many of the minority protections adopted at the time of independence. In response, Tamil legislators formed a solid political caucus as the Tamil United Front to present their concerns in the national legislature. To diminish the appeal of a growing militancy among their youth, they also sought greater autonomy at the district level, to give them greater freedom and voice in those northern districts where they were in the majority.

The landslide victory of the United National Party in the 1977 elections took away the Tamil United Front's leverage as a critical voting block at the national level. With the need to resettle some 130,000 families displaced by the new dams in the Mahaweli River Project, the UNP pursued policies that placed more Sinhalese in redefined districts in the northern part of the country. The Tamils then found them-

selves also losing political power at the district level.

The Tamils' loss of political protection during the 1970s fanned the fires of some 36 militant student groups, youthful and eager for social and political change. Among them, the most ruthless and disciplined was the Liberation Tigers of Tamil Eelam (LTTE). It organized and carried out a sustained reign of terror throughout the northern regions of the country. In 1983, the LTTE ambushed a Sri Lankan army unit, inciting anti-Tamil riots in Colombo and across the south. Close to 2,000 Tamils were killed, 100,000 became internally displaced persons (IDP), and 130,000 fled to India as refugees. Civil war had begun.

Unable to control the violence, President Jayewardene invited the government of India in 1987 to send an Indian Peace Keeping Force (IPKF) to Sri Lanka. Faced with the IPKF's ineffectiveness and unpopularity, and with growing violence against the Tamils by the Sinhalese youth group JVP, Jayewardene did not seek reelection in 1988. His United National Party won the elections, and his successor, Ranasinghe Premadasa, asked the Indian Army to withdraw.

The Indian Peace Keeping Force left the LTTE weakened but no less resolved to seek independence for a separate Tamil state at any cost, including through drug trade and suicide bombing. This militant group was implicated in the assassination of President Premadasa on May 1, 1993, by a human time bomb, the same way Rajiv Gandhi, Prime minister of India, was killed while campaigning in south India in 1991.

The LTTE asserted its control in the northern Jaffna District by calling for a boycott of the 1994 national legislative elections. Less than 10 percent of the electorate in that district voted. In other parts of Sri Lanka, war-weary voters sought a political rather than military solution to the conflict between the Tamil insurgents and the Sinhalese majority. In hopes for peace, they elected a fragile coalition of leftist parties called the People's Alliance, led by Chandrika Kumaratunga.

Mrs. Kumaratunga was no stranger to politics. She was the daughter of S. W. R. D. Bandaranaike, the popular prime minister, leader of the Sri Lanka Freedom Party in the 1950s. Her mother, Sirimavo Bandaranaike, became leader of the SLFP after his assassination in 1959. She served as the nation's first woman prime minister from 1960 to 1965 and from 1970 to 1977, and as president from 1996 until her retirement in 2000. Mrs. Kumaratunga's husband, a popular film actor, was also active in national politics until his assassination, purportedly by a Sinhala nationalist group, while a presidential candidate in 1988.

Mrs. Kumaratunga initially proposed talks with the LTTE for a cease-fire. When they did not materialize, the Sri Lankan army undertook a major offensive to remove the LTTE from its stronghold in the ravaged city of Jaffna. Her efforts to end the conflict by force did not bring peace.

Although weakened and further isolated from any political base, the LTTE continued to carry out guerrilla attacks in the northeastern coastal region of the country. It recaptured the town of Killinochchi on the vital highway to Jaffna in September 1998 and defeated the Sri Lankan forces in the Elephant Pass in April 2000. Its reign of terror included the assassination of two Tamil mayors of Jaffna to protest the attempt of a more moderate Tamil United Liberation Front to reestablish civil order there.

ACHIEVEMENTS

With extensive international help, the country has made substantial recovery from the 2004 tsunami. The Army has effectively defeated the LTTE. The nation looks for restoration and peace from a conflict that has devastated and displaced many of its Tamil minority.

In 2001, the United National Party, campaigning to renew efforts toward peace in the national legislative elections, defeated Kumaratunga's People's Alliance. Prime minister Ranil Wickremesinghe picked up on initiatives for mediation by the Norwegian government to enter into a full cease-fire agreement with the LTTE in February 2002. In July, his government fulfilled a vital precondition of the LTTE to enter into peace talks by withdrawing the ban placed on the LTTE as a terrorist organization. Formal talks with the LTTE then began with Norwegian facilitation in Thailand in September. At a later round of talks in December 2002, the Norwegian mediators offered a proposal called the Oslo Statement to explore an acceptable formula for limited autonomy for the Tamil people within a united sovereign Sri Lanka. It proved problematic for both parties, and the peace process stalled.

The LTTE did not want to discuss any proposal that presupposed a united, sovereign country. They wanted first to establish an Interim Self Governing Authority for the Tamil-speaking Northern and Eastern Provinces. Once accepted as separate, then they would talk about assurances to make it possible for them to join in a shared governance of the island as a whole.

On the other side, in the national legislative elections held in November 2003, a roused Sinhala nationalist opposition defeated the United National Party. It asserted that Prime Minister Wickremesinghe was making too many concessions in the Norwegian negotiations.

At the end of November 2004, to push its agenda for self rule, the LTTE held "Heroes Week" demonstrations in the northeast region, to commemorate 17,800 Tamils who had died in their 20-year civil war. Alleged security force interference with the demonstrations led to a one-day strike in some northern cities. The cease-fire remained fragile, with UNICEF accusations of child recruitment by the LTTE, and with fighting erupting among factions within the LTTE.

On December 26, 2004, the Indian Ocean tsunami hit the east coast of the country from the tip of Jaffna in the north to the city of Galle in the south. The immense power of its wave killed 30,240 people, and left 833,780 homeless. The survivors of Sri Lanka were overwhelmed by the indiscriminate devastation and heavy toll of the tsunami disaster and then by the incredible outpouring of relief provided by so many from all parts of the world.

Bickering over relief efforts, intensified by the LTTE's dominant control over the northeastern region of the country, quickly dissolved the hope that a shared national calamity might bring the warring sides together.

In the presidential election in November 2005, Mahinda Rajapakse's United Peoples Freedom Alliance was a coalition of Sinhalese nationalist parties that took a hard line for a unitary rather than federalist solution to the civil conflict. The LTTE, which saw more advantage to its cause for self-rule in a hard line opposition in Colombo, enforced a boycott of the election in the region of the

Timeline: PAST

500 B.C.
Migration of people of India

247 B.C.
Mahendra (Asoka's son) introduces Buddhism

A.D. 1815–1948
British colonial rule

1948
The independence of Ceylon, as a British Commonwealth dominion

1972
A new Constitution establishes Sri Lanka as a democratic republic

1977
The United National Party wins elections by wide margin

1978
The Constitution is modified to establish an independent president

1982–1988
Junius Jayewardene serves as president; anti-Tamil riots break out; Indian Peace Keeping Force

1990s
Efforts to achieve a cease-fire between LTTE and Sri Lankan military forces and to negotiate a settlement in the dispute between the Tamil minority and Sinhalese majority fail

PRESENT

2000s
Sri Lankan economy hit by civil war and the Indian Ocean Tsunami

2001
The government and LTTE agree to Norway brokered cease-fire and to talks to restore peace.

2004
Indian Ocean Tsunami hits, leaving 30,240 dead and 883,780 homeless.

2006
With death toll of civil war rising to 67,000 since 1983, peace talks between government and LTTE break down.

2008
Sri Lanka army, with help of LTTE dissident, routs LTTE forces out of Eastern Province, and government holds provincial elections, won by dissident's party. Sri Lanka army begins major offensive against LTTE in its strongholds in Northern Province.

2011
The Cabinet decided to reclaim and develop 10 islands between five to 10 hectares in lagoons in Male atoll

island under its control. That stance assured Rajapakse of success at the polls.

The Sri Lanka Monitoring Mission (SLMM) reported in August 2006 an increasing number of major violations in the Cease Fire Agreement in the North and East. United Nation's estimates report more than 3,000 deaths and 225,000 made homeless by terrorist and military action in 2006, and a meeting of both sides in Geneva to resume peace talks in October got nowhere.

To reaffirm his unitary position, President Rajapakse initiated a shared common policy with the United National Party toward firming a strong negotiating position in Norwegian sponsored peace talks. But with the collapse of the cease-fire, he began a major military campaign to eliminate the LTTE from its entrenchment in the Northern and Eastern Provinces, which had been combined during the Indian Army Peacekeeping Force's attempt at reconciliation in 1987. When they were separated by a decision of the Supreme Court in 2006, with the help of a LTTE dissident, Colonel Karuna, the Sri Lanka army forced the LTTE sufficiently out of the Eastern Province to allow provincial elections in May 2008. Chandrakanthan, deputy leader of Karuna's political party (TMVP), was elected Chief Minister of the Provincial Assembly.

Building on this apparent success in the more ethnically diverse Eastern Province, President Rajapakse turned the army's efforts toward the more Tamil dominant Northern

Province. The threat of this operation to the lives and relief of the more than 300,000 displaced persons in this area roused great concern and calls for a cease-fire from India.

In response to this concern for the safety of the civilian population during this intensifying military operation, the Rajapakse government assured renewed efforts to pursue a political solution to the conflict and further development efforts in the Tamil dominant regions of the country.

But in 2007, Rajapakse had already created a multi-ethnic panel called the All Party Representative Committee (APRC) to recommend a form of genuine power sharing which could accommodate minorities that have been sidelined and alienated from the state, while preserving the unity, sovereignty, and territorial integrity of the state. When the panel issued its report, dissension among the 17 members who created it was clearly evident. That the more militant Tamil minorities will accept Rajapakse's unitary proposals as an effective avenue for negotiations for peace does not appear promising.

For even if the army succeeds in routing out the LTTE militarily, the expectation of guerrilla warfare and terrorist attacks, which are continuing in the Eastern Province, holds out little hope to those in the Northern District who have been so ravaged and displaced by these many years of civil war.*

Sri Lanka's experience in seeking an inclusive national identity as a democracy is taking a heavy toll among its people.

*Thomas Fuller, "Sri Lanka War Nears End, but Peace Remains Distant," *New York Times,* February 17, 2009.

India's Central Asian Struggle

SREERAM CHAULIA

Central Asia is the most coveted area in the world for strategic influence. By virtue of its location at geopolitical crossroads and its vast mineral treasures, the region of the six 'stans' (Afghanistan, Tajikistan, Uzbekistan, Kazakhstan, Kyrgyzstan and Turkmenistan) has been a prized object of contention for great powers of different eras. In the 13th century, Mongolia's Changez Khan's swept across the area, killing 15 million people and plundering its resources. Changez's imperialism in the Caucasus and Russia was facilitated by his control of the Central Asian steppes.

In the 19th century, Russia and the British Empire locked horns over Central Asia in the 'Great Game', an intense rivalry for mastery of the region. For London, Afghanistan was a staging post for the Russians to invade India, the jewel in the Victorian crown. For the ambitious Czars, subjugating the Muslim khanates of Central Asia was necessary for Russian traders to carry their wares westwards to lucrative markets.

The late 20th century revival of the 'Great Game' between the United States and the USSR centered on the swing state of Afghanistan. Moscow's 1979 invasion of Afghanistan was aimed at shoring up the former's 'southern frontier' against American destabilisation. The ensuing American arming of the *mujahideen* forces via Pakistan turned Central Asia into a deciding ground of the Cold War. The Russian defeat in Afghanistan in 1987 was instrumental in determining the final outcome of the Cold War.

Since the end of the Cold War, the world has witnessed the rise of two new great powers in Asia—China and India. These two giants made remarkable economic progress in the last two decades and began to be acknowledged as important players in their own right, not as satellites of the US or Russia. Apart from the perennial strategic stakes in Central Asia, China and India saw the 'stans', host to the largest untapped oil and gas reserves on the planet, as potential sources of energy.

Chinese and Indian quests for energy are complicated by their mutual competition for greatness. Indian Prime Minister Manmohan Singh echoed this fact by saying, "China is ahead of us in planning for its energy security. India can no longer be complacent." China and India add to the pre-existing energy-driven melee in Central Asia that pits the US against Russia. Russia has been ably countering the American attempt to 'free' Central Asian oil and gas from the Russian stranglehold through a proposed Trans-Caspian Pipeline. The Sino-Indian scramble for Central Asian energy works under the larger rubric of a Russo-American 'new Cold War'.

Islamic fundamentalism is a new factor motivating great powers to seek leverage in Central Asia. The anti-Soviet jihad of the 1980s unleashed a powerful tool of political mobilisation based on *jihad*. From Afghanistan, the virus of violent Islamism spread to the Uzbeks, Tajiks, Kazakhs, Kyrgyz and Turkmens, turning the entire area into a nursery for global terrorism. All the four major contenders in Central Asia— the US, Russia, China and India—have a direct interest in managing the threat of Islamism emanating from the 'stans'.

India's struggle for gaining a foothold in Central Asia rests on two legs—Afghanistan and Tajikistan. In the former, India has an abiding interest in neutralising the Taliban-Al Qaeda duo. The direct links between the Taliban and Pakistan-based anti-India terrorist formations like the *Lashkar-e-Tayyaba* and the *Jaish-e-Muhammad* imply that India can never be secure until *jihadis* from Central Asia are silenced.

The American-led overthrow of the Taliban government in 2001 opened a window of opportunity for New Delhi to boost ties with the new Afghan government of Hamid Karzai, which was eager to repel Pakistani dictation of Afghan politics. India's generous economic and infrastructural assistance to the Karzai government has won the appreciation of the authorities in Kabul. The closeness between India and Afghanistan is underlined by a common animosity for Pakistan's sponsorship of cross-border terrorism on two fronts—the Durand Line to the west and the Line of Control to the east.

A striking example of India-Afghanistan partnership is the road construction venture by New Delhi's quasi-military Border Roads Organisation (BRO) to connect distant corners of Afghanistan and strengthen its territorial integrity. India is paying the price for this initiative not only financially but also in blood. In April 2008, Taliban terrorists killed two Indian construction workers of the BRO in a suicide attack. In December 2005, the Taliban kidnapped and killed an Indian BRO driver with a demand that all Indians should leave the country. Following this incident, India dispatched 300 paramilitary forces of the Indo-Tibetan Border Police (ITBP) to provide security to the Indian workers in Afghanistan. The move rang alarm bells in Pakistan about Indian military presence in Afghanistan for the first time since Pakistan's creation as a nation state.

The Taliban, who operate with impunity with the connivance of Pakistani intelligence, carried out another suicide attack in January 2008 that killed two ITBP personnel. The Islamist hatred for India's sincere attempts to shore up the Karzai government has not been limited to attacking official government-of-India personnel. In April 2006, the Taliban abducted an Indian engineer working for a Bahraini telecommunications company in Afghanistan and decapitated him.

The targeting of Indians in Afghanistan exemplifies the hurdle posed by Pakistan to New Delhi's ambitions. A shadow of doubt hangs over the reliability of Pakistan as a transit state for oil to be transported to India from Turkmenistan or Iran. At every step, Islamabad is determined to prevent India from making inroads in Afghanistan. India has expressed grave reservations at the Yusuf Raza Gilani government's recent negotiated deal with the Taliban, wherein the Pakistani army will halt campaigns and hand over arrested Taliban members in return for a cessation of terrorist attacks on Pakistani soil. The essence of this pact is that the Taliban will be free to go berserk in Afghanistan as long as they do not cause havoc inside Pakistani territory. Attacks on NATO coalition troops in Afghanistan as well as on Indian BRO and ITBP staffers are likely to escalate as a result of this agreement. A previous ceasefire between General Musharraf's government and the Pakistani Taliban in 2006 yielded a similar crop of violence in Afghanistan.

In Tajikistan, India faces an equally strong set of obstacles as in Afghanistan. Since the late 1990s, India operated a field hospital at Farkhor, southeast of the capital Dushanbe, as part of its role in helping Afghanistan's Northern Alliance in the fight against the Taliban regime.

This facility was upgraded into a military outpost and eventually an air base in 2003, becoming the first of its kind for India on foreign soil. The Ayni air base was to be established close to the Afghan border with the permanent presence of the Indian Air Force and Army. Since the Indian base was supposed to be "co-located" alongside the Russian base at Ayni (which counters American designs), the agreement between New Delhi and Dushanbe was probably facilitated by Russia.

In 2007, though, the Indian base in Tajikistan ran into trouble. The Tajik government, reportedly under Russian pressure, ordered the eviction of Indian forces from the base. The diversification of India's arms imports away from Russia towards the US had apparently miffed Moscow. Although this narrative was denied in Moscow and New Delhi, the uncertainty about India's continued hold over Ayni reflected the competitive fragility that characterises Central Asia. In 2008, matters seemed to return to normal after India delivered promised development aid to Tajikistan. The Tajik defence minister announced that Dushanbe had "temporarily stalled" India's ejection from Ayni after New Delhi released the financial assistance. One would assume that Russia too has eased its objections to the Indian base at Ayni in the interests of continued diplomatic and military cooperation with New Delhi.

It bears mentioning here that the Ayni base is also desired by the US and China. The Chinese military journal, *Bingqi Zhishi*, argued in 2004 that India's forays into Central Asia are "containing Pakistan and pinning down China's development." The Beijing-Islamabad nexus will expectedly leave no stone unturned in rolling back India's attempt to become a prominent actor in the 'stans'. China intends to use the Shanghai Cooperation Organisation (SCO) and pipeline diplomacy to impress its own hand on Central Asia. Since Russia is unwilling to cede the keys to the region to any power, be it the US or China, India will be a balancing necessity, and New Delhi will have to cultivate this aspect of its friendship with Moscow.

The desolate terrain of Central Asia has for time immemorial enticed greedy great powers. India's advent is the latest arrival on an already crowded scene akin to a 'Hare and Hounds' game among lead states and pursuer states. Unless New Delhi plays its diplomatic cards with Russia and the US more adeptly, its struggle to obtain a toehold in Central Asia will be in vain.

Critical Thinking

1. Why is India's Ayni base, located in Tajikistan, of interest to the U.S. and China?

2. Discuss how India's relationship with Afghanistan is viewed by the Taliban.

3. Besides security, why is it critical for India to establish leverage in Central Asia?

SREERAM CHAULIA is a researcher on international affairs at the Maxwell School of Citizenship in Syracuse, New York. He can be reached at sreeramchaulia@hotmail.com

From *The International Indian*, June 2008, pp. 22–23. Copyright © 2008 by Chaulia Sreeram. Reprinted by permission of the author.

Does India Seek the Largest Nuclear Arsenal Possible?

Ashley J. Tellis

Because the U.S.-Indian civilian nuclear cooperation agreement does not terminate the production of fissile material for India's nuclear weapons program—an agreement that had such an effect could never have been concluded—there is truly no way of determining *a priori* what the eventual size of India's nuclear arsenal will be. The government of India has repeatedly affirmed its desire for only a "minimum credible deterrent," but has refused to quantify publicly what this concept means in terms of numbers and types of weapons. It is, in fact, entirely possible that not even the government of India itself knows what the notion of minimum deterrence precisely entails, because in a situation where India's rivals, China and Pakistan, are both continuing to build up their nuclear arsenals in the absence of any clearly defined force posture goals, policy makers in New Delhi would want to keep their options open in regards to their own strategic response. No one, therefore, can say with any certainty whether the eventual Indian nuclear arsenal will be large, medium, or small in size, because that magnitude will depend, at least in part, on the eventual—and as yet unknowable—strength and character of the Chinese and Pakistani nuclear inventories. What can be said, however, with reasonable confidence, is that the fundamental assumption inherent in the maximalist version of the critique of U.S.-Indian nuclear cooperation—that India seeks to build the largest possible nuclear weapons inventory it could develop through use of its indigenous resources—is simply not borne out by the record thus far. In fact, as Secretary of State Condoleezza Rice emphasized in her testimony before the Senate Foreign Relations Committee on April 5, 2006, the most interesting feature of the Indian nuclear weapons program historically has been its restraint, not its indulgence.

A few details help to place this judgment in perspective. The Indian nuclear weapons program is not transparent enough to enable analysts on the outside to determine conclusively when its nuclear establishment began producing fissile materials for weapons and with what efficiency, although it is universally agreed that India's two research reactors, the Canadian-supplied CIRUS and the indigenously constructed Dhruva, have been the principal production foundries used for this purpose. Based on the known information about the history, technical characteristics, and fissile material production potential of these two reactors, several analysts have offered educated judgments about the size and quality of India's fissile material stockpile but, in the absence of authoritative data from the government of India, all these assessments are clouded to some degree or another by uncertainty. One of the best Western assessments, produced in the immediate aftermath of India's 1998 nuclear tests, concluded that New Delhi possessed about 370 kilograms of weapons-grade plutonium (WGPu) at the time, and that its weapons-related fissile material stockpile, deriving principally from the output of the Dhruva (and to a lesser extent, CIRUS) reactor, was growing at a rate of some 20 kilograms annually. If India is classified as a country with "low" technical capability as far as nuclear weapons design is concerned, meaning that a weapon with a 20 kiloton yield would require at least something on the order of 6 kilograms of weapons-grade plutonium, the notional Indian nuclear stockpile stood at about 61 weapons in 1998. A well-connected Indian journalist, R. Ramachandran, who reportedly was given access to several confidential government briefings on the subject, concluded that India's inventory of weapons-grade plutonium in the aftermath of its 1998 tests consisted of approximately 280 kilograms—sufficient for about 46 weapons. Furthermore, he reported that this inventory grew traditionally at the rate of about 12–16 kilograms per annum or, in other words, sufficient for slightly less than three new nuclear weapons annually.

In the aftermath of India's 1998 tests, the government of India directed its nuclear establishment to increase the production of fissile materials over historical rates for two reasons: first, to provide Indian policy makers with the option of deploying a larger nuclear arsenal than originally intended, if China and Pakistan were to increase their own nuclear targeting of India in the future; and second, as insurance in case a global fissile material cutoff regime, which could require India to immediately terminate the production of weapons-grade fissile materials, were to unexpectedly materialize. Consistent with this injunction, India's nuclear managers pursued several diverse initiatives concurrently: recognizing the age and increasing inefficiency of the obsolescent CIRUS reactor, they sought its replacement by advocating the construction of a new 100-megawatt Dhruva-type research reactor that would be dedicated to the production of weapons-grade plutonium. Simultaneously, they explored the idea of using at least some of India's power reactors in a "low burnup" mode to increase the production of weapons-grade plutonium and possibly to produce tritium as well. Finally, using their existing research reactors, they increased the rate of production of both weapons-grade plutonium—the primary material for India's nuclear weaponry—and tritium—the boosting agent required for its advanced nuclear weapons—above the previous norm, while paying increased attention to the manufacture of other byproduct materials and nonfissile components required by its nuclear weapon stockpile.

Discussions with Indians familiar with their nuclear establishment indicate that the new post-1998 practices have resulted more or less in a "doubling" of the weapons-grade plutonium production rate known to obtain historically. Although tritium production is believed to have increased as well, no Indian interlocutor could provide any sense of how the current production rate of this byproduct material compares with the past. If David Albright's and R. Ramachandran's data pertaining to weapons-grade plutonium are treated as previous benchmarks, then it must be inferred that India's new production rate has bequeathed the country with between 40 kilograms and 24–32 kilograms of this material annually since 1998. Obviously, these yearly increases are unlikely to have been either consistent or uniform, and every marginal increase in the fissile material stockpile is also unlikely to have been immediately fabricated into cores for usable nuclear weapons; yet, these numbers do provide a point of reference that illustrates the growth in the Indian fissile materials inventory (and, by implication, the size of its national nuclear weapons stockpile) since New Delhi's last round of nuclear tests. If the conclusion about "doubling" were in fact veracious—as is likely—then the Indian fissile materials inventory in 2006 would range from some 550 kilograms of weapons-grade plutonium (extrapolating from Albright's 1998 estimate) at the high end, to some 388–424 kilograms of weapons-grade plutonium (extrapolating from Ramachandran's 1998 estimate) at the low end. Most knowledgeable Indians suggest that the figures at the low end of these estimates probably convey a more accurate picture of India's current holdings than the data at the high end, but in any event these inventory sizes translate into a national stockpile of some 91–65 simple fission weapons.

What is remarkable about these numbers is that they repudiate the first key assumption that many critics of the U.S.-India nuclear cooperation agreement holding the maximalist view appear to make, namely that New Delhi seeks the largest possible nuclear arsenal it can lay its hands on. For starters, the relatively slow—even if increased—pace of production of weapons-grade plutonium indicates that the government of India appears to be in no hurry to build the biggest nuclear stockpile it could construct *based merely on material factors alone*. Most observers of the Indian nuclear weapons program, both U.S. and Indian, invariably underscore the conspicuous

inefficiencies that still characterize many aspects of India's production regime; this reality no doubt accounts for some of the languid pace witnessed even in the post-1998 epoch, but it cannot be a sufficient explanation because the production of other byproduct materials and nonfissile components required by India's nuclear devices has apparently increased during this same period.

The best explanation that accounts for the slow accumulation of primary fissile materials required by the weapons stockpile, therefore, is New Delhi's choices—which are driven more by what it believes are necessary to deter its adversaries without unnecessary arms-racing than by some automatic need to maintain the largest possible arsenal simply because technical factors permit it. In other words, it is India's strategic preferences—born out of its traditional penchant for political moderation—and not simply its infrastructural capacity that defines the size of its extant and prospective arsenal. Other practical considerations appear to play a role as well: conversations with senior Indian military officers involved in the strategic program indicate that the country's immediate priority is not to maximize the production of weapons-grade materials per se even if technical conditions allow it, but rather to successfully integrate the modest capabilities India already possesses into an effective deterrent. This involves, among other things, producing the delivery systems, institutionalizing the procedural systems, and codifying the ideational systems in order to ensure that the weapons New Delhi already has in the stockpile can be used as intended in situations of supreme emergency.

At any rate, and irrespective of what the precise determining influences are, the conclusion remains the same: India appears content to produce less than the maximum quantity of weapons-grade materials it otherwise could based on material constraints alone. Translated, this means India's restraint is rooted in choice, rather than forced upon it by successful foreign strategies of denial. This fact is corroborated incontrovertibly by a simple detail: each of the major Indian reprocessing facilities at Tarapur (PREFRE) and at Kalpakkam (KARP) have a nominal capacity to reprocess at least 100 metric tons of spent fuel per year; the smaller reprocessing plant at the Bhabha Atomic Research Center in Trombay has a nominal capacity to reprocess some 50 metric tons of spent fuel annually. All told, then, India has the nominal capacity to reprocess at least 250 metric tons of heavy metal per year (MTHM/yr) in these three facilities, far more than the quantities it is currently reprocessing to yield the 24–40 kilograms of weapons-grade plutonium now produced annually for its weapons program. The evidence, therefore, repudiates the first assumption made by those who advance the maximalist criticism of the U.S.-Indian civil nuclear agreement: not only is the Indian "nuclear bomb lobby" not in any hurry to produce the largest possible arsenal that it is often accused of desiring, it is in fact separating far less weapons-grade plutonium than it could technically through its current reprocessing facilities—a detail that cannot be explained away simply due to the age and condition of the Trombay reprocessing plant.

Lest it be imagined that the slow pace of plutonium production is justified by some accelerated Indian activity relating to uranium enrichment, nothing could be further from the truth. The Indian Rare Earths uranium enrichment plant at Rattehalli in Mysore has been plagued by technical problems since its inception and represents one of the most sorry stories of mismanagement in the Indian nuclear program. In any event, the enriched uranium produced in this facility is intended primarily for fuelling the reactors associated with India's nuclear submarine program and not for developing a new series of uranium-235-based fission weapons. Enriched uranium would obviously have great utility for thermonuclear weaponry, which India is known to be avidly pursuing, but all the information openly available suggests that India's thermonuclear designs still emphasize plutonium-based devices supplemented as necessary by deuterium, tritium, and lithium deuteride.

The bottom line, therefore, remains unchanged: there is no evidence so far that India is seeking to build the biggest nuclear arsenal possible. The data adduced above suggests that New Delhi is in fact producing far less weapons-grade plutonium than it is capable of, given its current capacity. Consequently, the notion that India seeks to inexorably expand its nuclear arsenal does not stand scrutiny because New Delhi's weapons program even today is not operating at its maximum potential.

Critical Thinking

1. India has used restraint in the past in regards to its nuclear arms program. What role does China and Pakistan play in India's need to increase its arsenal?

2. What two major reasons were cited by India's government for directing the increase of production of fissile materials?

3. Is there reliable evidence available to assess India's actual production of weapons-grade material?

From *Atoms for War? U.S.-Indian Civilian Nuclear Cooperation and India's Nuclear Arsenal*, by Ashley J. Trellis (Carnegie Endowment for International Peace, 2006), pp. 11–15.

The Problem Is in Pakistan, Not Kashmir

SUSHANT K. SINGH

A FEW days before he won the 2008 US presidential elections, Barack Obama raised not a few hackles in the subcontinent by revealing that he considered appointing Bill Clinton as a special envoy on Kashmir. After it emerged that Hillary Clinton is the front-runner for the office of secretary of state, Henry Kissinger dismissed the idea of Mr Clinton's appointment saying "there is a limit to the number of Clintons you can appoint" at one time.

Now, key officials of the Bush administration—from the defence secretary to the intelligence chief—not to mention Mr Obama himself, have identified Afghanistan and Pakistan as their topmost priority. However some commentators have tried to deflect the attention from the real issue—Pakistan's reluctance to act against jihadi militants—by dragging Kashmir and imaginary fears of Indian aggression into the debate. The terrorist attacks on Mumbai put paid to this theory by demonstrating how it is the jihadis that are the true cause of Pakistan's insecurities.

In a report published in early November, the Center for American Progress (CAP), a think-tank headed by John Podesta, co-chairman of the Obama transition team, contends that "any regional approach must address Pakistan's security concerns with India, specifically related to Kashmir and Afghanistan." This argument is only partially true: it rightly holds that the cause of instability in Afghanistan is in Pakistan. But the implied corollary that Pakistan needs jihadis to ameliorate its military handicap vis-a-vis India is fallacious.

Pakistani Army's Relationship with the Jihadis

The root cause of Pakistan' indifference to fighting terror is not India, but the institutional interests of the Pakistani military establishment. The Pakistani army is unwilling to take on Islamic militant groups because they have been used to wage proxy wars against India and Afghanistan. The incontrovertible proof of an ISI hand in the bombing of Indian embassy in Kabul, where the Karzai government is perceived to be close to New Delhi, is testimony to Pakistani army's belief that it can get away with the use of Islamic terrorists for political and diplomatic purposes.

The relationship with the Taliban is part of the Pakistani military establishment's "strategic games." The military brass remains obsessed with the prospect of Indian domination of Afghanistan should US and NATO forces leave the country.

The Taliban are seen as a counterweight to Indian influence and Pakistan wants to hedge its options by turning a blind eye towards the jihadi elements. The Pakistan military establishment nurtured this relationship with the jihadis believing that it can manage the militants, but numerous terrorist incidents targeting the armed forces after the storming of Islamabad's Lal Masjid in 2007 suggest that this belief is misplaced. Yet, the feeling in the army's officer corps, as in the rank-and-file, is to rationalise the jihadi fury as wages of Pakistan's relationship with the US.

Another reason for the tacit Pakistani support to Islamic militants is to play up the threat of Taliban and other jihadi elements for financial gains. This allows the Pakistani military to garner billions of dollars in aid, part of which is then used to improve conventional military capabilities. The US Congressional Research Service has noted with concern that "a lot of the military assistance has been much more useful for a potential war with India." A CAP report of July 2008 has assessed that 70 percent of US military aid has been "misspent" on purchasing systems that are inappropriate for the counterinsurgency struggle.

Indeed, if it panders to purported Pakistani concerns over Kashmir and India, the Obama administration would legitimise, sanction and promote the fraternising of an already radicalised Pakistani army with Islamic militants. On the contrary, the United States should focus on disabusing Islamabad of its use of terrorism as a diplomatic and military tool. Pakistani society is already beginning to be convinced about the dangers of continuing with this dangerous liaison. This is a welcome development that both the Obama administration and the next Indian government should seek to reinforce.

An Islamised and Unprofessional Army

Many Western experts have been taken in by the portrayal of the Pakistani army as a modern and professional force. This is no longer the case, with the growing Islamisation of its rank and file. This religious indoctrination of the officers and soldiers, which metastasised in the Zia-ul-Haq era, can be forcefully leveraged by the military leadership against its "Hindu" enemy, India. However the senior Pakistani military leadership, despite under tremendous pressure from the United States, finds it difficult to mobilise the army and ISI to act against the Taliban and other Islamic militants inside the country.

The Pakistani army has lost every single war it has ever fought, and, in periods of military rule, its record has been far from glorious. Moreover, the Pakistani army isn't trained for counterinsurgency operations. Its record in the counterinsurgency operations in tribal areas since 2004 has been pathetic. Indeed, the Pakistani army views the battles it is fighting against the extremists very differently from Western strategists and policy-makers—with the sole aim to do as little as possible—only to maintain its primacy as the premier instrument of the state and to secure its own political and economic interests.

The incoming Democratic administration must recognise the fundamental truth that even if the Pakistani army somehow miraculously generates the intention to take on the Islamic insurgents inside its own borders, it no longer has the capability to undertake effective counterinsurgency operations. Thus the expediency of placating the Pakistani army to meet short-term security goals, as opposed to the long-term plans for strengthening Pakistani society, polity and economy, is deeply flawed and a recipe for another US foreign policy disaster.

The long-term goal of the Obama administration to transform Pakistan into a modern, democratic state can only begin with an unconditional disowning of jihadis, religious fundamentalism, commercial interests and political overreach by the Pakistani army. In their present state, neither the Pakistani army in general nor the ISI in particular can be a part of any viable short-term or medium-term solution, whereas a long-term solution is largely about dismantling and then recreating these institutions from scratch.

MD Nalapat, professor of geopolitics at Manipal University, rightly suggests that despite the obvious history, the Pakistan army's desires are been once again sought to be equated with the needs of the entire nation. What the army seeks and what Pakistan needs are totally different. This hyphenation of the army with the people of Pakistan is the source of many a flawed policy. The incoming Obama administration must recognise and stay away from this fundamental fallacy.

Afghanistan, Not Kashmir

The contention that Kashmir lies at the 'core of Pakistani nationhood' and the Pakistani army will brook no changes is an overused notion that has been carried over from the previous century. It has little significance in the geopolitics of the twentyfirst century and the existing ground realities.

Many previous Democratic administrations have tried to draw comparisons between Kashmir and the Middle East or Northern Ireland peace processes. These parallels are not apt as today, neither India nor Pakistan desire outside intervention. In fact, substantial progress has been made in recent years as a result of bilateral negotiations—the current back-channel negotiations between India and Pakistan are the first since 1962–63. A US intervention will rapidly shrink the domestic political space for India in its negotiations with Kashmiri political leaders. In fact, perceptions of US prodding could well vitiate the entire spectrum of India-US exchanges, to the detriment of both sides.

The fact is that Kashmir is no longer the epicentre of instability in South Asia. The successful conduct of assembly elections in Kashmir against the calls of the separatists is a sign of normalcy that US officials in charge of Iraq and Afghanistan would perhaps give their right arm for. Militancy and infiltration figures have dipped in the state, the ceasefire is holding and initiatives to soften borders in Kashmir by facilitating cross-border trade and movement are gaining greater traction.

There is a risk that all these gains will be lost if the new US administration shifts its focus from Afghanistan to Kashmir. Hopes of US incentives being offered on Kashmir are bound to encourage the Pakistan army to harden its stance against the current peace process with India. It will result in the Pakistani army and its jihadis cohorts controlling developments on both fronts—Afghanistan and Kashmir.

Another related idea that has been recently doing the rounds is to assuage Pakistani fears by garnering an Indian security guarantee underwritten by the United States. Yet, a better guarantee already exists, implicitly in the deterrence provided by the nuclear weapons. The idea that the Pakistani army is unable to focus on insurgency due to threats of an Indian aggression is absurd when there are nuclear weapons on both sides.

A security guarantee causes a moral hazard problem. It encourages the Pakistani army to undertake another misadventure against India in Kashmir, just as a perceived guarantee of international intervention factored in Pakistan's initiation of wars against India in 1965, 1971 and 1999. The same was at play during the recent Georgia-Russia conflict, which was instigated by the Georgians acting under the assumption of NATO or EU security guarantees.

The Road Ahead

To succeed in Afghanistan, the Obama administration must initiate and see through a comprehensive reform of Pakistani army. The economic and development assistance plan, under the Biden plan, will be effective only if it is tied to this goal. Otherwise, as Jim Hoagland put it, it will merely amount to "dropping cash from helicopters."

An objective reading of the subcontinent's geopolitical reality suggests that Indian and US interests are closely aligned over Afghanistan. The Obama administration should court greater Indian support in Afghanistan, including facilitation of a co-operative relationship with Iran (which provides an alternative land corridor to Afghanistan). Kashmir is a red herring which could derail an emerging India-US strategic partnership. Finally, if the US does not keep India on its side in Afghanistan, then who has it left?

Critical Thinking

1. Why is the Pakistani army reluctant to fight Islamic militants?

2. What is the major obstacle in U.S. efforts to transform Pakistan into a democratic state?

3. Why is it important that the United States not shift its focus from Afghanistan to Kashmir?

Sushant K Singh is a resident commentator on the *Indian National Interest*.

From *Pragati: The India National Interest Review*, December 2008, pp. 12–14. Copyright © 2008 by The Indian National Interest. Licensed under Creative Commons Attribution 2.5 India license: http//creativecommons.org/licenses/by/2.5/in/

The Elusive National Counter-Terrorism Policy

Ajit Kumar Doval

That the absence of a coherent and time consistent policy is responsible for India's failure on the counter-terrorist front is a common refrain of many well meaning critics. The parallels with United States' success in securing its homeland following the 9/11 attacks, as against repetitive attacks in India, are largely attributed to this infirmity. While the logic of the two comparisons is faulty on the fundamentals, it cannot be denied that despite having bled profusely, India's response to terrorism has not been in pursuance of a grand policy.

The Indian response generally has been episodic and disjointed, mostly reacting to situational challenges in the aftermath of major terrorist actions. Short-term and tactical, the response is primarily driven by an anxiety to reduce political costs in the wake of popular resentment and media onslaught, achieve quick results in identifying and neutralising the culprits and dish out brave statements to boost public morale, all in the hope that these will be seen as government's bold new policy initiatives.

Arguably, this is the time for fast and smart tactical actions to generate heat on the terrorists and not for policy-making which is a long and cumbersome exercise of defining objectives, building capacities, re-defining inter-agency role and responsibilities and restructuring systems. While one can justify the immediate taking precedence over the important to meet the problem at hand, it is baffling that even after the initial outburst subsides the important continues to remain as elusive as before. The system settles down to the rut of the routine till the next event triggers the cycle all over again.

People start believing that the government lacks the intention, capability or both to address the problem. Once their expectations of the government grappling the problem from a higher plane with a long term policy perspective, strategic vision and systems-driven co-ordination are belied, widespread cynicism sets in.

It would be absurd to presume that any government in power would not wish to deliver—if for no other reason than for its own political benefit. It also can not simply be attributed to bureaucratic apathy or insensitivity of the security apparatus. The latter are perhaps the worst sufferers of non-policy and would very much like to be led by definitive policy guidelines, if they only had the capability and opportunity of having one. The question that begs an answer is why does this happen in a country that is the world's biggest victim of terrorism. There has to be something more fundamentally amiss in the Indian system which is responsible for this. It is important to identify these causes to bring about the required correctives.

Policy-making in government is a process through which those in power translate their political vision into plans and programmes to achieve certain defined objectives. Existence of political vision is thus at the centre of policymaking. Yet in the fractious contemporary Indian polity, political vision has been overcast by electoral calculations and the need to pander to the perceived sensitivity of vote-banks. Maximising electoral advantages by serving the national interest best is no more considered to be the politics that pays. Commitment to the national good and ideological convictions, visible in early years of independence, has been taken over by politics of compromise and short-term expediency. In recent times, coalition compulsions have further accentuated the problem, constricting policy making only to a small residual area which does not hurt political interests of even a small constituent, as withdrawal of parliamentary support could lead to collapse of the government. This minimal area of consensus is too small to formulate policies in respect of challenges which require national response at maximal level. As many security issues, including terrorism, fall in this category they have been the worst hit.

For instance, the North-East is India's most vulnerable strategic region with more than 99 percent of its boundary being international. Over 88 percent of this international border is with countries with which India faces one or the other security related problem. Due to geo-historical reasons, the area is still secluded from national mainstream and has witnessed more than two dozen insurgencies since India's independence. It also provides an easy route for smuggling of weapons from Pacific Rim countries and drugs from the Golden Triangle area. In this setting, securing its borders and making them impregnable should have been the nation's prime security priority.

However, what we did was just the opposite. In 1984, Assam which was worst hit by the massive demographic invasion was taken out of the purview of Foreigners Act through enactment of Illegal Migrants Determination by Tribunal Act (IMDT Act). The Act facilitated uninterrupted illegal migration of Bangladeshis into Assam and, from there, to the rest of the country.

The illegal immigration also provided an opportunity to jihadi terrorists to find easy access to India. These illegal immigrants were constituted into a major vote bank, a consideration which for the Congress Party took precedence over national security interests.

Twenty-one years after this Act was passed, the Supreme Court in 2005 observed that it was "wholly unconstitutional and must be struck down." Calling it as an "aggression", it added that "the presence of such a large number of illegal migrants from Bangladesh, which runs into millions, is in fact an aggression on the state of Assam and has also contributed significantly in causing serious internal disturbances in the shape of insurgency of alarming proportions. The IMDT Act and Rules had been so made that innumerable and insurmountable difficulties are created in identification and deportation of the illegal migrants."

The serious security implications of millions of illegal immigrants settling down in a region, challenged by high internal and external threats was eclipsed by electoral considerations. More alarming was the fact that immediately after such a severe indictment by the Supreme Court, the UPA government issued the Foreigners Tribunal Order in February 2006, reintroducing the provisions of the IMDT Act through the back door. It took another Supreme Court intervention on a public interest litigation to strike down the order.

Political Vision, Bipartisan Approach

There can be no effective policy making in security matters unless those in power develop a political vision in which national security takes precedence over short-term political gains. In a competitive electoral politics, this will entail pursuing a bipartisan approach so that the national interest does not become politically unaffordable. A political discourse at a higher plane among major political parties on critical security issues, including terrorism, would be necessary for achieving this objective.

Even in the settings where political will and vision exists, policy making does not accrue as an automatic by-product. It requires an institutionalised knowledge base, expertise both of the issues involved and the art of policy-making, the capacity to optimally leverage given constants and variables to the nation's best advantage and a highly competent and committed civil service. The Indian security management system is deficient in this respect. Though there are individuals with high capabilities and commitments, but as a system, they are not able to achieve what the nation otherwise is capable of. This invites snide remarks of India being a "soft-state" implying that its policy-making and policy-executing capacities are disproportionately low to the sum total of its comprehensive state power.

Both policy-making and policy-execution in India is mired in a bureaucratic morass where there are more brakes than accelerators. Policymaking has to pass through cumbersome processes which are slow, militate against change, are fettered by antiquated rules and procedures whose rationale has long been lost, and is beleaguered by inter-department rivalries. Worst still, at different stages, it is handled by people who lack the required knowledge, skills and decision-making capabilities, and are not accountable. They are not stakeholders in the success or failure of policies, a burden that has to be borne by the executive agencies. They are safe as long as they do not violate rules and procedures.

While policy-making has evolved into a fine professional discipline changes have eluded the Indian system of governance. To compound matters, modern security issues are no more unidimensional in character and require multidisciplinary understanding and application. For instance, tackling of terrorism in India would require a sound understanding of plans and strategies of neighbouring countries sponsoring terrorism, the nuances of their intricate politico-strategic relations with India, the ideological and collaborative linkages of terrorist groups, inter- and intragroup relationships, tactics and technology of modern-day terrorists, and an understanding of centre-state relations and legal frameworks, to name just a few.

Moreover, there is a plethora of knowledge and ideas outside the government which should be factored in imaginatively for good policy-making. In a democracy this should further include trends in public thinking, views of political rivals and interest groups, opinions of think tanks and such-like. With the declining standards of governance, a perceptible decline in these capabilities is discernible at a time when security challenges have become most acute.

A Federal Fix

The second challenge to counter-terrorist policymaking emanates from the structural architecture of India's legal-constitutional framework itself. When designed, it did not foresee the type of complex internal security problems, like terrorism, emerging with trans-national and inter-state connectivities. With wars increasingly becoming cost ineffective and unpredictable instruments of achieving politico-strategic objectives, the modern world is witnessing emergence of fourth generation warfare—where the enemy is 'invisible'—as a substitute. Even the small and weaker states can take on their more powerful adversaries in this asymmetric warfare which largely targets internal security, with terrorism as its most favoured weapon. India has been witnessing the Pakistani onslaught of covert action now for nearly there decades.

In India, while national security, including internal security, is the responsibility of the Centre, most of the instruments—like powers to maintain law and order, the criminal administration system, police and prisons—are controlled by the constituent states. The states, keen to preserve their turf and apprehensive of the central government's political interference are unwilling to provide any space to the Centre that could empower it to take direct action in security related matters. This renders the task of a holistic tackling of internal security threats difficult.

While the states lack capabilities to cope with these threats on their own they are unwilling to allow any direct intervention by the Centre. This seriously limits the Centre's ability to formulate, execute, monitor and resource national counter terrorist policies in an effective and comprehensive manner. In this setting while the Centre's actions get confined to dishing out advisories, apprising the states of the threats in a generic way and providing funds for capacity building, the states operate in a tactical mode aimed at maintaining the law and order. This leaves little scope and space for formulating comprehensive national level counterterrorist policies. To make the matters worse, at times, the Centre sees even the bonafide requests of the states through a political prism undermining their genuine efforts towards capacity building. The Centre's refusal for over four years to clear the state legislations against organised crimes in Gujarat and some other BJP ruled states is illustrative. Incidentally, the draft Acts sent by them for approval was similar to an Act that exists in Maharashtra, a Congress-ruled state.

Framing the Counter-Terrorism Problem

Thirdly, the very nature of the terrorist phenomenon makes policy-making difficult. The first task of policy making is defining the objectives in tangible and positive terms that are sought to be achieved. But in fighting terrorism, the state largely achieve negative goals—preventing what the terrorists wish to do from happening. This list may include for instance, averting dismemberment or degradation of the state, preventing breakdown of the constitutional machinery, frustrating terrorist plans to kill citizens and their leader, and striking at vital installations. It will appear ridiculous for a government to claim all that has not happened as the list of their achievements. Success can not be computed on the basic of political goals denied, the innocent citizens who the terrorists could not kill, the leaders who were not attacked and vital installations which the terrorists wanted to destroy but could not.

Terrorist don't kill in the hope that their depredations will lead to attainment of their political goals, they kill to break the will of the government. Correlation between the policy initiatives taken by the government and their real impact on terrorism is also vague, diffused and a matter of subjective interpretation. For example, the efficacy of counter-terrorist laws, structural changes in the security apparatus, role of diplomatic initiatives, political engagement are all difficult to determine, at least in a short run. This provides scope for political decision-makers to take positions on political considerations as there are no clear policy rights and wrongs in the battle against terrorists.

The impediments and problems notwithstanding, gravity of the threat and its grave implications for India's security demand a policy-driven comprehensive national response. To make it happen there is a need for the two major political parties to develop a bipartisan approach towards response to terrorism. These parties should also take upon themselves the responsibility of convincing the state governments where they are in power to support legislative measures that could enable the Centre to play a more active role in handling terrorism and allied threats. A serious national debate was already overdue before November 26th, 2008. It has become vital now.

Critical Thinking

1. In what way has India's lack of a political vision compromised its counter-terrorism efforts?

2. How is India's internal framework itself a challenge to counter-terrorism policy making?

3. Why is a bipartisan approach to terrorism necessary in developing a policy-driven response?

Ajit Kumar Doval was formerly the head of India's Intelligence Bureau.

Imagining India: Ideas for the New Century

Vir Sanghvi

Over a year ago, at lunch in New York, Nandan Nilekani told me about his book. The idea of the book, he said, was ideas. If that sounded circular or complicated, it wasn't. Nandan's contention was that nations, societies and civilizations are shaped by ideas. And yet despite the fact that India itself is an idea, Indians are strangely reluctant to delve too deeply into the realm of ideas.

I provided a knee-jerk response: had Nandan been influenced by the success of *The World Is Flat*, the Thomas Friedman bestseller which took a cheerful look at globalisation and became, in itself, a global success story? The book had emerged out of a conversation with Nandan ("the world is flat," is his term) and contained many of his ideas.

Certainly, an Indian World Is Flat would work. The market is full of what we could call 'high concept' books in which the author takes a single idea (such as "the internet allows as greater access to products desired by a minority" or "intuitive judgments are the best ones") and turns it into a book, padding the pages with travelogues, anecdotes, gee-whiz! statistics and simplified versions of other people's theories or research.

But the more I spoke to Nandan, the clearer it became that what he had in mind was far more ambitious than a high concept bestseller. His model was less The World Is Flat and more Ramachandra Guha's masterly history of modern India. (And, in fact, Nandan thanks Guha in his acknowledgments as his 'mentor'. . . . . who stayed the course with me and was extraordinarily helpful. . . . .") But while that book concentrated on events, Nandan wanted to approach India through ideas.

A year later, when the first draft was ready he sent it to me (full disclosure: he has been my friend for nearly three decades which is why this does not pretend to be an objective review written by a disinterested critic) and I was staggered by the scope, range and ambition that the book displayed.

The first part looks at traditional ideas and how they've changed over the years. From worrying about our population, we've now gone to praising it as our human capital. And we've changed our minds about economic regulation too.

The second part examines ideas that are in the throes of change. For instance, we've accepted now that all that stuff about 'the real India is the India of the villages' is an incomplete vision. So, slowly but surely, we are coming to terms with urbanisation.

The third part deals with the clash of ideas—to use Nandan's words, "between people who see reforms as empowering and those who see them as exclusionary."

And the final section deals with the ideas that will shape our future: on health, energy, the environment etc.

In the book's 500-odd pages, Nandan deals with these issues in a manner that's neither condescending or simplistic. There are no profiles and travelogues here. There are precious few anecdotes and only the odd jokes. This is not designed to be some mass-market bestseller, read by purchase managers on plane journeys when they want to trade up from John Grisham. This is a big, serious and important book, one that requires attention and concentration while reading and one where the research (much of it by Devi Yesodharan) shows up on every page.

And yet, I think it will be a bestseller. I'm not a fan of the book's packaging (it is hideous; a complete aesthetic nightmare) but I can see why Penguin has put a soulfull picture of Nandan on the front cover: every intelligent young Indian has respect for his enormous achievements. I can also see why there's a very long quote from Thomas Friedman on the back cover too—everybody who bought *The World Is Flat* will want to buy this book. (Though the quote only tells half the story. Yes Nandan is a 'great explainer' but his real strength is as an original thinker.)

But I don't think the commercial considerations worry Nandan. Much has been made of the advance that Penguin paid him: the highest-ever paid for a non-fiction book. But frankly, such is his personal wealth that Nandan could probably buy Penguin India before breakfast and not notice.

I think he will be happy when the book becomes a bestseller because it will reach thousands of people. But his real concern is not with sales figures, it is with the ideas in the book. He wants them to provoke debate, to set off storms and to make us rethink some of our beliefs. As he says in his introduction "I hope this book is read by my peers, by people in business, media and the government—even if they only brandish it above their heads while loudly refuting my arguments. I would welcome the debate."

That sentiment is somehow typical of Nandan—and perhaps of the company he helped found. I find it interesting that his boss Narayana Murthy never wanted to be known as a corporate titan who created one of India's best companies. Rather, he wanted to be known for his views on Indian society and how we should live our lives.

So it is with Nandan. Though he describes himself as a 'stunted IIT nerd,' he has rarely made much of Infosys' success. His real passion lies in the world of ideas. He once told me (in an interview for the **HT**) that the biggest thrill for him was not when his company declared record profits but when his ideas entered the public domain and spurred discussion and debates.

I don't think it is a coincidence that his wife Rohini and he give away so much of their money each year. When the time comes to assess Nandan Nilekani's legacy, it's not the billions he wants us to count—it is his contribution to the world of ideas that matters.

And judging by this book, it is a contribution that will be remembered.

From *Hindustan Times*, December 22, 2008. Copyright © 2008 by Hindustan Times House. Reprinted by permission of HT Media Ltd.

Eight Top Managers Convicted over Bhopal Gas Leak Disaster

JAMES LAMONT

A court in the Indian city of Bhopal yesterday convicted one of the country's top industrialists and seven others of criminal negligence over the devastating gas leak at a Union Carbide plant that killed thousands of people more than 25 years ago.

The former members of Union Carbide's senior management in India were sentenced to two years in jail and fined Rps 100,000 ($2,100).

The sentence was met with derision by campaigners who said it showed how expendable Indian lives were in the face of corporate negligence and a fumbling judicial process.

The surviving seven defendants—one died as the case proceeded—may still be years away from any imprisonment as appeals are expected.

The December 1984 industrial accident at the pesticide plant in Bhopal was one of the world's worst industrial accidents.

The gas leak took the lives of more than 8,000 people within three days and left thousands more suffering toxic after-effects. The area still suffers from a high incidence of birth defects and chronic illnesses.

Today, Bhopal's plight highlights the perils of lax safety regulations and poor accountability in a country that is one of the fastest growing large economies in the world. Manmohan Singh, the prime minister, has described the accident as one that still "gnaws" at the collective conscience.

A $470m compensation payment agreed between Union Carbide and the government has been dogged with accusations that it was not fully disbursed to victims.

The most senior executive to be convicted was Keshub Mahindra, former chairman of Union Carbide's Indian subsidiary. He is currently chairman of Mahindra & Mahindra, one of the country's foremost industrial conglomerates.

Indian campaigners and state prosecutors have also pursued Warren Anderson, the 89-year-old former chairman of Union Carbide corporation in the US, over the past two decades.

But the US refused a request to extradite Mr Anderson in 2004. "The message of this [judgment] is that you can come here, play hell with people's lives and get away scot free," said Satyanath Sarangi, president of the Bhopal Group for Information and Action.

Union Carbide, now a subsidiary of Dow Chemical, yesterday said its former executives were not responsible for the misfortune of its Indian subsidiary.

"Union Carbide and its officials are not subject to the jurisdiction of Indian courts since they did not have any involvement in the operation of the plant, which was owned and operated by the UCIL (Union Carbide India Limited)," it said.

The convictions come as parliament weighs a nuclear liability bill that would cap compensation in case of an accident.

Critical Thinking

1. Do you feel the Union Carbide executives received a fair ruling in this case?

2. What role did the Indian government play? Was it diligent or lax in its response?

3. Does Union Carbide's (Dow's) reason for not assuming responsibility for the leak viable?

4. What strategies besides imposing stronger regulations and accountability should be implemented to address these types of issues in the future?

A Harvest of Water

Long at the mercy of the monsoons, some Indian farmers are sculpting hillsides to capture runoff, enriching their land and lives.

SARA CORBETT

Farmers in India do a lot of talking about the weather—especially, it seems, when there is no weather in sight. During the month of May, when the land heats up like a furnace and most fields lie fallow, when wells have run dry and the sun taunts from its broiling perch in a cloudless sky, there is no topic more consuming or less certain than when and how the summer monsoon will arrive. The monsoon season, which normally starts in early June and delivers more than three-quarters of the country's annual rainfall in less than four months, will begin gently, like a deer the farmers saw and later it will turn into a thundering elephant. Or it will start as an elephant and then turn into a deer. Or it will be erratic and annoying right through, like a chicken. In other words, nobody really knows. But still, everybody talks.

This was the case one day in 2008 when an extended family of farmers from a village called Satichiwadi climbed up to the hilltop temple of their village goddess, planning to ask her for rain. It was mid May and 106 degrees, and Satichiwadi, a village of 83 families that sits in a parched rural valley in the state of Maharashtra, about a hundred miles northeast of Mumbai, hadn't had any significant rainfall for seven months. Most of India at this point was caught in an inescapable annual wait. In New Delhi, the heat had triggered power cuts. Dust storms raced, unmitigated by moisture, across the northern states. Tanker trucks clogged the rural highways, delivering government sponsored loads of drinking water to villages whose wells had run dry. Meanwhile, radio newscasters were just beginning to track a promising swirl of rain clouds mining over the Andaman Islands, off the southeast coast.

All day, villagers had been speculating about those distant clouds. It was gambling time for rain-dependent farmers across India. In the weeks leading up to the monsoon, many would invest a significant amount of money, often borrowed, to buy fertilizer and millet seeds, which needed to be planted ahead of the rains. There were many ways to lose this wager. A delayed monsoon likely would cause the seeds to bake and die in the ground. Or if the rain fell too hard before the seedlings took root, it might wash them all away.

"Our lives are wrapped up in the rain," explained a woman named Anusayabai Pawar, using a countrywoman's version of Marathi, the regional language. "When it comes, we have everything. When it doesn't, we have nothing."

In the meantime, everyone kept scanning the empty sky. "Like fools," said an older farmer named Yamaji Pawar, sweating beneath his white Nehru cap, "we just sit here waiting."

IF THE PEOPLE OF SATICHIWADI once believed the gods controlled the rain, they were starting to move beyond that. Even as they carried betel nuts and cones of incense up to the goddess's temple, even as one by one the village women knelt down in front of the stone idol that represented her, they seemed merely to be hedging their bets. Bhaskar Pawar, a sober-minded, mustachioed farmer in his 30s, sat on one of the low walls of the temple, watching impassively as his female relatives prayed. "Especially the younger people here understand now that it's environmental," he said.

Satichiwadi lies in India's rain shadow, an especially water-deprived swath of land that includes much of central Maharashtra. Each year after the summer monsoon pounds the west coast of India, it moves inward across the plains and bumps against the 5,000-foot peaks of the Western Ghats, where the clouds stall out, leaving the leeward side punishingly dry.

In an effort to lessen their dependence on the monsoon, the villages residents had signed on to an ambitious, three-year watershed program designed to make more efficient use of what little rain does fall. The program was facilitated by a nonprofit group called the Watershed Organization Trust (WOTR), but the work—a major relandscaping of much of the valley—was being done by the villagers themselves. Teams of farmers spent an average of five days a week digging, moving soil, and planting seedlings along the ridgelines. WOTR, which has led similar projects in more than 200 villages in central India, paid the villagers for roughly 80 percent of the hours worked but also required every family to contribute free labor to the project every month—a deliberate move to get everyone invested.

From the vantage point of the temple, the effort was evident: Beyond the small grids of tile-roofed mud homes and the sun-crisped patchwork of dry fields, many of the russet brown hillsides had been terraced, and a number of freshly dug trenches sat waiting to catch the rain. If only, of course, the rain would come.

In Satichiwadi the anticipation was high. "Very soon," Bhaskar said, "we will know the value of this work."

COMPLEX AND CAPRICIOUS, the South Asian monsoon—widely considered the most powerful seasonal climate system on Earth, affecting nearly half the world's population—has never been easy to predict. And with global warming skewing weather patterns, it's not just the scientists who are confounded. Farmers whose families for generations have used the Panchangam, a thick almanac detailing the movement of the Hindu constellations, to determine when the monsoon rains are due and thus when to plant their crops, lament that their system no longer works reliably.

"It is a bit of a puzzle," said B. N. Goswami, director of the Indian Institute of Tropical Meteorology, based in Pune. After studying five decades of rain gauge data for central India, Goswami and his colleagues concluded that although the amount of rainfall has not changed, it is coming in shorter, more intense bursts, with fewer spells of light rain between, mirroring a larger pattern of extreme weather worldwide.

Groundwater has helped some farmers cope with erratic rains. But India's water tables are dropping precipitously, as farmers who now have access to electric pumps withdraw water faster than the monsoon can replenish it. According to the International Water Management Institute, based in Sri Lanka, half the wells once used in western India no longer function. "Thirty years ago we could strike water by digging 30 feet," said the village chief in Khandarmal, a dusty settlement of about 3,000 people perched on a ridge about 20 miles from Satichiwadi. "Now we have to go to 400 feet." Even that is chancy. Over the years the villagers have drilled a total of 500 wells. Ninety percent of them, he estimated, have gone dry.

Water shortages throw farmers into an unrelenting cycle of debt and distress, driving many—by one estimate up to a hundred million each year—to seek work in factories and distant, better irrigated fields. During the dry months, between November and May, you see them on the roads: families creaking along in bullock carts, truck taxis jammed with entire neighborhoods of people on the move. The stakes can seem impossibly high. According to government figures, the number of suicides among male farmers in Maharashtra tripled between 1995 and 2004.

One afternoon outside a sugarcane processing factory not far from Satichiwadi, I met a boy named Valmik. He was 16, with a sweet smile and out-turned ears, wearing a brown T-shirt and pants that were ripped across the seat. Standing in front of his bullock cart loaded with two tons of freshly cut sugarcane, he explained that he had driven his two-oxen cart 110 or so miles with his older brother and widowed mother to spend five months working in the fields with a sickle. His arms and hands were heavily scarred from the work.

Speaking softly, Valmik detailed one of the crueler paradoxes of rain dependence. A year earlier his family had borrowed 40,000 rupees (about $800) from a moneylender to cover expenses such as seeds and fertilizer for their fields at home

and hadn't been able to pay it back. Why? Because there hadn't been enough rain, and the seeds had broiled in the ground. What would they do when the debt was paid off? The same thing they'd done for the past three years after a season of cutting sugarcane: They would borrow again, plant more seeds, and revive their hopes for a decent monsoon.

GIVEN THE ENORMITY of India's water issues, encouraging single villages to revive and protect their own watersheds can seem a feeble response to a national crisis. But compared with controversial top-down, government-led efforts to build big dams and regulate the wanton drilling of deep wells, a careful grassroots effort to manage water locally can look both sensible and sustainable. When I visited Khandarmal with Ashok Sangle, one of the civil engineers who works for WOTR, the people there described a failed $500,000 development project to pump water several miles uphill from the nearest river. Sangle shook his head. "What is the logic of pulling water up a slope," he asked, "when you can more easily catch the rain as it flows down?"

The idea behind watershed development is simple: If people cut fewer trees, increase plant cover on the land, and build a well-planned series of dams and earthen terraces to divert and slow the downhill flow of rainwater, the soil has more time to absorb moisture. The terracing and new vegetation also control erosion, which keeps nutrient-rich topsoil from washing or blowing away, and this in turn boosts the productivity of agricultural land.

"Where the rain runs, we make it walk; where it walks, we make it crawl," explained Crispino Lobo, one of WOTR's founders, using an analogy the organization often employs when introducing the concepts behind watershed work to farmers. "Where it crawls, we make it sink into the ground." Runoff is reduced. The water table for the whole area rises, wells are less apt to go dry, and especially with some simultaneous efforts to use water more efficiently, everybody needs to worry less about when it will rain again.

The benefits—at least hypothetically—spool outward from here. More productive farmland means more food and better health for the villagers, and it opens the possibility of growing cash crops. "The first thing people do when their watershed regenerates and their income goes up," Lobo said, "is to take their kids out of the fields and put them in school."

Lobo began working on water issues in the early 1980s through a development program funded by the German government. WOTR is now directed by Marcella D'Souza, a medical doctor and Lobo's wife, whose efforts to involve women in watershed redevelopment have earned international recognition. They believe there is an important emotional dimension to watershed work as well. "If people are able to improve the land and restore the soil, you start seeing a change in how they see themselves," Lobo said. "The land reflects some hope back at them."

To be clear, this is not always easy. Since the late 1990s, both the Indian government and a variety of nongovernmental organizations have funneled some $500 million annually into redeveloping watersheds in drought-prone rural areas. But experts say many such endeavors have fallen short of their goals or proved unsustainable, in large part because they have focused too much on the technical aspects of improving a watershed and too little on navigating the complex social dynamics of farming villages. In other words, no effort gets very far without a lot of hands-on cooperation. And if you're wondering what could possibly be so complex about a smallish group of marginal farmers living in the middle of nowhere, you should go to Satichiwadi and spend some time with the Kales and the Pawars.

SATICHIWADI LIES several miles off a two-lane road that crosses a high, semiarid plain dotted with meager-looking farms and drought-resistant neem trees. The road to the village, completed last year, remains little more than an axle-smashing series of dirt switchbacks descending some 600 vertical feet from the high bluffs to the flat valley floor. Many of the villagers still come and go the old-fashioned way, making a 45-minute, sweaty hike up a vertiginous footpath.

Members of the Pawar family like to say they got here first, about a hundred years ago, when this was a mostly uninhabited, forested place, and great-grandfather Soma Pawar, a nomadic shepherd belonging to the Thakar tribe, made his way down from the high buttes and liked what he saw. Sometime after that—precisely how long is in dispute—great-grandfather Goma Genu Kale, also a Thakar, is said to have ambled in and taken up residence as well.

For a time the Kale and Pawar families got along just fine, living close together in a small group of thatched-roof, mud-brick homes built near the temple. Working together, they cleared trees and tilled the land to grow rice and other grains. Then, about 40 or 50 years ago, the Kales abruptly moved to the other side of the valley. The reason is also in dispute: The Kales say they simply got tired of tromping the half mile or so back and forth to their millet fields. The Pawars say, somewhat huffily, that the Kales got sick of the Pawars.

Whatever the case, the two families—despite being separated by no more than 500 yards of fields—stopped talking. They held their own independent holy weeks to celebrate the goddess Sati and pointedly stopped attending one another's weddings. The Pawars stopped calling the Kales by name, referring to them instead as the "Fed Up People." The hamlet where the Kales now live is known simply as Vaitagwadi, Fed Up Town.

As Satichiwadi's harmony deteriorated, another kind of diminishment began. Sheep and cows trampled the grassland; the last of the trees disappeared. Crops too began to falter. Farmers gave up growing rice, which required so much water. By March each year, most of the wells across the valley had dried up.

With both food and income scarce, villagers started migrating to work on sugarcane plantations, on road crews, and in brick factories. "If you had come even three years ago during the dry season," Sitaram Kale, a farmer who also owns a small shop in Satichiwadi, told me, "you would have found only very old people and very small children living here."

The villagers did not easily come around to the idea that they could work together and revive the valley. Getting them to set aside their differences took months of meetings, several

exploratory "exposure visits" to other villages where WOTR's watershed programs had been successful, and the diligent attention of a high-energy young social worker named Rohini Raosaheb Hande, who hiked the path into Satichiwadi every other day for six months. Hande was the second social worker WOTR had sent to Satichiwadi; the first had quit after a few weeks. "She told me it was a place without hope," Hande recalled. "Nobody would even talk to her."

Such resistance is common. In the village of Darewadi, where the watershed work was completed in 2001, one villager had chased WOTR employees away with an ax. Because the organization encourages simultaneous social reconfiguration and environmental change, its efforts often initially rub farmers the wrong way. WOTR mandates, for example, that village-level water decisions include women, landless people, and members of lower castes, all of whom might ordinarily be excluded. To give the local greenery a chance to recover, villagers must also agree to a multiyear ban on free-grazing their animals and cutting trees for firewood. Finally, they must trust the potential benefits of watershed work enough to sign on to the sheer tedium it entails—three to five years spent using pickaxes and shovels to move dirt from one spot to another to redirect the flow of rainwater.

In Darewadi an elderly farmer named Chimaji Avahad, who lives with his extended family in a brightly painted two-room home hemmed in by sorghum fields, recalled the early difficulties of adjusting to the new rules. He was taken aback, he told me, by the talkative women who filled his life. "Each one of them—my wife, daughters, daughters-in-law, and even granddaughters—has an opinion," he said, amused. His wife, Nakabai, a tiny woman with a face wizened by years working in the fields, immediately chimed in, "It was a very good change."

A walk around Darewadi confirms this. By all accounts a grim and waterless place before the project began more than a decade ago, it now boasts bushes and trees and fields of wild grass. The village's wells now remain full, even at the height of the dry season. With more water, Darewadi's farmers are getting their first taste of prosperity, moving from producing only enough millet to feed themselves to growing onions, tomatoes, pomegranates, and lentils and selling the surplus in nearby market towns. Avahad now puts about 5,000 rupees (about a hundred dollars) a year in the bank. Darewadi's women have used their new influence to ban the sale of alcohol and also have formed women's savings groups—a common feature of WOTR projects—that collect a small monthly fee and in turn loan money to members who need it to pay for weddings or veterinary care or the solar lights that now dot the village at night.

WHEN I RETURNED TO SATICHIWADI in January, the villagers were finding some hope in their own land. The young trees on the ridgetops were green and thriving. The hills and fields had been contoured with small dams and trenches, looking like tidy ripples arcing across a brownish pond. Bhaskar Pawar—the farmer who had sat in the temple with me eight months earlier, waiting to see whether the watershed work would pay off—excitedly reported that the water level in the village wells was about ten feet higher than normal. And this was a good thing, because the monsoon had once again confounded the villagers. Not a drop had fallen over the valley during the month of June or in the first three weeks of July. Their millet seeds had withered and died. "It was a miserable time," Bhaskar recalled.

And yet when the rain did come—in torrents in late July—they were ready to catch the water and put it to use. They'd spent the fall months harvesting tomatoes. Now they were working on onions and sorghum. And they were also harvesting something less tangible: a newfound, tenuous harmony.

One morning I watched as Sitaram Kale, the shopkeeper and one of nine members of the Village Watershed Development Committee, rode his bike over to the Pawars' settlement to spread the word about a watershed-related meeting to be held later in the dusty schoolyard on his side of town. He passed the news to a voluble, grandmotherly woman named Chandrakhanta Pawar, who disseminated it by ducking her head into several of her neighbors' homes, assuring that each would come and participate. "There's a meeting later this morning over in Fed Up Town," she announced. "One of the Fed Up People just came over to say so."

Critical Thinking

1. What are the major advantages of a watershed program?

2. Why isn't the annual monsoon season itself enough to provide an adequate supply of water?

3. How does the social role of the farmer affect the success of watershed programs?

From *National Geographic*, November 2009, pp. 110–127. Copyright © 2009 by National Geographic Society. Reprinted by permission.

The Loom of Youth

James Lamont

In Stanford University's MBA class of 2001, Jyotiraditya Scindia joined almost every business group he could. The Maharaja of Gwalior, central India, lent his name to the venture capital club, high technology club, private equity club and the entrepreneur club.

Today, as minister of state for commerce and industry, the same youthful enthusiasm for business combined with experience as an investment banker at Morgan Stanley has matured into something strikingly purposeful.

His spreadsheets and daily updated "to do" lists are a refreshing break from a more familiar image of slow-moving files and socialist policies in the world's largest democracy. Yet his business-like approach, and that of some of his young peers, is appropriate for a fast-growing large economy outstripped only by China. One way of reaching double-digit economic growth is, he says, to improve the country's governance and delivery.

"No form stays on my desk for more than 10 minutes," he says, BlackBerry in hand and with an eye on rolling news on a nearby plasma screen. "There is a quick turnover."

It is not just bureaucratic process in the throes of a turnround. The 39-year-old Mr Scindia is an example of a broader change taking place in the upper echelons of the world's largest democracy: the emergence of a generation of politicians that hopes to steer India's global integration and rising economic power in coming decades.

More than 70 percent of the population of 1.2bn is under the age of 35—a statistic some claim puts the country at an advantage to aging societies in China, Japan and Europe.

"Every 25 years there is a generational shift in politics," says Mr Scindia. "But what's different this time around is the huge demographic dividend in India. It's a unique opportunity."

The most prominent of the new generation is Rahul Gandhi, 39-year-old great-grandson of Jawaharlal Nehru, India's first prime minister. Others include the children of ministers and parliamentarians, and the daughter of a Bollywood actor turned politician. Many have been educated abroad, often in North America, have worked for multinational corporations and share a pro-market world view.

They are also more likely to grasp the benefits technology can deliver in a country where fast-growing mobile technology and television is helping deliver information and aspirations to hundreds of millions for the first time. At the same time they are careful to describe themselves as "agriculturalists"—a clear appeal to the large rural population (and electorate).

"These younger people are very much in sync with what is happening at the cutting edge in India and the world, particularly how young people think and respond," says Amit Mitra of the Federation of Indian Chambers of Commerce and Industry. "They may be able to connect with ideas and perhaps debate ideas about tomorrow's India."

For international investors, keen to tap the country's considerable potential but often bewildered by complex social and political structures, the emergence of this younger, well travelled generation is welcome. Their support for opening up the economy wins plaudits from those long thwarted by barriers implemented by earlier generations.

Executives passing through New Delhi, the capital, now like to include meetings with MPs such as Agatha Sangma, minister of state for rural development, Tathagata Satpathy of Orissa or Dushyant Singh from Rajasthan, in their schedules.

Such recognition has yet to be fully matched in politics. Few of the younger generation have yet made it to the Lok Sabha, the national parliament, where the average age of an MP is 53; the cabinet is filled with people in their 60s and 70s. However, with the left-of-centre Congress party of Prime Minister Manmohan Singh expecting to be in power for the next decade, members of the business-savvy younger generation are confident of becoming central actors.

Their mix of competence and international experience is seen as desirable to their party in a country seeking to increase its share of trade, investment and global output. Mr Singh has appealed to young people in the diaspora to return to take up jobs in public service and politics. Congress, led by its party president Sonia Gandhi, has embarked on a campaign to bring young leaders into its ranks and swell party membership in opposition-held states such as Uttar Pradesh, one of the poorest; industrial Gujarat; and Punjab, the grain belt.

Yet for all their promise, many of the cohort remain reluctant to view themselves as part of an emphatic shift down the age pyramid, stressing the valued mix of youth and experience in a government where the prime minister is 77, his finance minister 74.

In Indian politics, and society at large, age counts. Atal Behari Vajpayee, former prime minister and head of the Hindu nationalist Bharatiya Janata party government, once pointed out that an Indian politician is born at the age of 50, becomes a teenager at 60 and a young man at 70.

Young politicians are seldom given much responsibility in government. "Among the elders who run the parties there is a dictum that they are reluctant to give cabinet jobs to young politicians . . . on the grounds that experience counts and that you need to be tried and tested for the big jobs," says Karan Thapar, a political analyst. "There is an attitude to hold the young back."

That view is being challenged. As Sachin Pilot, a 32-year-old minister, puts it: "We are going to see a civil society accepting a leadership that doesn't have to have an experience of 40 years."

But the new generation still faces considerable hurdles. In the past month, one novice politician has come to grief. Shashi Tharoor, 54, a quick-witted former UN official, was elected in last year's parliamentary polls as a first-time MP. His free-talking, irreverent style and embrace of modern technology—he likes to Twitter—earned him enemies long before he became embroiled in a cricket scandal that cost him his job.

Indian businesspeople and commentators frequently explain the behaviour of their people with the analogy of crabs in a box. If one tries to climb out, others will pull him back down. Mr Tharoor was hauled back down.

Nonetheless, Congress party strategists have clearly seen the potential of youth. They have sought to harness the power of India's demographics in a way that the BJP has not.

The champion of the movement is Mr Gandhi, scion of the Nehru-Gandhi dynasty and a central figure in Congress's plans to stay in power. Rather than taking executive office, he has devoted himself to bringing young people into the party, reviving its internal democracy and travelling the land with a message of renewal. The strategy has paid off. He is in part credited with Congress's strong victory in the 2009 general election.

The BJP, among whose own youthful leaders are Mr Gandhi's cousin, Varun, and Manvendra Singh, son of a former finance minister, has yet to come up with an answer.

Yet as long as Mr Gandhi, the "*yuvraj*" or prince as he is known, remains out of cabinet, none of his peers will be allowed to take a big executive job. "It's a problem to rise ahead of the heir apparent," says Mr Thapar. "The Congress party will have been in power for 10 years and it didn't build a future prime minister by putting him through the top portfolios."

The impetus for greater recognition of youth comes from Mr Gandhi's mother, Sonia, to whom some of the party's rising stars ascribe their ascent. The Italian-born wife of assassinated prime minister Rajiv has proved a shrewd operator in reviving her family's party's fortunes. She is also nostalgic for the era of her husband's rule in the 1980s, when he drew around him thinkers, including friends from his days at India's elite Doon School. Today, she is handpicking leaders such as Mr Pilot and Priya Dutt, a rising star in Mumbai politics.

Malvika Singh, the editor of *Seminar Magazine* and a Delhi-based political pundit, says Mrs Gandhi has skilfully turned around old enmities. Mr Pilot's father served under former prime minister Narasimha Rao, who tried to reduce the influence of the Gandhi family in Congress party politics. The father

of Jitin Prasada, minister of state for petroleum and natural gas, was a close adviser to Mr Rao. Ms Sangma's father was the speaker of parliament and a leader of a splinter from the Congress party, the Nationalist Congress Party.

"Everyone who has attacked her, she has gone on to make peace with their children," says Ms Singh.

The flaw in the design is India's inability to break with dynasty. The widest criticism is that the new generation's advancement is a result of family pedigree. Many started careers in business only, in some cases after personal tragedy, to heed a political calling similar to their parents'.

Ms Sangma, from a political family in the northeast, acknowledges the benefits of family ties. She says she has achieved a ministerial job in her 20s while someone without her pedigree could take 30 years just to get a parliamentary nomination.

The leg-up draws scorn in some quarters. "Politics is just like business and Bollywood in this country," says Bharat Kewalramani, a Mumbai-based businessman critical of the political order. "It just runs in the family."

However, he predicts that rising incomes will disrupt family political franchises within as little as 12 years, and that ruling families will find potent challengers for their pocket boroughs. As the middle class grows, he says, these voters will want to see people more like themselves in the Lok Sabha, and not simply younger offspring of established families.

Mr Scindia is already anticipating an era where performance will score higher than lineage. He overhauled the post office with a strategy called Project Arrow, supported by McKinsey and advertising agency Ogilvy and Mather, in his previous job. Today, his focus is cutting transaction costs to boost the competitiveness of Indian industry.

The university clubs of Stanford and the voters of Madhya Pradesh never knew they had so much in common.

The Gandhi Scion Tipped to Be Prime Minister Who Eschews Office for Now

Rahul Gandhi (above), 39. Son of Rajiv Gandhi, the assassinated former prime minister, and Sonia Gandhi, the president of the Congress party, he is the scion of India's most powerful political family. He has eschewed ministerial office to focus on youth politics and reviving Congress's fortunes in Uttar Pradesh, the most populous state. His constituency in the state is Amethi, a family seat held by Feroze Gandhi—his grandfather, husband of Indira Gandhi—and he is strongly tipped as a future prime minister. Mr Gandhi travels constantly across the country but is regarded by his peers as a modern thinker able to take breaks from a consuming political life. Although his education was interrupted by security concerns following his father's murder in 1991, he attended Doon School, India's equivalent of Eton, Rollins College in Florida and Cambridge University, where he took a postgraduate degree in development economics. He also worked for three years in London at the Monitor Group, a management consultancy.

Sachin Pilot, 32. Minister for telecommunications and information technology. One of the most promising new leaders and a close ally of Rahul Gandhi. Urbane and accessible, he gave up a career at General Motors to go into politics after his father, a former air force pilot and internal security minister, died in a car crash. Educated at the universities of Delhi and Pennsylvania, he is an accomplished marksman, pilots small planes and has written a book in honour of his father. Sara, his wife, is sister of Omar Abdullah, chief minister of Kashmir. His constituency is in Ajmer in Rajasthan.

Omar Abdullah, 40. Chief minister of Jammu and Kashmir. Ministerial goals including keeping a lid on secessionist violence in the territory disputed with Pakistan and scaling down presence of the Indian army, cause of much resentment. British born and educated in India and Scotland, he comes from one of Kashmir's leading families. His grandfather founded the Muslim Conference in 1932; his father is a government minister. Became MP for Ganderbal in Kashmir 12 years ago and has also served as minister for commerce and industry.

Jitin Prasada, 36. Minister for petroleum and natural gas. Though his recent wedding to a former television presenter won bigger headlines than his ministerial work, he has held two portfolios, including minister for steel. Previously worked in banking but decided to follow his father, former vice-president of the Congress party and adviser to prime ministers Rajiv Gandhi and Narasimha Rao, into politics. He was educated in India at Doon School, the Shri Ram College of Commerce at Delhi University and the Indian Management Institute. His constituency is in Uttar Pradesh.

Priya Dutt, 43. Health activist. Combines a political pedigree with the glamour of Bollywood. As a Congress party MP, she has earned a reputation for facing down local communal politics. Her father was an actor turned politician; her brother is one of the most familiar faces in Indian contemporary film. A sociology graduate of Mumbai University, she was encouraged to enter politics by Sonia Gandhi and remains loyal to the Congress

party president. Represents Mumbai North in India's financial capital.

Agatha Sangma, 29. Minister for rural development. The youngest government minister comes from one of the best-known political families in the northeast. Her father was the speaker of parliament and her siblings are all involved in politics in her home state of Meghalaya, where they belong to the Nationalist Congress party. She trained as a lawyer in Delhi has a diploma in environmental development, and now has responsibility for water and sanitation. She also represents the aspirations of the northeast, often viewed as a marginal part of the country. Her constituency is Tura in Meghalaya.

Varun Gandhi, 30. National secretary of the Bharatiya Janata party. Rahul Gandhi's first cousin is seen as the black sheep of the Nehru-Gandhi dynasty. Broke with family tradition to join the Hindu nationalist BJP, and stirred controversy with remarks seen as anti-Muslim during the 2009 general election campaign. Acclaimed in the BJP for strong leadership qualities and is a trump card in its fight to neutralise power of Gandhi brand. Has written on national security and holds an economics degree from London University. His constituency is in Uttar Pradesh.

Jyotiraditya Scindia, 39. Minister for commerce and industry. One of the most experienced young politicians, already in his second ministerial post. Entered politics after a career in investment banking following the death of his father—who was seen as a possible prime minister—in an air crash in 2001. Studied at Harvard and Stanford Business School. Helped set up Morgan Stanley's India office and maintains interest in venture capital through Mumbai—based Scindia Investments. Inherited the title Maharaja of Gwalior and is MP for Guna in Madhya Pradesh, central India.

Critical Thinking

1. In what way is demographics in India an advantage in its economic/business realm?

2. What role does age play in Indian politics?

3. What are the pros and cons to India's strong family ties in politics?

On Using the Final Argument

Harsh V. Pant

The hijacking of the ship MV *Stolt Valor* with 18 Indians aboard underlined the need for a proactive stance by the Indian Navy in protecting India's sea-borne trade as well as deterring piracy alongside other navies deployed in this crucial region. But for long the Indian government continued to make a show of its usual dithering. The Defence Minister explicitly ruled out hot pursuit of pirates "as a policy" because "it has wider implications." After having finally decided to send its naval warships to the Gulf of Aden, it is to be hoped that Indian political and military leadership will now evolve coherent policy towards the use of force in securing Indian economic and strategic interests.

There is a broader issue at stake. India is increasingly being perceived as a global player, a power whose military capabilities are expanding and which has always had highly professional armed forces well-ensconced in a liberal democratic polity. A rapidly growing economy has given India the ability to spend on its defence readiness like never before. India has emerged as one of the largest arms buyers in the global market in the last few years. In line with India's broadening strategic horizons, its military acquisitions are seeing a marked shift from conventional land based systems to means of power projection such as airborne refueling systems and long-range missiles. But it remains unclear under what conditions India would be willing to use force in defending its interests.

This question needs some immediate answers and the nation's civilian and military leaderships have let the nation down by not articulating a vision for the use of Indian military assets. If at all some suggestions are being made, they have verged on being facile. For example, ruling out sending of troops to Afghanistan, the army chief had suggested that "India takes part only in UN approved and sanctioned military operations, and (since) the UN has not mandated this action in Afghanistan there is no question of India participating in it." Such displays of lack of appreciation of underlying international politics make it easier for the Indian government to ignore the military leadership when making decisions. The army chief's statement demonstrated a fundamental misreading of Indian security policy.

Much like other nations, India has tended to accept or ignore the United Nations as per the demands of its vital national interests. India cannot cede authority to international organisations as ineffective as the UN on matters of national security and if history is any guide India has done exactly that.

However, the Indian leadership has in recent times given an impression that the role it sees for India in global security is not shaped by its own assessment of its interests and values but rather by the judgements of global institutions like the UN. The Indian armed forces remain concerned with China and Pakistan while the civilian leadership lacks any substantive and sophisticated understanding of the role of force in foreign and security policy.

Military power, more often than not, affects the success with which other instruments of state-craft are employed as it always lurks in the background of inter-state relations, even when nations are at peace with each other. Military power remains central to the course of international politics as force retains its role as the final arbiter among states in an anarchical international system. States may not always need to resort to the actual use of force but military power vitally affects the manner in which states deal with each other even during peace time despite what the protagonists of globalisation and international institutions might claim.

A state's diplomatic posture will lack effectiveness if it is not backed by a credible military posture. In the words of Thomas Schelling, "Like the threat of a strike in industrial relations, the threat of divorce in a family dispute, or the threat of bolting the party at a political convention, the threat of violence continuously circumscribes international politics." Even in the age of nuclear weapons, contrary to suggestions in some quarters that the utility of force has declined, military strategy has merely morphed into the art of coercion, of intimidation, a contest of nerves and risk-taking and what has been termed as "the diplomacy of violence."

Such diplomacy of violence, however, has been systematically factored out of Indian foreign policy and national security matrix with the resulting ambiguity about India's ability to withstand major threats of the future. Few nations face the kind of security challenges that confront India. Yet, since independence, military power was never seen as a central instrument in the achievement of Indian national priorities, with the tendency of Indian political elites to downplay its importance. Even though the policy-makers themselves had little knowledge of critical defence issues, the armed forces had little or no role in the formulation of defence policy till 1962. Divorcing foreign policy from military power was a recipe for disaster as India realised in 1962 when even Nehru was forced to concede that "military weakness has been a temptation, and a little military strength may be a deterrent." A state's legitimacy is tied to its ability to monopolise the use of force and operate effectively in an international strategic environment and India had lacked clarity on this relationship between the use of force and its foreign policy priorities.

A lot of attention is being paid to the fact that India will be spending around $40 billion on military modernisation in the next five years and is buying military hardware—such as C-130 transport planes, airborne refuelling tankers, and aircraft carriers—useful for projection of power far beyond its shores. But such purchases in and of themselves does not imply a clear sense of purpose. Indian armed forces are today operating in a strategic void under a weak leadership unable to fully comprehend the changing strategic and operational milieu. At a time when Indian interests are becoming global in nature, India cannot continue with its moribund approach of yore. It is up to the civilian leadership to come up with a credible policy on the use of armed forces and it is up to the military leadership to provide them sound guidance.

India has always been a nation of great ambition but today more than ever it needs to answer the question: What is the purpose behind its ambition? India wants to rise, but what for? It's not clear if India's political elite understand the implications of their nation's rise. India can no longer afford to sit on the sidelines of unfolding global events that impinge directly on vital Indian interests.

Critical Thinking

1. What are the implications of having a strong military program without a vision behind it?

2. Is it realistic for a country to allow the UN to determine its policies?

3. Besides trade and the threat of piracy, what other reasons warrant India having a strong military presence to protect its borders?

HARSH V PANT teaches at King's College London.

From *Pragati: The India National Interest Review*, December 2008, pp. 19–20. Copyright © 2008 by The Indian National Interest. Licensed under Creative Commons Attribution 2.5 India license: http//creativecommons.org/licenses/by/2.5/in/

Pakistan, the State That Has Refused to Fail

DAVID PILLING

Just 18 months ago Hillary Clinton declared there was an "existential threat" to **Pakistan.** The Taliban had occupied the picturesque Swat valley and imposed sharia law only 100 miles from Islamabad. With militancy on the rise in almost every corner of the country and bomb blasts thundering across its cities, the nuclear-armed state did indeed appear to be in peril.

Only weeks after the US secretary of state's intervention, Pakistani troops poured into Swat. Several hundred militants were killed and more than 2m refugees fled in the biggest internal displacement of people since the Rwandan genocide. The Swat campaign was "a watershed moment," according to Salman Taseer, governor of Punjab and an ally of the civilian government of President Asif Ali Zardari. "It was a battle for life and death. If we hadn't survived that, who knows?"

Who knows indeed. Yet watershed moments are hardly a rarity in **Pakistan,** a state that lurches from crisis to crisis like a bus stuck in first gear (and lacking brakes and headlights to boot). Since the army imposed a tenuous order on Swat, **Pakistan** has been buffeted by the mother of all floods, a fresh wave of suicide bombings and what Maleeha Lodhi, former ambassador to the US, calls "layer upon layer of economic crises."

Yet **Pakistan** has survived. In its partial victories against Islamist militants it may even have made some kind of progress. It is all too easy to think of **Pakistan** as a failing—even a failed—state. But it might be better to see it as the state that refuses to fail.

To appreciate just how remarkable this is, cast your mind back to this dangerous year's catalogue of fire and brimstone. First, following its victory in Swat, the army turned its attention on South Waziristan, bombarding militants in lawless areas bordering Afghanistan. Many considered that an important step, given the well-documented links between the Inter-Services Intelligence (ISI) spy agency and tribal militants, part of **Pakistan's** quest for "strategic depth" in Afghanistan.

Second, and partly as a result of the army's offensives, there has been a wave of counterattacks on hotels, mosques and police stations. Last October, militants mounted a brazen raid on the supposedly impregnable headquarters of the 500,000-strong army. That led to alarm that men with beards and a less-than-glowing feeling towards America were getting perilously close to **Pakistan's** nuclear arsenal.

Third, **Pakistan** has had to adapt to a dramatic shift in US policy towards Afghanistan. In December, President Barack Obama ordered a surge of 30,000 extra troops, a military intensification that has sent militants scurrying across the border into **Pakistan.** Worse from Islamabad's point of view, the US president has committed to drawing down those troops from next summer, a retreat, if it happens, that would once again leave **Pakistan** alone in a nasty neighbourhood.

Fourth, the economic outlook remains precarious. **Pakistan** just about avoided a balance of payments crisis which, at one point, saw its reserves dwindle to just one month's import cover. But respite has come at the cost of being in hock to the International Monetary Fund, which has extended some $7bn in loans. With tax receipts at a miserable 9 percent of output, it is unclear how it will make ends meet.

As if these man-made calamities were not enough, **Pakistan** has been drowning in the worst floods in its history. At one point, no less than one-fifth of the country was under water. Imran Khan, the cricket idol turned politician, describes seeing buffalo swept up in the engorged rivers like pieces of paper. With crops failing, millions made homeless and the threat of disease looming, many warned that the flood would prove the final straw for **Pakistan.**

Remarkably it has not been. Why not? A partial explanation for **Pakistan's** staying power is that it has become an extortionary state that thrives on crisis. Islamabad is well versed in the art of prising cash out of panicked donors by sidling ever-more convincingly towards the abyss. Not even the most ardent conspiracy theorist could accuse **Pakistan** of manufacturing its own floods. But, as documents released by WikiLeaks confirmed, the state has long maintained a deeply ambiguous relationship with the very elements threatening to tear it apart.

There are more benign explanations too. The strength of civil society has helped. Many refugees from the floods, like those from Swat, have found temporary shelter with the networks of friends and relatives that bind the country together. The army's response to the floods has also underscored, for better or worse, the efficiency of the state's best-run institution. Even the civilian administration, weak and discredited as it is, has clung on. If, as now seems plausible, Mr Zardari can survive, power could yet be transferred from one democratically elected administration to another for the first time in **Pakistan's** 63-year history.

One should not overstate **Pakistan's** resilience. The world is rightly alarmed at the mayhem that rages at its centre. But, if you care to look on the bright side, you might conclude that, if **Pakistan** can survive a year like this, it can survive anything.

Critical Thinking

1. Why was the Swat campaign a "watershed moment"?

2. Paksitan endured several crises over the past year alone. Discuss them and their larger implications.

3. What are some reasons for Pakistan's resilence?

US-Pakistan Relations

The Geo-strategic and Geopolitical Factors

JEHANGIR KHAN

US-Pakistan relations are greatly indebted to the geo-strategic and geopolitical significance of the latter. There is no denying the fact that geography controls the political environment of a country and the same is true about Pakistan. Besides opportunities, the geography poses some challenges too. There is no escape from one's geography and from its impact on one's policies. The security of a state largely depends upon the extent to which it adopts a vigilant policy towards her neighbors that postulates a sound frontier policy. It is also stated by the scholars of international politics and diplomacy that the defense and foreign policies of the 'small' and 'weak' states do contribute to shape regional and international politics. All these are true for Pakistan. Looking at the past, it can be seen that owing to the strategic worth of South Asia, it has always been the focus of world attention and after the partition of Indian subcontinent in 1947 into two independent states of Pakistan and India, its importance remained the same. Both the states were viewed as key players in checking the influence of communist threat emanating from both Soviet Union and China.

In 1947, possessing a unique geographical location, Pakistan consisted of two distant parts; the West Pakistan, in the Indus River basin and the East Pakistan (later on became Bangladesh in December 1971) located more than 1000 miles (1600 kilometers) away in the Ganges River delta. Separated from each other, these two wings had 1000km wide Indian territory between them. On the West, Pakistan borders with Afghanistan, whose one kilometer narrow *Wahkhan* strip kept the defunct Soviet Union away from Pakistani frontiers. To the North, she has the Peoples Republic of China. The oil rich heart of the Persian Gulf region–Iran, is in the northwest of Pakistan. In the South, the Arabian Sea, the northwestern extension of the strategically important Indian Ocean washes Pakistan's coastal shores. The vitality of the Indian Ocean has remained unquestionable throughout the known history as it provides not only a commercial and trade link between Europe and the Far East but has also remained a key to the seven seas. The East Pakistan was separating the Pacific Ocean from the Indian Ocean and bordered Burma on the East. Thus, looking from the strategic point of view, Pakistan was and is still at the crossroad of Central, South and Southwest Asia and is the easiest link between the oil-rich Persian Gulf and the East Asia. In short, Pakistan is situated in the region called 'fulcrum of Asia' the strategic centre on which the stability of the Asia depends. Apart from enjoying the proximity with the strategically significant regions, Pakistan, until the disintegration of the Soviet Union, faced the grave geopolitical realities on the ground as it was in the most troublesome region where the clash of interests between the two superpowers of that time was imminent. There were also certain intra-regional conflicts that were startling Pakistan and added much to her agonies. The circumstances of Pakistan's origin and the composition as well as the unique geographical features (especially from 1947 to 1971) had made it particularly a security-conscious country. At the same time she was faced with economic deficiencies as a newly independent state.

Looking at the geostrategic scenario of the region, it becomes obvious that Pakistan was faced with a generally hostile geopolitical and geo-strategic environment because of the pattern of her relationship with her immediate neighbors i.e. India and Afghanistan. The Indo-Pak relations had always been characterized by mutual distrust, hostility and serious disagreements on regional and international political issues since day one of their creation in 1947. India had not accepted Pakistan and she was constantly engaged in weakening Pakistan. The Indian leaders wanted the hegemony of India over the entire subcontinent. To achieve that end, they were openly striving to merge Pakistan with India. The forceful annexation of the Muslim States of Hyderabad (Deccan) and Kashmir in 1947–1948, the deployment of a massive part of her army and all her armor on Pakistani border and imposition of a war, just within a year of partition, were clear indications of the Indian hegemonic designs. India was applying not only warfare tactics but was also exerting political and psychological pressure of relentless propaganda against the very *raison d'être* of the origin of Pakistan. Indian leadership, with the help of some other countries, was also engaged in isolating Pakistan from the comity of nations. Pakistan was in a real stalemate and she had to look for an external ally to check the Indian designs. Therefore, the entire edifice of Pakistan's foreign policy was based upon Indian fear.

Pakistan's relations with her western neighbor–Afghanistan, had also been far from cordial due to the *Pukhtoonistan* issue. It was in 1947, that the Afghan government denounced the 1893's Anglo-Afghan treaty of the demarcation of an international boundary between Afghanistan and India (then a British colony). She also launched her irredentist claim over the North Western Pukhtoon populated area and started supporting secessionist elements in Pakistan. Afghanistan was also pampered by India by extending support on this issue. Afghanistan also had the Soviet Union on her back. Moreover, Afghanistan was the only country to vote against Pakistan's admission into the United Nations. This wave of tension kept creeping under the carpet but was not allowed by King Zahir Shah, the then Afghan king, to take a violent form although his cousin Sardar Mohammad Daud was fanning it. However, Pakistan had a perception of resurrection of this issue.

This precarious geopolitical situation confronted Pakistan with two-fold security concerns. This fear was further aggravated due to the narrow strategic waist of Pakistan as all her major cities were border outposts especially one of her provincial capitals, Peshawar, was just next to the border.

In such a grim geopolitical milieu, Pakistan needed a strong, modern, well-equipped and hard-hitting army capable of combating any threat arising from her western or eastern border that could jeopardize her national security and territorial integrity. Pakistan had a number of options for making her security invincible and to keep her national integrity intact. But the common democratic ideals, the westernized bureaucratic set-up and, above all, the inclination of her armed forces towards the United States pushed Pakistan to opt for a close US-Pakistan relationship in order to get a strong external equalizer against the regional threats to her national security and territorial integrity. Pakistani leaders were fully aware of the strategic importance of this nascent state. These leaders even could not afford to ignore the geopolitical compulsion of their country for they had influenced the course of Pakistan's foreign policy throughout the history. Moreover, the economic needs of the country were considered to be best catered by the economically potent United States.

Pakistan, therefore, started efforts to win the United States' strategic and economic support. But till 1949, the United States did not respond in the same coin, as the focus of world-politics, at that time, was Europe. Europe was passing through a very critical situation and there was a race between the United States and Soviet Union to win its support. Therefore, the United States was giving much importance to Europe than any other region in the world. However, during 1949–1951, just after the communist triumph in China, the war on the Korean Peninsula, and the volatile political situation in the Middle East, the strategic analysts in the United States started to realize the importance of Pakistan's geographic location. The US State Department, in a policy statement, recognized the leading role of Pakistan in the Middle Eastern region and viewed it as a potential balancer in the South Asian power paradigm but

looked at India as a Japan's successor in Asiatic imperialism. The United States desired the use of air bases and other facilities in Pakistan during any possible combat with the communist countries, especially Soviet Union and China. Formerly, the US administration had tried to build up India as the leader of Asia to check the flow of communism from China into Asia but on calculating Indian tilt towards non-alignment, her reluctance to join the US camp, her role in Korean War, a visible change came into US policy. Keeping in view the catastrophe of the spread of communist dogma from Soviet Union into the South and Southwest Asia and into the oil rich Middle East region, the United States seriously diverted her attention to these areas and decided to form a ring of alliances in order to curb this menace. The rapid political changes in the Middle East were also adding to the US discomfort. In these circumstances, the United States found Pakistan as the most important, comfortable and valued asset. Pakistan was also ready to fulfill US strategic objectives not only due to the peculiar geopolitical requirements but also in order to gain economic and military assistance that was essential for her national security and territorial integrity. But still the United States did not want to antagonize India. The officials of the State Department were not in favor of giving any military assistance to Pakistan because they said, "India is the power in South Asia. We should seek to make it our ally rather than cause it to be hostile to us. Pakistan is distressingly weak." The US ambassador went to the extent of saying: "It is a bad arithmetic to alienate 360 million Indians in order to aid 80 million Pakistanis who are split into two sections." The US President, Eisenhower, and Secretary of State, Foster Dulles, were also not dismissive of these views but the vital strategic interests in the Middle East were considered more important by them. The upheavals in the Middle East and a perception of threat to the West's control over the strategic oil resources necessitated a new policy requiring cooperation of Pakistan in arrangements for the defence of the region. The induction of a nationalist government in Iran and nationalization of the Anglo-Iranian Oil Company testifying to the decline of British power and prestige triggered the new US policy of direct involvement in the defence of the region. Therefore, by 1952, Pakistan came to be looked upon as a potential partner in the arrangements aimed at the containment of the Red Peril, the Soviet communism. Testifying before a congressional committee, Secretary of State John Foster Dulles described Pakistan as 'a real bulwark' and remarked that the religious convictions and martial spirit found in Pakistan can play a pivotal role against communism. On June 1, 1953, in an address to the American people, the US Secretary of State expressed the same feelings and it was perhaps the first official introduction of Pakistan to the American people. In other words, it was the geopolitical and geo-strategic importance of Pakistan which brought her into the limelight of world politics and there established a close strategic partnership between Pakistan and the United States in early 1950s. The United States regarded Pakistan not only as a major player in the containment of communism but envisaged the military of Pakistan as a 'stabilizing force', in the Middle East, and, even in Southeast Asia. The United States established close ties with the Pakistan Army to curb any possible anti-US or pro-communist popular movement in Pakistan, to keep the country's policies in line with the United States and grab power itself if the politicians show signs of derailing the US interests. In 1958, when there was felt a mounting popular and political pressure for bourgeoisie democratic reforms and withdrawal from US backed defense pact, the Pakistan army led by General Ayub Khan staged a coup, abrogated the constitution and banned all political parties. This military coup gave support to the American and British interests. Ayub Khan, the then military ruler had, later on, revealed that he had consulted officials in Washington, including the CIA Chief, Allen Dulles, before declaring Martial Law in Pakistan. Ayub Khan had also spoken about his visits to the United States in May 1958 and he said that he had held extensive discussions with General Nathan Twining and Services Chiefs. This US-backed military take over retarded the already delayed progress of constitutional development in Pakistan, politicized the army and increased the role of the army at the cost of civilian and democratic institutions. Neil H. McElroy, the US Defense Secretary, who was present in Karachi just one day before the military's taking control of power, defended the military coup in the Senate Committee on Foreign Relations in 1959. The US State Department also termed Pakistan-military as "the greatest stabilizing force in the county." These statements fully endorsed the active US involvement in the military and polity of Pakistan that was in the US interests. In early 1950s, Pakistan, under the bureaucratic-military oligarchy, had joined the US-backed alliances, SEATO (1954) and Baghdad Pact (1955). The latter was subsequently renamed as CENTO. One of the major reasons for Pakistan's participation in these pacts was propounded as the desire to strengthen her defense vis-à-vis India. Pakistan, with the US support, wanted to check the Indian hegemonic tendencies and prevent India from becoming a regional power by usurping the independence of her small neighbors and putting their territorial security and national integrity at stake. Thus, it becomes obvious that the United States had a global agenda while Pakistan had a narrow regional security perception. But in spite of all the divergence of interests, the geo-strategic significance of Pakistan brought the United States in close strategic collaboration with the former. It was an arrangement between two 'unequal partners.' Ironically, this collaboration was at the cost of Pakistan's relations with her two neighboring states; People's Republic of China and the Soviet Union. The aforementioned US-backed pacts alienated Pakistan from the Soviet Union and the latter got closer to India. The Soviet leaders supported the Indian stance over the Kashmir issue and backed the Kabul regime on the issue of Pukhtoonistan. Resultantly, the Kashmir issue found no solution under the 'United Nations Resolutions' due to the overwhelming opposition of the Soviet Union. On the Kashmir issue, the Soviet leaders clearly stood by the Indian claim when, in November 1955 during a visit to Srinagar, the Soviet leaders declared it as an integral part of India. In 1962, the Soviet veto to the resolution submitted in the United Nation's Security Council for the solution of the longstanding Kashmir issue was the direct outcome of close US-Pakistan relationship that had sowed seeds of distrust and antagonism between Pakistan and the Soviet Union. Apart from India,

Afghanistan also remained hostile to Pakistan. During the Ayub era (1958–1969), Pakistan adopted an anti-China policy in the footstep of the United States and even on the UN forum voted against the People's Republic of China. All these arrangements could not even provide Pakistan with any leverage against India as the United States and Western powers were afraid of annoying India. It is evident from the fact that when India approached the United States for clarification of the Pakistan Foreign Office's interpretation of the 1959's US-Pakistan Mutual Assistance Agreement, the United States assured India that this agreement could not be used against her. It was a clear indication that the United States was exploiting the geo-strategic significance of Pakistan for the sake of her own security interests but was not ready to defend the latter against Indian aggression that was the main concern and the cornerstone of Pakistan's foreign policy. Pakistan was the only country that could facilitate the United States to have a close watch on the Soviet and Chinese activities through her espionage technology system and which could enable her to counteract them. Therefore, this urgency to get an air-base in Pakistan made the United States sign an agreement with Pakistan in 1959. As a result of the close US-Pakistan partnership, an American airbase was established near Badabher, a village in the suburb of Peshawar. Pakistan got nothing in return except increasing her burden of geopolitical compulsions and problems. That is why the United States has always preferred military dictators over democratically elected governments in Pakistan. But this nexus of Pakistan army with the CIA and Pentagon (headquarter of the US army) brought a great havoc to the democratic and judicial institutions of Pakistan. It politicized a military that, in turn, undermined the democratic and political culture in Pakistan and resulted in the dismemberment of the Eastern wing of the country in 1971, as it created a sense of deprivation due to prolonged military rule (1958–1971). Moreover, the establishment of the US-military base in Pakistan made the latter more vulnerable to the Soviet incursion when the Soviet leaders warned Pakistan of the dire consequences after the shooting down of U-2 reconnaissance aircraft which had taken off from that base. According to *The New York Times,* Pakistan would have been the direct victim, had any conflict taken place between the United States and Soviet Union. Thus, the defense problem of Pakistan not only remained unresolved but also became more critical while the military as an institution got strengthened.

The other determining factor in the US-Pakistan relationship was the precarious and volatile geo-strategic scenario in the Middle East. In the late 1950s, Arab nationalism got a new impetus in the Middle East when Jamal Abdul Nasir became the president of Egypt and united the two important countries; the Egypt and Syria, into the United Arab Republic in 1958. Moreover, in the wake of WW-II, the British withdrawal from the Suez Canal had given way to a power vacuum and to the Anglo-Egypt confrontation over the nationalization of strategically important Suez Canal. These and some other developments urged the United States to focus more on this region. The United States was already alarmed by the Korean War (1950) and the socialist revolution in China and the nationalization of US oil companies in Iran. She had also faced a humiliating defeat in Vietnam and could not afford to lose ground to the Soviets in the Middle East, the vital strategic zone of world politics. Therefore, the United States and her Western allies envisaged a plan for setting up a Middle East Defence Organization (MEDO) on the pattern of NATO but geopolitical environment in this region was different from Europe and the idea of collective security could not get fame in the Arab States of the Middle East. But the non-Arab pro-US states such as Pakistan, Iran and Turkey, took it as a blessing in disguise and overwhelmingly provided their shoulder to carry on this US agenda. Pakistan enjoyed the status of most valued ally in the region and reaped some benefits but the costs incurred were greater. Her defense dilemma remained intact but got some confidence in the face of Indian threat. The deep sense of insecurity on the part of Pakistan lessened when Pakistan's army organized and modernized itself due to sufficient US-arms supply and military training facilities under the above-mentioned pacts. This military aid also strengthened the position of the military at the domestic level as it had the resources, hierarchal system, discipline and *esprit de corps* which made it the most influential and modernized segment of the society.

The unique geo-strategic location of Pakistan has played a key role in attracting the United States towards Pakistan. The US has always come closer to Pakistan to win support of the latter to carry out the US international agenda or to eradicate a menace threatening the US interests directly or indirectly. Thus, whether it was the containment of communist advance in South Asia, the protection of the US interests in the oil-rich Middle East or the US war against terrorism, the US has desperately needed Pakistan because the fulfillment of these objectives was not possible without Pakistan's support. Pakistan has also sought to compensate her weak military position vis-à-vis India through close military ties with the United States. The US economic aid and political support were also needed by Pakistan. But looking at the equation of benefits, the United States has benefited more than Pakistan. The US triumph over the former Soviet Union, which made her the sole power, was indebted to Pakistan's unqualified support during the last phase of the Cold War. The present US hold over Afghanistan is due to the marvelous intelligence and logistic support extended by Pakistan. On the other hand, Pakistan's gains had remained only marginal. Through US support, Pakistan could never safeguard her national frontiers from frequent Indian aggressions, which was stated as the main objective of Pakistan's strategic support to the US, nor could it prevent dismemberment of her Eastern wing in 1971. The two major benefits that Pakistan reaped were; the successful nuclear technology by turning off the US pressure in 1980s and the military strength got through US support. As far as the nuclear gains are concerned, Pakistan cannot claim herself secure even in the presence of the nuclear umbrella. The build up of a strong and well-disciplined military institution is the other gift of the close US-Pakistan relationship that has every now and then uprooted the democratic institutions of

the country and obstructed the way of evolution of a national solidarity among the federating units of the country. It is also a fact that military has not been successful in defense of the state, which was its prime duty, and it is quite evident from the fall of Dhaka (1971) and misadventurism in Kargil Operation (1999). However, a strong Pakistani military was needed by the US as a stabilizing force to promote US interests in the Middle East and to crush any anti-US sentiments in Pakistan. This US objective has been successfully achieved by the Pakistan army. However, the main drawback of the US-Pakistan relationship is its flimsy nature. The root-cause of this fragility in relations lies in the fact that the main driving force behind the intermittent close US-Pakistan relationship has not been the convergence of interest but the need to accomplish their separate, different and sometimes divergent interests through mutual collaboration. Only the geo-strategic factor cannot turn the alliance among unequal partners into a durable and long-standing partnership and the same has proved true for the volatile US-Pakistan relationship. Each time the evaporation of strategic relevance of Pakistan has not only resulted in a cleavage in the US-Pakistan relations but also put the latter under much political, economic and diplomatic pressure than before.

Since 9/11, Pakistan has once again become instrumental in the US strategic war against terrorism due to the strategic worth arising from her geographical proximity to Afghanistan, her military superiority in the region and sophisticated intelligence and logistic facilities. Analyzing the history of Pakistan's engagements with the United States, it can be predicted with a greater degree of authenticity that this new phase will meet the same fate as in the past i.e. the US strategic interests in Pakistan will diminish as soon as her agenda gets materialized. At the end of this unmatchable relationship, Pakistan may face a number of dreadful consequences both at home and abroad. Once the US military hold over Afghanistan gets firm, the very existence of nuclear Pakistan will be put at stake. The United States would need an uninterrupted flow of hydrocarbons from the mineral-rich Caspian basin. Only the Pakistani ports of *Gawader* (constructed with Chinese support), and Karachi can provide the easiest routes for their direct and economical transportation. A peaceful, stable and sovereign Pakistan could become a hurdle to the smooth transit of the US shipments. The peace in Afghanistan would ultimately turn the US attention towards Pakistan and she would not leave any stone unturned in making her interests secure.

Critical Thinking

1. What challenges does geography impose upon Pakistan, particularly in its relationship with India and Afghanistan?

2. Why did Pakistan want U.S. support? How does this play out today, in light of current events?

3. How is the Middle East a determining factor in the U.S-Pakistan relationship?

Floods Leave Zardari Marooned from People

MATTHEW GREEN AND FARHAN BOKHARI

The stage seemed set for a lynching: a man sat down in the road to block a car carrying a pair of government officials through a camp housing 3,000 people who had lost their homes in Pakistan's floods.

Within seconds a mob had surrounded the vehicle. "You're enjoying yourselves while we're suffering," a man yelled. Another climbed on to the bumper.

The crowd was angry at official attempts to regulate a chaotic relief effort by local charities, fearing the authorities would steal supplies. "If you hand over any aid to the government then nothing will reach the ordinary people," said Hasan Zia, a doctor.

After a heated discussion the crowd dispersed and the officials escaped unscathed, but the incident in the north-western town of Nowshera this week reflects the growing sense of alienation between millions of Pakistanis and their state.

The UN confirmed the first case of the deadly waterborne disease cholera, in Mingora, the main town in the northwest's Swat Valley, on Saturday.

But the disaster does not immediately threaten the two-year-old administration of Asif Ali Zardari, president, who has begun visiting flood victims after being criticised for a visit to the UK and France. But Pakistan's 170m people want their leaders to do more than muddle through. So does the west.

The disaster has struck as the Obama administration is increasing aid in a drive to shore up a civilian leadership emerging from decades of army rule, undercut an Islamist insurgency and win greater co-operation over Afghanistan.

The army is playing the lead role in rescue efforts but has pledged not to divert forces from the battle against Islamist militants.

The insurgents, meanwhile, have said they are halting operations during the floods.

"The jihadists have also been affected in terms of their operations—floods do not discriminate," said Kamran Bokhari, an analyst with Stratfor, the global intelligence company. However, he cautioned: "What they will benefit from is the difficulties that the state is going to face."

Islamic charities, some with ties to militant groups, have set up relief efforts in some areas, raising concerns that the groups will gain sympathy for their extremist ideology.

Criticism of the government's flood response may fuel concerns about its ability to harness effectively a projected influx of $7.5bn (€5.8bn, £4.8bn) in US aid to combat poverty over the next five years.

"People say they have simply lost confidence in our leaders," said Sardar Naeem, a volunteer with the privately run Edhi ambulance service, helping victims around Nowshera, one of the hardest-hit areas.

Officials say any country would have struggled to cope with the floods that have either swamped or otherwise affected about a third of the country. Six million people are in urgent need of emergency relief, and aid agencies are warning of the risk of disease among an estimated 14m affected by the deluge.

The bitterness among those awaiting help, however, stems from a broader failure that is reflected in a litany of woes, from a power crisis to economic stagnation, that has provided fertile ground for militancy. Mr Zardari says his government has made significant progress in dismantling the vestiges of military dictatorship. But the military's main role in the relief effort is a reminder it remains the country's most powerful institution.

The civilian leadership will bear responsibility for tackling underlying problems that have been exacerbated by the catastrophe, in particular in the agriculture sector. Robert Zoellick, World Bank president, said the floods were likely to have destroyed crops worth about $1bn. Pakistan has said it will miss this year's 4.5 percent gross domestic product growth target.

Until the floods, much of Pakistan had been preoccupied by water shortages. Population growth in the eastern Punjab province led to the diversion of water for farming, reducing the once-mighty Indus river to a puddle in parts of the southern Sindh province, says a 2009 study by the Woodrow Wilson International Center for Scholars, a US think-tank. Climate change is worsening the situation, the study says, as does Pakistan's failure to adopt effective policies.

Michael Kugelman, an associate at the centre, says a political class rooted in landowning dynasties has little incentive for reform. "These vested interests are the single biggest obstacle to moving forward in a sustainable and long-term way. It's not just on the water problems, but also food insecurity, agricultural problems and also the energy crisis."

On the central reservation of a highway linking Peshawar and Lahore, a tented village has mushroomed. "The rain came from heaven and our fate lies in heaven," said Ata Gul Jan, a farmer, fighting back tears. "No one can save us but God."

Critical Thinking

1. How has the Pakistani government's response to the flood impacted concern over forthcoming U.S. aid distribution?

2. In what ways have broader failures increased the gap between militancy and civilians?

Another Restoration of Democracy

PLABAN MAHMUD

Bangladesh is at a critical juncture as it walks towards the long awaited election in December which is expected to put democracy back on track. The military-backed caretaker government is committed to hold the election by end-2008 (there is also a court order ordering them to) but there was much uncertainty whether all parties would participate. While most of the parties are prepared to contest the election, the Bangladesh Nationalist Party (BNP) and its coalition partner Jamaat-e-Islami has alleged that Election Commission (EC) has deprived them of a level playing field.

Bangladeshi democracy had suffered a derailment on 11th January 2007 (referred to as 1/11) when a parliamentary election under a nonpartisan caretaker government was cancelled and a military backed government took power. A state of emergency was declared and elections were deferred.

But what led to this situation? 2001–2006 was BNP's second term in power after parliamentary democracy was reinstated in 1991. Most of the parliamentary sessions were boycotted by the opposition Awami League (AL), making them ineffective. The Awami League complained that because BNP and its alliance had a majority, most of the opposition demands were either ignored or sidelined. Meanwhile, the country reeled under constant strikes and political acrimony.

The era saw the rise of fundamentalist forces, who received political backing. There were many bomb attacks, reaching its peak in 2005. On 21st August 2004, grenades were thrown at an Awami League rally targeting Mrs Hasina. Twenty-one people were killed, including Ivy Rahman, the party's secretary for women affairs. Awami League leaders like former finance minister Shah AMS Kibria and Ahsanullah Master were assassinated. The Awami League alleged a long term plan of the Khaleda-Nizami led BNP-Jamaat government to annihilate its leadership. Investigations into these assassinations were politically compromised. The caretaker government filed charges against 22 persons including top Harkat-ul-Jihad Islami (HUJI) leader Mufti Abdul Hannan and BNP leader and former deputy minister Abdus Salam Pintu.

The fact that the attackers had held two meetings at the BNP minister's residence to make a decision about the attack proves that a section of BNP was involved in the assassinations. Towards the end of the BNP coalition tenure, the government tried to ensure its re-election by politicising all important government posts.

It is alleged that the main players behind the 1/11 bloodless coup were a mixture of some local intellectuals and ambassadors of some foreign countries. They facilitated the change of government using the armed forces to prevent the country's descent into chaos, with the Awami League boycotting the election, accusing the BNP's set-up of engineering the elections. At the same time the kingmakers could restrain the army with the threat that lucrative UN mission jobs would disappear if there was a military dictatorship.

The new caretaker government took some populist measures like cracking down on politicians on charges of corruption. The revamped anticorruption commission has investigated and brought hundreds of charges against politicians, businessmen, and bureaucrats. Some of them were arrested, tried, and convicted. A big step was taken to cleanse the election process of corruption. A new national ID-card cum voter-ID project was initiated.

But its measures were not free of controversy. Most of the arrests were made under the emergency act, without charges. Proper investigation and charges against the accused would have been more effective in securing convictions. In the event, many of the arrested found their way out of the jails after the judicial process.

The caretakers also tried to reform the main political parties. Their much criticised 'minus two theory' was to keep the two begums out of the leaderships of the main two parties. Former prime ministers Khaleda Zia and Mrs Hasina were arrested on different politically motivated charges and detained. Family members and relatives of both the members were also put behind bars. But because of protests and their own resilience, the government was forced to release them on bail.

The Awami League is now in the position the Democrats were in during the US elections in November. People want to see a change of government. Some believe that General Moeen U Ahmed, the army chief, supports the League. The Awami League leaders, however, may be overconfident about their prospects and have not vigorously countered BNP propaganda.

Meanwhile many pro-BNP and Jamaati supporters are alleging a conspiracy to bring the Awami League to power. Redrawing the constituencies according to demography by the Election Commission has affected the BNP adversely. The revised Representation of People Ordinance (RPO) 2008 enacted by the caretaker government bars those individuals who have defaulted on utility bills, have been convicted or are war criminals; from standing for elections. The BNP and the Jamaat are vehemently opposing it because some of their potential candidates will be disqualified. The main problem of the BNP is that most of its top leaders are either behind bars on corruption charges or are on the run. Sources of their wealth are in question, their bank accounts frozen or under scrutiny by the government, and they will need time to clear the mess. There are feuds within the party structure in almost all local divisions. Many of their leaders are not hopeful of winning. Leave alone a majority, they are not sure whether they will be able to form a strong opposition. Indeed, they are not even sure of their ability to post enough strong candidates in 300 seats across the country.

This is where BNP's coalition partner Jamaat-e-Islami comes into the picture. In the recent years it has gained poise and strength when most of the leaders of BNP and Awami League were reeling under charges of corruption. It is now bargaining with BNP to post at least 100 candidates for the coalition and if it wins most of those seats, the coalition will move to the far-right.

The other players in the political field, like the former dictator Hussein Mohammed Ershad's Jatiyo party, and ex-president, veteran ex-BNP leader Badruddoza Chowdhury's *Bikalpa Dhara* or Kamal Hossain's *Gono* forum are not seen as alternatives to those three main political parties.

The BNP, having realised that they have no option but to participate in the election, proposed that if election was deferred for 10 days to December 28th and their three point demands are met then they will participate. Their three points include

abrogation of Section 91E of RPO act which states that Election Commission can cancel the candidature of anyone who, on investigation, is found violating the electoral code of conduct. These measures had been put in place to add more teeth to the hitherto unenforced code of conduct.

The Election Commission acceded to the demands. It announced that the general election would be postponed to December 29th. The date for submission of nomination papers was also extended giving the undecided parties some more time to prepare for the election. The government had no other option: for if the BNP and the Jamaat did not take part in the election then strikes and violence would return to the streets of Bangladesh, making the incumbent government dysfunctional.

So what future awaits Bangladesh? Will the voters allow these two begums to regain the control of Bangladesh politics? Will Bangladeshis be able to disengage from the confrontational and polarised politics of Bangladesh? The final decision, wonderfully, lies in the hands of the voters.

Critical Thinking

1. Are the Bangladesh Nationalist Party's (BNP) grievances with the Election Commission (EC) justified?

2. Who are some of the alleged facilitators of the 1/11 coup?

3. What advantage does the Awani League have in the upcoming elections?

PLABAN MAHMUD is a EU-based commentator on Bangladeshi current affairs.

Sovereignty and Statelessness in the Border Enclaves of India and Bangladesh

REECE JONES

Along the northern border between India and Bangladesh there are 198 enclaves of one country's territory completely surrounded by the other. Most of the 106 Indian and 92 Bangladeshi enclaves are small and located several kilometers inside their "host country," the country that surrounds them, which has resulted in their complete loss of contact over the past 60 years with their "home country," the country that continues to claim sovereignty over them. The enclaves were originally created in 1949, two years after the partition of British India, when the previously non-territorial administrative system of the princely state of Cooch Behar was used to define the territorial boundary between India and East Pakistan (contemporary Bangladesh). While the home countries make formal claims of sovereignty over their enclaves, the enclaves are effectively stateless spaces due to the complete lack of contact with the home country and the absence of administration from the host country. Estimates of the total population in the enclaves on both sides of the border vary widely from 50,000 to 500,000 people because formal censuses have not been conducted since the early 1950s. Based on interviews with enclave leaders and previous estimates of the population, it seems likely that in 2009 there are approximately 100,000 people living in the enclaves.

Although a few of the larger enclaves have established local councils for basic administration, most of the enclaves have no form of government at all. All of the typical services provided by a government are either completely absent in the enclaves or are carried out by the residents themselves. Without a public school system, many children receive no education. Without a public works department, the few bridges that do exist are built by the residents from dirt and bamboo. Without hospitals or health clinics, many people die of curable diseases like cholera. Without a government to record them, official documents such as land titles or marriage certificates are drawn up by the enclave residents themselves. Without police or judges, vigilante justice is the only way to settle disputes. Even the most basic infrastructure of electricity, telephones, and roads, which are widely available in the neighboring areas of the host countries, is absent in the enclaves.

The enclaves are spaces that were effectively put on hold for the past 60 years as the territories of India and Bangladesh were incorporated into the modern sovereign state system. Because they are relatively small and remote, they garnered only meager attention in Indian and Bangladeshi political circles and the residents remained in a state of uncertainty since the partition of British India. They find themselves in an alternate space that is shaped by the processes of modernity but not incorporated into it. Indeed, the enclaves are spatially set outside the social, political, and economic processes that swept up their otherwise similar neighbors. In a time when many—in academia at least—foresee, or dream of, a post-modern world where the categorizing, ordering, and totalizing processes of modernity are challenged and transcended, the enclaves remain a counterpoint of spaces that have not joined the modern era.

Why do the enclaves continue to exist? The home countries never had control of the enclaves, they are not contiguous with the enclaves, and they never reaped any economic benefit from them. Indeed, the enclaves on both sides of the border consist of only subsistence farmland and do not represent a potential future economic asset. Not only do the residents not want to be reunited with their home country, the majority of the current residents, as will be described below, moved into the enclaves specifically to flee violence directed at them in their home country. A more palatable solution (at least from the perspective of the enclaves' residents) would be for each host country to absorb the enclaves that are within their territory through an exchange. Hypothetically, this should be achievable diplomatically—indeed an agreement has been in place on paper since 1958—but practically such an exchange has proven illusive; it does not appear that the political standoff is any closer to a resolution today than when the enclaves formally came into existence in 1949.

This article analyzes the continued existence of the enclaves along the border between India and Bangladesh and it explores the implications they have for understanding the uneven imposition of the modern sovereign state system around the world. The research is based on fieldwork conducted in India and Bangladesh from August 2006 through April 2007. The data includes discourse analyses of government documents and media reports as well as interviews and focus groups conducted in 15 Indian enclaves and in the surrounding Bangladeshi communities. These enclaves were chosen due to their varying size and their distance from the main international border. Due to visa restrictions and inaccessibility, Bangladeshi enclaves in India were not included in the interview process for this article. Secondary sources suggest the situation in the Bangladeshi enclaves is similar and it can reasonably be inferred that the experiences of enclave Indian residents described here also likely apply to the Bangladeshi enclaves inside India. All interviews were originally conducted in Bengali and were translated by the author in collaboration with a research assistant in Bangladesh.

The next section situates the India-Bangladesh enclaves within the study of political enclaves and it describes the process that led to their creation in 1949. . . . The article concludes that the failure to exchange the enclaves after 60 years demonstrates the powerful role nationalist identity politics of religion and homeland play in institutionalizing the concepts of sovereignty and territorial integrity, often at the expense of basic human rights.

Despite the interesting implications political enclaves have for understanding the contemporary sovereign state political system, they have received little attention in the literature. Indeed, the vast majority of references to "enclaves" do not refer to fragments of states at all, but rather are used to describe the spatial organization of ethnic communities, often in the United States. The lack of interest in political enclaves may be connected to the misconception that there are not very many enclaves left and that they are mostly disappearing as states normalize their borders. Despite these assumptions, in 2009 there are still over 280 "real" political enclaves/exclaves in the world, the vast majority of which were created in the 20th century.

Almost all of the enclaves worldwide emerged from three different periods when the sovereign state political system was implemented or reorganized in a particular region. The oldest group of enclaves, the 39 remaining in Western Europe, consists of pre-Westphalian feudal holdings that were never normalized, often due to their small size. The second group of over 200 enclaves, mostly in Asia, emerged during the period of decolonization in the mid-20th century as newly independent states were carved out of former colonies. The third event that resulted in the creation of over 20 enclaves was the dismantling of the Soviet Union and Yugoslavia in the early 1990s.

The majority of the literature on enclaves focuses on definitional issues and cataloging the enclaves around the world. The terms enclave and exclave are largely interchangeable but do have some minor differences. An enclave is a piece of territory completely surrounded by another state. An exclave is a piece of one country's territory that is separated from the mainland. Vatican City and San Marino are enclaves but not exclaves because they are single entities that are not detached from a larger home state. Kaliningrad and Ceuta are exclaves but not enclaves because they are separated from their home states but not completely surrounded by another state. All of the enclaves along the border between India and Bangladesh fit into both categories, however for clarity will be referred to here as enclaves.

While many of the better known enclaves in Europe and North Africa have received the majority of scholarly attention, fully 70 percent of the world's 280 enclaves are along the northern section of the border between India and Bangladesh. In addition to 173 regular enclaves, there are also 24 counter-enclaves (for example, a Bangladeshi enclave inside an Indian enclave inside Bangladesh) and what is believed to be the only counter-counter-enclave in the world (an Indian enclave inside a Bangladeshi counter-enclave inside an Indian enclave inside Bangladesh).

The enclaves along the India-Bangladesh border came into existence after the authorities used the boundaries of the princely state of Cooch Behar, which were last recorded in a treaty in 1713, as the new borders between India and Pakistan after the 1947 partition of British India. The original treaty was signed between the Maharaja of Cooch Behar and a local leader of the Mogul empire at a time when there was not a modern understanding of sovereignty or territoriality in South Asia. Even today, the only visual cues that a boundary exists are a few small concrete markers erected by the British in the 1930s, which are now mostly covered by vegetation or buried in embankments.

The obscure origins of the enclaves and the almost unbelievable complexity of the boundaries—just imagine the difficulties of owning property in a counter-counter enclave—have led many current residents to rely on colorful folktales to explain how they ended up in this predicament. By far the most common story, which is even repeated by Indian government officials, suggests that the enclaves resulted from the profligate gambling habits of the local Maharajas in the 18th and 19th centuries. The folk tale says that when the Maharajas would meet for a monthly night of drinking and gambling, if a Maharaja lost his money he would resort to gambling the rights to estates he owned in the area, which resulted in a patchwork of different sovereign rulers. Another apocryphal explanation is that a British officer decided to have a few drinks as he was finishing the partition boundary line in 1947. As he got drunk, he knocked over an ink bottle and it spilled across the map. The next morning his associates saw the markings, assumed it was an intended part of the partition award, and the enclaves were retained in the final draft.

The true story is a bit less exciting. After the 1713 treaty was signed between the Maharaja and the Mogul leaders, the political organization of the area was not substantially altered until the 1947 partition. The 1713 treaty stated that the hostilities would end and the areas controlled by the armies of each side would be taxed by that ruler. The arrangement had little impact on the daily lives of the residents; it only meant that some people's taxes and documents were handled in Cooch Behar while others were handled in the equally close Mogul towns of Jalpaiguri or Rangpur. Eventually the British conquered the Mogul empire but left the princely state of Cooch Behar as it was. The boundaries between Cooch Behar and the British Empire were finally surveyed and marked in the 1930s but the enclaves were left in place because there was local resistance to any changes to the tax system.

In 1947, the new border created by the partition of British India was drawn through the area of northern Bengal near the princely state of Cooch Behar. The partition boundary commission did not address the enclave issue because the partition agreement only applied to the areas that were directly controlled by the British government and did not decide the fate of Cooch Behar and the other princely states. Instead, the princely states were given the option of joining either of the new sovereign states. The Maharaja of Cooch Behar opted to join India on 20 August 1949, the date that marks the official creation of the enclaves. In the years since partition, the main border between India and East Pakistan (contemporary Bangladesh), which was not previously inscribed into the landscape, was marked with border stones in the 1950s, guarded by border security forces in the 1960s, and in the past decade large sections were fenced by India.

The leaders of India and Pakistan immediately recognized the enclaves as a problem and worked to develop an agreement to exchange the enclaves, which was eventually signed in 1958. The agreement was unpopular in India and the authority of the government to cede sovereign territory to another state was challenged in the courts. These cases represent the beginning of a protracted effort by the Hindu Right in India to prevent the transfer of any additional territory to what it perceives to be illegitimate governments in Pakistan and Bangladesh, a process that will be analyzed further below. Nevertheless, the Indian Supreme court eventually ruled on 29 March 1971 that the agreement to exchange the enclaves was valid. Unfortunately for the enclave residents, Bangladesh had declared independence from Pakistan three days earlier on 26 March 1971, and once it gained its independence later that year, the agreement had to be renegotiated with the new government. The new agreement was signed in 1974, ratified by the parliament of Bangladesh, and Bangladesh fulfilled its obligations by transferring the disputed territory of Berubari to India. Berubari is a small territory located in the same general area as the enclaves that was mislabeled in the partition award. The text of the award said it was to go to India but the map showed it as part of Pakistan. The 1958 agreement had resolved the dispute by splitting it in half but the 1974 agreement was revised to transfer all of Berubari to India in order to partially equalize the land area of the enclave exchange. Despite these concessions by the government of Bangladesh, the Indian parliament has not ratified the agreement. The fate of the enclaves is still in doubt 35 years after the India-Bangladesh treaty, 51 years after the India-Pakistan treaty, and 60 years after the creation of the enclaves.

The only exception to the lack of progress is the creation of the Tin Bigha corridor between the large Bangladeshi enclave of Dahagram/Angarpota and the mainland of Bangladesh. Dahagram is unique among the enclaves because it was able to maintain contact with its home country. It has a population of over 16,000 people and is separated from Bangladesh by the Tista River to the west and a stretch of only 175 meters of Indian territory to the east. Both the 1958 and 1974 agreements allowed the enclave to remain under the sovereignty of Bangladesh by creating a corridor to the mainland through the Indian territory. Even the creation of the small corridor is contentious because the Indian village of Kuchlibari is connected to the mainland of India through the same corridor. Therefore, if the corridor is in use by Bangladeshi residents of Dahagram, the Indian residents of Kuchlibari are cut off from India in what, in effect, becomes a new enclave. In 1992, the governments eventually reached an agreement that allowed India to maintain sovereignty over the corridor but allowed Bangladesh to rent access to it in perpetuity. The agreement was protested by the Bharatiya Janata Party (BJP) of India, which claimed the arrangement effectively ceded sovereignty over Indian territory to Bangladesh.

Strict adherence to the concept of territorial integrity, then, not only prevents a rapid solution to the enclave issue, but also results in protests over any arrangements that could be perceived as threatening the state's sovereignty, even if it is only over a tiny strip of land in a remote part of India. But what is it about sovereignty that makes these small territories crucially important? . . .

The transformation of a former colony into an independent sovereign state is often represented as the transition from the premodern world into modernity. An important part of this transformation is the rescaling of identity category towards the newly defined state territoriality. In South Asia, as with a multitude of other places around the world, this is a fraught process where previous social connections, cultural practices, and political formations are made illegitimate as the new state sanctioned categories of national citizenship are introduced. In order to ease this transition, the new social boundaries between peoples, and the territorial boundaries of the sovereign state, are made to seem natural by placing the divisions on "natural" physical boundaries, by practicing them through markers, fences, and patrols, and by representing them on maps.

In India and Bangladesh, however, the existence of almost two hundred islands of foreign territory along the border undermines the claim of tight and inviolable linkages between the states, their territories, and their peoples. Beyond officially asserting their sovereignty, neither India nor Bangladesh has enacted or practiced sovereignty on the ground in the vast majority of the enclaves along the border. Neither country includes the residents in official censuses nor represented the enclaves on official maps. Perhaps most importantly, neither country has made any effort to enact the boundary on the ground by marking or patrolling the borders of the enclaves. And yet, the strict adherence to the concept of sovereignty also prevented India from renouncing its claim to territories it never possessed and prevented Bangladesh from violating that claim by providing basic services and rights to human beings that desperately need its help.

The general neglect of the enclaves perpetuates the status quo and the lines created by the 1713 treaty continue to order the local residents' experiences. And yet, even that order is transgressed on a daily basis by the residents themselves. Many of the original families that resided in the Indian enclaves in 1949 were displaced over the intervening 60 years by Muslim families fleeing India. The current enclave residents routinely cross the "international" border between the enclaves and the host countries to go to the market, visit friends, and take their children to school. Some of the large enclaves have even established their own elected councils, which operate completely outside the authority of the state that asserts sovereignty over the enclave.

The lack of modernization within the enclaves highlights both the good that the modern sovereign state system brings with it through the establishment of law and order and the problems it causes by territorializing those basic social protections. In the neighboring areas of Bangladesh, the benefits of the modern state are clear: paved roads, concrete bridges, government subsidies, police, judges, and laws. And yet, the residents of the enclaves live in a space that is completely unregulated, but was created by the same boundary-making process. While the residents of the enclaves can use the facilities of Bangladesh in their daily activities, the enclaves lack a legal authority to settle disputes, to normalize social interactions, and to control individuals who behave inappropriately. When the residents need a sovereign authority the most, it is not there. Without these basic social protections, violence is an accepted way of life and is the only option for protecting family and property.

After living for many years in stateless spaces, the enclave residents do not identify with the categories of nation and state that organize modern political imaginaries. The enclave residents live in stateless diasporic spaces where they are denied the benefits of citizenship in both their home and host countries, which results in ambivalent and unsettled feelings of belonging. The enclave residents identify with neither their home state, which they lost contact with and received no support from, nor their host state, which their lives are intimately tied to but whose citizenship they are excluded from. Instead, the enclave residents identify with the category that has been forced upon them: *chitmahal bashi* [enclave dweller]. And yet, the residents also want to simply be accepted as a citizen of one of the two sovereign states.

At the global systemic level, the existence of the enclaves as spaces that are still not incorporated into the sovereign state system furthers recent critiques that untangle and contest the often assumed connections between sovereignty and the state.

As spaces that are bounded in by and excluded from the sovereign state system, the enclaves expose the cracks and fissures in the fiction of coterminous nations, states, and territories and displace the notion of the absolute sovereignty of the state over its people and territory. And yet, their continued existence 60 years after their creation also demonstrates the power that the notion of territorial integrity maintains in that system. While humanitarian crises and the doctrine of contingent sovereignty have raised questions about the absolute authority of the state to carry out its internal affairs without intervention, these openings have still not resulted in a broad reassessment of the foundations of the current state system.

The solution of an enclave exchange seems easily achievable—indeed, a treaty between the countries has been agreed upon, most maps already represent the area as if an exchange has occurred, and in many ways in practice the enclaves already operate as part of the host countries. And yet, the exchange also proves illusory as nationalist identity politics are more important than the lives of a hundred thousand people who suffer in the enclaves. In the end, it is irrelevant that the Indian enclaves inside Bangladesh have never actually been part of the Indian state, do not have any economic value for the state, and are populated by Muslims that chose to leave India. Their existence is not what really matters. What matters is the symbolic effect the act of relinquishing them would have on the narratives that justify the legitimacy of the Indian state and the idea of a larger Hindu homeland. It would demonstrate that the territorial integrity of India is not inviolable and it would further solidify the position of Bangladesh as a legitimate sovereign state in what the Hindu Right claims as its historic homeland. For these reasons alone they remain.

Critical Thinking

1. Discuss ways in which the continual existence of enclaves illustrates the sovereignty of states.
2. Why did people choose to move to the enclaves?
3. Bangladesh continues to encourage an exchange of the enclaves with India. Why is India reluctant?

Nepal Hits Back at Foreign Intervention

JAMES LAMONT AND PRATEEK PRADHAN

Nepal's prime minister has hit back against pressure from the European Union and other foreign powers to form a coalition of national unity with the country's Maoist opposition ahead of an impending deadline for passage of a new constitution.

"If [parts of the international community] want to teach us, or to some extent instruct us, this is not acceptable to us," Madhav Kumar Nepal told the *Financial Times*.

"They should mind their own business. . . . No one is overlord here. We don't want any new colonisers here. We will not tolerate any high-handedness. Instruction, interference and undiplomatic words are not acceptable to us."

International concern heightened this month when a general strike called by the Maoists brought the capital and other areas to a standstill for a week. Ahead of the strike, the EU called on parties "to work together for national unity."

The Maoists fought a bloody civil war for 10 years before signing a peace agreement in 2006. The Unified Communist Party of Nepal (Maoist) won parliamentary elections in 2008, but quit government last year after a power struggle with the country's president over control of the armed forces.

The interim constitution implemented in the wake of the peace agreement is set to expire on May 28, but little progress has been made on a permanent replacement.

Despite Mr Nepal's rejection of foreign intervention, Kathmandu last week successfully convinced the United Nations Security Council to extend the UN peace mission in Nepal until September.

Mr Nepal, who represents the Communist Party of Nepal (Unified Marxist Leninist), said the international community had to be careful not to take sides.

He warned against trying to appease the Maoists, in retrospect calling the decision to bring the party into the political process before disbanding its armed forces and paramilitary wing "a big mistake."

He said the country was now "paying the price" economically and socially for a botched peace process.

"The [Maoists'] transformation is very slow. They still have extreme-left thinking," he said. "They have the authoritarian mindset."

The fate of the Maoists' combat forces is the biggest source of disagreement between the party and the government as the army has balked at integrating its former foes into its ranks as set out in the peace agreement.

The Maoist combatants, estimated at about 19,600 people, remain in camps across the country under UN monitoring.

Another area of mistrust is whether the Maoists are committed to multi-party democracy.

Mr Nepal's hard line is likely to fuel tensions with the Maoists, who have been agitating for their leader Puspa Kamal Dahal, otherwise known as Prachanda, to return as prime minister.

Krishna Bahadur Mahara, a Maoist politburo member and former cabinet minister, said a return to war in one of the world's poorest countries was a possibility if there were no compromise between the parties.

"There may be no alternative for us but to go back to war," he warned. "This is our compulsion, not our will."

Mr Mahara said his party was unable to "dissolve the [People's Liberation] army overnight."

He blamed machinations by India, which has traditionally had a close relationship and an open border with Nepal, with hindering a settlement among Nepal's leading parties.

"India is a problem. They want to keep Nepal in their command," he said. "Delhi has the idea to keep south Asian countries under their control."

Nepal's economy, which depends on remittances and tourism, has been badly hit by the political uncertainty.

Economic growth is expected to slump to 4 percent this year, less than half the rate of neighbouring India and China. Some Nepalese banks face a liquidity crunch as anxious citizens put money in property, gold or Indian deposits. Foreign investors are staying away.

"What's happening is that the money being brought back by remittance sources, and domestic sources, is not being put sufficiently into the banking system," said Yuva Raj Khatiwada, governor of the central bank.

"The deposits in the banking system are not growing commensurate with the money coming in. The liquidity crunch is a consequence of that," Mr Khatiwada added.

Critical Thinking

1. In what ways has the political climate affected Nepal's economy?

2. Do you agree that the EU should "mind its own business"?

3. What purpose in there in the EU's forming an alliance with the Maoist opposition?

Last Footfall in Nepal

ETHAN TODRAS-WHITEHILL

The path is wide, the terrain easy, yet I keep losing my footing, tripping over stones and my own feet because I can't watch the trail. My eyes refuse to leave the white mountain filling the sky before me, the 24,786-foot Himalayan peak Annapurna III. It dominates the horizon as surely as a sunset does, but with millenniums-old glaciers ringing its crest like a necklace of diamonds, it feels more dazzling than even the brightest setting sun.

Just over a third of the way through the legendary 150-mile Annapurna Circuit trek, circling the Annapurna massif in Nepal, I have finally reached a height where no smaller mountains obscure my sightlines to the peaks. Ahead, four days on, lies Thorong La, a daunting 17,769-foot pass, the high point of the circuit and start of the trail back down. But I've already reached euphoria. Annapurna III is too everything—tall, close, imposing, beautiful—to be true.

Everyone who's been to Nepal tells you the Himalayas are big. But nobody prepared me for the reality of breathing hard at altitudes already near those of some Rocky Mountain peaks, only to see a mountain rise another full height of the Rockies above me.

If my fiancee, Jen, and I had driven this same route in a jeep, my memories now and forever after would be a blur of trees and far-off villages, the mountains beautiful but remote, hardly more vivid than those seen in nature documentaries or computer wallpaper. Instead, as we approach the base of Annapurna III after a week of walking, my head is swimming with images seen close up: swaying footbridges over thunderous gorges; rocky footpaths jammed with goats, donkeys and water buffalo; terraced rice paddies thrusting green shoots against the olive hillsides; narrow stone Gurung villages filled with shrieking children, chatty shopkeepers and the low hum of chanting monks seeping out of brightly colored Buddhist monasteries.

And the mountains. Day by day, we've hiked in the company of the Annapurnas, admiring them from a distance in their shifting costumes of sun and shadow, sighing each time they hid behind clouds and cheering when they emerged. They feel like our mountains, our friends. Our Annapurnas.

It is a shame, then, that by 2012 a road will have been built on this path, destroying this experience and, according to many, placing the last nail in the coffin of what was once the greatest trek on earth.

Many walks lay claim to the title of World's Greatest Trek—the Milford Track in New Zealand, Mount Kilimanjaro in Tanzania and the Inca Trail in Peru are a few. But none of those are epics through valleys surrounded by five-mile-high peaks, staying every night in teahouses run by local villagers and stocked with good kitchens, cold beer and Snickers bars. The Annapurna Circuit marries natural grandeur, cultural immersion and relative luxury in a union found nowhere else.

The circuit is a tale of two river valleys: up the steep, lush Marsyangdi, then over the pass and down the wide, arid Kali Gandaki. But in recent years a road, usable by buses and four-wheel-drive jeep-like vehicles, was completed that runs up the Kali Gandaki to the base of the pass. On that side, most trekkers now opt to ride in the jeeps rather than walk in their dust, and as a result, the time needed to complete the circuit has shrunk from 17 days to 11. In the coming years, with the road now being built on the Marsyangdi side, the undeveloped portion of the trek will shrink again, to just four days.

Roads are the bane of trekkers, most of whom—myself included—want to visit places where only their own two feet can take them. On trekking blogs and message boards, purists are already mourning Annapurna's demise. So when I walked the Annapurna Circuit this past October, I decided to test this trekking prejudice: with Jen, a guide and a porter, I would walk the 17-day trail, even if it meant mingling with jeeps, and find out first-hand if all the doomsaying was warranted.

Thorong La is the highest altitude reached by many trekkers in their lifetimes, a few hundred feet higher than Everest Base Camp and eclipsed on the popular-treks list only by Kilimanjaro's 19,331 feet. October, after the usual monsoon months, is prime trekking season because it is typically the driest month.

For pretty much every trekker in Nepal, whether headed to Annapurna, Everest or any of the other fabulously scenic regions, the preparation starts in the Thamel neighborhood of Katmandu, where every third storefront overflows with knock-off trekking poles, nylon pants and packs at prices half to a third of those elsewhere. (Our guide, a 30-something, thin-mustached Gurkha, called it "Chinese North Face.") Thamel has no sidewalks, so our every foray into its streets was a tooth-and-nail battle with rickshaws, cars and mopeds.

Then the bus ride from Katmandu: careering along cliffside roads, passing slower vehicles whenever a mouse hole of an opening presented itself, accompanied by a constant soundtrack of honking horns. Essentially, by the time we arrived in the town of Bhulbhule at the start of the trek, the idea of walking around a mountain range seemed downright tame.

The first day started out misty and wet, and although I was excited when after 13 miles our guide announced that the night's teahouse was around the corner, I was anticipating a bowl of rice and lentils for dinner and a dung-burning hovel in which to sleep. A couple of decades ago, when enterprising Nepalese villagers had only recently begun offering tea and space on the floor to passing hikers—giving rise to the term "teahouse trekking"—I might have been right. But since 1993, over 60,000 people on average have visited the Annapurna region every year, drastically altering the hospitality landscape.

Our stop that night, the Waterfall View Guesthouse, was a two-story pink and aquamarine motel-like structure and restaurant overlooking a lofty cataract. The double rooms had foam mattresses, pillows and electricity, and the four-page restaurant menu included fresh-baked bread and imported beer. For hikers accustomed to dehydrated meals and wet tents, it was almost too much. I stuffed myself with vegetable lo mein and an Indian potato curry, washed down with Nepali masala milk tea.

The next day the trail began to climb, and we passed pairs of middle-aged trekkers, dropping them one by one with our younger legs. Soon huge masses of schist, granite and sandstone rose on either side of us, daubed with green moss and brown lichen and dripping with cascades of black fungus that grow in the runoff of the monsoon rains. It was as if Jackson Pollock had been given an entire mountainside as his canvas.

That night, it began to rain in earnest. A drenched, forgettable next day took us to Chame, the largest town this side of the pass. We were happy to hang our clothes and dry our boots by the Shangri-La Guesthouse's stove, which the proprietor finally lighted after much prompting. It poured all that night, too, and with the other guests, we stayed on the following day, passing the time and hoping the driving downpour would stop. It is precisely to avoid rains like this, supposedly rare in the fall, that nearly three times as many people walk the trail in October as in the summer monsoon season. We had caught the anomaly.

The next morning the sun returned and luckily did not desert us for the rest of the trip; we needed every minute of it to melt the snows that the storm had deposited higher up. Leaving Chame, we caught our first glimpses of Annapurna II and IV, then Annapurna III the next day (the peaks are numbered by height, not placement in the range), gasping each time at the angle at which we had to hold our heads to view them. But the trickle of trekkers heading the opposite way, retracing their route after giving up on making it over Thorong La, soon grew to a stream, keeping us sober-minded with their snow reports. "Chest-deep on the pass—no one's crossing," a lone Israeli said. "Knee-high in Manang," a British couple announced.

The sun did its work, and when we arrived two days later in Manang, a landmark town on the trek, the snow there had largely melted. Most trekkers stay over an extra day in Manang, partly because at 11,600 feet it's at the perfect height for acclimatizing, but mostly because at the head of a valley crowned with several heart-stopping peaks, it's a simply perfect place to be. If Manang were in Colorado or Montana, Robert Redford

and Ted Turner would already have bought every acre they could get their hands on.

Hundreds of trekkers were in town, backed up from waiting out the rain and snow, running into fellow travelers they had met at other points on the trail. Most of the crowd had soon coalesced into groups, newly formed clans of six to eight united by age, language or sheer happenstance. Jen and I found ourselves splitting thermoses of tea and playing cards with four Australian professionals, a South African management consultant and a Canadian occupational therapist (the only woman among them), all in their early to mid 30s.

Although we would recognize it only afterward, the laughs and the fledgling nicknames—the sense of everyone banding together against the cold, fatigue and thinning air—were as great a joy during our time in the Marsyangdi River Valley as the Annapurnas themselves.

Before leaving Manang, we stopped in for the afternoon lecture at the Himalayan Rescue Association, staffed that season by volunteers from Bozeman, Mont., a doctor and her husband, a civil engineer. They stressed the importance of ascending slowly toward Thorong La and drinking water copiously to avoid altitude's dangers: headaches, bloody lungs, cerebral edema and even death.

After Manang, our new group of eight trekkers (with three guides jostling for primacy) slept one night at 13,000 feet and another at 14,500 at the base of Thorong La, walking only two or three hours a day to follow the Bozeman doctor's advice. Two of the Australians were already suffering a little, taking each step as though slogging through a bog of molasses. The drifts on the pass were still high, but by the time we arrived, people had been going over for a day or two, packing the snow into a path with each bootfall.

Crossing Thorong La was by far the hardest day of the trip: a 3,200-foot climb to the summit, followed by a 5,200-foot descent to the Hindu and Buddhist pilgrimage site of Muktinath on the other side. Everything over 15,000 feet was covered in snow and ice. We rose at 3:30 A.M., intending to reach Muktinath before a powerful wind began blowing up the valley there as it does every afternoon. It was so cold my Camelbak hose— the hiker's lifeline for water—froze within 10 minutes as the lights of our teahouse faded to black below.

But Jen and I, both under 30, were fit and had been close to these heights before, and as the predawn light hit the snowscape, we realized that our worries about altitude sickness and the impassable snows had been needless. We said hello to Annapurna III as it reappeared after days of hiding, now far off, and stopped for a hot lemonade at one of the three teahouses we were shocked to encounter above 15,000 feet.

At 18,000 feet, the air holds half the oxygen it does at sea level, a phenomenon I learned the hard way as we tried to pass frustratingly slow trekkers in the deep snow. The effort so drained me that for the last 500 vertical feet I became one of them, Jen impatiently dragging me upward and stuffing energy bars into my mouth.

We reached the pass at 7:30, too tired to jump with the joy we felt. After a half-hour of taking the obligatory snaps with the pass marker and prayer flags, verifying the altitude on a GPS and catching our breath, we headed down. Boot-skiing, butt-sledding and mud-running, we made it into Muktinath around lunchtime. The whole day of trekking was only seven and a half miles, but it had taken us over nine hours. (The molasses-boggy Australians did it in 12.)

Feeling destroyed in body but renewed in spirit, we sat down in a restaurant for lunch; I ordered yak steak. At the table with us sat three other young English-speaking travelers, and we settled into the same slow dance of smiles and pleasantries that in previous days had led to enjoyable evenings of conversation and beer followed by exchanges of e-mail addresses.

Suddenly one of the travelers' friends popped her head into the restaurant. "The jeep driver says he won't wait!"

The three immediately packed their things. Handing some money to the restaurant owner, one explained, "We don't want to be stuck here all day." Then they were gone.

The road up the Kali Gandaki to Muktinath was begun in 2004 and completed a couple of years ago. The road taking shape on the Marsyangdi side is to be completed to Chame, where we waited out the rain, by 2011 and to Manang by 2012, according to Lal Prasad Gurung, director of the Annapurna Conservation Area Project, a governmental agency that opposes the development.

Local people who make their money from tourism are firmly against the road, Mr. Gurung said, but they make up only 15 to 20 percent of the populace. The rest—"those who are involved in agriculture, those who go overseas for work," said Mr. Gurung—"they want the road."

And it's not even clear that vehicle accessibility will hurt the region's long-term tourism prospects. As jeeps and maybe someday cars take over, Muktinath and Manang will most likely only grow as tourism hubs, attracting new visitors content to ride up to the peaks. The only clear losers in the equation are the trekkers.

Walking down through the Kali Gandaki was a very different experience from the one we had on the way up. Then, we could barely go a hundred yards without bumping into another group of trekkers. Now the only human companions our group found on the road were Nepalis hauling goods too bulky and cheap to be worth transporting by vehicle, usually in giant wire-frame cargo containers cantilevered on their foreheads. The days were long and dusty in a dry landscape of mountainsides and fields rendered in a monochromatic palette of tan, beige and taupe. The towns were more developed and less charming. The eight of us clung together as the last stalwarts of the bygone Annapurna Circuit bonhomie.

"The people you see give the trail a kind of vibe," said James Rait, the South African management consultant. "When all those people disappear, that vibe just goes away."

I tried hard to appreciate the beauty of the Kali Gandaki. In the town of Kagbeni, Jen and I visited a Buddhist monastery and got lost in the winding, catacomb-like streets of the old city. We navigated back using odd markers: children playing a version of marbles, a brown calf poking its head out of a doorway, and a 10-foot orange fertility idol built into an archway, his male bounty pointing in the direction of our hotel. Back on the road, we found consolation in getting to know a new

set of mountains: the bladelike ridge of Nilgiri and the perfect pyramid of Dhaulagiri, at 26,795 feet the seventh-tallest peak in the world.

But I would be lying if I said that every time I saw a jeep or a bus picking up passengers, I wasn't tempted to jump on and end what, as we coughed in the dust of motor vehicles, was beginning to feel like a pointless exercise.

By the time we reached the hot springs town of Tatopani, four days out of Muktinath, everyone was emotionally and physically spent. From there the Annapurna Circuit leaves the road and climbs 6,500 feet to Poon Hill before losing the altitude again over the last two days to trail's end. It was our last chance to take the jeep.

Poon Hill would be a hard slog, and because it's at a junction point with several other popular treks in the region, we knew it would be blanketed with tourists. The Australians and the Canadian—tendons, knees, backs and feet aching—took the jeep. James, Jen and I took the climb.

Atop Poon Hill, we found an impossibly beautiful panorama. But mingling among the hundreds of other trekkers there at dawn, hearing them marvel over these peaks that they were seeing for the first time and bond over the altitude and their surprise at the good teahouse food, I felt like a two-week-old artifact. Our time in Annapurna had come to an end. Our journey was, like the soon-to-be-obliterated circuit itself, merely a snapshot in time. I took a long, last look at the Annapurnas, glowing now with the first fiery rays of morning, and began the descent.

If You Go

Most trekking in Nepal begins in Katmandu. Flying there from the United States generally requires changes along the way. A recent search for flights from New York to Katmandu in April turned up an Air India flight with a long layover in Delhi starting at $1,295 and a one-stop flight on Etihad, a United Arab Emirates-based airline, with a nearly full-day layover in Abu Dhabi from $1,213.

A guide is not necessary for the Annapurna Circuit, but hiring one can make the trip simpler. Many travelers also use porters; they are usually young Gurkha men who speak little English but can carry up to 50 or 60 pounds. A 23-day itinerary within Nepal (including arrival, departure and travel days) that includes a guide, porter, all lodging, all transport and permits and all meals can be booked starting at around $1,000 a person. Most trekking companies allow the guide to keep your unused budget, so it is important to clarify up front exactly what aspects of meals are covered (for example, appetizer, entree and tea might be included, but no soda, beer or candy).

The Thamel neighborhood of Katmandu is literally overflowing with trekking agencies; it is best to make arrangements beforehand but certainly possible to do so upon arrival.

We used Himalayan Glacier Trekking (977-1-4411387; himalayanglacier.com), a tightly run outfit providing all relevant services.

Earthbound Expeditions (977-1-4701051; enepaltrekking .com) has a good reputation as well. Most agencies can customize their services to your specifications—for example, providing permits, transport and porter but not lodging or meals, if you prefer to arrange your own.

Critical Thinking

1. Besides accommodating trekkers, are there other advantages to not allowing the road to be constructed?

Crackdown Provokes Fears for Sri Lanka's Democracy

Lydia Polgreen

In a part of the world better known for the interruption of democracy than its stubborn endurance, **Sri Lanka** has always been something of an oddity. A small country that suffered through one of the world's nastiest recent wars, it nevertheless remained for the most part a vibrant multiparty democracy.

Last spring the government of President Mahinda Rajapaksa decisively defeated the Tamil Tiger insurgency that had terrorized **Sri Lanka** for the better part of three decades. Last month, voters rewarded him with a landslide victory that gave him a new term.

So it is all the more surprising that his government decided to arrest the longtime ally who became his main rival for the presidency, Gen. Sarath Fonseka.

That arrest, and the harassment of journalists and opposition politicians and their supporters, are raising **fears that Sri Lanka's** democracy is faltering just as the long-awaited peace begins.

War has a way of chipping away at the foundations of even the strongest democracies. But what has surprised many people in **Sri Lanka** and beyond is the way that **crackdown** has endured well beyond the government's battlefield triumph, and has, in some ways, even intensified and become routine as Mr. Rajapaksa and his family have tightened their grip on government.

"**Sri Lanka** has been on a clear path towards the consolidation of power in the hands of very few people, many of them related to each other," said Alan Keenan, an analyst at the International Crisis Group who specializes in **Sri Lanka.**

The events of the past week have been so unsettling that some influential supporters of the president have questioned the arrest. In a highly unusual rebuke, a group of leading Buddhist monks, one of Mr. Rajapaksa's most stalwart constituencies, criticized the arrest of General Fonseka in a letter to the president, saying the general had "made enormous sacrifices to unite and safeguard the territorial integrity of the country."

Dayan Jayatilleka, a former diplomat, political analyst and ally of Mr. Rajapaksa, wrote in a deeply critical essay on Groundviews, a popular citizen journalism Web site, that the arrest of General Fonseka was a "clumsy melodrama" that was "obscuring the clear, conclusive electoral victory handed to Mahinda Rajapaksa by the masses."

Even Rajiva Wijesinha, secretary general of **Sri Lanka's** peace secretariat and a staunch defender of the Rajapaksa government, admitted in an interview this week that "the timing could have been better," adding that "it might have been better after he lost so badly to let him go."

Top officials insist that General Fonseka posed a grave threat.

Gotabaya Rajapaksa, the president's brother and the defense secretary, told *The Straits Times*, a newspaper based in Singapore, that General Fonseka had planned to topple the government, and that acting to stop him was the only way to preserve democracy. "He was planning on a military rule," the newspaper quoted him as saying.

Mr. Rajapaksa and General Fonseka were once united in their determination to crush the Tamil Tiger insurgency at virtually any cost. Mr. Rajapaksa gave the military a free hand to prosecute the war, and the army's size and budget ballooned.

The president's defenders say that at the end of the war Mr. Rajapaksa tried to reassert civilian control, alienating the general. Rumors that General Fonseka was plotting a coup have swirled for months, though many dismissed them because **Sri Lanka** has no history of military intervention in its politics.

Some analysts have contended that he was arrested because he was hinting that he might give evidence of war crimes committed in the final battle against the Tamil Tigers, and the arrest was a way to keep him quiet. No charges against General Fonseka have been announced, and it remains to be seen if he will be tried in military or civilian courts.

The election has featured the clearest signs yet that the government does not feel bound by the rule of law, analysts said. Despite clear directives from the country's beleaguered elections commissioner, state-controlled news media continued to favor the president overwhelmingly.

Parliamentary elections are scheduled for April, and many people worry that General Fonseka's arrest will have a chilling effect on the vote. Mr. Rajapaksa's party has made it clear that it seeks a two-thirds majority that will allow the president and his allies to reshape the Constitution.

The opposition coalition that backed General Fonseka, meanwhile, is crumbling. The biggest opposition party, the center-right pro-business United National Party declared Monday that it would run on its own in parliamentary elections. But its ability to draw voters is in question; it failed to deliver its urban stronghold, Colombo, the capital, for General Fonseka.

The other large opposition party, a Marxist organization that dabbles in virulent Sinhalese nationalism, is also on the wane.

The fact that these disparate parties chose to champion General Fonseka is a sign of just how weak and ineffective they have become. Not one had a candidate within its ranks who could rival Mr. Rajapaksa.

General Fonseka proved a wooden candidate and had the temperament of a hard-charging military officer, according to people who have worked closely with him.

As a candidate he pressed the government to release Tamil civilians held in closed camps, but government officials said that as army commander he had resisted calls to resettle civilians quickly. That record, along with his role in the bloody final stages of the war, makes him an unlikely martyr. But Mr. Rajapaksa seems determined to make him one, contended one political analyst who did not want to be quoted criticizing the government.

The president could have simply settled for a victory, the analyst said, but by making the general a target, Mr. Rajapaksa has only given him more credibility.

Critical Thinking

1. Did the arrest of General Sarath Fonseka by President Mahinda Rajapaska help or hurt Rajapaska's position?

2. What motives could have been a factor in Fonseka's arrest?

3. What, if any, threat to Sri Lanka's government exists in light of the waning of opposition groups?

Muslim Geographies and the Politics of Purification in Sri Lanka after the 2004 Tsunami

Shahul Hasbullah and Benedikt Korf

When the Indian Ocean tsunami of 26 December 2004 wreaked devastation on Sri Lanka's coastal regions, a global space of compassion and generosity opened up, bringing large flows of aid money, volunteers and aid professionals to Sri Lanka and other affected countries in Asia. This global wave of compassion and aid has been likened to another type of 'tsunami after the tsunami' one that triggered ambivalent experiences and impacts. Indeed, as we will argue in this paper, in Sri Lanka's multiethnic east, the politics of aid and humanitarianism 'after' the tsunami accentuated, or fell prey to, the historical genealogy of what we will call the 'politics of purification'—the fragmented ethnic politics and the spatial politics of purifying space into (ethnically) homogenous territorial entities.

Interestingly, Edward Simpson reports similar dynamics occurring after the 2002 earthquake in Gujarat, India, where Hindu nationalists set out to reimagine the shape and purpose of the state, thereby playing into a political economy of nostalgia that enlivened Hindu nationalist foundational myths which distanced Hindus from a 'secretive' Muslim minority. In both instances, of Sri Lanka's east coast and Gujarat, it is arguable that even a momentous natural disaster did *not* create a space of disjuncture, a rupture of 'politics as usual' or a space of opportunity for opening up politics towards inclusion. Instead, the natural disaster as an event provided an opportunity for the reimagining of the state as a purification mechanism.

In Sri Lanka, the politics of purification entail geographical imaginations of a 'nation' as 'the same people living in the same place' (from James Joyce's *Ulysses*), but also anxieties and concerns about the intrusion of alien discourses and values into these imaginary 'pure' spaces of Muslimness, or Tamilness, or the Sinhala-Buddhist nation. As Jonathan Spencer has argued, Sri Lanka has experienced a constant movement of people in colonial and postcolonial times that mark this politics of purification. Purification is the attempt to maintain fictive separations based on the illusion that 'a nation is the same people living in the same place.' Sankaran Krishna calls these

'fictions of homogeneity', referring to the manifest geographical imaginations of an ethnically pure territorial space in Sri Lanka, such as a 'Sinhala-Buddhist Sri Lanka' or a 'Tamil Eelam' or a Muslim homeland in Sri Lanka's southeast.

Following Spencer and Krishna, purification is a *fiction*. Spencer takes the metaphor of 'the work of purification' from Bruno Latour as 'it provides a suggestive frame for interpreting the disparity between powerful self-images of modernity . . . and the far messier picture revealed by careful ethnography and historical research in which the boundaries are routinely transgressed and hybrids abound.' In the Sri Lankan context, the suggestive frame of the (ethno) nation as pure territorial container conceals the more complex reality that careful ethnography reveals. Ethnic boundary marking as a purification discourse exists *within* the three ethnic constituencies, making purification a highly fraught and contested exercise.

The politics of purification is evidenced by certain geographies of post-tsunami housing relocations. When the Sri Lankan government declared a coastal buffer zone or 'setback area'—a defined territorial strip at the coastline wherein reconstruction of damaged or destroyed property was forbidden—large numbers of tsunami displaced people who had lived close to the coastline had to be relocated to ostensibly safer places further inland. As Ruwanpura points out, the relocation of families from the designated buffer zone was more than just 'putting houses in place'. The government's buffer zone policy opened up new grounds for continuing, in some cases completing, the work of purification as it required the movement of people to different places. By offering the possibility to enhance the 'purification' of territories, the 'apparent geographical "fix" [of the buffer zone] served . . . to fan the flames of political controversy between the major political parties and among the various ethno-national groups.'

This paper explores the practices of purification and their antinomies in one place, Maruthamunai, a Muslim village located in Kalmunai Divisional Secretariat (DS) division on the coast of Amparai District in southeast Sri Lanka. We read the politics behind the relocation of Muslim families from the buffer zone into new places as a continuation of a politics of purification driven by the geographical imaginations (or fictions) of ethnically purified territories. The post-tsunami imperative for suitable land to relocate people provided an opportunity for territorial realignments influenced by differing political 'purification' agendas. The sheer magnitude of post-tsunami aid money tended to strengthen certain forms of patronage based on place-based politics, which also fragmented the notion of a spatially contained Muslimness.

The Muslim community have perceived themselves as the weakest link in the Sri Lankan polity, more so after being sidelined in the peace talks held after 2002. Subsequently too their voices were marginalized in the post-tsunami discourses on aid distribution that created a dichotomy between the state and the then prevailing separatist Liberation Tigers of Tamil Eelam (LTTE)—or between 'south' ('Sinhala') and 'north' ('Tamil'). This was patent in the highly publicized public debates about the appropriateness of channelling aid into then LTTE controlled areas of the interior heartlands of the north (the Wanni). The binary grievances of 'north–south' or 'Tamil–Sinhala' temporarily obscured the suffering and plight of those tsunami devastated communities on the east coast, notably the Muslim community in Amparai, who sustained one of the highest death tolls in the whole of Sri Lanka.

Our case study of place-based politics of tsunami aid is located in Kalmunai DS division within the thin coastal strip of Amparai District comprising a densely populated mosaic of Tamil and Muslim settlements. Maruthamunai village lost about one tenth of its population to the tsunami wave, of whom women and children made up two thirds. The worst affected were the settlements closest to the sea where mostly poor subsistence dwellers, including fishing families, had been living in makeshift houses and huts that were easily washed away. After the tsunami, more than two thirds of the survivors in Maruthamunai had to be evacuated, some temporarily, some permanently. The northwestern part of the village was particularly affected with almost 600 houses being completely destroyed, but further inland, seawater intrusion also caused considerable damage to house and properties.

Our empirical material is based on a long-term engagement with Muslim politics in Amparai and with Sri Lankan aid politics more broadly. Co-author S.H. Hasbullah, who has been involved in research and political activism in the area for some time, was on the spot in Maruthamunai one day after the tsunami struck and has repeatedly visited the place since then. Ongoing participant observation and key informant interviews and informal group discussions with tsunami affected families, local bureaucrats, mosque leaders and aid workers were conducted intermittently on various occasions over 2005 and 2006. In May and June 2006, we administered a semistructured questionnaire that covered approximately 200 tsunami affected families, collecting data on their current status, their opinions on

aid delivery and their anxieties and expectations of the future. This augmented data we had previously collected from interviews and informal conversations with a number of provincial bureaucrats and aid workers, both Sri Lankan and foreign, in Trincomalee and in Colombo in June and October 2005.

This paper draws particularly on those parts of the material that are based on participant observation, informal talks with key figures and selected key informant interviews beginning in the immediate aftermath of the tsunami event. This research is critical for understanding and reconstructing the spatial politics of aid—and to connect 'local' politics to the broader spatial dimensions of political violence in the east, national discourses on aid delivery and emergent debates on Muslim geographies in the east. However, we recognize the limitations of the material. First, the narratives that we use to reconstruct the spatial politics of post-tsunami aid are mainly based on informal encounters, observations and 'being-in-the-field' while situations were unfolding. Due to the highly sensitive politics, particularly relating to then mounting Muslim–Tamil tensions, we have not used direct quotes from our interviewees, although we do indicate differing dominant discourses. Second, our positionalities as male researchers restricted our access to women, particularly in the context of small Muslim communities where women (including the many widows) are often reticent about publicly expressing their viewpoints to researchers. Indeed we noted a tendency for husbands to provide answers on behalf of their wives in interview settings. While we could make up for this, partly, by triangulating with key informant sources, our understanding of women's perspectives remains limited.

We map out three trajectories of the continued politics of purification after the tsunami. First, we discuss how a local 'nonpolitical' space of relief distribution that was organised by the mosque federation (*pallivasal samasam*) was considered as an interruption of what is popularly summed up as 'politics'—a disjuncture of the politics of purification. Second, we describe the reemergence of this taken for granted workings of 'politics' through the advent of international humanitarian aid, which provided the material resources for a competitive politics of purification and, equally, how this provided an impetus for the Muslim polity to fragment deeper into place-based patronage politics. Third, we explain the territorial politics of purification, that is, the political practices of keeping or expanding territories as pure ethnic containers. While these practices are shaped by 'fictions of homogeneity', the Muslim geographies that emerge out of these practices are contradictory and fragmented rather than purified.

Critical Thinking

1. In what way has the aid given to Sri Lanka after the 2004 tsunami contributed to territoriality?

2. Describe the politics of purification.

From *Singapore Journal of Tropical Geography*, July 2009, pp. 248–252. Copyright © 2009 by Department of Geography, National University of Singapore. Reprinted by permission of Wiley-Blackwell via Rightslink.

Bhutan, Borders, and Bliss

David A. Andelman

Thimphu, Bhutan—The Druk (dragon) Air flight from Bangkok via Dacca banks into its final descent to Paro Airport's landing strip at 7,333 feet. Nestled in a high valley, surrounded by peaks ranging to 18,000 feet where planes thread their way deftly, it serves as the sole passenger airport in this tiny Asian kingdom. Those fortunate enough to be sitting in a left-hand window seat during the approach can spot the unmistakable majesty of Mt. Everest. Stretching off into the distant east is the remainder of the far Himalayas. Many of these mountains, which surpass 23,000 feet in altitude, remain unnamed. Most have never been conquered, out of respect to the spirits that are believed to make their homes there.

Beyond this year-round wall of snow and ice that forms Bhutan's entire northern and much of its western boundary lies China, specifically the Tibet Autonomous Region. It is one of the most formidable and impassable borders in the world, whose legitimacy may be traced to the efforts in the first decade of the twentieth century of Sir Arthur Henry McMahon, the army colonel who served as foreign secretary of the British Indian government, the Raj. Today, this boundary that he traced, following the ridge line of the Himalayas, and the entire nation that lies south and east of it, serves as a strategic buffer between the two most populous countries on earth—China and India—whose common frontier would otherwise be extended another tense 292 miles. This function is, of course, only one of the reasons Bhutan has been able to survive as an independent kingdom, indeed until two years ago one of the world's last absolute monarchies. But the reasons for its survival, while so many others in this part of the world have disappeared or been swallowed up—Sikkim and Cooch Behar come immediately to mind—are a compelling object lesson as to precisely what constitutes a nation in today's world. For Bhutan, it is a complex amalgam of geography, religion, language, and culture. And ultimately, all come together in what may be its unique legacy to the world—Gross National Happiness.

Above all, Bhutan serves as a contemporary model for other nations, or wanna-bee states, living in the shadow of great powers—from Chechnya to Baluchistan, Kurdistan to Kosovo, and on to Georgia, Abkhazia, and the Ossetias, not to mention a host of tribal territories scattered across Africa—as to just what constitutes a viable, secure, and prosperous country.

If there were ever an example of geography as a central element of nationhood, it is Bhutan. Certainly the Bhutanese are far more a Himalayan than an Indian people, geography notwithstanding. Only a few narrow passes, each above 15,000 feet, allow entry to the north into remote Tibet and China; the south is a broad flat plain stretching on for thousands of square miles into India. Indeed, India trains its mountain troops in the high Himalayas of its Bhutanese neighbor, while China has made few efforts to encroach on Bhutan.

"We are here because we cannot be anywhere else, but you must handle this in a way that is balanced. Then you start to have interactions," Bhutan's elegant foreign minister, Lyonpo Ugyen Tshering, tells me at lunch in a private dining room of the Taj, the capital's lavish Indian-owned hotel. "You cannot choose your neighbor, but you can deal with your neighbor. The short answer is that we always have to be afraid, and that should be our maxim. But you must take every opportunity to make the situation better. At the same time, we must not lose the idea of who we are. You must understand where you are standing, which side is the hard ground and which side is the soft ground."

The hard fact, however, is that Bhutan is a landlocked nation some 450 miles from the nearest port—and that path to the sea lies directly through India. So, not surprisingly, it is the interactions with India that are defining Bhutan's present and, most likely, will continue to frame its future. Indian investments, workers, markets, and its educational and legal system have built modern Bhutan. The vast hydroelectric network—a system of dams, generators, and transmission facilities, all built by India—supply the bulk of Bhutan's electric power, while the export of this electricity via hundreds of miles of high-tension lines, accounts for the nation's largest single source of hard currency. Indian engineers and workers have built what there is of a national highway system, including most of the single west-east highway (often barely one-and-a-half lanes wide, snaking through the Black Mountains that bisect the nation). Much of the nation's food supply (beyond the basic homegrown staples of red-hot chilis, cheese, rice, and potatoes) not to mention the very plates they are eaten on are a product of India or have arrived from the nearest port, Kolkata. There is no natural boundary with India. Bhutan's flat southern plains and those of India's north are all but indistinguishable physically—each flowing seamlessly into the other. Indeed, the only real point of contention was a 2.6 square mile tract around Dewathang, ceded by Bhutan to India in the Treaty of Sinchula in 1865 and restored in 1949 when the newly independent India finally and definitively recognized Bhutan's independence.

Today's Indian ambassador to Bhutan, Pavan Varma, a gentle, professional diplomat of enormous intellectual accomplishment and deep personal understanding, nevertheless has inherited a position and a residence that places him in a position that can only be likened to an ancient Roman proconsul of the outlying possessions—tenuously linked to the empire but essential to its ultimate survival and prosperity. The residence, called India House, is a vast 70-acre tract in the middle of Thimphu, surrounded by a high chain-link fence topped with razor wire and patrolled on the inside by Indian troops. Within its perimeters may be found a golf course, tennis court, basketball court (the 30-year-old king is quite an accomplished basketball player, as it happens), and soon a hot stone bath, not to mention the palatial ambassador's residence and the embassy offices.

When Bhutan's national library needed a re-make, the ambassador rang up a friend in New Delhi who heads India's library system. He was on the next flight north to launch a whole new network with augmented resources and computerized registry. But the interactions at all levels are vastly more complex. Since Bhutan has no law school, all the nation's lawyers and by extension its judiciary head to India for their legal training, with a yearlong "post-graduate . . . orientation in our law," as Supreme Court Justice Dasho Tshering Wangchuk explains to me. "India uses British common law," he continues. "But we were never colonized, so we developed our own laws."

Indeed, the absence of a colonial past is a source of enormous pride and as it turns out national cohesion as well. Bhutan has really never been conquered. Geographically a string of lush, but narrow, often v-shaped valleys (even today, few even have enough flat territory at the bottom to allow for an airport landing strip), each separated from the next by steep mountains, what is today Bhutan began as a collection of fiefdoms, each ruled by the local *penlop.* Even today, the Crown Prince is on occasion referred to as the Penlop of Trongsa, the initial post held by the founder of the House of Wangchuck. The nation itself dates back to the early seventeenth century, when Shabdrung Ngawang Namgyal, the Tibetan lama and military leader, a victim of religious persecution at home, swept down from Tibet, building a fortress, or *dzong,* at the entrance to the strategic Thimphu valley, then moved ever eastward, consolidating his control. Since it often took days to make the arduous journey from valley to valley, the *penlop* system persisted until 1907 when the first king was unanimously chosen by his peers as hereditary monarch and the dynasty was formed. Four of his descendants mounted the throne, each identified by his numerical rank in the succession. Today, the 30-year-old fifth *Druk Gyalpo,* or dragon king, Jigme Khesar Namgyel Wangchuck, educated at Phillips Academy at Andover, Wheaton College, and Magdalen College at Oxford, rules a thoroughly united nation that all but worships him and the institution he represents.

Throughout its history, the region that is now a unified Bhutan has successfully resisted a succession of would-be foreign invaders, from early Tibetan forces to several centuries of an uneasy truce, punctuated by a few brief, violent confrontations with the British Empire. Today, neighbors India and Bhutan are both democracies, though of dramatically different sizes—and derivations, one emerging from a colonial heritage, another from a centuries-long monarchy.

Their friendship is clearly a great tribute to their individual, indeed divergent histories and cultures. India is without question the dominant nation in the South Asian region and has accumulated few friends. Pakistan, from which it was carved when the British pulled up stakes in 1947, is a Muslim nation, deeply suspicious of the motives and goals of its far larger Hindu neighbor. When India acquired a nuclear weapon, Pakistan was not far behind. Today, these two nuclear powers maintain larger armed forces across their nominally peaceful frontier than anywhere else on their peripheries. Other nations India has either absorbed or ignored. And then there's Bhutan.

"The reason we get along so well is that India treats us an equal," observed a member of Bhutan's Senate over coffee. "There is no condescension on their part. And for our part, we recognize everything they have to offer." An equal? Scarcely. But a nice fiction that both parties find thoroughly opportune to sustain.

Imagine for instance, India deciding it was somehow to its advantage to absorb Bhutan. Ignore the opprobrium that would descend on this democracy from all sides in the region and the world. Still, its hand would be stayed by one overwhelming reality. Faced with such a *fait accompli* on what would become its new border with an ancient adversary, China could then see itself free to claim portions of India that it coveted. The scattered Sino-Indian conflicts of past decades would be a mere *amuse bouche* for the resulting battle of the nouveau superpowers.

With China, Bhutan has had a long and tortuous relationship. "You have to understand we dealt with the Tibetans not with the Chinese for all these years, for all these centuries," Foreign Minister Tshering tells me. "It is only since 1959 that you actually had Chinese people. And here again, we are learning to live together." But beyond a religion and heritage shared with the people of Tibet, there were other, more fraught issues with China. That nation's communist rulers "came at a time when there was a beginning of the Cultural Revolution," the foreign minister continues. "And Bhutan, as another Buddhist country, could not accept the damage to the Buddhist heritage in Tibet. Tibet historically has been the closest country, with which there have been lots of differences but also a lot of interaction."

The goal was a simple one as far as Bhutan was concerned. Clearly, it was not going to persuade China to let Tibet remain a Buddhist state. But equally, it was determined that there would be no hostilities. And there have not been. While the iron curtain has in theory descended along the roof of the world that forms this, the world's highest continuous frontier, the people on both sides of the border continue their interactions. "Officially, today the border is closed," Tshering continues, then smiles gently. "But you do have some clothing going across, there is some cross-border trading, there are TVs being carried over the mountains, and these communities are becoming very rich. But we try to keep the best relationships and China respects that also."

Underlying the entire relationship, there will always be the undercurrent of religion.

From Monarchy to Democracy

Until two years ago, Bhutan was officially one of the world's last absolute monarchies. The House of Wangchuck has been blessed by a succession of gifted rulers and heirs. Each has endeared himself to his 700,000 subjects. From the beginning, the kings have traveled, crisscrossing the entire country, making themselves personally accessible to the lowliest individuals. Even before there was a single passable road, they would trudge for hundreds of miles at times on foot, at times on horses, or at higher elevations on yaks, seting off with their retinues for the most remote hamlets. In December, in the wake of a catastrophic earthquake, the fifth king set off in a dozen automobiles for the collapsed villages, across the Black Mountains. On such visits, the king would distribute his land (the royal lands comprise the vast bulk of unsettled territory in the country) to worthy or needy individuals. At a stroke, he has been able to settle disputes, award citizenship or even marriage licenses (as he did to the parents of one friend of ours in Thimphu), and distribute largesse of all types.

But two years ago, Bhutan left the realm of absolute monarchies, elected a popular parliament and became a democracy—though the fifth king remains the head of state. His father, the fourth king, had initiated the process. Still, across the nation, even at many of the highest levels of this democratic government, there is a quiet admission that if a referendum were held on the question tomorrow, the overwhelming choice of the people would be to scrap democracy and return to an absolute monarchy.

"They see what has happened in other democracies, even in India," explains one leading politician. "And they worry."

But of far greater worry to the fourth king, according to several of those who have advised him, was what is generally referred to as the genetic imperative. Bhutan has been blessed by a succession of capable, even dazzling rulers. But can it always count on that? The future of the nation, perhaps its very survival, cannot rest on a genetic roll of the dice. What if the next heir somehow falls short of the attributes of his predecessors? Democracy, it seemed to the fourth king, was the only alternative. Perhaps.

But if the monarchy is sold on democracy, the people still have some profound reservations. In the first parliamentary election two years ago, voters sent to Thimphu 45 members of the government party and two members of the opposition. As Prime Minister Jigmi Thinley tells me in the course of an hour-long conversation in his offices decorated in lavish Bhutanese style in the parliament building, "I guess what the people wanted was continuity with the past. And I think between the two parties they felt that our party represented continuity, in the sense that there were five of us from the previous government and many of us were directly trained by the fourth king and served the fourth king from the day he was crowned. And

the other party had only two, of which one of them had been with his majesty the king soon after he came to the throne.. . . The thrust of our campaign slogan was "NOT SO MUCH CHANGE." The other party emphasized change and I think they placed too much emphasis on the *need* for change, while not being able to clearly convince the people. So what people saw, I think, was reason for the fear of the unknown."

Which is not to say there are not those with some reservations about the true benevolence, as well as the power, of the monarchy. On our way back west from Mongar, we are stopped for an hour or so at a roadblock. Road workers are repairing a section of the highway that had been washed away. We wander down toward the work site.

On the left of the road, next to a pile of large rocks are squatting a dozen women. Using metal hammers, they are, one by one, breaking up the rocks into smaller rocks and creating a pile of large-scale gravel. It is hard, backbreaking labor. The most elderly, and clearly the most outspoken, tells me she's been doing this every day for some 40 years. She is not very bitter at her lot. The work has allowed her to raise a lovely family, of whom she is clearly quite proud. What does irk her, however, is a deeper slight that has been festering for years. Over the past decades, she has applied several times for a grant of land from the king so that she might find a way back to the village where she was raised.

Each time, she has been either refused or ignored. No reason is ever provided. None is required either by law or tradition. But she sees others from her village who have been so favored. Still, she goes back to work each day. Breaking rocks. Is she happy, I ask? She shrugs. Sure. She is happy. Buddhists are rarely unhappy with their lot in life. But she could be happier. Perhaps the largest question facing Bhutan is how to keep its people happy—or, better yet, make them even happier.

Gross National Happiness

Indeed, beyond Buddhism and the monarchy, happiness is the other glue that holds this nation together and that has made Bhutan best known far beyond its borders. Sometime during the reign of the fourth king, he decided that Bhutan's place near the bottom of the world's nations by the traditional measure of gross national product (GNP) did not quite reflect the quality of life in his kingdom. Another measure of success was necessary. He hit upon the concept of Gross National Happiness, or GNH.

Basically, the concept, which has evolved into a complex system to measure the state of mind of every individual, from the most remote hamlet to the capital, is assessed by a series of 72 indicators organized in nine domains ranging from psychological wellbeing and community vitality to the economy, the environment, and security. Every government initiative, every law, every investment must be run past the GNH Commission. If it doesn't pass muster, it doesn't happen. When American entrepreneur Daniel Spitzer was launching his investment in hazelnut production, with the intention of bringing 25,000 trees to Bhutan, it had to stand the test of GNH. It did.

"Our task is to make GNH ever more concrete so it can guide policy in the government, so that all actions are consistent with this policy, and so that we are able to attain Gross National Happiness as required by the Constitution," says Dasho Karma Tshiteem, secretary-general of GNH.

Every two years, a group of carefully-trained pollsters will be fanning out across the country to assess the nation's GNH. The first such effort did not take place until 2007 and it was very much a work in progress. This first round selected 350 families, with one member taken through a list of questions, some 128 pages in length. It took eight hours to administer the poll, and each respondent was paid 250 nultrums ($5.38) for their participation. At times, it took the pollsters eight hours of walking to reach the more remote locations. Over the next two years, the poll was refined. Now, it's just 54 pages and takes two hours to administer, as it was last year to 950 families. They will do it again later this year, with a vastly expanded group of 8,000 respondents.

What did they learn? "People who are earning more are actually happier than those who aren't," says Tshoki Zangmo, who helps administer the poll at the Center for Bhutan Studies. "Also, people in Thimphu are the ones who are the most stressed and who don't socialize much with their family."

What this means in terms of policy, is quite clear to Zangmo. "We cannot just let our people be led by their illusion that money is everything," she says. "Our government has to try" to broaden the definition of happiness.

Out in the provinces, where the rubber meets the dirt road, officials like Sherab Tenzin, the governor of Mongar, are trying to do just that. The biggest problem for the governor is how to keep his people down on the farm. Ultimately, that means how to keep them happy. "Mongar is basically agricultural countryside," he says. "But if your activities are not productive, no matter what I feel, what the government feels, they will not stay on the farms. I would like to see by and large that people maintain their values. People will get educated and modernized. What we have done is to show people that if we don't support our customs, our institutions will also go very fast. We must stay in touch with our values. This is our top priority."

Indeed, it is a priority that small nations like Bhutan must learn if they are to continue to survive, even prosper, rather than being ground between or absorbed by far larger and more prosperous neighbors.

Or as Foreign Minister Tshering puts it, "The role of Bhutan is to be silent and do what we must in the small place called home. And not have to be too worried with the broader universe." Perhaps this is the true secret of happiness.

Critical Thinking

1. What is the role of geography in India's influence on Bhutan?
2. How is religion a factor in Bhutan's relationship with China?
3. In what way would China be a consideration should India decide to take over Bhutan?

From *World Policy Journal*, Spring 2010, pp. 103–107, 108–111. Copyright © World Policy Institute. Reprinted by permission of Sage Publications via Rightslink.

Remote Bhutan Aims to Draw Investors to the Himalayas

PATRICK BARTA

Thimphu, Bhutan—The government of this remote Himalayan nation, which didn't have television until the late 1990s, has a message for the outside world: Bhutan, once largely closed to foreigners, is open for business.

Among the world's most isolated places, Bhutan was ignored in the rush to emerging markets in recent decades. Tourists weren't allowed until the 1970s and even today, only a few thousand visit each year, with just a handful of major foreign investments to date. There are no traffic lights in the capital of Thimphu, and laws require residents to work in traditional dress, which for men includes multicolored knee-length robes. Top officials often wear swords.

Life still moves at a different pace than the rest of the world. Businessmen often spend large portions of the day competing in archery tournaments and families take picnics in the evenings in their rice fields. While neighboring China and India rack up world-leading growth rates, the government here measures economic progress by a complex local measure known as "gross national happiness."

But change is coming fast since Bhutan's revered monarchy engineered a peaceful transition to parliamentary democracy in 2008. With an economy dominated by agriculture and government work, elected officials are concerned democracy won't survive unless Bhutan's 700,000 people have more high-paying jobs and development. So Bhutan now hopes to join the global mainstream.

Officials are pushing an array of projects, including a new domestic airline, an information-technology park, and a $1 billion-plus "education city" they hope will attract investments from major universities in India and possibly the U.S.

Bhutan will use its own funds and money from investors to fund projects. It also hopes to make Bhutan a convention destination.

Although many parts of the plan—including the education city—are still in early stages of development, the government is dispatching officials for foreign-investment road shows abroad and has retained McKinsey & Co., the consulting firm, to help.

All that is stirring anxiety, especially among residents who believe Bhutan's peace and stability—and its unique culture—will be jeopardized if it opens its gates much further.

"If we go too quickly, I think it will bring problems," says Pema, a 28-year-old tour guide who, like many Bhutanese, goes by only one name. "We'll become like Nepal," a nearby state plagued by poverty, unrest and unstable governments in recent years, he says.

"The government is going all out with economic growth targets—but how much of that is going to generate jobs?" says Tshering Tobgay, Bhutan's opposition leader. Bhutan is "doomed" if projects like the education city take off, he says, because they'll make impossible demands on Bhutan's labor and infrastructure.

As for McKinsey, he says, the consulting firm "represents the best of corporate America." But when it comes to Bhutan, with its emphasis on happiness over growth, "I don't think McKinsey has a clue what we're talking about." A McKinsey spokesperson declined to comment.

Backers of the development program, including Prime Minister Jigme Thinley, say Bhutan has little choice but to accelerate its entry into the global economy. Some 23 percent of the population lives below international poverty standards, he says. Many residents are migrating from rural hinterlands to urban areas such as Thimphu, a ramshackle town of rugged buildings with tigers and other animals painted on the walls. Its population has shot to about 100,000 from 45,000 a decade ago; land values have climbed 150 percent over the past three years.

"In a democracy, I think the government, or the leadership, does not have the luxury of time to meet the needs and aspirations of the people," Mr. Thinley said in a recent interview with *The Wall Street Journal*, in a government complex near Thimpu's main dzong, or local royal citadel. "What matters to us is that unemployment doesn't become an unmanageable problem. Our economy has to grow."

Mr. Thinley and other officials say they are intent on preserving Bhutan's culture and are only targeting investments that are compatible with the country's unique circumstances.

"If someone comes to us with a plan for cutting timber, we will not be interested," says Damber S. Kharka, executive director of Druk Holding and Investments, set up in 2007 in part to better manage state companies such as the national airline, which has two planes, and make them more competitive in a global economy. "We'll be very selective. We'll not go for the real industrialization that damages the environment." Either way, the "outside world will be a key player" in Bhutan's development, he says.

Bhutan has long struggled to balance outside intrusions with its inward-looking instincts. It fought against Tibetan invaders in past centuries and tussled with the British during colonial times. It retained its independence, and its isolation, in part because of a rugged mountain landscape that makes it hard for outsiders to get in.

It also had a series of kings who made it a priority to preserve Bhutan's Buddhist-oriented culture. The fourth king, Jigme Singye Wangchuck, popularized "gross national happiness" as an alternative to the growth-at-all-costs mindset of other countries. It has used extensive surveys—with questions such as "How stressed are you?"—to provide what Bhutanese officials believe is a more meaningful measure of a society's development over time.

The king also pressed for Bhutan to become more democratic, which he felt would be more sustainable than a monarchy. Although he handed the throne to his son in 2006, the position is now largely ceremonial.

The changes to Bhutan's tourism industry are among the most controversial.

Currently, the country assesses a levy of $200 a visitor, which helps keep tourist numbers low. McKinsey presented options to the government that could have included rethinking the fees and targeting 250,000 visitors per year within five to seven years.

After a testy town hall meeting in February, the government settled on compromises in which the levy would remain—and

increase to $250—but officials would press ahead with plans to hit 100,000 arrivals by 2012.

To get there, they're opening remote parts of the country once closed to outsiders and planning three domestic airstrips and a new airline beginning in spring 2011. Officials are weighing proposals from three bidders, including a team with Nepalese investors, to run the carrier.

They're also forcing hoteliers to upgrade facilities to make them more appealing to foreigners and conventioneers, and making arrangements for what officials say will be the country's first credit-card transaction later this year.

The education city, to be built from scratch at a site to be determined, is likewise stirring debate. The idea is to use Bhutan's reputation as a green, relaxing place to attract foreign universities to set up satellite campuses there. Officials say they are organizing a team of international experts, including a board member from Indian conglomerate Tata Group, to help and that the government has held preliminary discussions with several universities with a focus on attracting major schools from India.

Critical Thinking

1. What are possible long-term implications for Bhutan if it becomes an active player in the global economy?

2. Are Prime Minister Jigme Thinley's arguments for justification of Bhutan's fast-forward move into commercialism valid?

3. Is it possible for the people of Bhutan to maintain their present low-stress lifestyles once tourism and big business come to town?

A Look at America's New Hope: The Afghan Tribes

Ruhullah Khapalwak and David Rohde

For three decades now, Communism, civil war and Islamic fundamentalism have laid siege to Afghanistan's tribes. In many ways, Afghanistan's tribal structure is arguably the weakest it has been in the country's history.

Nonetheless, American civilian and military leaders are turning to some of these tribes as potentially their best hope for success against the resurgent Taliban after being frustrated by the weak central leadership of President Hamid Karzai.

Tribes have existed for millennia in the area that is present-day Afghanistan. They emerged over centuries in various sections of the country, taking form along extended kinship lines. Led by councils of elders, tribes provided their members with protection, financial support, a means to resolve disputes, and punishment of those who had committed crimes or broken tribal codes of conduct.

For Pashtuns, the country's largest ethnic group and the Taliban's primary source of support, tribes are particularly important. Successfully turning Pashtun tribes against the Taliban—or perhaps families or sub-tribes if they deal with the government on their own—could deliver a serious blow to the insurgency and potentially create a means of stabilizing the long-suffering country.

Some Afghans, though, warn that the tribal system is not a panacea and fear that the United States is adopting a quick-fix approach that will not create long-term stability. They see the tribes as inherently anachronistic, sexist and corrupt—a system that further undermines the already extraordinarily difficult task of creating multiethnic, merit-based national institutions. They warn that the country would be thrown into the hands of myriad tribal militias that the central government could never control.

Last week, the importance of the tribes to American strategy became clear when the leaders of the Shinwari tribe in eastern Afghanistan agreed to work with the government and forbid cooperation with the Taliban. The pact was announced as a major first step for the American effort to win over the tribes.

It was not the first time outsiders have turned to Afghanistan's tribes as allies and surrogates. The British, who fought Russia for control of the region in the 19th century, brought with them a practice of enlisting local leaders. After the British departed, Afghan kings in Kabul relied on the tribal structure to maintain stability and order in remote areas.

But then came Communism in the mid-1970s, which viewed tribes as archaic obstacles to social progress and, most important, as a potential threat to party leaders' hold on power. Hundreds of tribal elders were taken from their homes and killed in a series of brutal crackdowns.

At the same time, the United States, backed by the Saudi and Pakistani governments, unleashed its own assault on Afghanistan's tribes. American-backed Wahhabi fundamentalism created hundreds of thousands of young mujahadeen "holy warriors" to attack Soviet troops in Afghanistan. Religiously indoctrinated and flush with American cash, these young Afghan fighters viewed Muslim clerics and mujahadeen commanders—not tribal elders—as their true leaders.

Once the Soviets left—and in turn the Americans—mujahadeen commanders turned on each other and the Taliban emerged as a force that, though repressive, at least provided law and order. The Taliban emphasized Islam as the organizing principle for society and government, not tribes. Across the country, little-known Muslim clerics ran government ministries, provinces and cities. Tribal elders were again ignored.

Since being toppled in 2001, the Taliban have mercilessly targeted tribal elders who support the Karzai government, apparently viewing them as one of their greatest potential rivals. At the same time, President Karzai's weak government has struggled to protect and strengthen tribal elders, hundreds of whom have been killed in assassinations and bomb attacks.

One hallmark of the American agreement with the Shinwari tribe is that $1 million in American development aid will go directly to Shinwari elders. The money will bypass Karzai government officials, whom Shinwari elders dismiss as corrupt and ineffective.

Critical Thinking

1. Is Afghanistan's tribal system a realistic means for the United States in creating stability?

2. Why is the U.S. strategy of using tribes a concern to many Afghans?

3. What is the significance of the U.S. pact with the leaders of the Shinwari tribe?

Afghans' Distrust of Officials Poses Threat to Military Successes

ALISSA J. RUBIN

Jalalabad, Afghanistan—Nearly a year into a new war strategy for Afghanistan, the hardest fighting is still ahead, but already it is clear that the biggest challenge lies not on the battlefield but in the governing of Afghanistan itself.

That has been the early lesson of the American-led offensive in February in Marja, in Helmand Province, where most Taliban insurgents either were beaten back or drifted away. Since then, Americans and Afghans have struggled to establish a local government that can win the loyalty of the Afghan people, something that is essential to keeping the Taliban at bay.

The success of the far larger offensive in the coming weeks in Kandahar, the Taliban heartland, may well depend on whether Afghans can overcome their corrosive distrust of President Hamid Karzai's government.

Mr. Karzai was confronted with that issue when he met with American officials this week, including President Obama on Wednesday. The two leaders seek to repair months of badly strained relations and come together at a crucial moment, both for the NATO countries involved in the fighting and for Afghanistan itself. Mr. Obama plans to begin withdrawing American forces a little more than a year from now.

If the timetable is not daunting enough, an April report by the Pentagon to Congress found that by most measures, the country is, at best, only a little better off now than it was a year ago. Progress so far appears well off pace to meet the American goals.

The insurgency has spread to some new places, notably the north and northwest of the country, although it has diminished in a few areas. It is now made up of more than half a dozen groups with different agendas, making it that much harder to defeat, or negotiate with, even if the Americans and Afghans could agree on a strategy for doing so.

In 120 districts that the Pentagon views as critical to Afghanistan's future stability, only a quarter of residents view the government positively. And the government has full control in fewer than a half dozen of these districts.

Despite the commitment of more troops by Mr. Obama and a new strategy that has emphasized the protection of Afghan civilians, few in Afghanistan believe that a functional government that holds the country together can be created on the timetable outlined.

"It was very unrealistic to think that in 18 months they would be able, with the Afghan government, to secure a very large part of the country which is insecure today," said Nader Nadery, a commissioner on the Afghan Independent Human Rights Commission, who travels extensively around the country. "Look at only Marja. It took such a long time just to secure that area."

The timeline also leaves many Afghans reluctant to back the Americans and the Afghan government, because they fear that the members of the NATO coalition may be leaving soon, Mr. Nadery said. The point was echoed by European diplomats.

"I did not anticipate the increasing sense of uncertainty among Afghans that Americans and Europeans will pack their bags and leave the country in the coming weeks and months," said Vygaudas Usackas, who recently arrived in the country to serve as the European Union's special representative to Afghanistan.

"We all understand we can't succeed by 2011," Mr. Usackas said.

Even as American troops clear areas of militants, they find either no government to fill the vacuum, as in Marja, or entrenched power brokers, like President Karzai's brother in Kandahar, who monopolize NATO contracts and other development projects and are resented by large portions of the population.

In still other places, government officials rarely show up at work and do little to help local people, and in most places the Afghan police are incapable of providing security. Corruption, big and small, remains an overwhelming complaint.

"People are tired of the Taliban, but they also don't want cops to shake them down, they don't want power brokers who are so corrupt they impact their lives and livelihood," said a senior officer who works closely with Gen. Stanley A. McChrystal, the NATO commander for Afghanistan.

The challenges are clearly visible in eastern Afghanistan, where the military has come to recognize the limits of American power in this wild terrain. The United States abandoned two combat outposts in the east over the past year—one in Nuristan and the other in the Korangal Valley, in Kunar Province.

Col. Randy George of the Fourth Brigade Combat Team, Fourth Infantry Division, who has responsibility for the four easternmost provinces, tries to build relationships with tribal leaders in most of his territory, at gatherings called shuras, although he has given up ground to the insurgents in some areas.

The strategy inevitably means allowing the insurgents some havens, as long as those are in sparsely populated areas where the insurgents are unlikely to have much impact. Colonel George said he hoped that if he could embolden Afghan citizens to combat corruption in the more populated river valleys and provincial towns in their areas, they would at least create a government they could support, rather than help the insurgents who attack it.

"We're not worried about corruption in itself, but we are worried about governance," Colonel George said.

"Part of that is making sure that we are continuing to connect the Afghan people to the Afghan government as a whole, and when you've got a rotten piece of that, the people don't want to connect to it," he said.

Over the past year, elders in the east banded together in three districts in Laghman Province to force out three corrupt police chiefs, and in Kunar and Nuristan, they forced out two district governors.

But entrenched officials, some of them Karzai allies, sometimes undercut the efforts, and tribal dynamics are infinitely complicated. In Nangahar, a major effort by the military to persuade a large tribe to sign on to a pact to keep out the Taliban drew criticism from the powerful provincial governor, Gul Agha Shirzai, who appeared to fear that the pact would undercut his power. Since then, no similar pact has been approved.

Such pacts and agreements to oust local leaders require multiple meetings with villagers and elders. Several days a week, Colonel George flies to remote districts to meet with tribal elders, listen to their complaints and try to cajole them into supporting the Afghan government.

This is retail politics; valley by valley, village by village. In a meeting earlier this spring in Asmar, a remote district near the border with Pakistan, elders berated him for giving money earlier in the year to corrupt district leaders—underscoring how difficult it is for the Americans to pick reliable local allies. And by the time the Americans know who is who, they are on the verge of rotating out of Afghanistan.

One village elder at the outdoor meeting looked at Colonel George and said: "You are giving the money to individuals and not to the community. Look at the directors of government agencies, look at the cars they are driving, look at the houses they build—where does that money come from? It's our money."

Diplomats who have spent years in the country working with Afghans give the Americans credit for trying, but they warn that it is easy to underestimate the complexity of Afghan tribal relationships and the profound antipathy for the government.

"One of my Afghan friends always says, 'You want a shura, I can organize one for you in 24 hours,'" said Thomas Ruttig, a former German diplomat in Kabul and an expert on the country who founded the Afghanistan Analysts Network. "The problem is, do you have the right people?"

"When you give out money, you might end up supporting one side in a local conflict—and not realizing that it's roulette," Mr. Ruttig said.

Critical Thinking

1. What are the larger implications in the Afghans mistrust of government on U.S. military efforts in Afghanistan?

2. What further frustrations are encountered once areas are safe from militants?

3. How can the Afghanistan government regain the trust of its people?

The Maldives

Kingdom of a Thousand Isles

ANDREW FORBES WITH KEVIN BISHOP

Geography and Wildlife

The Maldives is a chain of low coral atolls no more than 128 kilometres (80 miles) wide and stretching some 765 kilometres (475 miles) from north to south, running from latitude 7°N to just south of the equator. The country actually forms the central part of the Laccadive-Chagos Ridge, a submerged mountain range which is mostly about 300 metres (985 feet) deep, but increases to more than 1,000 metres (3,280 feet) deep between the main part of the country and the two southernmost atolls.

The total land area is less than 300 square kilometres (115 square miles)—a tiny fraction of the 90,000 square kilometres within its official territory. The Laccadive, Minicoy, and Amindivi Islands to the north—known collectively as Lakshadweep—belong to India, while the Chagos Archipelago to the south forms the British Indian Ocean Territory. The Maldives consists of well over 1,000 islands—as many as 2,000 if all permanently exposed banks and reefs are included. Only nine are larger than two square kilometres (one square mile), and the biggest, Fua Mulaku, is just 4.5 kilometres (three miles) at its longest point. Nowhere in the Maldives is more than four metres (15 feet) above mean sea level, so there are no hills or rivers and only two small freshwater lakes, both on Fua Mulaku.

Atoll Formation

The great English naturalist Charles Darwin first expounded the theory of atoll formation in 1842. Although he never visited the Maldives, Darwin made a close study of charts and other information about the area and described the differences between barrier and fringing reefs, and explained the creation of isolated atolls. In fact, the English word 'atoll' is derived from the Dhivehi word *atholhu*.

Darwin's revolutionary view was that an atoll is not the coral-encrusted rim of a volcanic crater, as had been thought, but is formed when a small volcanic island, or tip of a mountain peak, gradually subsides into the sea.

Coral grows in the warm, shallow water around this island, and as the sea level effectively rises, the coral growth keeps pace. Eventually, the original land disappears beneath the sea, leaving only the doughnut-shaped coral reef, or string of islets, enclosing a central lagoon. The top part of the encircling reef is mostly exposed, and covered with accumulated coral sand and other debris. It has now become an island, or a series of islands, itself. There are channels through the reef, linking the lagoon with the open sea, which are normally on the leeward side. (There is some disagreement about whether the land actually sinks, or whether the sea level rises, but this is relatively unimportant as both processes are probably involved in long-term atoll formation.)

In the last year of his life, Darwin expressed the hope that some 'doubly rich millionaire' would confirm his theory by making borings into a coral atoll. In due course, in 1952, the US Atomic Commission undertook just such a series of borings at Eniwetok Atoll, in the Pacific. The coral extended down for 1,220 metres (4,000 feet), and the underlying rock was found to contain fossilised shallow-water creatures, sure evidence that the rock had indeed changed position.

To this day, the atolls of the Maldives are considered the classical examples of coral atoll formation. Also, the Maldives has the largest true atoll in the world, Huvadhoo Atoll, which has a lagoon 112 kilometres (70 miles) in diameter, with a maximum depth of 86 metres (282 feet).

Coral

What we think of as coral is actually the external skeleton formed by a community of millions of tiny animals called polyps. These coral polyps are diminutive members of a group of sea creatures, the coelenterates, which include jellyfishes, sea anemones, and sea fans. Snorkellers and divers usually cannot see the coral polyps, partly because they are generally extremely small, but also because they are mostly nocturnal and therefore retracted during the daytime. But if you have the necessary experience, do try a night dive, when you will see them expanded with their tentacles waving gently in the current. The tentacles are armed with stinging cells—nematocysts—which they shoot into passing prey to immobilise them. The prey, which are mostly microscopic planktonic creatures, but can also include tiny shrimps and even juvenile fish, are then dragged by the tentacles into the mouth of the polyp.

But the life of the coral polyp has another important aspect, which helps explain its incredible reef-building powers. Inside the tissues of the polyp are symbiotic algae, that is, tiny plants literally 'living together' with the polyp to the mutual advantage of each. The algae use the sun's energy to convert carbon dioxide and water into oxygen and carbohydrates through the process called photosynthesis—and the coral polyp in turn makes good use of this supply of oxygen and extra food.

The limestone skeleton of the hard coral remains even when the polyps die, and it is this which forms the permanent structure we know as a coral reef. The reefs of the Maldives—and, indeed, they are the very foundation of the country—have been constructed over millennia by huge armies of tirelessly energetic coral polyps. Over 200 different species of hard coral are found in the Maldives—which contribute to the diversity of the reef, and of course create an endless variety of habitats for an astonishing range of colourful underwater creatures.

Besides the so-called 'hard corals,' described above, there are also 'soft corals' which are somewhat similar but do not have the massive external skeleton. Instead, they produce a kind of internal skeleton formed in limestone crystals. And some of the soft corals do not have the symbiotic algae of the hard, reef-building corals. One further point is that since algae depend on sunlight, and sunlight is quickly absorbed by seawater, it is rare to find much hard coral growing deeper than 30 metres (100 feet). After that, soft corals, sponges and other organisms that do not depend on the sun's rays start to take over.

The coral reef as a whole is an immensely complex ecosystem, and the interactions and survival strategies of its inhabitants are endlessly varied—and deeply fascinating for those underwater explorers with the inclination to observe and try to understand their behaviour. Most relationships that are likely to be seen by the diver are based on predator-prey interactions, however, there are some other relationships which are more harmonious. These include the association between clown fishes and potentially lethal anemones, and the mutually beneficial system known as 'cleaning symbiosis.'

Clown fish are brightly coloured, usually yellowish with a distinctive blue stripe, found hovering above or often half-hidden amongst the venomous tentacles of sea anemones: The fish protects itself from harm by secreting a mucus that disguises its own chemical composition, and at the same time covering itself with the anemone's own mucus. Thus, the anemone is deceived into thinking that the fish is actually part of itself. The benefit to the clown fish of this arrangement is that the anemone's tentacles protect it. While the benefit to the anemone is not quite so obvious, it is probable that potential predators do not bother the anemone because the presence of the brightly coloured clown fish warns them away.

Swimming around the reef, one can soon spot established 'cleaner stations' where small fish are diligently at work cleaning parasites, dead tissues, and fungus off larger species. The cleaners work over their customers' bodies, including the gill cavities and even inside the mouth, without risk of harm. In fact, the client species often seem to enjoy the experience, and are protective towards the cleaners (who also benefit by getting a meal in the process). Sometimes quite large numbers of bigger fishes will gather at the cleaning stations and it is amusing to see them wait their turn in an orderly fashion.

Besides full-time cleaners (usually species of cleaner wrasse in the Maldives), there are some which only perform this function on a part-time basis and others, such as angelfish and butterflyfish, that do it only while they are juveniles. The cleaners also include invertebrates, especially shrimps.

Fish Large and Small

Apart from the beauty of the reefs themselves—and many people consider the reefs of the Maldives to be among the most beautiful in the world—probably their greatest attraction is the dazzling variety and number of fish that inhabit them.

Firstly the lagoon, which in a typical atoll is surrounded by a protective outer reef. A surprising variety of fish can be found here, often at depths of no more than 1.5 metres (five feet). Though the bottom is mainly sandy—not normally a good place to find fish—there are outcroppings of coral that act as magnets for fish. Here you will see damselfish and clown fish, including the blackfooted clown fish which is unique to the area, and juveniles of many other colourful reef species, especially surgeonfish, triggerfish, and wrasse. You may also encounter young whitetip reef sharks in this nursery area. If you have never met a shark before, and are uneasy at the prospect, this is a good place to start, as the youngsters may only measure a metre (three feet) or so, and should allow you to conquer your fears in readiness for the big-time world of the reef itself.

Once outside the lagoon on the seaward side of the protective reef, everything changes. At first you will be awed by the sheer number and diversity of fish. More than 1,000 species have been recorded from the Maldives and the surrounding ocean, so it is one of the most species-rich marine areas of the world. With this abundance you may find your first experience of fish watching bewildering. What you can be sure of is that each dive will be different, bringing new, colourful and sometimes surprising sights. You will want to keep returning again and again.

There are fish of all sizes in the Maldives, from very small ones like the brilliant-coloured fire goby to the massive manta ray and the gigantic humphead wrasse which is the length of a tall man but much heavier, up to 190 kilograms (420 pounds). If you are lucky, you might encounter the largest fish of all, the harmless, plankton-feeding whale shark, which can attain a length of about 12 metres (40 feet) and weigh more than 20 tonnes.

But more likely you will meet those colourful and characteristic reef fish, the angelfish and their close relatives the butterflyfish; the former are mostly seen on their own, while schools of pennant butterflyfish numbering several hundred are not uncommon. There are plenty of large groupers, of which a striking example is the vermilion rock cod, bright red or orange and decorated with a maze of blue spots. Schools of surgeonfish graze the coral walls of the reef (look for the beautiful powder-blue surgeonfish), while large-eyed, nocturnal soldierfish and their cousins the squirrelfish, hang out under ledges. And you can be sure to see jack, snapper, goatfish, fusilier, anthias, coral-crunching parrotfish (you can actually hear them doing it), and a host of others.

145

There are some special sights to look forward to in the Maldives. Unicornfish are fairly common here, though not so elsewhere. The aptly named cowfish, a member of the boxfish family, has one pair of 'horns' pointing forwards. The large red-faced batfish is a companionable creature, and it is not unusual for a group of them to escort divers while they explore the reef.

Sharks and turtles—green, loggerhead, leatherback, and especially hawksbill—are relatively common, and an underwater encounter with one of the great amphibians is an outstanding experience. Ungainly on land—and it is only the females who ever return to the beach to lay their eggs—some turtles can reach speeds of 50 kph (31 mph) or more in the sea.

Among other denizens of Maldivian reefs are slow-moving lionfish, beautiful but poisonous—though easy to avoid—and sharp-toothed moray eels poking out of holes in the coral. Although quite harmless unless you harass them, it is probably wise not to tempt fate by touching a moray eel, as some people do, for it has a grip of steel and you would never be able to pull free if it did choose to bite your arm. Starfish, brittle stars, feather stars, sea urchins, sea cucumbers, sea squirts and hermit crabs are just some of the other life-forms to be seen and enjoyed.

Land Animals and Birds

Compared with the astonishing richness of the marine life, the terrestrial fauna of the Maldives is very limited, in common with other small oceanic islands. Nevertheless, it is quite interesting, though as yet little studied.

Most of the animals have come to the Maldives from India or Sri Lanka, and indeed all of the mammals and reptiles are also found in those two countries except the fruit bat, or flying fox, which is judged to be a distinct Maldivian sub-species. The fruit bat no doubt made its own way to the Maldives, but the other mammals—the black rat, house mouse, and Indian house shrew—were almost certainly introduced by man or came on ships. There are also a few cats and goats, but no dogs (or indeed pigs) as these are prohibited for religious reasons.

The reptiles, which may also have been introduced, include two nocturnal house geckos, a colourful agamid lizard that is fairly common on some islands, a skink, and two non-poisonous snakes. In addition, there is one species of frog and one toad. Little is known about the invertebrates, but there are nearly 70 species of butterflies.

Birds are more numerous, with more than a hundred different kinds recorded, but only a small proportion of these breed in the islands.

The two commonest land birds are the house crow and the koel, a type of cuckoo that depends on the crow as host for its eggs. These are present on most of the inhabited islands, including Malé, and the resort islands. The crow has increased to pest proportions but no effective method of control has yet been found. The koel by contrast is seldom seen, though its varied and remarkable repertoire of calls (some sound like a girl screaming) are unmistakable.

There is a total absence of small passerine birds. However, the non-indigenous rose-ringed parakeet, bright green with a red bill, is a colourful sight on Malé and nearby islands. The only other land bird likely to be seen is the rather elusive white-breasted waterhen, which nests under low bushes and rank vegetation in the centre of some islands in Malé Atoll.

Some 13 different herons are found in the Maldives. The commonest is the large grey heron, which stands on the outer reefs of most islands waiting patiently for a suitable meal to swim by. Some of the other herons are thought to be endemic sub-species.

Most numerous are the seabirds, among which are several terns including the graceful fairy tern (though this is confined to Addu Atoll in the south). Two frigate birds breed in the Maldives in small numbers, the great and the lesser; two noddies (which fishermen watch out for as they indicate where the tuna are); Audubon's shearwater; and one of the most elegant of seabirds, the white-tailed tropic bird. It is possible the red-tailed and red-billed tropic birds also breed here.

A number of migrant birds, and others that have been blown off course, visit the Maldives at various times of the year. They include petrels, ducks, shearwaters, various birds of prey, and such birds as whimbrels, plovers and sandpipers.

Flora

As with animal life, the Maldives are not rich in terrestrial plant species. Of about 600 species, more than half were probably introduced for food or other human use, such as herbs, in medicine or as ornamental plants or shade trees. Others are common tropical plants that are often found in association with man. It has been estimated that fewer than 100 species might have colonised the islands before the arrival of man.

Even including all the introductions, the Maldives have far fewer plant species than it has islands, unlike the situation in most tropical island groups. The explanation may be that in the low-lying Maldives there are not many different ecological niches available, and thus only limited possibilities for plant colonisation.

One very interesting point, which has been noted by Dr Dennis Adams of the Natural History Museum in London, is that most of the common native plants of the Maldives are also found on similar islands in the Pacific, but are rare or absent in between. He suggests that they reached the Maldives from the Pacific, rather than the other way round.

Only five of the Maldivian plants are said to be true endemic species (not found anywhere else), and these are the local varieties of pandanus, or screw pine. The question is still open, however, as it seems unlikely that these trees alone should be endemic, especially as their seeds are very well adapted for oceanic dispersal. Furthermore, the Maldivians themselves do not recognise five kinds of pandanus but three, which they identify as small, medium and large.

As for cultivated plants, the visitor may see breadfruit, mango, tamarind, areca nut palms, lime, watermelon, pineapple and banana. Crops include millet, some sorghum, sweet potato, taro, manioc, and Indian arrowroot. It should be noted that nowadays relatively few islands go in for agriculture and to spot these crops is pretty rare. Rice is not grown, but substantial quantities are imported.

Theorising 'Small' and 'Micro' State Behaviour Using the Maldives, Bhutan and Nepal

Amalendu Misra

While there is no disputing that many states in the developing world are weak, paradoxically, these entities are often endowed with a strong social base. Consequently, social forces exhibit forms of resistance when the state or the governing regime attempts to introduce forms of negative social control. The existence of this social base, therefore, is a deterrent to predatory governance. In this context, owing to the limitations imposed by geography and the prevalent interconnectedness among individuals and families, society in small and micro states is far more cohesive than in their larger counterparts. This social endowment gives members greater strength to withstand forms of negative social control imposed on behalf of the state.

While social cohesion in small and micro states exists, one cannot expect a similar degree of power available to oppose the state. This anomaly is best explained if one takes into account the nature of the society itself. Geographical limitations often create a homogenised social pattern. The society, then, can be described as a large extended family where each individual is linked to the other through a network of bonds. Their kinship may include a common history, bloodline, religion and appreciation of what one might describe as a singular cultural way of life. This is best described as a patrimonial model, where the state is caught in the trap of a 'clientele effect (clan, ethnic religious, territorial and other segregation and/or favouritism)'. Owing to this quirk, inheritance, individuals and society sleepwalk into a form of governance best described as a patron–client relationship.

Locked into this form of a power relationship, the citizenry of small and micro states may find it hard to forge alternatives to challenge various forms of social control imposed by the ruling house, government or regime. Essentially, these are police states where freedom of speech is compromised. Leadership, in this context, ranges from hard to soft authoritarianism. Another peculiarity is the continuation or dominance of one party or one person rule that steamrollers all opposition.

Modelled directly after the political culture mentioned earlier, the Maldives and Bhutan are its authentic representatives. The Maldives' president and the Bhutanese monarch are both into their third decades of their respective rule. While it is true that, under their leadership, both countries have witnessed some prosperity and stability, both the Maldives and Bhutan exhibit the political paranoia associated with authoritarian leadership.

The Maldives are a republic only in name, as the defining character of state power and authority is channelled through personal rulership. A running joke among critics of the Maldives goes:

Question: 'Who wouldn't like to be a prisoner in a paradise island?'

Answer: 'The Maldivians themselves'.

Although the country managed to rid itself of the old sultanate system, sultanism exists under a new guise. Even a cursory glance at the nature of Maldivian polity reveals what Weber described as 'Sultanism without Sultans'. In this context:

the person or individual exercising authority is not a 'superior' but a personal 'chief'. His administrative staff does not consist primarily of officials, but instead personal retainers . . . What determines the relations of the administrative staff to the chief is not personal obligation of office, but personal loyalty to the chief.

By electing himself for a record sixth five-year term in a yes/no referendum in which voters are presented with a single candidate chosen by the *Majlis* (parliament), Maumoon Abdul Gayoom has fulfilled some of the notions presented within the Weberian interpretation. As the president is responsible for appointing members of the cabinet and the judiciary, as well as close to one-fifth of the *Majlis*' members, it forces one to appreciate the timelessness of Weberian notion of Sultanism without Sultans in this particular situation. Weber also reminds us that, whenever there is a strain in the patron–client relationship in such polities, the ruler takes unprecedented measures to stifle opposition.

Interestingly, there are no political parties in the Maldives despite the absence of an official ban on political activity. Journalists, media persons and the press are permitted limited criticism of the state, but the government still has the power to shut these media outlets. Given that all media outlets are either government owned or state controlled, it is not particularly a hard task to indoctrinate everyone into the language of 'sultanspeak'. Interestingly, in recent years, those Maldivians who have refused to give into this form of self-censorship are labelled as 'drug addicts' by no less a personality than the country's president.

Apart from the patrimonial and pre-capitalist inheritance, there is another significant reason why micro and small states opt for authoritarian modes of governance. The authoritarian solution (benign or otherwise), it could be argued, guarantees economic stability. Defending this deeply personal and authoritarian policy, the Maldives' president has gone on the record to underscore that 'his country's limited democracy has helped create strong economic growth'. This sentiment is echoed within a section of Maldives' society that has benefited enormously from this patron–client relationship. Those who have missed out, however, are less certain of this form of benevolent authoritarianism.

There is no denying the fact that it is relatively easy to exercise what Weber would call 'genuinely patrimonial authority' in a small or micro state. The existence of a single clan, tribe or ethnic group fulfills the socio-biological necessities or preconditions that are crucial to the maintenance, furtherance and survival of patrimonial authority. This form of patrimonial authority is best suited, according to Weber, in a 'pre-capitalist' society; a state or society that decides to step back into history, that is.

A globalised world, however, clearly makes the idea of the continuance of pre-capitalist structure outmoded. Is there any escape route from this inevitable force? Insularity is often a great asset for those states that wish to continue with their traditional ways of governance or preferred way of life. By hermetically sealing the country from outside or external influence, a society could perhaps retreat into this pre-capitalist structure of existence. This is made possible if it is exercised through authoritarianism and the citizenry feels committed (for several different reasons that are often overlapping, such as: a perceived threat to life and property; indoctrination; or a genuine sense of togetherness expressed through a singularity of identity made possible by common ethnicity, religion and history).

Two states in the annals of contemporary international society are genuinely committed to a pre-capitalist structure of governance. One is North Korea and the other is Bhutan. In both cases, the reasons behind such ideological and structural preferences are somewhat different. Yet the common thread that runs through these two disparate polities is the patrimonial factor. As Weber reminds us, 'the political administration in a pre-capitalist patrimonial order is treated purely as a personal affair of the ruler and political power is considered part of his personal property.'

The monarchy in Bhutan not only exercises a patron–client relationship with its citizenry, but also affirms a pre-capitalistic logic. In order to consolidate the ethno-cultural homogeneity of the state-forming ethnos (which never fully existed in the country), the Bhutanese monarchy has regularly embarked on controversial policy implementations that are, at best, discriminatory and, at worst, culturally genocidal. Notwithstanding the avowed ethno-cultural prefernces of to the regime, there has been scarcely any attempt to modernise the state as modernisation actively threatens to dislocate the traditional authority of the monarch.

The retreat to this discriminatory and pre-capitalist mode of governance in the case of the Maldives and Bhutan has very little rational legal justification. Some small states might adopt such extreme policy preferences if confronted by genuine internal or external threats. Neither the Maldives nor Bhutan face such challenges to their sovereignty. That said, why do they exhibit such paranoia; why this utter disregard for true democratic ideals? The answer to this can be traced, once again, to Weber's interpretation. The explanation one can draw by using his thesis is a deceptively simple one: a traditional, patrimonial, and pre-capitalist polity is enslaved to an individual or family. Consequently, the overall governance is subject to that individual's, or persons', whims and fancies. Since this individual or person is not a 'legal rational authority' in the modern sense of the term, there exists very little scope for that actor to take into consideration or give due attention to egalitarian ideals.

Clientelism and Corruption

Conventional wisdom suggests that small states, due to their size, are more transparent by nature. The socio-economic and political process in these states is much more exposed to public scrutiny. It is probable that any decision-making process or transaction will be leaked into the public domain. Therefore, the regime, the bureaucracy and the elite tend to be more conscious of their public transaction. This, at least, is the theory. In practice, however, small states are no different from their big counterparts. If anything, they are more corrupt and engage in such practices relatively unhindered under the guise of what is often called clientelism.

According to Transparency International, most developing states are vulnerable to corruption and nepotism. Indeed, they constitute the core of the corruption index prepared by Transparency International. In the case of large developing states, accusations of corruption and nepotism lose their intensity in proportion to their size. Could it be that, although the same levels of irregularities exist in small states, owing to their smallness such issues are magnified several times over? The answer is likely to be yes. But there is no denying that occurrences of corruptness, bribery, kickbacks and favouritism are rampant in small states.

In most small states, there is often collusion between the ruling authority and the upper levels of the society. Therefore, the leadership, bureaucracy and elite in a great majority of these countries, scoff at 'western notions of transparency'. They adopt various ways and methods to counter any allegations of wrongdoing. They either 'buy off their critics' if enough money is available or 'come down heavily on their detractors' during the lean period.

Small states are especially vulnerable to extreme levels of corruption and economic nepotism. Deborah Bräutigam and Michael Woolcock argue that a 'close-knit political arrangement and centralisation can lead to higher levels of corruption in such states as both the ruling regime and its officials may be more accessible to clientelist and "old boy" network pressure'. A cursory look at cross-country comparison of South Asian small states shows that the aforementioned two complementary processes are at work. Taken together, they can be defined either as clientelism or, for lack of a better word, corruption.

The affluent world's hunger for paradise islands under the sun has radically altered the profile of the Maldives. These erstwhile specs of sand and fishing outposts are now one of the most sought-after destinations in the itinerary of pleasure-seeking tourists. The country has exploited this opportunity in earnest. Although the tourism industry is now well entrenched, and is currently the mainstay of the Maldives' economy, it is dominated by a select few individuals. Major contracts on hotels and the ancillary service sector are dished out to the inner coterie of the president, members of the *Majlis* and the powerful elite residing in the capital. Profits made by the tourism industry are unevenly distributed. Those close to the president and his coterie are given opportunities to engage in this sector according to the terms of clientelism while those outside it often have very little or nothing.

Male, the capital, being on a significant piece of land and the centre of all government activities, has also assumed the character of a metropole. Decades of revenue from tourism and its concentration in the city have corrupted its society and eroded the work ethic of its residents. Unsurprisingly, those in various outlying inhabited islands have remained on the periphery, both in the literal and developmental sense. The 'Male mafia', as one Maldivian dissident puts it, has cornered all the largesse from tourism.

The centre-periphery or metropolis-satellite analogy used to describe the levels of corruption and wealth concentration in the Maldives is equally evident in Nepal. In a study conducted in the 1970s, a group of British anthropologists and developmental economists found that 22 percent of Nepal's population held almost 93 percent of all the higher civil service and political posts. While there is no accurate figure available for current state of affairs, it is widely held that there has not been any significant change in earlier statistics—hence the rise in left-wing insurgency and its ideology of radical socio-economic transformation. 'It is probable that in terms of its gross domestic product (GDP), Nepal has received more foreign aid per head than any other country in the world'. Nonetheless, the per-capita average annual income is one of the lowest in the world, touching barely US$250. There can be several explanations of this contrasting picture, the most important being the distribution and accumulation of wealth according to caste hierarchy and geographical positioning.

Most of Nepal remains a periphery of the Kathmandu valley and is dominated by upper-caste Bahuns, Chhetris and Newars.

They hold all key government posts and have a stronghold in the private sector. Social, economic and political exclusion of lower castes and those inhabiting the areas beyond Kathmandu valley is institutionalised. The Nepalese themselves admit that, even after the restoration of democracy in 1990, caste discrimination in the country is on the rise. The level of corruption is blatant, and the current monarch and his coterie control the lucrative hotel and tourism industry.

William Easterly has argued that 'good institutions can help mediate the latent social conflicts associated with ethnic and economic inequality'. For all practical purposes, Nepal's indigenous institutional set-up is blighted by inefficiency and corruption. Perhaps one naturally turns to the external bodies to intervene and thus, for decades, Nepal has attracted hordes of non-governmental organisations and international non-governmental organisations. Even then, argues Alan Macfarlane, 'most of the money was recycled back to the donor countries in the form of large salaries to their "experts" and to pay for machinery and goods from the donor country'. The country's elite, often the intermediaries in many projects, were responsible for mismanaging the remainder of any allocated funds. A nearly decade-long civil war and an ineffective government have scared off major international investments and infrastructural developments. This balance sheet on Nepal indicates that it risks being the first failed state of South Asia. . . .

In the event that a small state does not recognise this status, dominant powers can wilfully ignore the security needs of the former and let it plunge into chaos. Such accusations are common from small states. The question, therefore, is how they confront internal threats and meet their security challenges. Small states often wallow in prolonged periods of insecurity, and experience bouts of turmoil before they attract any regional or external intervention for the furtherance of peace and order. The civil war in Nepal and the response of India and China to unfolding events in the Himalayan kingdom is a case in point.

Nepal is one of a handful of Asian countries that escaped European colonisation. At a time when the underlying principle behind intervention is linked to the issue of historical or postcolonial responsibility, Nepal's inheritance sits at odds with its current predicament. Tucked between two great Asian powers that refuse to tolerate outside forces next to their frontiers, Nepal is forced to undergo a painful process of slow disintegration. Although New Delhi has the power to curb the Maoist uprising in Nepal, it has dragged its feet on the matter.

Having failed to elicit support from its neighbours, Nepal has begun to approach distant powers for help. Britain, the European Union and the United States are unanimous in their belief that the internal disorder in this small state is a threat both to Nepal itself and to the larger world. The United States, for its part, 'has decided that the only way to prevent Nepal from becoming a "failed state" or, worse still, a "rogue nation" is to increase the flow of military aid'. US Ambassador to Nepal Michael Malinowski, contemplating the Maoist insurgency, has argued that, although the country is 'a long way from the United States . . . we're concerned that areas in Nepal don't get out of control, don't become a vacuum where terrorist groups can move into and use Nepal for whatever'. Thus, as stated earlier, a security situation in a small state has the potential to affect regional as well as global peace.

Small states also are at risk from natural threats. Small island states are among the most susceptible areas in the world to environment extremes, and they constantly face the high economic, social and environmental consequences of cyclones, hurricanes, tidal waves, and so on. Small island states also face serious physical challenges owing to global environmental pollution. Global warming is considered one of the most alarming of threats to their survival as rising sea levels may lead to the partial loss of territory of small island states—or even their complete disappearance under the rising waves.

Modernisation and the pressures of overpopulation is another factor posing a serious thereat to the physical survival of small island states. Although global warming is one of the main culprits, 'the phenomena of shrinking' also may be attributed to modernisation projects undertaken by that particular state. In their attempt to attain a better standard of life, many communities have embraced ways and means that actually contribute to the problem. Pumping out ground water, using sand for construction, and thinning out indigenous greenery are all responsible for damaging the fragile ecosystem of these already vulnerable small island states.

The environment must be understood as a key national security issue for most states. However, trying to map out different trajectories to environmental challenges in the context of South Asian small states is not an easy task. There are both alarmists and those who maintain a blasé attitude to the entire subject. For instance, if survey reports, newspaper articles and documentaries provide credible proof, the Maldives is on the way to extinction in the next few decades due to global warming and unregulated exploitation of nature by its native population. A government White Paper on the state of the environment in the Maldives, however, describes meticulous efforts to protect its fragile ecosystem. Nevertheless, increased tourist activity, new developmental projects, and the upwardly mobile lifestyle of the islanders continue to contribute irreparable damage to the ecology of the Maldives.

Like the Maldives, Nepal also has its fair share of misfortune when it comes to environmental degradation. However, unlike the Maldives, which is primarily hostage to external factors, the damage done to the environment in Nepal is mostly man-made. Of all South Asian states, environmental degradation is most grim here. In Nepal, abject poverty leads to predatory ecological practices, while the absence of any coherent environmental policy planning and erratic climatic conditions also have contributed to a gradually unfolding environmental nightmare. Perpetual landslides, flooding and changed rainfall patterns have seriously undermined the physical and socio-economic security of a substantial portion of the Nepalese population.

Democracy and Development

Small states that consciously adhere to democratic procedures reap long-term benefits. Democracy complements economic development and ensures social cohesion and stability, and the small island state of Mauritius exemplifies this model. Since the early 1970s, it has religiously embraced modern democratic ideals and norms in its political process. The observance of such practices and procedures has put Mauritius on a par where British political and civil liberties are concerned. The political stability ensured by democracy has allowed the state to spend almost 40 percent of its budget on social expenditures (including education, health care, universal old age pensions, housing, social assistances, and food subsidies). This egalitarian economic policy in Mauritius has spanned almost four decades. Although the country itself has a diverse population, both in religious and ethnic terms, it is one the most stable polities in Africa—and a very successful small state.

Note, however, that popular democracy is not a prerequisite for social and economic development; rather, a healthy socio-economic base creates impetus for the furtherance of an effective democracy. For underdeveloped micro and small states, such a policy recommendation can be a conundrum as the absence of a viable economic structure and a backward economy opens the door for various forms of authoritarianism: 'Democracy as a stable state . . . is highly desirable, but democratisation, or the process of getting to such stable democracy, can trigger highly undesirable side effects'. Some societies that attempt to shrug off non-democratic practices find themselves in a painful transition. A decade and half ago, the Nepalese embraced the logic of democracy and constitutionalism over absolute monarchy. This new ideology, however, has had difficulty striking roots in the country's body politic; for instance, from 1990 to 2004, there have been twelve governments and ten prime ministers.

With a democratic government bungling its response to societal ills and a deteriorating economy, Nepal may be the first failed state in South Asia. 'Failed states', argues Martin Doornbos, 'are fragile states suddenly facing deteriorating economic conditions which seriously affect the livelihood of a large majority of the population, leading to a breakdown of state institutions.' The unfortunate truth is that Nepalese socio-economic well-being has fallen since its democratisation. Nepal is currently one of the poorest countries in the world with a standard of living equal with some states in sub-Saharan Africa.

In Nepal, one response to failing development has taken the form of a revolutionary people's democracy. This alternative ideology offered by a section of disaffected society in the past ten years is new, untested and uncertain of its long-term viability. Unsurprisingly, those towards whom this experiment is projected remain difficult customers. They neither fully embrace the logic of subversion nor remain committed to constitutional deliberative democracy. The ensuing result is a long and drawn-out violent struggle. Uncertainty is rampant in Nepalese society as left-wing rebels vying for a new political system and structure of governance stir unrest. Doornbos warns that 'a state undergoing a major struggle over power and over the political and cultural orientation and organisation of society is a potentially failed state'. If the current state of affairs in Nepal is anything to go by, the population of this Himalayan kingdom are sleepwalking towards a very dark future indeed.

The crude truth that emerges from our assessment of democracy project in the Maldives, Bhutan and Nepal is that the hasty introduction of Western-style democracy may not be conducive to certain societies. Indeed, small states that have introduced democracy in small measures have succeeded in avoiding a general breakdown of order, while small states with authoritarian or illiberal democratic regimes have been able to maintain a higher standard of life for their people.

Avoiding the Inevitable

If we are to comprehend the pervasive patterns of failure in many of the small states in South Asia, we must focus on the character and capacity of the concerned state, the forms of governing structure that they posses, and the institutional mechanism that sustains them. William Easterly and Aart Kraay argue that small states can avoid a slow slide down the path of state failure by 'opening up more to international capital markets'. Although there is merit in this argument, not all small states are in a position to diversify their economy nor reach out to international capital markets. Small states, as highlighted earlier, often have a monocultural economic base that restricts diversification.

That said, some small states have succeeded in registering higher economic growth. A number have benefited from travellers: 'since the 1960s, tourism has grown in excess of 5 percent per year . . . [to] become the largest global industry, accounting for 10 percent of the world GDP and 7 percent of capital spending'. Many small states, especially in the Caribbean Sea, have adopted new forms of economic activity that have released them from a reliance on traditional monocrops (such as sugar, copra, and fish), and those with good natural resources and a more cohesive population have been better able to adapt to change. However, in small states, such positive economic growth depends on their being endowed with an enticing natural landscape, possessing an industrial and infrastructural base capable of diversifying, having access to preferential trade arrangements, and enjoying relative political stability. In the absence of some or all of these features, a small state may remain committed to a pre-capitalist economic structure and, therefore, be susceptible to economic uncertainties that affect their political process.

The three small states in South Asia under discussion possess only some of the characteristics already highlighted. The Maldives continues to reap the benefits of worldwide tourism. The isolationist policy of Bhutan, however, has deterred the growth of a tourist industry in the country. Nepal, once a favourite destination for adventure tourism, has grown out of favour as the decade-long left-wing insurgency has led to the growth of antisocial attitudes towards foreigners. The paucity of industrialisation coupled with overt dependence on India for trade and commerce has stifled the economies of Bhutan and Nepal. Little wonder, then, that Nepal have shown negative growth in the economic sector and has continued to slip in the economic ranking of states.

While Easterly and Kraay suggest that small economies can 'take advantage of opportunities to diversify away their special risks since they are currently not particularly financially open and the shocks they receive are relatively uncorrelated with those experienced by the rest of the world', this is not a convincing argument. In the face of rapid economic globalisation, it is almost impossible for any state, regardless of size, to engage in any form of protectionism. On the other hand, argue Bouayad-Agha and Fernandez, an economic arrangement marked by:

> high foreign trade dependence, especially if based on a limited number of export commodities and sectors, can leave a country highly exposed to external economic developments. A sharp decline in the world price of the main export commodity, or the withdrawal or reduction of trade preference in a major export market or shifting of preference as with tourism, can have a devastating impact on the economy of a small country.

In short, the smallest fluctuation in the international financial market has far-reaching effects, where the originating ripple grows into a tidal wave by the time it reaches bottom-rung or small economies. Therefore, contrary to Easterly and Kraay's position, the economies of small and micro states are actually more in jeopardy and are less able to rebound than their larger counterparts. Indeed, these states have always been more vulnerable in the global economy not only because monocultural 'trade comprises a larger proportion of their economic activity than it does in large states, but also because they lack the power to set any of the terms or make any of the rules that govern globalisation'.

Although foreign investment can stimulate development in small backward economies, this escape route is strewn with insurmountable challenges. Small states commonly suffer from a lack of confidence by investors who tend to regard them as riskier choices than larger ones. Attracting external capital inflow also requires complete autonomy that some of these countries may not possess. Bhutan and Nepal's landlocked status and preferential trade agreements with India imply that any form of large-scale industrialisation or acceptance in the international capital market will have to be negotiated with New Delhi. This requires considerable good will from India, as well as a willingness of external investors to endow Bhutan and Nepal with investments. Since India is currently attracting massive foreign direct investment and is itself undergoing a renewed process of industrialisation, the chances of its small neighbours receiving similar attention is remote.

The remoteness and insularity of small states is one of the greatest hindrances to their development. Indeed, 'isolation from major centres of trade and commerce makes it difficult for them to turn to world markets'. One might argue that, since both Bhutan and Nepal have access to an ever-expanding market in India, they do not necessarily need access to the world market beyond. While a valid argument, their reliance on India creates a dependency circle that necessitates them to gear their respective economies to a monocultural structure akin to a form of economic imperialism.

The Effects of Globalisation

Globalisation favours large states with huge economies while making it extremely difficult for small states to be influential players in the global arena. Globalisation has exposed many well-established, self-sufficient small states to an external environment in which they have little or no control. Globalisation, argues Halldor Asgrimsson:

> calls for adaptation from domestic self-sufficiency to an international market economy, e.g. in the areas of trade, culture, transport and communication. This radical change could prove difficult for many smaller states because their existence is often based on the individual characteristics of the nation state and their economies often lack the resilience which is the fruit of diversity.

Challenges emanating from the economic sector are the most worrisome for many small states. As they are handicapped by small domestic markets and suffer from backward economies, small states, although outward-looking, are dependent on their more powerful neighbours 'to meet some of their very basic necessities'. Moreover, their extreme economic dependence on other states often jeopardises the independent decision-making process of small states.

However, all is not lost. Globalisation need not destroy small states if, write Bräutigam and Woolcock, 'they are able to combine economic competitiveness, continual innovation, and increasingly higher value-added production, with reductions in poverty and improvements in key socio-economic indicators such as health, longevity, literacy, and social violence'.

Yet, of the three small states in South Asia discussed in this study, only one has shown some measure of adaptability to changes in the global economic environment. The Maldives has made progress in developing its infrastructure and industries, both in the tourist and fisheries segments, and has been mindful of investing in social sectors such as health and education. Even so, the country remains seen as highly vulnerable in terms of issues related to its environment. Bhutan faces a worrisome future in both the economic and environmental terms, while Nepal, with a very low GDP and rapid environmental degradation, has the most to improve of all three.

Critical Thinking

1. In what ways does an authoritarian form of government guarantee economic stability?

2. Is it more difficult for small states to become corrupt due to their obvious transparency?

3. How is U.S. military aid seen as a solution to Nepal's problems?

Glossary of Terms and Abbreviations

Adivasi Literally, "first dweller"; members of India's tribal population, officially recognized in the Constitution as Scheduled Tribes eligible for placement up to a designated percentage in schools and government jobs.

Al-Qaeda "The Base"; a loose collection of Islamic terrorist cells held together by their fundamentalist zeal to resist the encroachment of Western secularist power and values on the Muslim community (Ummah), and by financial support from contributions to Salafiyyah mosques throughout the world and from patrons like Osama bin Laden (died on May 2, 2011).

Asoka A Mauryan emperor in northern India from 268 to 232 B.C. Overcome with remorse about deaths caused by his military conquests, he abandoned warfare as an instrument of imperial power and adopted the Buddhist Dharma as the standard for his rule. He enforced this expectation in a series of edicts carved into stones and pillars throughout his kingdom. His example is recognized today in the adoption of the lion capital on one of his pillars as the insignia of the Republic of India.

Ayodhya, Uttar Pradesh A small city in the eastern part of India's largest state which is a national pilgrimage center as the birthplace of Lord Ram with the rise of Hindu religious nationalism in the 1980s. The destruction of the Babri Mosque there by Hindu pilgrims in 1992 led to communal riots throughout India and abroad. *See* Babur.

Babur The first of the Mughal emperors, who established the Mughal empire in India in 1516.

Bharatiya Janata Party (BJP) "Indian Peoples Party" grew as a Hindu nationalist party out of the heartland of the Ganga (Gangetic) plain to become the only party to challenge Congress Party hegemony on a national level. Led by Atal Behari Vajpayee, it attained leadership in Parliament with the support of a 19-party coalition in 1998, and with a 24-party coalition in 1999. Riding high on a platform of Hindu nationalism and economic reform, it lost to the Congress Party in the elections in 2004.

Brahmin The priestly class, ranked highest on the varna caste scale.

Buddhism A religious faith that started in India in the sixth century B.C. by Siddhartha Gautama, who renounced his royal heritage to seek enlightenment for the salvation of all humankind. The attainment of Nirvana (his death) is placed at 483 B.C. This faith extended throughout Asia in two major traditions: Theravada ("Teaching of the Elders") to Sri Lanka and Southeast Asia; and Mahayana ("Great Vehicle") to China and Japan. Tibetan Buddhism is a subset of the Mahayana tradition. Theravada has been called Hinayana ("Lesser Vehicle") by Mahayana Buddhists to distinguish that tradition from their own.

Congress Party As the successor of the Indian National Congress in 1935, under the leadership of Jawaharlal Nehru, it led to the independence of India in 1947, and to the Republic of India in 1950. The party remained in power in Parliament for 45 years, led by Nehru's daughter, Indira Gandhi, after his death in 1964, and by his grandson Ranjiv Gandhi, after her death in 1984. Narasimha Rao became prime minister after the death of Ranjiv Gandhi in 1991, until 1996. Nehru's granddaughter-in-law, Sonia Gandhi, elected president of the party in 1998, led it to victory in the parliamentary elections in 2004.

Dalits The "broken" or "oppressed"; this is the name preferred by those traditionally known as scheduled castes, outcastes, or untouchables, members of the lowest-rank communities in the classical caste system, below the four ranks of priests, warriors, peasants, and laborers on the varna social scale. Mahatma Gandhi, deeply concerned about removing their oppression, called them *Harijans,* "children of God."

Deccan Literally, "southern"; refers to the plateau between the eastern and western mountains (ghats) and south of the Vindhya Mountains in peninsular India.

Dharma Translated as "law, justice, duty, cosmic order," the moral standard by which society and an individual's life are ordered and given meaning.

Godhra, Gujarat A small city in a growing industrial state in which Mahatma Gandhi was born, where a gang of slum dwelling Muslims set fire to a railway car full of pilgrims returning from Ayodhya on February 27, 2002. The death of 59, including women and children, led to violent reprisals against Muslims in the city, which killed more than 1,000 Muslims and left many more homeless.

Green Revolution An upsurge in agricultural production that followed the introduction of high-yielding hybrids of rice and grains, developed by the Rockefeller Foundation in Mexico and the Philippines, into South Asia during the 1950s and 1960s.

Harappa and Mohenjo Daro The two largest cities excavated during the 1920s and 1930s in the Indus River Valley to reveal an ancient urban culture that began around 3000 B.C. It flourished for 1,000 years and then inexplicably disappeared.

Hindi The prevalent language and literature of northern central India.

Hindu One who follows the faith of Hinduism.

Hinduism The dominant religion of India, emphasizing Dharma, with its ritual and social observances and often mystical contemplation and ascetic practices.

Hindutva "Hindu-ness"; a political platform of the Hindu nationalist Bharatiya Janata Party, which aspires to rule India according to the classical norms of Great Tradition, i.e., pre-Islamic, India.

Hurriyat Conference The consolidation of some 23 Kashmiri Muslim insurgent groups in 1993 to seek an end to Indian military occupation and an independent Islamic Kashmiri homeland. Many in these groups are committed to finding a peaceful resolution and are in dialogue with the government of India. Others have received monetary support, arms, and training from Pakistan as well as the support of *jihadis* from all over the Islamic world.

Indian National Congress An association of educated Indians and sympathetic Europeans who gathered in Bengal in 1885 to seek admission for qualified Indians into the British Indian Civil Service. In the early twentieth century, this association became the bearer of the independence movement of the subcontinent from British colonial rule. Following the establishment of a provisional government in 1935, it evolved into the Congress Party.

Islam A religious faith started in Arabia during the seventh century A.D. by the prophet Mohammad.

Islamization A policy adopted by General Mohammad Zia-al-Haq of Pakistan in the late 1970s to win political support for his martial rule from a growing Islamic fundamentalist movement in his country, spurred by the Soviet military incursion into neighboring Afghanistan.

Jain A religious faith started in India by Mahavira in the sixth century B.C. Its primary teachings include the eternal transmigration of souls and the practice of nonviolence toward all living creatures.

Jajmani A barter system of economic activity in the village, in which villagers provide their services on a regular basis to particular land owners—their patrons—in exchange for fixed portions of the annual harvest.

Jati An extended kinship group, usually identified with a traditional occupation, that defines the parameters of accepted marriage relationships. It is the unit that is ranked in the hierarchical social (caste) structure that moves within that structure.

Jihad "Struggle"; the quest to become part of a pure Muslim community (*Ummah*) by practicing an exemplary religious life in submission to Allah and by protecting it from all that would deny or destroy it. In the twentieth century, it took on the obligation among fundamentalist Muslims to become religious warriors, *jihadis*, on behalf of the faith.

Khalistan An independent state movement in the South Asian subcontinent for Sikhs.

Koran The sacred scripture of the Islamic faith, the teachings of Allah (God) as revealed to His prophet Mohammad in the seventh century A.D.

Ladakh The easternmost and highest region of the state of Jammu and Kashmir, inhabited mostly by Buddhists.

Lama A leader of a Tibetan Buddhist monastic community (sangha).

Lashkar-e-Taiba (Militia of the Righteous) A militant wing of a large Pakistan Sunni religiously fundamentalist organization, Markaz-ud-Dawa-wal-Irshad. Committed to restoring Islamic rule over all of India, it has been actively supporting the insurgency in Kashmir to free Muslims from Indian military occupation since 1993. It was declared a terrorist organization by the United States in 2001 and banned by the Pakistan Government in 2002. Identified with many terrorist acts in India, including the bombing of commuter trains in Mumbai on July 11, 2006, it played a major role in fund raising and relief work following the massive earthquake in Pakistan in October 2005. It is also known as Jamaat ud-Dawa (Party of the Calling).

Liberation Tigers of the Tamil Nation (LTTE) The militant separatist organization of Tamil-speaking Hindus in northern Sri Lanka. This insurgency sprang up in the 1980s under the leadership of V. Pirapaharan to seek by force a homeland independent of Sinhalese domination. Its violent ravaging, including suicide bombings, continued until it declared a cease-fire in December 2001 and entered into peace negotiations under Norwegian auspices with the Sri Lankan government in September 2002.

Lok Sabha and Rajya Sabha The two houses of Parliament in the Republic of India: "The House of the People" (Lok Sabha) has 545 members elected directly by voters on the district level; "The Council of States" (Rajya Sabha) has 250 members, 12 appointed by the president and 238 elected by state legislatures.

Loya Jirga A council of Afghan chieftains and clan leaders called by claimants to regional power to recognize their authority to rule. Such a council was convened in June 2002 under United Nations auspices in Kabul to create a provisional government to restore civil order to the war-ravaged country of Afghanistan.

Mahabharata The Great Epic of India, with more than 90,000 stanzas, composed around the third century B.C. The longest poem in the world, it is the story of five brothers' struggle to wrest their father's kingdom from their cousins. This epic contains the *Bhagavad Gita,* a discourse between one of the brothers, Arjuna, and his charioteer, Krishna, on the eve of the culminating battle with their cousins, when Arjuna is overcome by concerns about appropriate behavior and quality of life.

Mahar A depressed (untouchable) community in the state of Maharashtra, which converted to Buddhism in October 1956 as an initiative to free themselves as a community from the social burden of untouchability, under the leadership of Dr. B. R. Ambedkar.

Mahatma Literally "great souled one"; a title given to Mohandas Gandhi by Rabindranath Tagore in 1921 and adopted by the people of India to express their belief in Gandhi's saintliness.

Mandal Commission Established by the government in India in 1979 to identify backward communities eligible for reserved access for placement in schools and government jobs and to recommend quotas for reservation.

Mandala An intricate visual symbol developed in the Tibetan Buddhist tradition, revealing elaborate patterns of many shapes and colors, intended to lead its creator and observer into supranormal levels of consciousness.

Mohajirs "Immigrants"; those Muslims who moved from their homelands in India at the time of partition in 1947 to settle in Pakistan. Because they have retained many of the customs as well as the language (Urdu) of their former homes, even today they remain a distinctive community and political force, as the Mohajir Quami Movement (MQM) in Pakistan.

MMA (Muttahida Majlis-e-amal) A coalition of 5 Islamist political parties that won control of the North-West Frontier Province of Pakistan in the 2002 elections. It used this base to push its fundamentalist, anti-American agenda nationally until its defeat by the Awami National Party in the 2008 elections.

Monsoon Literally means "season." An annual torrential rainfall, which normally begins during the month of June, when the prevailing winds shift to the west, gather clouds with water from the Arabian Sea, and deluge the subcontinent with rain as the clouds rise over the Himalayan Mountains. The dramatic shift from the torrid dry heat of late spring to this stormy wet season and the lush growth that it provides has an immense impact on the economies, the literature, and the consciousness of South Asian peoples. Raja Rao gives a brief, gripping description of the coming of the monsoon on page 50 of his novel *Kanthapura* and in his notes, pages 215–216.

Mughals Islamic invaders of Mongol descent who established the longest dynastic imperial rule in South Asia, from A.D. 1526 to 1857.

Mujahideen Militant tribal leaders in Afghanistan who joined in alliance to protect their authority from national and foreign (Soviet) incursion.

Muslim One who submits to the supreme will of Allah (God), as revealed to the prophet Mohammad; one who practices Islam. Sometimes spelled Moslem.

NATO (North Atlantic Treaty Organization) Established in 1949 as an alliance of now 26 North American and European countries "to unite their efforts for collective defense and for the preservation of peace and security."

Naxalites A loose collection of militant groups in central and eastern India inspired by the Maoist revolution in China, who attack any element of the Indian establishment in the name of the landless and the tribal people of that region. Their name comes from an uprising of a tribal community in the village of

Naxalbari in western Bengal in 1967. Though mostly active in the 1960s and 1970s, now largely fragmented, small bands of the People's War Group or the Maoist Communist Centre still attack landlords and politicians sporadically in Chhattisgarh Andhra Pradesh, Jharkhand, Orissa, and Bihar.

Nirvana Literally, "blowing out, extinguishing"; the ultimate enlightenment of Buddhism: departure from the relentless trans-migratory cycle of births and deaths into nothingness.

Panchayat Literally, "council of five." This traditional leadership of elders in the jati kinship group was adopted in the Panchayat Acts in state legislatures during the 1950s as the appropriate form of democratically elected village government in the Republic of India.

Parsi A member of the Zoroastrian faith, the ancient religion of Persia. Most of the Parsis in South Asia live in Mumbai (Bombay) and Karachi.

Pathans A group of peoples in the northwest section of Pakistan who speak the Pushtu language.

Punjab Translated as *panch* ("five") and *ap* ("water"), designates the land in the western portion of the Indian sub-continent through which the five rivers forming the Indus River System flow. The province was divided between India and Pakistan in 1947.

Raj Translated as "rule" or "kingdom," a term that designates political sovereignty. (The word *reign* comes from the same Indo-European root.) "Raj" is used with "British" to identify the British colonial government in India; it is used with *maha* ("great") to identify rulers of the Indian princely states; and it is used with *swa* ("self") to mean self-rule or independence.

Ramayana An epic Sanskrit poem, composed around the second century B.C. and attributed to Valmiki, describing the ordeals of the ideal prince Rama. The text describes his ultimately successful quest for his faithful wife Sita, who was abducted by the demonic King Ravana.

Rg Veda (Rig Veda) The first of the four Vedas, which are the earliest and most sacred of the writings of the Hindus. Around 1000 B.C., it was compiled into an anthology of 10 books containing 1,028 hymns.

Salafiya Movement to advocate a fundamentalist reform of Sunni Islam, began in the late ninteenth century in Egypt to protest the imposition of Western secular thought. Based on a literal interpretation of the Koran, it espouses severe puritanical behavior and punishment for any apostasy from their rigid beliefs.

Salt March An act of nonviolent civil disobedience (*satyagraha*) led by Mahatma Gandhi in 1930. He and his followers marched from his *ashram* at Sabarmati 241 miles to Dandi on the coast to evaporate salt from the sea, in order to protest the British tax on salt.

Sangha A Buddhist community of holy men and women who follow the Buddha's path called Dharma. The Buddha, Dharma, and Sangha are called the "three jewels of the Buddhist faith."

Sanskrit Translated as "made together, formed, perfected," as descriptive of the classical language of India as structurally perfected.

Satyagraha Literally, "holding the truth," the name that Mahatma Gandhi adopted while in South Africa to describe his nonviolent civil protest against the South African government's oppression of the people from India. Gandhi's translation of this term as "soul force" affirms that, even early in his public career, he understood such action to be primarily religious and only secondarily political.

SEWA (Self-Employed Women's Association) Began as a union of textile workers by Anasuya Sarabhai in Ahmedabad in 1920, following upon Mahatma Gandhi's successful strike of textile workers in 1917. It became registered as a trade union in 1972. Under SEWA's General Secretary, Ela Bhatt, it has grown to seven hundred thousand members, the largest member-based organization of poor working women in India.

Shariah "The Path to the Water Hole"; Islamic sacred laws, based upon the Koran as revealed to Mohammad and the *Sunnah,* the record of his exemplary life. These laws are affirmed by the Sunni followers of Islam to be divinely inspired and immutable guides for Muslims' everyday life.

Sherpa Literally "eastern people"; an ethnic group in Nepal who live in the high Himalayan region, but also a name applied to any Nepali who is skilled in climbing and navigating the mountain peaks.

Shiva Literally, "auspicious"; the name of one of the three main Gods One of the two main sects of Hinduism: Shaivism (from Shiva) and Vaishnavism ("followers of Vishnu").

Sufi A person of the Islamic faith who affirms through religious discipline and mystical experience the spiritual union of self with God.

Sunnah "Custom"; practices of the Prophet Mohammad remembered by his early followers as the guide for an ideal Islamic life.

Sunni A sect of Islam. The tradition of the majority of Muslims, based on strict adherence to the Sunnah of the Prophet Mohammad.

Taliban "Seekers of religious knowledge"; members of a militant and exceptionally conservative freedom force named after the Pathan students of Islam from Kandahar who started a fundamentalist crusade to free Afghanistan from foreign and modern corruptions of their faith and traditional way of life.

Tsunami An enormous ocean wave created by an earthquake on an ocean floor. Occurring with some frequency in the Pacific Ocean, the Indian Ocean tsunami on December 26, 2004, was the result of a totally unexpected earthquake that measured 9.0 on the richter scale along the Sunda trench west of Sumatra in Indonesia. The worst tsunami in history, it extended across the entire Indian Ocean to the coast of Africa, causing death and damage in 13 countries. Indonesia reported a death toll of over 110,000. On the eastern shore of Sri Lanka it killed 38,000; along the coast of Tamil Nadu, in India, 7,968 and the Indian Andaman and Nicobar Islands, 1,837, with 5,625 missing; and in Thailand, an estimated 11,000 deaths. In 2011, a tsunami in Japan caused enormous destruction.

Varna Originally translated as "color," later as "class"; the fourfold division of classical Indian society, ranked on a purity–pollution scale: priests, warriors, peasants, and laborers. The untouchables and tribals are a fifth group, known as outcastes, ranked below the laborers.

Vishnu Receiving somewhat minor attention as a solar deity in the *Rg Veda,* Vishnu became recognized as Supreme Lord of the universe, its creator and preserver during the classical period (in Indian history) (A.D. 300–1200). He is worshipped widely throughout Hinduism through his incarnations (*avatars*), of whom Rama and Krishna are the most prevalent.

Wahabism A fundamentalist tradition of Islam initiated by Muhammad ibn Abd-al-Wahhab in the Eighteenth century, adopted as the national religion of Saudi Arabia after the collapse of the Ottoman Empire in the early Twentieth century.

Yoga Literal meaning "union." A highly disciplined set of exercises to identify, nurture, and develop different parts of one's natural body, breathing, nervous system, and consciousness. Practice of this discipline leads to the integration of one's total self—physical, mental, and spiritual, the unconscious as well as the conscious.

Bibliography

SOURCES FOR STATISTICAL REPORTS

C.I.A. *World Factbook* (2009–2010).
World Bank *World Development Reports* (1978–2009).
UN *Population and Vital Statistics Reports* (2011).
UN Human Development Report (2010).
World Health Organization (WHO) Statistics (2008).

GENERAL

A. L. Basham, *Wonder That Was India,* (Picador, 2005).
Sumit Ganguly, *Conflict Unending, India-Pakistan Tensions since 1947,* (Columbia University Press, 2002).
Sumit Ganguly and Devin T. Hagerty, *Fearful Symmetry: India Pakistan Crises in the Shadow of Nuclear Weapons,* (Oxford University Press, 2006).
Ayesha Jalal, *Partisans of Allah: Jihad in South Asia,* (Harvard University Press, 2008).
Jonathan M. Kenoyer, *Ancient Cities of the Indus Valley Civilization,* (Oxford University Press, Islamabad: American Institute of Pakistan Studies, 1998).
Todd Lewis and Theodore Riccardi, *The Himalayas: A Syllabus of the Region's History, Anthropology, and Religion,* (Association of Asian Studies, 1995).
Ann Leonard, *Seeds: Supporting Women's Work in the Third World,* (Feminist Press, 1989), Chapters on Credit Organization in Madras, India; Non-craft Employment in Bangladesh; and Forest Conservation in Nepal.
Jane McIntosh, *A Peaceful Realm: The Rise and Fall of the Indus Civilization,* (Westview Press, 2001).
Francis Robinson, (ed), *The Cambridge Encyclopedia of India, Pakistan, Bangladesh, Sri Lanka, Nepal, Bhutan, and the Maldives,* (Cambridge University Press, 1989).
Francis Robinson, *Islam and Modern History in South Asia,* (Oxford University Press, 2001).
Joseph Schwartzberg, *A Historical Atlas of South Asia,* (Oxford University Press, 1993).
Stanley J. Tambiah, *Leveling Crowds, Ethno-Nationalist Conflicts and Collective Violence in South Asia,* (University of California Press, 1997).
David Gordon White, *Kiss of the Yogini: "Tantric Sex" in its South Asian Contexts,* (University of Chicago Press, 2006).

INDIA

Joan Bondurant, *Conquest of Violence,* (Princeton: Princeton University Press, 1988).
William Dalrymple, *The Last Mughal: The Fall of a Dynasty, Delhi, 1857,* (Knopf, 2007).
Dennis Dalton, *Mahatma Gandhi, Nonviolent Power in Action,* (Columbia University Press, 1995).
Nicholas Dirks, *Castes of Mind: Colonialism and the Making of Modern India,* (Princeton University Press, 2001).
Diana Eck, *Darshan—Seeing the Divine Image in India,* (Columbia University Press, 1985).
Ainslie, Embree, *Utopias in Conflict, Religion and Nationalism in Modern India,* (University of California Press, 1990).
Bill Emmott, *Rivals: How the Power Struggle Between China, India, and Japan Will Shape Our Next Decade,* (Harcourt, 2008).

Eric Ericson, *Gandhi's Truth,* (Norton, 1970).
Mohandas K. Gandhi, *An Autobiography: The Story of My Experiments With Truth,* (Beacon, 1957).
Rajmohan Gandhi, *Gandhi: The Man, His People, and the Empire,* (2008).
Sumit Ganguly (ed), *India as an Emerging Power,* (Frank Caso, 2003).
Sumit Ganguly, Larry Diamond, and Marc F. Plattner, *The State of India's Democracy,* (Johns Hopkins University Press, 2007).
Ramachandra Guha, *India After Gandhi: The History of the World's Largest Democracy,* (Harper Perennial; Reprint edition, 2008).
Arthur Herman, *Gandhi and Churchill,* (New York: Bantam Books, 2008).
Thomas Hopkins, *The Hindu Religious Tradition,* (Belmont, CA: Dickenson, 1971).
Tarun Khanna. *Billions of Entrepreneurs: How China and India Are Reshaping Their Futures—and Yours,* (Harvard Business School Press, 2008).
David Knipe, *Hinduism, Experiments in the Sacred,* (Harper, 1990).
Edward Luce, *In Spite of the Gods: The Rise of Modern India,* (Anchor, 2008).
Suketu Mehta, *Maximum City: Bombay Lost and Found,* (Alfred A. Knopf, 2004).
Maria Misra, *Vishnu's Crowded Temple: India Since the Great Rebellion,* (Yale University Press, 2008).
Aditya Mukherjee, Mridula Mukherjee, and Sucheta Mahajan, *RSS, School Texts and the Murder of Mahatma Gandhi: The Hindu Communal Project* (([Response Books]), Sage Publications Pvt. Ltd, 2008).
V. S. Naipal, *India: A Million Mutinies Now,* (Viking, 1992).
Jawaharlal Nehru, *The Discovery of India,* (John Day, 1946).
Martha C. Nussbaum, *The Clash Within: Democracy, Religious Violence, and India's Future,* (Harvard University Press, 2007).
Arvind Panagariya, *India: The Emerging Giant,* (Oxford University Press, 2008).
Raja Rao, *Kanthapura,* (New Directions, 1963). A novel describing the impact of Mahatma Gandhi on a South Indian village.
Lloyd and Suzanne Rudolph, *The Modernity of Tradition,* (University of Chicago Press, 1984).
Srirupa Roy, *Beyond Belief: India and the Politics of Postcolonial Nationalism,* (Duke University Press, 2007).
Amartya Sen, *The Argumentative Indian: Writings on Indian History, Culture, and Identity,* (Allen Lane, 2005, Farrar, Straus & Giroux, 2005).
Vikram Seth, *A Suitable Boy,* (Perennial, 1994). A monumental novel about pursuing the choice of a husband in 1950s north India.
Spear & Thapar, *A History of India, 2 vols.* (Penguin, 1965).
M. N. Srinivas, *Social Change in Modern India,* (University of California Press, 1969).
Alex Von Tunzelmann, *Indian Summer: The Secret History of the End of an Empire,* (Henry Holt, 2007).
Asutosh Varshney, *Ethnic Conflict and Civic Life: Hindus and Muslims in India,* (Yale University Press, 1993).
William Wiser, Charlotte Wiser, and Susan Wadley, *Behind Mud Walls,* (University of California Press, 2001). A classic description of an Indian village in 1930 and 1960, with a new chapter on 2000.
Stanley Wolpert, *Nehru, A Tryst with Destiny,* (Oxford University Press, 1996).

R. C. Zaehner, *Hinduism,* (Oxford University Press, 1970).

Heinreich Zimmer, *Myths and Symbols in Indian Art and Civilization,* (Harper, 1946).

AFGHANISTAN

Steve Coll, *Ghost Wars: The Secret History of the CIA, Afghanistan, and Bin Laden, from the Soviet Invasion to September 10, 2001,* (Penguin ([Non-Classics]) 2004).

Sarah Chayes, *The Punishment of Virtue: Inside Afghanistan After the Taliban,* (Penguin ([Non-Classics]) 2007).

Robert D. Crews (ed) and Amin Tarzi (ed), *The Taliban and the Crisis of Afghanistan,* (Harvard University Press, 2008).

James F. Dobbins, *After the Taliban: Nation-Building in Afghanistan,* (Potomac Books Inc., 2008).

Martin Ewans, *Afghanistan: A Short History of Its People and Politics,* (Harper Perennial, 2002).

Khaled Hosseini, *The Kite Runner,* (Riverhead Books, 2003). A novel of an emigrant's childhood in Kabul and his return during Taliban rule.

Robert D. Kaplan, *Soldiers of God, With Islamic Warriors in Afghanistan and Pakistan,* (Vintage, 2001).

David Macdonald, *Drugs in Afghanistan: Opium, Outlaws and Scorpion Tales,* (Pluto Press, 2007).

Ahmed Raashid, *Taliban: Militant Islam, Oil and Fundamentalism in Central Asia,* (Yale University Press, 2001).

Barnett R. Rubin, *Afghanistan's Uncertain Transition from Turmoil to Normalcy,* (Council on Foreign Relations, 2007).

Barnett R. Rubin, *The Fragmentation of Afghanistan: State Formation and Collapse in the International System,* (Yale University Press, 2002).

Rosemarie Skaine, *The Women of Afghanistan Under the Taliban,* (McFarland, 2001).

Mohammad Yousaf, *Battle for Afghanistan,* (Pen and Sword Books, 2007).

BANGLADESH

David Bornstein, *The Price of a Dream: The Story of the Grameen Bank,* (Oxford University Press, USA, 2005).

Hanifa Deen, *The Crescent and the Pen: The Strange Journey of Taslima Nasreen,* (Praeger Publishers, 2006).

Katy Gardner, *Global Migrants, Local Lives: Travel and Transformation in Rural Bangladesh*

Katy Gardner, *Songs at the River's Edge: Stories from a Bangladeshi Village,* (Pluto Press, 1997).

Amitav Ghosh, *The Hungry Tide: A Novel,* (Mariner Books, 2006).

Maneeza Hossain, *Broken Pendulum: Bangladesh's Swing to Radicalism,* (Hudson Institute; 1st edition, 2007).

Rokeya Sakhawat Hossain, *Sultana's Dream,* (The Feminist Press, 1988). Bengali Muslim writer on purdah and a dream of its reversal.

Taslima Nasrin, *Meyebela: My Bengali Girlhood,* (Steerforth, 1998).

Sufia M. Uddin, *Constructing Bangladesh: Religion, Ethnicity, and Language in an Islamic Nation,* (The University of North Carolina Press, 2006).

Muhammad Yunus, *Banker To The Poor: Micro-Lending and the Battle Against World Poverty,* (PublicAffairs; 2003. Corr. 2nd edition, 2003).

BHUTAN

John Berthold, *Bhutan: Land of the Thunder Dragon,* (Wisdom Publications, 2005).

Russ and Blyth Carpenter, *Blessings of Bhutan,* (University of Hawaii Press, 2002).

Britta Das, *Buttertea at Sunrise: A Year in the Bhutan Himalaya,* (Summersdale Publishers, 2006).

Michael Hutt, *Unbecoming Citizens: Culture, Nationhood, and the Flight of Refugees from Bhutan,* (Oxford University Press, USA, 2005).

John Wehrheim, *Bhutan: Hidden Lands of Happiness; Texts and Photographs,* (Serindia Publications, 2008).

Richard Whitecross, *Bhutan,* (Lonely Planet; 3rd edition, 2007).

Jamie Zeppa, *Beyond the Sky and the Earth: A Journey into Bhutan,* (Riverhead Trade, 2000).

MALDIVES

Asian Centre for Human Rights, *Maldives: The Dark of the Life,* (2006).

Maumoon Abdul, Gayoon, *The Maldives: A Nation in Peril* (Ministry of Planning Human Resources and Environment, Republic of Maldives, 1998).

NEPAL

Monica Connell, *Against a Peacock Sky,* (Viking Press, 1991).

John N. Gray, *Domestic Mandala: Architecture of Lifeworlds in Nepal,* (Ashgate Publishing, 2006).

Jonathan Gregson, *Massacre at the Palace. The Doomed Royal Dynasty of Nepal,* (Miramax Books, 2002).

Mahendra Lawoti, *The Maoist Insurgency in Nepal: Dynamics and Growth in the Twenty-first Century,* (Routledge, 2009).

PAKISTAN

Stephen Cohen, *The Idea of Pakistan,* (Brookings Institution Press; 2nd edition, 2006).

Husain Haqqani, *Pakistan: Between Mosque And Military,* (Carnegie Endowment for International Peace, 2005).

Arif Jamal, *Shadow War: The Untold Story of Jihad in Kashmir,* (Melville House, 2009).

Adrian Levy, *Deception: Pakistan, the United States, and the Secret Trade in Nuclear Weapons,* (Walker & Company, 2007).

Greg Mortenson, *Three Cups of Tea,* (Penguin ([Non-Classics]), 2007).

Ahmed Rashid, *Descent into Chaos: The United States and the Failure of Nation Building in Pakistan, Afghanistan, and Central Asia,* (Viking Adult, 2008).

Mary Anne Weaver, *Pakistan, In the Shadow of Jihad and Afghanistan,* (Farrar, Straus and Giroux, 2003).

SRI LANKA

William Clarance, *Ethnic Warfare in Sri Lanka and the U.N. Crisis,* (Pluto Press, 2007).

R. B. Herath, *Sri Lankan Ethnic Crisis: Towards a Resolution,* (Trafford Publishing, 2006).

Pradeep Jeganathan, *At the Water's Edge,* (South Focus Press, 2004).

Michael Ondaatje, *Anil's Ghost: A Novel,* (Vintage, 2001).

John Richardson, *Paradise Poisoned: Learning About Conflict, Terrorism and Development from Sri Lanka's Civil Wars,* (International Centre for Ethnic Studies, 2005).

Stanley Jeyaraja Tambiah, *Sri Lanka—Ethnic Fratricide and the Dismantling of Democracy,* (University of Chicago Press, 1991).

Margaret Trawick, *Enemy Lines: Warfare, Childhood, and Play in Batticaloa,* (University of California Press, 2007).

Mark P. Whitaker, *Learning Politics From Sivaram: The Life and Death of a Revolutionary Tamil Journalist in Sri Lanka,* (Pluto Press, 2007).

Deborah Winslow and Michael D. Woost (eds.), *Economy, Culture, and Civil War in Sri Lanka,* (Indiana University Press, 2004).

Index

Index

Martial law, in Pakistan, 80, 81, 82-84
McMahon Line, 9
Mehta, Geeta, 4
"Minute on Education" (Macauly), 8
Mughal Empire, 7–8
Mujahideen, 14
Mumbai (Bombay), 38
Musharraf, Pervez, 25
Muslim League, 78
Muslims
   In India, 36, 39
   In Maldives, 66, 67-68
   In Pakistan, 15, 77, 80
   In South Asia, 7, 11
Muttahida Majlis-e-Amal (MMA), 14, 82, 83
Muttahida Quami Movement (MQM), 15

N
Naipaul, V.S., 39, 44
Najibullah, Muhammed, 54
Naseem, Evan, 68–69
Nasheed, Mohamed, 69
Nasir, Amin Ibrahim, 68
Nasreen, Taslima, 59
National Democratic Front of Bodoland (NDFB), 26
Naxalite Maoists revolutionary movement, 26
Nehru, Jawaharlal, 16, 41, 42
Nepal, 19, 28, 71-76
   challenges today, 76
   climate, 71
   economy of, 72
   environmental concerns, 71
   ethnicity in, 71
   geography of, 71
   government system in, 72
   historical timeline, 75
   languages, 71
   map of, 71
   politics in, 73–75
   population, 71
   social diversity in, 73
   terrorism in, 28
   instability in, 19
Nepali Congress Party (NCP), 73
New Delhi, 7, 8, 36, 37
New York Times, 22, 42
Nirvana, 5, 27

P
Pakistan, 17-18, 25, 77-84
   and Afghanistan border (Durand Line), 9
   climate, 77
   democracy: 1971-1977, 80–81
   democracy: 1988-1999, 81–82
   economic conditions in, 17–18
   economy of, 78
   environmental concerns, 77
   establishment of in 1947, 9
   ethnicity in, 77
   geography of, 77
   government system in, 78
   historical timeline, 83
   independence movement in, 78–79
   independence of, 10, 17

   internal challenges, 84
   Islamic extremism in, 17
   languages, 77
   map of, 77
   martial law: 1958-1971, 80
   martial law: 1977-1988, 81
   martial rule since 1999, 82–84
   politics in, 79–80
   population, 77
   religions in, 77
   terrorism in, 25
Pashtuns, 52
Passage to Peshawar (Reeves), 24
Pathans, 9
Patna, 37
People's Democratic (Communist) Party, 53
Philosophies of India (Zimmer), 5
Proshika, 60
Punjab, 7, 38

Q
Qanuni, Yunus, 55

R
Rahman, Mujibur, 22, 59
Rahman, Ziaur, 22, 58
Ramayana, 5, 30, 45
Rao, Narasimha, 46
Refugees, 27-28
Reeves, Richard, 24
Rg-Veda, 4, 5
Royal Manas National Park (Bhutan), 64
Rubin, Barnett R., 24
Rushdie, Salmon, 24

S
Salafiya, 14
Samajwadi Party (SP), 41
Sangha, 12
Sanskrit, 4, 30
Satyagraha, or Soul Force, 29, 31
Sayeed, Mufti Mohammad, 47
Self-Employed Women's Association (SEWA), 15
Sen, Binayak, 26
Seven Party Alliance, 28
Shalimar the Clown (Rushdie), 24
Shiva, 12
Shore Temple, 39
Singh, Kushwant, 22
Singh, Manmohan, 26, 40, 45
Sinhalese, 18
Snakes and Ladders (Mehta), 4
Solidarity movement (Poland), 29
South Asia, 2-16, 20-28
   ancient civilization, 3–10
   Aryan migration in, 4–6
   British India in 1947, 21–22
   British Raj, 8–10
   climate, 3
   democracy in, 20–28
   geography of, 3
   geology of, 3
   independence of, 9–10
   linguistic diversity in, 10, 14–15
   map of, 2

   maritime commerce in, 4, 8
   Mughal Empire, 7–8
   national identity in, 21
   population, 10
   post-Colonial, 16
   religious diversity in, 10, 11–14
   river systems in, 3
   social diversity in, 10–11, 15–16
Sri Lanka, 18–19, 85-89
   civil war in, 19, 87–89
   climate, 85
   economy of, 86
   environmental concerns, 85
   ethnicity in, 85
   financial experts in, 19
   geography of, 85
   government system in, 86
   independence of, 10, 87
   languages, 85
   map of, 85
   population, 85
   religions in, 85
   religious conflict in, 15
Sri Lanka, Voices from a War Zone (Subramanian), 27
Sruti, 4
The Story of My Experiments with Truth (Gandhi), 30
Students Islamic Movement of India (SIMI), 26
Subramanian, Nirupama, 27
Sudra, 5
Sufis, 13
Sunni, 13
Sunni Muslim, 52, 58, 68

T
Tagore, Rabindra Nath, 31
Tajik people, 52
Taj Mahal, 7
Tala Hydroelectric Project, 64
Taliban, 14, 24, 25, 53, 54, 55
Tamil Tiger, 18, 27
Terrorism
   in Afghanistan, 24–25
   in Bangladesh, 22–23
   in India, 25-27
   in Nepal, 28
   in Pakistan, 25
Train to Pakistan (Singh), 22
Tsunami of 2004, 27, 38, 68

U
United Marxist-Leninist Party (UMLP), 74
United National Party (UNP), 87
United Nations (UN), 9
United Progressive Alliance, 40, 41
Urdu language, 79

V
Vaisya, 5
Vajpayee, Atal Behari, 41
Vale of Kashmar, 23, 24
Varanasi, 37
Varna, 5
Veda. *see* Rg-Veda
Vedic Age, 4, 6